Series Editors:
Steven F. Warren, Ph.D.
Joe Reichle, Ph.D.

Communication
and Language
Intervention
Series

Volume 5

Language Intervention

Also available in the Communication
and Language Intervention Series:

Communication
and Language
Intervention
Series

Volume 5
Language Intervention
Preschool Through the Elementary Years

Edited by

Marc E. Fey, Ph.D.
Associate Professor
School of Allied Health
Department of Hearing and Speech
University of Kansas Medical Center
Kansas City, Kansas

Jennifer Windsor, Ph.D.
Assistant Professor
Department of Communication Disorders
University of Minnesota
Minneapolis, Minnesota

and

Steven F. Warren, Ph.D.
Professor
Departments of Special Education and
of Psychology and Human Development
Peabody College of Vanderbilt University
Nashville, Tennessee

·P A U L·H·
BROOKES
PUBLISHING CO.

Baltimore • London • Toronto • Sydney

Paul H. Brookes Publishing Co.
Post Office Box 10624
Baltimore, Maryland 21285-0624

Copyright © 1995 by Paul H. Brookes Publishing Co., Inc.
All rights reserved.

Typeset by Signature Typesetting & Design, Baltimore, Maryland.
Manufactured in the United States of America by
The Maple Press Co., York, Pennsylvania.

This book is printed on recycled paper. ♻

Library of Congress Cataloging-in-Publication Data
Language intervention : preschool through the elementary years / edited by
    Marc E. Fey, Jennifer Windsor, and Steven F. Warren.
        p.   cm.—(Communication and language intervention series ; 5)
    Includes bibliographical references and index.
    ISBN 1-55766-168-5
    1. Language disorders in children.   2. Language disorders in children—
    Treatment.   I. Fey, Marc E., 1952–   II. Windsor, Jennifer, 1959–
    III. Warren, Steven F.   IV. Series.
RJ496.L35L367   1994
618.926855—dc20   94-13214
                                                                       CIP

(British Library Cataloguing-in-Publication data are available from the British
Library.)

Contents

Series Preface

T HE PURPOSE OF THE *Communication and Language Intervention Series* is to provide meaningful foundations for the application of sound intervention designs to enhance the development of communication skills across the life span. We are endeavoring to achieve this purpose by providing readers with presentations of state-of-the-art theory, research, and practice.

In selecting topics, editors, and authors, we are not attempting to limit the contents of this series to those viewpoints with which we agree or which we find most promising. We are assisted in our efforts to develop the series by an editorial advisory board consisting of prominent scholars representative of the range of issues and perspectives to be incorporated in the series.

We trust that the careful reader will find much that is provocative and controversial in this and other volumes. This will be necessarily so to the extent that the work reported is truly on the so-called cutting edge, a mythical place where no sacred cows exist. This point is demonstrated time and again throughout this volume as the conventional wisdom is challenged (and occasionally confirmed) by various authors.

Readers of this and other volumes are encouraged to proceed with healthy skepticism. In order to achieve our purpose, we take on some difficult and controversial issues. Errors and misinterpretations are inevitably made. This is normal in the development of any field, and should be welcomed as evidence that the field is moving forward and tackling difficult and weighty issues.

Well-conceived theory and research on development of both children with and children without disabilities is vitally important for researchers, educators, and clinicians committed to the development of optimal approaches to communication and language intervention. For this reason, each volume in this series includes chapters pertaining to both development and intervention.

The content of each volume reflects our view of the symbiotic relationship between intervention and research: Demonstrations of what may work in intervention should lead to analyses of promising discoveries and insights from developmental work that may in turn fuel further refinement by intervention researchers.

An inherent goal of this series is to enhance the long-term development of the field by systematically furthering the dissemination of theoretically and empirically based scholarship and research. We promise the reader an opportunity to participate in the development of this field through the debates and discussions that occur throughout the pages of the *Communication and Language Intervention Series.*

Editorial Advisory Board

Volume Preface

APPROACHES TO LANGUAGE INTERVENTION for children are constantly evolving. This evolution reflects many factors, including: 1) developments in our understanding of language, language development, and language impairment; 2) philosophical changes in education; 3) the outcomes of investigations of the effectiveness of methods in education and language intervention; 4) the experiences of service providers who constantly seek the most effective and efficient methods; and 5) legislative mandates for service provision. The 1980s marked a dramatic change in our views of what counts as a language impairment and what the goals, contexts, agents, and methods of intervention should be. Consequently, intervention programs of the 1990s look dramatically different from those of the '70s and '80s.

Although we view the openness to change as a healthy attribute of speech-language pathology, it seems important for us to pause and integrate the information we have on new developments in language intervention and carefully evaluate their effects. This book was planned and prepared with the need for such integration and evaluation in mind. Consequently, the volume is designed to meet three objectives: 1) to present and discuss key issues facing speech-language pathologists working with children with language impairments from preschool through elementary ages, 2) to critically evaluate approaches that have been proposed for children exhibiting a broad range of language impairments, and 3) to document research findings about the effectiveness of these approaches.

The book is divided into three sections. The first section focuses on language intervention with preschoolers. Our inclusion of this section in the book targeting elementary school–age children was based on two factors. First, preschoolers with communication disabilities now can be considered of school age because of legislation requiring schools to provide services to these children. Second, we now have sufficient information to predict that most preschoolers with significant language impairments during the preschool years will experience social, behavioral, and/or academic difficulties in school. Recognition of this awareness can and should motivate changes in intervention with preschoolers in an effort to minimize their risk for later educational difficulties. The chapters by Fey, Catts, and Larrivee (Chapter 1) and Cole (Chapter 2) focus on the need to modify traditional intervention approaches with preschoolers. These chapters also provide information and analysis on the types of intervention goals and procedures and the curricular and service delivery options that show promise in helping children to maximize their communication potential.

Part II includes six chapters, each focusing on one broad area that commonly is found to be deficient among school-age children with language impairments. Fey (1986) described such broadly based areas of intervention concentration as "basic goals." He argued that intervention plans are most efficient and effective when specific goals, procedures, and activities are developed after careful consideration of a child's level of social–conversational participation. When factors that function as obstacles to successful communication are considered first, all subsequent planning must necessarily be relevant to the child's development as a more effective communicator.

When children of school age are considered, it becomes clear that the notion of basic goals must be extended to include literacy and other classroom issues. The importance of literacy development in language intervention planning can be seen throughout Part II. Chapters in this section highlight six basic goals that frequently must be targeted with children who have language impairments. These goals include speech intelligibility (Camarata, Chapter 3), word finding (McGregor & Leonard, Chapter 4), syntax (Scott, Chapter 5), oral and written narratives (Gillam, McFadden, & van Kleeck, Chapter 6), conversation (Brinton & Fujiki, Chapter 7), and social skills (Windsor, Chapter 8). Each chapter provides a clinical description of children for whom the basic goal is appropriate, techniques that have been used to treat children who present such a clinical picture, and a critical evaluation of the efficacy of these intervention efforts.

Part III includes four chapters that address central issues in intervention with school-age children. Unlike the chapters in Part II, which focus on the intervention goals, procedures, activities, and contexts that may be subordinated to a particular basic goal, these chapters speak to broader concerns that cut across different basic intervention objectives. These objectives include literacy issues for students with developmental disabilities (Koppenhaver, Pierce, Steelman, & Yoder, Chapter 9), the use of computers as intervention tools (Schery & O'Connor, Chapter 10), intervention considerations for children from linguistically and culturally diverse backgrounds (Kayser, Chapter 11), and service delivery options (Cirrin & Penner, Chapter 12). While these four major issues do not exhaust the general concerns of interventionists working with school-age children, it is difficult to conceive of an employment setting in which these matters are not of major importance.

A major theme of the volume, which is reflected in each chapter, is the critical need for information documenting the effects and effectiveness of intervention with school-age children. It is not enough to rely on our intuitions or clinical impressions about language intervention efficacy. Careful research involving the cooperation and collaboration of clinicians and researchers is necessary. At present, the answers to all of the relevant questions regarding intervention efficacy are beyond our reach. However, the time seems right to evaluate critically the current state of knowledge and to lay the groundwork for the development and testing of new and exciting approaches designed to better meet the needs of school-age children with language impairments. This book has grown out of this spirit of self-evaluation and excitement for the changes that lie ahead.

REFERENCE

Fey, M. (1986). *Language intervention with young children.* Newton, MA: Allyn & Bacon.

Contributors .

The Editors

Marc E. Fey, Ph.D., Associate Professor, School of Allied Health, Department of Hearing and Speech, University of Kansas Medical Center, 3901 Rainbow Boulevard, Kansas City, KS 66160. Dr. Fey's research and clinical work includes typically developing children as well as children with speech and language impairments. He has special interest in the experimental evaluation of the efficacy of intervention with children with language and literacy problems.

Jennifer Windsor, Ph.D., Assistant Professor, Department of Communication Disorders, University of Minnesota, 115 Shevlin Hall, 164 Pillsbury Drive SE, Minneapolis, MN 55455. Dr. Windsor's primary research interest is in the morphological and lexical skills of school-age children with language impairments and with typical language skills.

Steven F. Warren, Ph.D., Professor, Departments of Special Education and of Psychology and Human Development, Peabody College of Vanderbilt University, Box 328, Nashville, TN 37203. Dr. Warren is also Deputy Director of the John F. Kennedy Center for Research on Human Development at Vanderbilt University and Co-director of the Center's Mental Retardation Research Training Program. He has conducted extensive research on communication and language intervention approaches.

The Chapter Authors

Bonnie Brinton, Ph.D., Professor, Speech-Language Pathology Area, Educational Psychology Department, Brigham Young University, 127 TLRB, Provo, UT 84602. Dr. Brinton's research has examined a wide range of topics related to conversational language impairment in children with language disorders and adults with mental retardation.

Stephen Camarata, Ph.D., Director, Scottish Rite Child Language Disorders Center, Bill Wilkerson Center, Nashville, TN 37232, and Assistant Professor, Speech and Hearing Sciences, Vanderbilt University School of Medicine, Nashville. His research has examined speech disabilities and language disabilities in children, and he has been developing and validating more effective intervention procedures for special populations.

Hugh W. Catts, Ph.D., Associate Professor, Intercampus Program in Communicative Disorders, Department of Speech-Language-Hearing, University of Kansas, 3031 Dole Hall, Lawrence, KS 66045. Dr. Catts's research interests include the early identification and remediation of language-based reading disabilities.

Frank M. Cirrin, Ph.D., Speech-Language Pathologist, Department of Special Education, Minneapolis Public Schools, Minneapolis, MN 55413. Dr. Cirrin is a resource teacher whose current duties include the development of classroom-based service delivery models for language intervention. He has served as the chairperson of the American Speech-Language-Hearing Association's Committee on Language-Learning Disorders.

Kevin N. Cole, Ph.D., Research Assistant Professor, Experimental Education Unit, Child Development and Mental Retardation Center, University of Washington, Seattle, WA 98195. Dr. Cole's work has examined the efficacy of various models of language facilitation, as well as individual differences in children's response to intervention.

Martin Fujiki, Ph.D., Professor, Speech-Language Pathology Area, Educational Psychology Department, Brigham Young University, 130 TLRB, Provo, UT 84602. Dr. Fujiki's research activities address conversational language difficulties in children with language impairment and adults with mental retardation.

Ron Gillam, Ph.D., Assistant Professor, Program in Communication Sciences and Disorders, University of Texas at Austin, Austin, TX 78712-1089. Dr. Gillam's research interests concern memory, language, and literacy in school-age children with language-based learning disabilities. He recently received a Clinical Investigator Development Award from the National Institute on Deafness and Other Communication Disorders to study modality specific memory mechanisms in children with specific language impairment.

Hortencia Kayser, Ph.D., CCC-SLP, Post-Doctoral Fellow, National Center for Neurogenic Communication Disorders, University of Arizona, Tucson, AZ 85721. Dr. Kayser was the coordinator of the bilingual program in speech-language pathology at Texas Christian University from 1985 to 1992. Her research has focused on the social language use of Mexican-American children who are language impaired.

David A. Koppenhaver, Ph.D., Director, Center for Literacy and Disability Studies, University of North Carolina at Chapel Hill, Chapel Hill, NC 27514. The mission of the center is to promote literacy learning in children and adults with developmental disabilities.

Linda S. Larrivee, Ph.D., Assistant Professor, Department of Communicative Disorders, University of Missouri–Columbia, 303 Lewis Hall, Columbia, MO 65211. Dr. Larrivee's research interests include language impairments and reading disabilities in school-age children. She has extensive clinical experience in promoting the language skills of children with language-learning disabilities.

Laurence B. Leonard, Ph.D., Distinguished Professor, Department of Audiology and Speech Sciences, Purdue University, Heavilon Hall, West Lafayette, IN 47907. Dr. Leonard has published widely in the areas of language and phonological disorders. In addition to his work on word-finding problems, he has studied the early lexical and phonological characteristics of children with language impairments, as well as the factors affecting the morphosyntactic abilities of these children.

Theresa U. McFadden, M.Sc. Doctoral Student, Program in Communication Sciences and Disorders, University of Texas at Austin, Austin, TX 78712-1089. Ms. McFadden's primary research interests relate to issues surrounding language assessment and intervention with school-age children.

Karla K. McGregor, Ph.D., Assistant Professor of Speech-Language Pathology, Department of Communication Sciences and Disorders, Northwestern University, 2299 Campus Drive, Evanston, IL 60208-3570. Dr. McGregor has published and presented several papers on assessment and treatment of word-finding disorders in children. Her research extends to phonological and morphosyntactic impairments associated with specific language impairment.

Lisa C. O'Connor, Ph.D., Assistant Professor, Department of Communication Disorders, California State University–Los Angeles, 5151 State University Drive, Los Angeles, CA 90032. Dr. O'Connor also serves as Director of the Robert L. Douglass Speech and Hearing Clinic. She designed and operates the Clinical Computer Laboratory for students and clients in the clinic.

Sharon G. Penner, Ph.D., Speech-Language Pathologist, Department of Special Education, Minneapolis Public Schools, Minneapolis, MN 55413. Dr. Penner provides classroom-based and collaborative language intervention to students with language-learning disabilities at Andersen Contemporary School in Minneapolis.

Patsy L. Pierce, Ph.D., CCC-SLP, Associate Director for Education, Center for Literacy and Disability Studies, University of North Carolina at Chapel Hill, Chapel Hill, NC 27514. Dr. Pierce holds a doctorate in early childhood special education and literacy and has been a practicing speech-language pathologist since 1982.

Teris K. Schery, Ph.D., Research Professor of Education and Human Development, Peabody College, Vanderbilt University, Box 90, Nashville, TN 37203. Dr. Schery teaches in the Human and Organizational Development program. Previously she was a Professor of Communication Disorders at California State University–Los Angeles and helped design and run a large program for children with language impairments through the Los Angeles County Schools.

Cheryl M. Scott, Ph.D., Professor and Department Head, Department of Speech and Language Pathology and Audiology, 120 Hanner, Oklahoma State University, Stillwater, OK 74078. Dr. Scott directs a language and literacy clinic for school-age children and adolescents. Her teaching and research activities address language disorders in school-age children and adolescents, particularly in the area of structural aspects of spoken and written language.

Jane D. Steelman, Ed.D., Associate Director for Technology, Center for Literacy and Disability Studies, University of North Carolina at Chapel Hill, Chapel Hill, NC 27514. Dr. Steelman holds a doctorate in instructional technology and is currently engaged in a pair of research and development projects involving interactive literacy software.

Anne van Kleeck, Ph.D., Professor of Speech Communication, Program in Communication Sciences and Disorders, University of Texas at Austin, Austin, TX 78712-1089. Dr. van Kleeck's teaching and research focuses on various aspects of language acquisition and language disorders in infants, toddlers, and preschoolers. She is currently studying the process of literacy socialization that occurs in homes in the years before children actually learn how to read.

David E. Yoder, Ph.D., CCC-SLP, Assistant Professor of Special Education and Chair, Department of Medical Allied Health Professions, University of North Carolina at Chapel Hill, Chapel Hill, NC 27514. Dr. Yoder is well known for his contributions to the field of augmentative and alternative communication. He established the Center for Literacy and Disability Studies with David Koppenhaver in 1990.

To Sandy and Alyssa (MEF)
To R. and W. Windsor (JW)
To Eva, Marie, and Lena (SFW)

Series Editors:
Steven F. Warren, Ph.D.
Joe Reichle, Ph.D.

**Communication
and Language
Intervention
Series**

Volume 5

Language Intervention

PART I

Language Intervention During the Preschool Years

1

Preparing Preschoolers
for the Academic
and Social Challenges of School

Marc E. Fey, Hugh W. Catts, and Linda S. Larrivee

MANAGEMENT OF THE SPEECH AND language problems of preschoolers usually has focused on the facilitation of speech and oral language skills necessary for successful participation in conversations (e.g., Fey, 1986). In this chapter, we take the position that it may be far more productive to view language impairment (LI) in preschoolers not only for what it is at present, but also for what it is likely to become as the child grows older. This normativist view of early language impairment (Fey, 1986; Tomblin, 1983) requires that professionals who deal with children with communication disorders be sensitive not only to the existing symptoms of the child's speech and language disorder but also to the problems in related areas of life function that are likely to develop as the child grows older. The purpose of this chapter is to present the empirical foundation for our position and to examine critically the types of interventions that may minimize the risk of later academic and social failure in preschool children with language impairments. The essential components of our position apply to all children with significant impairments in any language domain, regardless of their cognitive, emotional, or physical status. In this chapter, however, we focus our review and arguments on children who have language impairments as their primary deficit and who are functioning within the normal range of intelligence or who have only mild general developmental delays. Children whose problems appear to be language specific (e.g., specific language impairment [SLI]) or whose language-learning problems are complicated by more severe emotional, physical, or cognitive impairments (e.g., autism, Asperger's syndrome) are identified accordingly.

ACADEMIC AND SOCIAL PROBLEMS
OF CHILDREN WITH LANGUAGE IMPAIRMENTS

There is a substantial body of research indicating that children diagnosed with language impairment in the preschool years subsequently experience significant difficulties in school. Early retrospective studies documented a link between a clinical record of SLI and later educational problems (Aram & Nation, 1980; Hall & Tomblin, 1978; King, Jones, & Lasky, 1982). More recently, prospective longitudinal studies have identified children with SLI in preschool or kindergarten and have assessed their academic progress during their school years (Aram, Ekelman, & Nation, 1984; Bishop & Adams, 1990; Catts, 1991a, 1993; Magnusson & Naucler, 1990; Padget, 1988; Stark et al., 1984; Tallal, Curtiss, & Kaplan, 1989; Wilson & Risucci, 1988). For example, Larrivee and Catts (1992) reported that 83% of a group of 47 kindergarten subjects with specific speech-language impairments received remedial reading or learning disability services in first or second grade. Similarly, Padget (1988) reported that of her 21 preschool age subjects with SLI, 14 (67%) were identified as having learning disabilities and 6 (29%) maintained a diagnosis of speech impairment 3–5 years after their entry into kindergarten. Only one child with SLI was no longer classified as having a communication and/or a learning disability.[1]

The academic problems most consistently observed among children with SLI involve learning to read and write. Reading and writing rely heavily on the abilities to understand, formulate, and think about language (Adams, 1990; Catts, 1989, Kamhi & Catts, 1989; Perfetti, 1985). Children with SLI have deficits in some or all of the basic language abilities that are closely associated with reading success. These basic language abilities include lexical abilities (Catts, 1991a, 1993; Kail & Leonard, 1986; Kamhi, Catts, Mauer, Apel, & Gentry, 1988; Leonard & Fey, 1979; Rice, Buhr, & Nemeth, 1990; see McGregor & Leonard, chap. 4, this volume), syntactic production and comprehension (Johnston, 1988; Leonard, 1989; Rizzo & Stephens, 1981; Saxman & Miller, 1973; Shriner, Holloway, & Daniloff, 1969), narrative production and comprehension (Bishop & Adams, 1992; Bishop & Edmundson, 1987; Crais & Chapman, 1987; Ellis Weismer, 1985; Paul & Smith, 1993), and phonological awareness (Catts, 1993; Kamhi & Catts, 1986; Kamhi et al., 1988; Kamhi, Lee, & Nelson, 1985; Magnusson & Naucler, 1990). In all of these areas, deficits are readily observable well before children with SLI enter school. Thus, by the time they reach school age, many children with language impairments have not developed the rich linguistic foundation on which the development of written language depends. It is important to note that the language deficiencies of preschoolers with language impairments are not confined to conversation, the domain of most early intervention efforts, but extend to narrative discourse and metalanguage as well.

Preschool language problems appear to have another more direct influence on written language development. Positive experiences with print in children's

---

[1]The counts for subjects with SLI are taken from Table IV (Padget, 1988). One subject in this table, SP, was excluded because he left the project before a kindergarten placement was assigned. The results of our analyses at kindergarten are somewhat less optimistic than those reflected in Padget's chapter because we considered any decision to hold a child back from kindergarten (e.g., with another year of prekindergarten) as an alternative or "non-regular" placement.

books and from the environment during preschool years appear to be critical to the emergence of literacy (Adams, 1990; Schuele & van Kleeck, 1987; van Kleeck, 1990; van Kleeck & Schuele, 1987). Gillam and Johnston (1985) observed that 3- to 6-year-old children with SLI were less capable of pairing printed words with the objects they represented than were a group of same-age children who were developing typically. It is important to note that the differences observed did not seem to result from differences in quantity or quality of exposure to environmental print. Rather, the results suggested that deficits in print awareness were related to the children's overall language abilities. Thus, children with SLI appear to be less proficient in making use of the written stimuli that they encounter during the preschool years—the period during which early reading abilities are believed to emerge and attitudes toward reading tend to develop.

Successful transitions to school and later educational achievements depend on more than just the presence of strong verbal abilities, however. Social competence and teacher, parent, and self-perceptions of social, verbal, and academic maturity also are closely associated with early school success (Alexander & Entwisle, 1988; Ladd & Price, 1987; O'Brien, 1992). The social and behavioral problems characteristic of many children with language impairments are well documented (Beitchman, Nair, Clegg, Ferguson, & Patel, 1986; Brinton & Fujiki, chap. 7, this volume; Cantwell & Baker, 1987; Fundudis, Kolvin, & Garside, 1979; Silva, Williams, & McGee, 1987; Windsor, chap. 8, this volume). Although the precise relationship between early oral language impairment and social problems is unclear (Windsor, chap. 8, this volume), recent evidence indicates that social problems among children with language impairments are well established during the preschool years. For example, Rice and her colleagues (Hadley & Rice, 1991; Rice, 1993; Rice, Sell, & Hadley, 1991) have reported the results of several observational investigations of the social interactions of preschoolers with SLI in their Language Acquisition Preschool. The findings of these studies may be summarized as follows: 1) typically developing children were preferred partners for all children in the preschool; 2) the conversational initiations of children with SLI were ignored more frequently than were the children developing typically; 3) children with SLI were more likely not to respond to other children and adults than were children developing typically; and 4) children with SLI were more likely to initiate social contact with adults than peers, whereas children developing typically were just as likely to make bids to peers as to adults.

Gertner (1993) followed up the investigations of Rice and her colleagues with what is, as far as we know, the only sociometric evaluation of children with SLI. Children in the Language Acquisition Preschool were asked to indicate the three children in the playroom they would like to play with most and the three children they would like to play with least. They also were asked to rate how much they liked to play with other children in the classroom. The typically developing children were the most preferred playmates, followed by children who were learning English as a second language. The children with SLI were the least preferred on all three indices.

Rice, Alexander, and Hadley (1993) set out to determine the influence of preschoolers' speech and language problems on how they were perceived by adults. Adult judges, including speech-language pathologists and kindergarten teachers, listened to brief audiotaped samples of the children's verbal interactions and were asked to rate the children on intelligence, social maturity, prognosis for success in kindergarten, leadership abilities, popularity, and the level of education and socioeconomic status of the children's parents. On each of these variables, the adults rated the children with SLI lower than the children with isolated speech impairments, who were rated lower than the typically developing controls. The same ratings were obtained for estimations of parental education and social status. Thus, adults appear to develop negative assessments of many important capabilities of children with language impairments, as well as of their parents' educational and social status, based solely on their poor oral language performance. Given the importance of teacher ratings of verbal, social, and academic competence on a successful transition to school, such negative assessments contribute further to the list of factors that place children with language impairments at extremely high risk for early school failure.

LANGUAGE INTERVENTION EFFICACY: WHEN IS SUCCESS REALLY SUCCESS?

Fey and Cleave (1990) argued that how we judge the effectiveness of language intervention depends crucially on the types of treatment objectives the intervention was designed to meet. We can illustrate this notion by examining the grammar facilitation approach recently administered to a group of preschoolers with language impairments by Fey and colleagues (Fey, Cleave, Long, & Hughes, 1993; Fey, Long, & Cleave, 1994). The basic goals for the children in this program were: 1) to foster the children's more consistent usage of morphosyntactic forms they were using inconsistently or in limited contexts, and 2) to facilitate the acquisition and use of new forms not evident in the children's extant expressive grammars. Both of these basic goals required improved performance in meaningful conversational settings. The importance of improved conversational performance was highlighted by the fact that all measures of performance were based on analyses of parent–child conversations collected during free-play interactions.

After the 4½-month intervention, the Developmental Sentence Scores (Lee, 1974) of the subjects who received intervention were almost one full standard deviation greater than those of a control group of subjects who received no interventions over the same period. Furthermore, Fey et al. (1993) presented evidence that a continuation of the intervention for an additional 4½ months led to additional gains for many children, although these improvements were generally not as great as those observed for the first phase of intervention. Given the basic goals for our intervention approach, we believe that it must be regarded as highly effective.

But consider this approach from the broader perspective outlined in the introduction: Was the intervention sufficient to minimize or at least substantially reduce the likelihood that these children would experience early academic and social difficulties in school? Did the intervention provide them with all that it might have to prepare them for positive early educational experiences? Fey and colleagues did not ask these questions as a part of their investigation and, therefore, these questions cannot be answered definitively. However, we would wager that the answer to the second and, possibly, even to the first of these questions is "No." We believe that, although the experimental program of Fey et al. (1993) accomplished much of what it was designed to accomplish, this approach and all others that emphasize only the preschool child's oral conversational language (e.g., Camarata et al., 1991; Friedman & Friedman, 1980; Lee, Koenigsknecht, & Mulhern, 1975) lack the comprehensiveness necessary to meet what we now regard as a crucial basic goal for preschool children with language impairments: to prepare them for the written language and social demands of school.

Acceptance of such a broad goal brings with it some substantial challenges for language interventionists. We agree completely with Kirchner (1991) who stated, "The question for language intervention is whether it is possible to make use of or construct supported communicative intervention contexts that can address conversational management and discourse, specific linguistic structures, and early literacy at once" (p. 311). But if such a program could be created, what would it look like? What specific targets, if any, might be selected for direct instruction in such a program? If these specific goals are reached, is the probability of school success actually enhanced as predicted? If phonological and grammatical forms are not targeted directly, do these language forms develop spontaneously at acceptable rates as the result of other types of intervention? These are the types of questions that we believe all speech-language pathologists working with preschoolers should be asking.

IS IT POSSIBLE TO REDUCE RISKS
FOR ACADEMIC AND SOCIAL FAILURE IN SCHOOL?

In the previous section, we claimed that our own grammar facilitation intervention program was not sufficiently comprehensive to attain the basic goal of minimizing the risk for social and academic failure in school. This is because our intervention (and evaluative measures) failed to consider all of the linguistic social, behavioral, and literacy factors that contribute to positive early school experiences. Children with LI are likely to be deficient in these very areas. Therefore, our program, by itself, must not have been adequate to prepare our subjects for the academic and social demands of school. Despite the logic of this speculation, there has been very little research designed to study systematically the effects of preschool language intervention on the early and subsequent school performance of children with language impairments. There are virtually no prospective studies that have carefully monitored, much less controlled, the type, quantity, or quality of preschool interventions with children who have language impairments with the specific intent of observing the impact on measures of academic and social success. What, then, do we really know about the effects of early language intervention on the school performance of children with LI?

Most of the results that have been reported are consistent with our negative speculation about conversational language interventions used to prepare preschoolers with language impairments for school. For example, Aram and Nation (1980) reported that in their sample of 63 children identified as having language impairments during preschool, the duration of preschool intervention was not associated with ratings of speech, language, or academic variables 4–5 years later. Bishop and Edmundson (1987) also reported that the outcomes of their subjects with SLI at age 5½ were unrelated to the amount of intervention the children had received since their identification at age 4. These investigators noted that the outcomes of their subjects at 5½ depended mostly on their performance at age 4, with subjects who exhibited more severe early impairments more likely to have an impaired profile at 5½ than 4-year-olds with less severe impairments. However, the nature and quality of intervention was not monitored or evaluated in either of these studies. Although it is clear in these investigations that the interventions did not eliminate the risks for later school problems for these children, it may be that they nevertheless had a positive impact, making academic problems less severe than they otherwise might have been (Bishop & Edmundson, 1987; Paul & Smith, 1993).

Padget (1988) reported the results of a prospective investigation in which all subjects received daily individual speech-language intervention for at least 1 year before starting kindergarten as an adjunct to a preschool program. Few details are provided about the type of intervention the children received, but it is clear that individual sessions and "carry over" work in the classroom and home focused on speech and oral language and not on socialization, classroom behavior, or early literacy skills. Regular kindergarten placement was selected from a number of options as the initial educational placement for only 6 of the 23 subjects with SLI (26%) at the time of their kindergarten eligibility.[2] After 4 years in school (including kindergarten), only one of Padget's subjects had progressed normally through the academic ranks.

These sobering findings contrast somewhat with the more positive reports of Cooper, Moodley, and Reynell (1979) and Huntley, Holt, Butterfill, and

---

[2]These calculations on children with SLI are based on analyses of Table III (Padget, 1988). We excluded four subjects listed in that table (CH, CL, PT, and SP) from our counts because they left the district and records of diagnostic classifications were not available. Two additional subjects (RH and FT) were excluded in our calculations for children with SLI because of evidence that they had hearing impairments.

Latham (1988). The preschool intervention provided in these studies was the Developmental Language Program (Cooper, Moodley, & Reynell, 1974). One model for this program was delivered in small groups in a clinic context. Sessions lasted 2 hours per day, 5 days a week. Descriptions of the types of procedures and activities involved in the program are rather sketchy, but it is clear that the program focused primarily on oral language comprehension and production. Emphasis was also placed on children's attentional abilities, visual-motor skills (e.g., with building activities and puzzles), and the use of language to direct self-action. A much streamlined version of this program involved teaching the techniques to parents for use in daily living activities. After an intensive initial training of parents, the speech-language pathologist in this model saw the children and their parents only once every 6 weeks. Over a year-long intervention, most of the preschoolers with language impairments who participated in either version of the program made gains in language that exceeded their rate of development prior to program entry. These gains also appeared to be greater than those of a comparison group of children from an earlier investigation who received no intervention.

More important than the Cooper et al. (1979) report of gains in language measures is their claim: "Despite the initially severe language handicaps with which the children presented, and many associated handicaps of lesser degree, the teachers' reports indicated that 70% of the whole class sample (50 children) [i.e., the parent group] made average to good progress in ordinary school during the first year after transfer" (p. 59). In their follow-up of the Cooper et al. (1979) subjects, Huntley et al. (1988) found that 81% of the children in this study who did not have marked cognitive impairments at the end of intervention remained in regular schools 5 years later. These investigators do not report how many of these children had been retained in one or more grades, however, nor do they note how many of these children were receiving special services in the regular schools. The reading performance of the subjects (including children with cognitive impairments) was approximately one standard deviation below the mean of the standardization sample, however, and reading accuracy, reading comprehension, and spelling all were significantly lower than the subjects' measured nonverbal intelligence scores. Thus, although the language gains of the children in the Cooper et al. study remain impressive throughout the early school years, evidence suggests that many of these children still were having significant problems in school.

We believe that it is unrealistic to expect language intervention programs to eliminate altogether the language-learning problems and the risk of subsequent school-related problems among young children with language impairments. Nevertheless, several questions warrant immediate consideration. For example, what is the likelihood that we can do better with more comprehensive, broadly based interventions not confined to the facilitation of conversational behaviors? In what ways might existing programs be modified (or overhauled) to yield the largest and most consistent results? The answers to these questions are not known, but several areas of deficiency might be targeted in an effort to minimize risks associated with preschool language impairments. Specifically, there is some evidence that interventions designed to facilitate emergent literacy, to enhance phonological awareness, and to improve social-interactional performance could be useful in minimizing subsequent school-related problems. Therefore, in the next section, we examine whether the performance of children with language impairments can be improved in areas associated with later school success.

Facilitating Early Literacy Skills

One approach that researchers and clinicians have taken in the prevention of reading disabilities is the early introduction of reading materials. It is generally thought that exposing typically developing children and children with language impairments to literacy materials and activities during the preschool years can result in children getting off to a better start when formal reading instruction begins (Adams, 1990; Schuele & van Kleeck, 1987; van Kleeck, 1990; van Kleeck & Schuele, 1987). A primary component of most emergent literacy programs is joint parent–child storybook reading. Parents of children at risk for reading disabilities often are encouraged to read to their children on a daily basis. This practice draws much of its support from the results of the Commission on Reading, National Academy of Education (Anderson, Hiebert, Scott, & Wilkinson, 1985), which concluded that "The single most important activity for building the knowledge required for eventual success in reading is reading aloud to children. This is especially so during the preschool years" (p. 23).

As noted earlier, Gillam and Johnston (1985) found that preschoolers with SLI were less aware of environmental print than their peers with typical language abilities. Furthermore, children with SLI have been shown to have deficiencies in their knowledge of story structure and their ability to make inferences based on simple texts (Bishop & Adams, 1992; Ellis Weismer, 1985). Therefore, the suggestions that parents of children with language impairments should read more to their children would seem to be reasonable and prudent.

Unfortunately, the evidence supporting this suggestion is weak at best. Scarborough (in press) reviewed 27 correlational and experimental studies since 1960 that have examined the effects of joint storybook reading on language abilities, reading achievement, and emergent literacy skills (e.g., letter identification, print conventions, environmental print recognition). Although Scarborough concluded from her review that parent–preschooler reading experiences are associated with enhanced language and literacy skills, she noted that these improvements were variable across studies and generally far more modest than anticipated. It also appeared that the effects of changes in the quantity and/or quality of shared book reading during the preschool years are greater for oral language measures than for emergent literacy or later reading achievement. Nevertheless, even if these studies showed conclusively that the quantity and quality of early oral reading experiences reduced the risk of reading disabilities, it would be inappropriate to extend this conclusion to children with language impairments. None of the studies included children who had identified language-learning problems, although many involved children who could be considered at risk for language and reading delays. Furthermore, Gillam and Johnston (1985) found no evidence to suggest that the deficiencies in print awareness were the result of inadequate experience. Rather, their subjects with specific language-learning problems seemed to take less from the same amount of experience than did their typically developing peers.

Thus, it may be that clinicians who make the general recommendation that parents of children with language impairments read more to their children are adopting the strategy that more input is better input. There is little indication from the studies reviewed by Scarborough (in press) to expect that this strategy will be successful, at least for children whose parents already engage in regular shared reading. Furthermore, in other areas such as the acquisition of grammar there is evidence that the sheer quantity of input may be less important than factors such as the discourse function of the utterances containing target forms, the relationship of the input to the child's own production, and the child's state of readiness to learn a specific target (e.g., Farrar, 1990; Hoff-Ginsberg, 1990; Nelson, 1989).

Nevertheless, there are some reasons for optimism if parents modify their style of interaction as they read to their preschoolers with language-learning problems. There are several reports of story-based procedures designed to influence the oral language performance of preschoolers with typical and impaired language development. For example, Whitehurst et al. (1988) presented a dialogic reading training program to 14 typically developing children between the ages of 21 and 35 months. This program was based on three general procedures: 1) increase the child's participation through more frequent use of *wh-* questions that are open-ended and that require the child to elaborate on descriptions of the pictures and on prior text, 2) increase "informative feedback" such as expansions that fill in grammatical details and extend semantically the child's utterances, and 3) be sensitive to the child's developmental level (e.g., require object labels when the child is in the single-word stage but sentence fragments and entire sentences when the child is in later stages). Parents of children in both the experimental and control groups were told of the potential importance of early book reading, and all parents were instructed to audiotape their reading sessions at home three or four times a week. Parents in the experimental group were trained in the procedures over two sessions of approximately 30 minutes held 2 weeks apart. The entire intervention lasted only 4 weeks. The results indicated that the parents in the experimental group modified their interactions with their children in the manner specified by the program. Furthermore, the children in the experimental group had higher posttreatment scores on the verbal expressive subscale of the Illinois Test of Psycholinguistic Abilities (ITPA) (Kirk,

McCarthy, & Kirk, 1968) and the Expressive One-Word Picture Vocabulary Test (EOWPVT) (Gardner, 1979). Follow-up on a subset of the children 9 months after intervention revealed strong trends in the same directions for the same measures. There were no differences in the reported or recorded frequency of reading sessions between intervention and control groups. Thus, a brief and inexpensive parent storybook training procedure that modified the *quality* of parent–child reading appeared to contribute significantly to oral language gains of typically developing children.

The same procedures were employed as part of a more comprehensive intervention tested by Whitehurst, Fischel, Caulfield, DeBaryshe, and Valdez-Menchaca (1989). This 4-month parent intervention program involved 25 children, 24–40 months of age, with specific expressive language delays. The program included seven assignments, most of which targeted lexical forms and early word combinations and made heavy use of elicited imitation and social reinforcement procedures (e.g., "Good talking"). The subjects who received intervention made significant gains in comparison to nonintervention controls, based on scores from the EOWPVT and the verbal expressive subscale of the ITPA. The nature of the gains observed is difficult to determine because none of the outcome measures were based on conversational speech or narration. Furthermore, as was noted by Whitehurst et al. (1988), the design of this study made it impossible to isolate the effects of the book reading from other intervention variables.

Dale, Notari, Crain-Thoreson, and Cole (1993) attempted to remedy the problems of the Whitehurst et al. intervention in an investigation involving 33 preschoolers with mild to moderate language impairments. Parents were assigned to receive storybook training or conversational training over two sessions. The periods of parent-administered intervention following each parent training session were 3–4 weeks each, for a total of 6–8 weeks of intervention. The very brief parent training led to several nonsignificant trends that were consistent with the program's intent. Mothers who received storybook training tended to use more *wh-* questions, open-ended questions, and expansions during story reading than did the mothers who received conversational intervention. Only the children in the storybook group exhibited statistically significant gains in MLU following intervention, but these gains were not significantly different from those of the conversational training group. Thus, these results do not demonstrate that intervention that changes parent reading styles has a greater effect on the oral language development of children with language impairments than does parent intervention focusing on parents' conversational behaviors. The results suggest strongly, however, that such an intervention could be an important adjunct to a larger intervention program designed to facilitate the oral language abilities of children with language impairments (cf. Whitehurst et al., 1989).

The studies of Whitehurst and colleagues (1988, 1989) and Dale et al. (1993) focus on the use of adult questions and expanded or recast sentences in story reading to facilitate the oral language skills of children with language impairments. Kirchner (1991) described a different storybook method, called "reciprocal book reading," that relies more on the inherent structure of children's stories to foster children's language development. Although Kirchner's book-reading approach could be modified to incorporate the techniques found in the Whitehurst et al. (1988) program, she stressed the importance of selecting books that contain the child's target language forms and topics of interest and that are highly repetitive and predictable in form and content (see also Gillam, McFadden, & van Kleeck, chap. 6, this volume). Kirchner encouraged multiple readings of these texts individually or in groups to foster memorization of story lines. Once the story is committed to memory, the interventionist may create a cloze context by pausing and allowing the child to complete phrases and sentences. Ultimately, the child can tell the story, and the adult can play the child's role of finishing sentences. Kirchner suggested that this procedure may facilitate: 1) the child's development of new language forms, 2) increased participation in dialogues and improved use of turn-taking, and 3) knowledge of story structure. She presented a case study of a child with Asperger's syndrome to illustrate the potential of the technique with a broad range of children with language-learning problems.

One final illustration of a story-based procedure is that evaluated in a case study by Hoffman, Norris, and Monjure (1990). The two subjects of this study were brothers, ages 4 years, 1 month who were two-thirds of a triplet cohort. Based on the authors' description, these children had mild impairments of grammar and phonology. One child received an oral story-retelling approach and the other received phonological intervention only. In the story-retelling approach, the clinician first told the initiating event of a story, then talked informally about what the characters were doing and their motives, using a variety of language models. In the second step, the child was instructed to retell the story to a puppet listener. Whenever the child was unclear, inaccurate, or ambiguous, the puppet requested clarification. The required information was provided by the clinician, again using a variety of models, and the child was then instructed to retell the event. The clinician focused on inclusion of appropriate information rather than on the form of the child's utterances. Remaining story events were then told and retold in the same manner. After the sequence of events was completed, the clinician added elements that attributed additional motives to the characters' actions, associated causes with events, interpreted feelings, predicted future events, and drew inferences from the story content. This intervention was provided in 18 50-minute sessions spread evenly over 6 weeks. Changes in language were measured by having the subjects tell "The Three Bears" before and after intervention. Following intervention, the child who received the story-based intervention used more sentences related to the story; made fewer errors of syntax, tense, and phonology; and tended to use more complex utterances. He made no gains in pronoun usage. His brother, who received only phonological intervention, made significant gains only in phonology. Thus, this intervention appeared to have a significant positive impact on the grammatical and phonological form and on the semantic content of the stories told by one child with a mild language impairment.[3]

From all of these studies, it may be concluded that parents and probably teachers, aides, and other adults can be taught to modify their style of reading and telling stories to their children with language impairments. These modifications involve: 1) getting the child actively involved through open-ended questions, choral reading and completion of cloze sentences, and story-retelling; 2) providing feedback in the form of requests for clarification, sentence recasts, and the recasting and integration of story content; and 3) focusing joint attention on a mutually pleasurable story experience. Only a very small number of subjects have been studied to date. Nevertheless, whether presented by a parent or by a clinician, it appears that these types of story-based techniques have a measurable impact on the form of children's sentences and on their expressive vocabularies. There is some limited evidence that such techniques help children to include more relevant semantic details of the stories they tell. It seems that these methods will have the greatest impact when they are incorporated within a more comprehensive language intervention package (cf. Whitehurst et al., 1989).

The early reports of the effects of story-based techniques on the oral language form, content, and function of at least some children with LI are encouraging. Furthermore, the procedures are highly efficient because storybook reading is a common activity shared by many parents and their young children. Based on these reports, we can see many good reasons to modify the early adult–child reading experiences of children with language impairments. In most cases, we can see no harm in adding such a procedure to a comprehensive preschool language intervention program. But this recommendation begs two questions: First, does an increase in high-quality exposures to printed material better prepare children with language impairments to read, write, and spell? There are many reasons to think that the answer to this question is yes. Unfortunately, these reasons are based on assumptions and speculations rather than evidence. At present, the only evidence concerning this issue comes from correlational and intervention studies involving typically developing children, some of whom may have been at risk for later problems. As discussed earlier, this evidence does not provide strong support for the assumptions (Scarborough, in press). Second, should parents of children with language impairments who

---

[3]The results of a recent investigation by Fey, Cleave, Ravida, Long, Dejmal, and Easton (1994) call to question the conclusion that interventions such as that of Hoffman et al. (1990) that do not provide direct focus on phonology will have a significant impact on the phonological development of children with language impairments. In this experimental evaluation of a primarily conversation-based intervention designed to facilitate grammatical acquisition, no effects were observed on a measure of phonology despite large effects on morphosyntactic production. Studies with larger samples of children with language impairments are needed to test the indirect effects of naturalistic language interventions.

exhibit little or no interest in literacy materials be encouraged to read more to their children or to modify their style? Many studies suggest that a child's motivation to read is a significant factor in the child's development of literacy skills (see Scarborough, in press). Scarborough expressed concern that forcing children who are uninterested in reading materials to participate in shared book reading when they choose to do otherwise may have unanticipated negative effects. Prospective investigations that systematically test story-based procedures for their effects on emergent literacy skills and later written language achievement among children with language impairments are sorely needed. It is also important to learn the extent to which intrinsic factors, such as a child's motivation and attitudes toward reading materials, can be modified through intervention.

Enhancing Phonological Awareness

As noted earlier, children with LI often have deficits in their awareness of and ability to manipulate the syllables and phonemic segments of words (Catts, 1991a, 1993; Kamhi & Catts, 1986; Kamhi et al., 1985).[4] The letters of the alphabet are closely related to phonemic segments, and some explicit knowledge of this letter–sound relationship is common among good readers of all ages. There is now strong evidence that problems in phonological awareness are a major contributing factor in early reading disabilities (Catts, 1989; Stanovich, 1988; Wagner & Torgesen, 1987). Therefore, one intervention strategy that may be helpful in offsetting the reading problems of children with language impairments is early direct instruction in phonological awareness (Catts, 1991b).

Catts (1991b) has summarized the various types of procedures and activities that have been incorporated into phonological awareness programs. These include: 1) beginning speech-sound awareness activities such as nursery rhymes, songs, and finger play; 2) sound play activities such as creating sequences of rhyming words; 3) rhyme, alliteration, and sound judgment tasks (e.g., "Which words start with the same sound?"); 4) sound segmentation and blending tasks; and 5) sound manipulation tasks such as creating new words by substituting one sound or syllable for another in a target word. Although some interventions have been long and intensive, others have been short and time efficient. For example, a highly structured program tested by Lundberg (1988) was administered daily for 8 months while interventions evaluated by Ball and Blachman (1988, 1991) were presented to groups of children in four weekly 15- to 20-minute sessions for only a 7-week period.

---

[4]There is evidence that children with reading and spelling disabilities also have deficiencies in other areas of linguistic awareness, such as inflectional and derivational morphology (Carlisle, 1987; Leong, 1989; Tyler & Nagy, 1990). Although training of morphological awareness skills also may be shown to facilitate the development of reading, there is presently no information on the effects of such training, if any, on preschoolers. Therefore, morphological awareness is not considered further in this chapter.

The results of numerous investigations have shown that phonological awareness can be trained in kindergarten and first-grade children. More important, gains in phonological awareness have been associated with improved reading ability (Ball & Blachman, 1988, 1991; Bradley & Bryant, 1985; Byrne & Fielding-Barnsley, 1990; Cunningham, 1990; Fox & Routh, 1983; Lie, 1991; Lundberg, Frost, & Peterson, 1988; Torgesen, Morgan, & Davis, 1992). Studies have shown that teaching children to categorize words that rhyme or begin with the same sound improves their phonological awareness and subsequent reading ability (Bradley & Bryant, 1985; Byrne & Fielding-Barnsley, 1990). Others have found that teaching children explicitly to segment and blend phonemes in words can have a significant effect on reading and spelling (Ball & Blachman, 1988; Torgesen et al., 1992). Still other research indicates that explicit training in phoneme analysis and synthesis may have the most significant effect when combined with instruction in how the alphabet represents phonemes (Cunningham, 1990).

We are aware of only two studies in which children with documented language-learning problems participated in phonological awareness interventions. One intervention evaluated by Warrick, Rubin, and Rowe-Walsh (1993) led to unambiguous positive outcomes. Prior to the intervention, two groups of 14 kindergartners with SLI were significantly different from a group of 14 age-equivalent children who were developing typically. One group of children with SLI was provided with an 8-week program of intervention that involved direct instruction on syllable awareness, rhyming, and phoneme segmentation. The other groups served as no-intervention controls. The children attended two 20-minute sessions weekly. The first postintervention evaluation showed that only the group with SLI that received intervention exhibited significant gains on phonological awareness tasks. Furthermore, the gains of the subjects in this group were sufficient to make the group indistinguishable from the group of typically developing children on the phonological awareness tasks. More important, these gains were maintained at a second posttest one year after the first. In addition, while the children with SLI who did not receive intervention lagged significantly behind their typically developing peers on phonological awareness, reading, and spelling tasks, the children with SLI who received the intervention were no different than their typically developing peers on any of these measures. It must be noted, however, that none of the reading and spelling tasks administered tested the children's ability to read or spell units larger than a word. The impact of this intervention on these children's processing of written sentences or longer textual units is not known.

Although encouraging, the results of a study by O'Connor, Jenkins, Leicester, and Slocum (1993) were not nearly as positive as those reported by Warrick et al. (1993). These investigators presented either a sound-blending, rhyming, or word-segmentation training program to 47 4-, 5-, and 6-year-old subjects participating in an experimental preschool program. Eighty percent of the 47 were children with language impairments, but many had deficits in other areas as well. The mean mental age for the subjects was 3 years, 8 months. Instruction was provided for 10 minutes per day in groups of from three to five children for 7 weeks. Each type of training had a significant effect on the children's ability to perform the tasks on which they were trained. For example, children trained to blend sounds outperformed other children on blending tasks, and children trained to segment words into their phonemic constituents performed better on segmentation tasks. Gains in one particular skill (e.g., blending, rhyming) generally did not lead to gains in another, however. Furthermore, training on one task did not result in gains on other tasks even when the tasks involved the same types of skills. For example, instruction that helped children to blend protracted but continuous strings of sounds (e.g., Sssaaammm→Sam) did not lead to gains on other blending tasks (e.g., S-am or S-a-m→Sam).

There are many factors that might explain the differences between the results of the study by Warrick et al. (1993) and the results of the study by O'Connor et al. (1993). For example, the impairments of the subjects in the study by Warrick et al. were more specific to language than those studied by O'Connor et al. Furthermore, the subjects of the study by Warrick et al. apparently were functioning at higher cognitive levels than the children studied by O'Connor et al. They appeared to have less impairment in their language performance as well. In addition, the intervention of Warrick et al. was more comprehensive than that of O'Connor et al. It may be that broader interventions that combine phonological awareness activities (i.e., blending, segmenting, rhyming) may be necessary for at least some preschoolers with language impairments.

Although many questions remain about the stability and generality of the effects of phonological awareness training for preschoolers with language impairments, the evidence at hand leads us to conclude that it is reasonable, if not advisable, to include structured phonological awareness activities in a comprehensive intervention package for preschoolers with language impairments (see Blachman, 1991; Chaney, 1990). Nevertheless, clinicians who attempt such programs must be realistic about the outcomes that are likely to result from phonological awareness training. Reading requires more than the decoding of words, which is the aspect of reading related most directly to phonological awareness skills. Good reading depends equally on the higher processes of text comprehension, and these processes may be impaired in children with language impairments (Bishop & Adams, 1992; Crais & Chapman, 1987; Ellis Weismer, 1985; Paul & Smith, 1993). Lundberg (1988) reported that his highly successful phonological awareness program had no effect on his subjects' language comprehension skills. Therefore, it seems unlikely that enhancement of phonological awareness skills could have a large impact on reading success among children with language-learning problems unless their problems with the production and comprehension of texts, such as stories, also are addressed effectively. The studies of O'Connor et al. (1993) and Warrick et al. (1993) demonstrate convincingly that children with language impairments who had no other instruction in reading can learn to perform various phonological awareness tasks with very limited training. Research is needed to examine more closely the types of phonological awareness procedures and activities that are most effective for different subgroups of children with language impairments and to determine more precisely the influence of such instruction on subsequent reading achievement.

Facilitating Social-Interactional Skills

Given the social nature of language, it is not surprising that many children with communication problems have deficiencies in their social-interactional performance and have difficulty in developing positive peer relationships (Bryan, 1974; Craig & Washington, 1993; Gallagher, 1991; Gertner, 1993; Goldstein & Gallagher, 1992; Windsor, chap. 8, this volume). Somewhat surprising is that the social disadvantages associated with language impairments are demonstrable by as early as 3 years of age even among children whose language problems are not complicated by documented intellectual, emotional, or physical disabilities (Gertner, 1993; Hadley & Rice, 1991; Rice et al., 1991). Negative self-assessment of competency as well as low evaluations by peers and teachers are predictive of poor transitions to school (Ladd & Price, 1987; O'Brien, 1992). Thus, to reach the basic goal of minimizing risk for school failure, early interventionists must be concerned with the social-interactional performance of preschoolers with language impairments. But what types of interventions are effective in modifying the social-interactional profiles of these children or the attitudes of their parents and teachers? Furthermore, if effective intervention leads to improved social performance and more positive perceptions of the children's cognitive status and social maturity, are the risks of school failure diminished?

There are numerous strategies that might be expected to foster the social skills and status of children with language impairments. The most obvious candidate from the standpoint of speech-language pathologists is an intervention that targets directly the child's disorders of speech and language form. This would be a reasonable approach if it could be assumed that the child's social difficulties were caused by his or her weak linguistic skills *and* if it could be demonstrated that early language intervention results in rapid normalization of children's formal linguistic abilities. If a child with a language impairment could be made to communicate like a child who is developing typically, the child might not suffer the negative social consequences associated with early communication problems. Unfortunately, it is difficult to determine the nature of the relationship between a child's linguistic and social deficits (Rice, 1993; Windsor, chap. 8, this volume). Furthermore, as we have shown earlier, it appears that many preschoolers who have received language intervention primarily targeting language form do not catch up with their same-age peers in language or school achievement (e.g., Aram & Nation, 1980; Huntley et al., 1988; Padget, 1988).

Therefore, it is unlikely that such interventions will have the significant and rapid impact on early social performance and status that is desired.

Many methods have been suggested to facilitate social interactions among children with mild to severe social-interactional impairments. The basic goals of these methods are to increase the use of positive social behaviors, such as the initiation of conversational turns and contingent verbal responding to the social bids of peers, and to reduce the use of negative behaviors, such as stereotypic, non-contingent phrases (see Windsor, chap. 8, this volume). In general, the assumption is made that if the rate of positive social interactions between children with social problems and their peers can be increased through intervention, these social contacts will become naturally reinforcing. This will result in more spontaneous positive social interactions, which in turn provide the contexts in which new social and linguistic learning may occur.

Intervention procedures include: 1) manipulation of the physical and social contexts, such as providing children with toys that tend to encourage social play in a relatively small space and structuring the children's play activities by assigning roles and explaining teacher expectations; 2) group affection activities in which a teacher leads group games and activities that encourage friendship, cooperation, and positive social acts such has hugging, "high-fives," and complementing; 3) direct instruction such as modeling or coaching the child in the use of target behaviors; 4) incidental teaching, that is, teacher prompts to redirect a social initiation to a peer or to respond to another child's social bid; 5) adult praise and attention that is contingent on positive social behaviors; 6) script training to help children act out reciprocal roles in familiar events; and 7) the use of peers as confederates either as partners or in structured group experiences to initiate interactions with target children and to respond more favorably to their social initiations. These methods are discussed in other reviews (Brinton & Fujiki, chap. 7, this volume; Gallagher, 1991; Goldstein & Gallagher, 1992; Odom & Brown, 1993; Windsor, chap. 8, this volume). In general, whether used in isolation or in combination, these methods have been successful in increasing the use of positive social behaviors and decreasing the use of negative behaviors in preschoolers with disabilities in at least some contexts. With some socially isolated school-age children, gains in social skill have led to improvements on indices of peer acceptance (Ladd, 1981; Oden & Asher, 1977).

There are several factors, however, that limit the applicability of these findings to the planning of social interventions for the preschoolers with language impairments who are targeted in this chapter. First, in general, the positive effects of the intervention methods noted earlier have tended to diminish after intervention protocols are terminated, and generalization to contexts outside the intervention setting often has been limited. It is clear that generalization to common social circumstances must be the central consideration of any intervention targeting improvements in children's social interactions and status with peers (see Chandler, Lubeck, & Fowler [1992] for a comprehensive quantitative review of generalization in social skills research). Second, because investigators generally have been interested in demonstrating the power of the methods they are testing, children with autism and/or severe emotional, cognitive, or behavioral disorders commonly are the targets of intervention in these studies. Although it is reasonable to assume that interventions that are effective with children from these populations with severe disabilities also would have some effect on children with less severe and more language-specific disorders, it cannot be assumed that the same methods are necessary or that they would have the same effects upon children with milder impairments. This is especially true with regard to generalization. For example, it may be that certain interventions that do not lead to generalization in uncontrolled nonintervention contexts with children with autism are sufficient to trigger significant improvements in the socialization of children with less general impairments.[5] Third, when children who have language impairment as their primary disability have been included in studies, their speech, language, and communication characteristics generally have not been well described. Thus, the extent to which impaired language comprehension and/or expression abilities figure into the subjects' social problems or contribute to the outcome of intervention is impossible to determine.

Social Interventions

To illustrate the types of interventions that may be effective with the children targeted in this chapter, four kinds of social interventions are discussed in some detail here. The first two of these social interventions have the advantage that they are designed to be implemented entirely in integrated classroom contexts. Twardosz, Nordquist, Simon, and Botkin (1983) designed an approach referred to as group affection activities. In their first two studies of this approach, a teacher discussed with the entire group of children the notions of friendship and the importance of displaying affection toward their peers. Following these discussions, the teacher led the children in group games and songs that required peer cooperation and modeled and encouraged positive social behaviors. The two studies described by Twardosz et al. (1983) involved three socially isolated preschoolers, only one of whom was noted to have significant speech or language problems. Compared to pre-intervention performance, the subjects interacted with peers more frequently and displayed more positive behaviors such as smiling and affectionate touching in free play over the period in which intervention was administered. Performance was highly variable, however, and withdrawal of the procedures led to rapid reductions in production of positive behaviors for one child. McEvoy et al. (1988) demonstrated that affection activ-

---

[5]The same type of problem arises in studies in which subjects are described merely as "socially isolated" (e.g., Hodgens & McCoy, 1990; Ladd, 1981; Oden & Asher, 1977). Although it seems likely that many children in these studies had problems with speech and/or language form and content, these deficits are not described. Thus, the role of language problems in the subjects' social problems and in the intervention outcomes cannot be determined.

ities can have the same type of small but positive influence on the social interaction of children with severe impairments and that the discussion component, which may require sophisticated verbal skills, is not necessary to achieve a significant, positive effect (McEvoy et al., 1988).

Rice (1993) described a different kind of social intervention for preschoolers with SLI. This program employed incidental teaching within the Language Acquisition Preschool classroom, where the need for assistance in social situations arises naturally. Rice's research (described earlier in detail) revealed that children with SLI were more likely to direct social bids to adults than to peers. Therefore, in this intervention, child initiations toward adults were redirected by requesting the child to seek assistance from a peer. For example, in response to a child's statement, "Need some glue," the adult might say, "Oh yeah, well ask/tell Susan," or "Get Mark to help you." Rice reported two preliminary investigations that have shown this strategy to be effective in increasing initiations of preschoolers with SLI in the classroom. As has been the case for most procedures, generalization to nontraining contexts was found to be difficult for some children. Similar results have been obtained by other investigators who used incidental teaching with preschool children with more severe impairments (Brown, McEvoy, & Bishop, 1991).

In many cases, interventions that are more direct and more intrusive than group affection activity or incidental teaching may be necessary. These interventions may require some instruction or modeling for target children and/or typical peers outside the classroom context. For example, Gallagher and Craig (1984) reported a case of a 4-year-old boy, Clark, with SLI who used the stereotypical phrase "It's gone" to gain access to the play of other children. This phrase was not only unsuccessful, but the child's peers seemed to regard it as socially aversive. A language intervention program that focused on language structure also included efforts to teach Clark to say, "Let's play," to gain entry into the play of others. Goldstein and Gallagher (1992) reported that Clark's subsequent use of this phrase was received positively by his peers and led to a proportional reduction in his use of the negative behavior. Thus, direct teaching of social skills can be combined with intervention that emphasizes language form, apparently to the social benefit of the child (see Brinton & Fujiki, chap. 7, this volume).

Goldstein, Wickstrom, Hoyson, Jamieson, and Odom (1988) developed an intervention based on the principle that children are more likely to communicate when they share common scripts. These investigators taught scripts that involved three children in a routine event such as going to a fast-food restaurant. These scripts were taught directly to the children individually or in groups of three over as few as four 15-minute sessions. In one experiment, two children with expressive language and behavior problems took part in group sessions with typically developing peers. In the other experiment, all of the children had communication problems. Each child was taught to play each of three roles using specific prompts, which were faded as the child began to act independently in her or his role. After the script was learned in structured training, the children were encouraged to enact the themes from the script during play time. During play, teacher prompts reminding the children to stay in character were shown to be effective in getting the children to produce theme-related communicative behaviors. All of the children improved in their participation in the script during sessions, and most increased their use of socially directed, theme-related behaviors during teacher-structured free play, although teacher prompts were required to maintain high levels of target social acts. The investigators noted that because only a single script was used per group of three children, some children tired of the enactments.

Goldstein and Gallagher (1992) stressed that script training requires little time and can be readily incorporated into a broader preschool program. Thus, it is possible and perhaps desirable to develop many scripts that then could be selected by the children for enactment during play times. Goldstein and Cisar (1992) demonstrated with three preschoolers with autism that it may take less time to help children learn subsequent scripts after they learn to participate in their first script.

It is too soon to determine whether social interventions lead to lasting changes in the social performance of children with language impairments. Furthermore, there is no evidence to suggest that such interventions result in improved social status for preschoolers with language impairments as determined by sociometric measures. Nevertheless, given the importance of social skills in the development of peer relationships and in the development of a positive self-concept, we believe that the social maturity and status of preschoolers with language impairments can no longer be neglected in early language intervention programs.

Odom and Brown (1993) recommended that social interventions for children with disabilities be carried out in a hierarchical fashion. In this hierarchy, methods that may be carried out with all children in an integrated classroom are employed first. More intrusive, child-specific techniques are added only if a child does not respond to less directive methods. For example, the first step in the hierarchy for children with language impairments would be to consult with the teacher in designing classroom activities that foster peer interaction and that focus on the interests and spontaneous actions of each child (see the discussion below of Activity-Based Intervention). If the child remains isolated in this type of environment, group affection training could be implemented. If these activities do not result in significantly improved social interaction, Odom and Brown recommended planning special play groups in which the physical and social environments are manipulated to foster positive social interaction between a child and a select group of peers. Finally, if such structured play groups do not have the desired effects, more direct social interventions that involve teachers or peers employing procedures toward a specific child (e.g., modeling, coaching, teacher prompts and praise) may be used.

Three Implications for Intervention

This hierarchical method of employing interventions seems highly reasonable to us. We suspect that some direct and child-specific teaching methods are required for many children with language impairments. In this case, we believe that several things must be kept in mind. For example, Gallagher (1991) stressed the importance of peers in social interventions and extracted from the intervention literature three implications for intervention that seem to apply to all children, including those with language impairments:

1. ...intervention programs that focus exclusively on the target child's behaviors are insufficient and would result in limited changes because they do not address the precipitating and maintaining behaviors of peers.
2. Target children and their peers need to be involved in the change process.
3. The goals of intervention should address the behavioral and perceptual changes needed by both the target children and their peers. (p. 31)

Furthermore, we suspect that if real gains are to be made in the social status and peer relationships of children with language impairments, interventionists need to place some emphasis on showcasing these children's interests and talents so they can be recognized by their peers and teachers. For example, the effectiveness of strategies such as group affection training, incidental teaching, and script training might be most effective if the themes that are selected focus on the children's areas of strength and expertise. For example, suppose that a child with a language impairment who had problems in social interaction showed a special interest in baseball. Baseball scripts involving a coach or manager, a hitter, and a pitcher could be constructed easily. Many other baseball-related scripts also could be created, such as a child getting autographs from a favorite player or negotiating with his or her parents for a trip to the concession stand. It is conceivable that with themes that are especially familiar and pleasurable for the child with a language impairment, that child might even take the lead in helping others to learn their roles.

The same principle could be employed in a modification of the incidental teaching strategy. Suppose, for example, the activity involved organizing baseball cards into teams or separating star players from regular players. In such tasks, many opportunities should arise in which the teacher could turn to the child with a language impairment for assistance. In other words, requests for teacher assistance from peers could be redirected to the child with a language impairment. It seems plausible that children with language impairments would be most likely to produce positive social responses when they are requested by their peers to perform tasks and fill roles in which they possess some knowledge and ability. By showcasing the nonverbal strengths and de-emphasizing the verbal weaknesses of these children, typically developing peers might be helped to see their value as playmates and friends despite their communicative handicaps. Such activities also might serve as reminders to teachers that most children with language impairments are quite capable in at least some areas that do not depend primarily on verbal abilities. Some consideration of peer and teacher attitudes toward the competencies and potential of children with language impairments, such as that embedded in these activities, may be important components of early interventions (O'Brien, 1992; Rice, 1993). Evaluating the value of these suggestions regarding the thematic content of social intervention activities on children's social adjustment, peer acceptance, and peer/teacher attitudes is a fertile area for future research.

ATTACKING EARLY LANGUAGE, LITERACY, AND SOCIAL GOALS

In our discussion thus far of intervention procedures and activities for preschoolers with language impairments, we have stressed the importance of providing some focus on specific structural and pragmatic aspects of preschoolers' conversational language as well as on emergent literacy, phonological awareness, and social competence. In this section, we consider strategies for attacking objectives in these areas in a comprehensive intervention program.

The Continuum of Intrusiveness

Fey (1986) described intervention approaches as falling at some point on a continuum of naturalness. At this time, this continuum seems better conceptualized as a continuum of intrusiveness. Historically, the most common language intervention approaches have fallen at the extreme high end of this continuum. In these maximally agent-oriented approaches, some intervention agent is in full control of most manipulable features of intervention, such as the intervention targets, the context of learning, and the antecedent and consequent stimuli provided. In such models, the level of intrusion upon the child's attentional, behavioral, and communicative agendas is extreme. At the opposite end of the intrusiveness continuum lie maximally child-oriented approaches. In these approaches, the selection of what is learned, when it is learned, and, in many respects, how it is learned is left to the child, with the intervention agent serving only as facilitator. Instead of controlling intervention variables such as the selection of specific speech and language targets, the emphasis is placed on observing children in contexts designed to facilitate spontaneous communication and on responding to the child's acts in a nonintrusive manner that follows the child's attentional and communicative lead. Here, the intervention agent must be highly sensitive to the child's agenda and utilize naturally occurring contexts as the central point for deployment of intervention techniques. Falling between these two extremes on the continuum of intrusiveness are what Fey (1986) described as hybrid intervention approaches. Hybrid approaches may employ some of the attributes of maximally child-oriented and more agent-oriented models. The number of hybrids is potentially unlimited, and some will be more child- or agent-oriented than others.

Maximally Intrusive Approaches

Maximally agent-oriented approaches designed to meet our broad basic goal would be the simplest conceptually. In such approaches, the clinician would generate specific goals within several areas, including oral language, phonological awareness, emergent literacy, and social interaction, and create specific activities, exercises, or experiences designed to attain each goal independently of other goals. Thus, a child might attend a preschool program but then be moved alone or with a group of children to a treatment room or to some area of the classroom for direct instruction in each targeted area. Although agent-oriented interventions have a rich history in speech-language pathology (Fey, 1986), they are being supplanted by less intrusive, more child-oriented models of intervention. This change is occurring because skills that are acquired in intervention contexts often do not generalize to functional communicative contexts and because theoretical developments have led many interventionists to propose that dependencies may exist both within and across linguistic, social, and behavioral domains (Bricker & Cripe, 1992; Fey, 1986; Norris & Hoffman, 1993).

Minimally Intrusive Approaches

In contrast to a heavily compartmentalized agent-oriented strategy, a minimally intrusive, maximally child-oriented approach would have as its most immediate objective the creation of highly responsive social environments that provide frequent opportunities for the child to initiate communication. Within such a positive communicative context, what is learned would be determined more by factors internal to the child than by the clinician. No specific objectives would be targeted for direct instruction or special focus. Instead, the emphasis would be on the child's success in communication. Focusing intervention efforts at such a central level of communication is presumed to lead naturally to gains in more specific areas of language and communication.

The best examples of a maximally child-oriented approach to the facilitation of language, literacy, and social development for children with language impairments come from a whole language perspective. Whole language intervention involves the use of procedures that provide a scaffold for the child's ongoing attempts to comprehend and create meaning in activities that are relevant and interesting to him or her. Thus, expansions of the child's utterances and requests for the child to retell stories or to clarify ideas by repeating or modifying sounds, words, phrases, and sentences are suitable procedures. Use of these procedures should lead to learning that spreads throughout all domains of the child's language system (see Gillam, 1994; Gillam et al., chap. 6, this volume; Hoffman et al., 1990; Norris & Damico, 1990; Norris & Hoffman, 1990).

Activities are of paramount importance in whole-language approaches. The repetition and contextual familiarity that is deemed necessary for learning oral and written language can be created by building intervention activities around consistent themes. For example, children's favorite stories usually involve simple themes around which numerous intervention activities can be developed. A story can be reread, retold, and acted out, the character and specific events can be drawn by the children, and the attitudes, motivations, and actions of the characters can be talked about over a period of days, weeks, or months. Early emphasis on print might involve frequent listening to and telling stories, dictating new or "retold" stories to an adult for incorporation into books, and even "writing" stories, which in the beginning might amount to little more than scribbling or random formations of letters into pretend words. Written language activities would focus on the individual elements of print such as words, letters, or sounds only to the extent that these elements allow the child to clarify or have fun with the meaning or function of a message.

Although any aspect of speech or language that interferes with communication could be targeted within functional communicative contexts in a manner consistent with whole language philosophy (see the phonological intervention described by Hoffman, 1992), advocates of whole language reject direct instruction on specific speech or language targets identified by a clinician. This rejection includes direct instruction on specific speech sounds or phonological processes (e.g., Elbert & Gierut, 1986; Hodson & Paden, 1991), specific lexical items (e.g., Leonard et al., 1982; McGregor & Leonard, chap. 4, this volume; Wilcox, Kouri, & Caswell, 1991), specific syntactic or morphological forms (e.g., Camarata & Nelson, 1992; Connell, 1986, Fey et al., 1993), individual semantic relations (Schwartz, Chapman, Terrell, Prelock, & Rowan, 1985; Warren & Bambara, 1989), conversational skills (Dollaghan & Kaston, 1986) or phonological awareness (e.g., Ball & Blachman, 1988; Bradley & Bryant; 1985; Lundberg, 1988). This rejection of approaches that focus instruction on predetermined specific goals is based on the assumption that careful scaffolding of a child's communicative attempts in interesting, thematically related relevant activities will lead naturally to more lasting, meaningful gains in *all* of these areas. For example, Norris and Damico (1990) claim that "Working on isolated syntactic constructions or pronouns won't help a child learn how to tell a story, but engaging in successful storytelling will help the child learn how to use word order and pronouns" (p. 215).

Surprisingly, there is very little empirical support for such claims. We are aware of only one study that has examined systematically the influence of a whole language intervention on development across language domains in preschoolers with language impairments (see Gillam et al., chap. 6, this volume, regarding whole language approaches for older children). This one study is by Hoffman et al. (1990), which is described in the section on early literacy skills.[6] Following a brief story-retelling intervention, one 4-year old subject with SLI increased his use of sentences related to a test story and produced fewer errors of syntax, tense marking, and phonology than were observed prior to intervention.[7] Compared to the child's brother, who received intervention only on specific phonological targets, this child's "across-the-board" gains were impressive. Only one child received this version of whole language intervention, however. Furthermore, the children in this study had only mild impairments in speech and language production. Therefore, it is difficult to know the extent to which the results may be extended to other preschoolers with language impairments.

Studies of other approaches that minimize intrusiveness and are consistent in many respects with the whole language philosophy have not always had results as positive as those of Hoffman et al. (1990). For example, Fey (1986) reviewed studies of highly child-oriented interventions that had as their primary objectives improvements in children's social-conversational participation. He concluded that, although these interventions are successful in helping nonassertive or nonresponsive children to become more active conversational participants, there is insufficient support for the use of such approaches when the basic goal is to promote gains in language form. More recent and better controlled investigations of Girolametto (1988) and Tannock, Girolametto, and Siegel (1992) with children with developmental delays with language impairments lend support to this early conclusion. The maximally child-oriented approaches reviewed by Fey (1986) were primarily conversation- rather than narrative-based, however, and involved mostly children with developmental delays. Furthermore, these interventions typically have taken place in homes rather than in the classroom context and have not utilized print materials. None have maintained the thematic consistency across tasks and sessions that is central to the whole language approach. These factors may be responsible for the failure of some minimally intrusive approaches to lead to broad gains in children's language acquisition and use.

However, even if whole language methods result in broad gains that cut across all language components, it still must be shown that they are more successful than other methods in achieving posited outcomes in social adjustment and academic achievement in school. There is some evidence that whole language programs are more successful than basal reading programs in helping kindergarten children to acquire early literacy skills such as awareness of print conventions. But the advantages of whole language on the development of reading may disappear when the approach is provided to first graders (see Stahl & Miller, 1989, for a review). More important, available studies have not involved

---

⁶Although the intervention of Hoffman et al. (1990) clearly observes many whole language principles, it is not consistent with some others. For example, the subject in this investigation might have been allowed to select his own stories or at least the themes for his own stories (cf. Gillam et al., chap. 6, this volume). Thus, this approach is more intrusive and less child-oriented than the whole language perspective outlined in this section. This does not imply that the approach is not as good as a less intrusive, more child-oriented whole language intervention. Judgments of relative efficacy are open to empirical test. But this problem in terminology illustrates the dangers inherent in grouping all approaches that have a strong child orientation or all approaches called "whole language" into a single unidimensional category.

⁷Contrary to the specific hypothesis of Norris and Damico (1990), this child made no gains in pronoun usage.

children with language impairments. Some critics of whole language have argued that the applied whole language philosophy withholds from such children the very types of instruction (e.g, direct instruction on phonological awareness tasks) they need most to learn to read (Blachman, 1991; Chaney, 1990).

At present, we believe whole language methods should be regarded as promising but untested for preschoolers with language impairments. There is little empirical support for the claim that the general language stimulation provided in naturalistic oral and written language experiences is sufficient to lead to dramatic gains across all language domains with these children. Nevertheless, the whole language philosophy represents one of the most serious challenges to more traditional agent-oriented or hybrid forms of treatment.

Hybrid Intervention Approaches

Between the extremely intrusive and nonintrusive approaches just discussed, there are many hybrid approaches that could be created to reach our basic language intervention goal for preschoolers with language impairments. Any two hybrid approaches likely will differ in their level of adult control or intrusiveness on the child's behavioral and communicative agenda. In reality, there is a great deal of common ground between whole language interventions for children with language impairment (e.g., Gillam et al., chap. 6, this volume; Hoffman, 1992; Hoffman et al., 1990; Norris & Damico, 1990; Norris & Hoffman, 1990, 1993; Schory, 1990) and the hybrid interventions that currently are gaining favor. For example, Bricker and Cripe (1992) recently articulated a hybrid approach to early intervention that is highly child oriented but controls certain aspects of intervention that are left to the child in less intrusive approaches, such as whole language. This general approach is referred to as activity-based intervention (ABI). According to Bricker and Cripe:

1. The focus of the activity-based intervention approach is often directed to the group as opposed to individual children. Individual children's objectives are recognized and coordinated within activities.
2. The activity-based intervention approach goes beyond communication and language. This comprehensive approach addresses all major curricular areas (e.g., social, self-help, motor, cognitive, and communication).
3. The primary vehicle for training is the use of activities that children choose or enjoy. (p. 29)

The major point of dispute among advocates of whole language intervention and hybrid approaches such as ABI is whether the thematic repetition and general stimulation inherent in whole language intervention provides sufficient focus on specific (meta)phonological, lexical, and grammatical targets to foster oral and written language development in children with language-learning problems (Chaney, 1990; Gillam et al., chap. 6, this volume). Because of concern that such general learning does not occur spontaneously, ABI places intervention emphasis on specific intervention targets (in language and all other areas) and stresses the importance of experiential focus on these targets. Thus, Bricker and Cripe (1992) state: "Activity-based intervention does not preclude the use of individual teaching that may be needed for the acquisition of a new skill. Instead, it is a context for intensive practice and a vehicle to assist in generalization" (p. 56). The language interventionist functioning in an ABI program would work with the child's teachers to identify relevant language, social, metaphonological, and emergent literacy goals. Activities then would be selected that provide focused stimulation with models of these targets and multiple opportunities for the child to attempt to use the target behaviors. Thus, the procedures of milieu language intervention (Kaiser, Yoder, & Keetz, 1992), as well as even less intrusive conversational models of intervention employing focused stimulation of specific language targets (e.g., Camarata & Nelson, 1992; Fey et al., 1993; Nelson, 1989), could be embedded easily into a broader framework of ABI. Although there is considerable evidence that these language intervention methods can be highly effective in reaching oral language objectives, there are no studies of their use within a broad program of intervention such as ABI. Thus, the effectiveness of such an approach remains an open question.

CONCLUSION

We have claimed that any evaluation of language intervention efficacy depends on the breadth of the goals the intervention was designed to reach. From this perspective, it is possible to view an intervention as fully effective at one level yet ineffective or only partially effective at another. This was the case for the grammar facilitation interventions of Fey et al. (1993). These interventions were shown to be successful in facilitating grammatical expression among subjects with language impairments. Nevertheless, we believe they are inadequate to meet the broader basic goal of minimizing the risk that preschoolers with language impairments will fail in their social adjustment and academic achievement upon entering school.

So, what can we do to attain this broader goal? Our review of the literature shows clearly that although we have a number of clinical hunches and theoretically motivated approaches, we have no definitive answers to this question. It seems likely, however, that intensive interventions carried out in preschool classrooms will be necessary. It also seems necessary to identify basic linguistic, social, and early literacy goals in order to address adequately all legitimate concerns for these children. Programs such as this are costly, however, and it must be stressed that there are no studies that clearly demonstrate the superiority of intensive preschool-based approaches over limited contact "out-patient" services for any group of children with language impairments (see Cirrin & Penner, chap. 12, this volume; Cole, chap. 2, this volume).

We are encouraged that broader intervention efforts that address the social and literacy, as well as the linguistic and communicative, needs of preschoolers with language impairments will have a significant impact on these children's later social, emotional, cognitive, and academic adjustment and performance. However, as we have demonstrated throughout this chapter, many important issues remain to be addressed in future research. The basic questions that motivated our discussion in this chapter also must underlie these research efforts with preschoolers with language impairments. First, does the approach lead to clinically significant gains in the specific oral language, literacy, or social domains it was designed to influence? Second, does intervention in a single domain lead to general developments within that domain? For example, does focus on the meaning components of oral and written language facilitate developments in other linguistic components such as grammar and phonology? Third, does intervention that focuses on only one or two domains (e.g., oral language and social skills) lead to spontaneous gains in other domain(s) (e.g., written language)? Fourth, how are the components of intervention best packaged and what level of adult control of intervention variables is most effective and efficient? Fifth, do improvements in preschoolers' oral language, emergent literacy, and social skills significantly reduce the risks for linguistic, academic, and social problems during the primary-school years and beyond? And finally, what type of intervention milieu leads to the most significant gains? For example, it is unclear whether services are most effective if carried out exclusively in full inclusion preschools with typically developing peers, in self-contained language-based classrooms, or in either type of classroom in combination with services provided outside the classroom.

These are very broad questions that have no simple answers. Until the answers to questions such as these are known, individuals working with preschool children with language impairments cannot be fully satisfied that their approaches are the very best ones possible.

REFERENCES

Adams, M.J. (1990). *Beginning to read: Thinking and learning about print.* Cambridge, MA: MIT Press.

Alexander, K.L., & Entwisle, D.R. (1988). Achievement in the first 2 years of school: Patterns and processes. *Monographs of the Society for Research in Child Development, 53* (2, Serial No. 218).

Anderson, R.C., Hiebert, E.H., Scott, J.A., & Wilkinson, I.A.G. (1985). *Becoming a nation of readers: The report of the commission on reading.* Washington, DC: National Institute of Education.

Aram, D.M., Ekelman, B.L., & Nation, J.E. (1984). Preschoolers with language disorders: 10 years later. *Journal of Speech and Hearing Research, 27,* 232–244.

Aram, D.M., & Nation, J.E. (1980). Preschool language disorders and subsequent language academic difficulties. *Journal of Communication Disorders, 13,* 159–179.

Ball, E.W., & Blachman, B.A. (1988). Phoneme segmentation training: Effect on reading readiness. *Annals of Dyslexia, 38,* 208–225

Ball, E.W., & Blachman, B.A. (1991). Does phoneme awareness training in kindergarten make a difference in early word recognition and developmental spelling? *Reading Research Quarterly, 26,* 49–66.

Beitchman, J.H., Nair, R., Clegg, M., Ferguson, B., & Patel, P.B. (1986). Prevalence of psychiatric disorders in children with speech and language disorders. *Journal of the American Academy of Child Psychiatry, 25,* 528–535.

Bishop, D.V.M., & Adams, C. (1990). A prospective study of the relationship between specific language impairment, phonological disorders and reading retardation. *Journal of Child Psychology and Psychiatry, 31,* 1027–1050.

Bishop, D.V.M., & Adams, C. (1992). Comprehension problems in children with specific language impairment: Literal and inferential meaning. *Journal of Speech and Hearing Research, 35,* 119–129.

Bishop, D.V.M., & Edmundson, A. (1987). Language-impaired 4-year-olds: Distinguishing transient from persistent impairment. *Journal of Speech and Hearing Disorders, 52,* 156–173.

Blachman, B.A. (1991). Early intervention for children's reading problems: Clinical applications of the research in phonological awareness. In H. W. Catts (Ed.), *Topics in language disorders, Vol. 12, Reading disabilities: Early identification, assessment, and remediation* (pp. 51–65).

Bradley, L., & Bryant, P. (1985). Rhyme and reasons in reading and spelling. *International Academy for Research in Learning Disabilities Monograph Series* (No. 1). Ann Arbor: University of Michigan Press.

Bricker, D., & Cripe, J.J.W. (1992). *An activity-based approach to early intervention.* Baltimore: Paul H. Brookes Publishing Co.

Brown, W.H., McEvoy, M.A., & Bishop, N. (1991). Incidental teaching of social behavior: A naturalistic approach for promoting young children's peer interactions. *Teaching Exceptional Children, 24,* 35–38.

Bryan, T. (1974). Peer popularity of learning disabled children. *Journal of Learning Disabilities, 7,* 621–625.

Byrne, B., & Fielding-Barnsley, R. (1990). Acquiring the alphabetic principle: A case for teaching recognition of phoneme identity. *Journal of Educational Psychology, 82,* 805–812.

Camarata, S.M., & Nelson, K.E. (1992). Treatment efficiency as a function of target selection in the remediation of child language disorders. *Clinical Linguistics and Phonetics, 6,* 167–178.

Camarata, S., Nelson, K.E., Welsh, J., Butkowski, L., Harmer, M., & Camarata, M. (1991). The effects of treatment procedures on normal language acquisition. *Asha, 33,* 152.

Cantwell, D., & Baker, L. (1987). *Developmental speech and language disorders.* New York: Guilford Press.

Carlisle, J.F. (1987). The use of morphological knowledge in spelling derived forms by learning disabled and normal students. *Applied Psycholinguistics, 37,* 90–108.

Catts, H.W. (1989). Phonological processing deficits and reading disabilities. In A.G. Kamhi & H.W. Catts (Eds.), *Reading disabilities: A developmental language perspective.* Newton, MA: Allyn & Bacon.

Catts, H.W. (1991a). Early identification of dyslexia: Evidence from a follow-up study of speech-language impaired children. *Annals of Dyslexia, 41,* 163–177.

Catts, H.W. (1991b). Facilitating phonological awareness: Role of speech-language pathologists. *Language, Speech, and Hearing Services in Schools, 22,* 196–203.

Catts, H.W. (1993). The relationship between speech-language impairments and reading disabilities. *Journal of Speech and Hearing Research, 36,* 948–958.

Chandler, L.K., Lubeck, R.C., & Fowler, S.A. (1992). The generalization and maintenance of young children's social skills: A retrospective review and analysis. *Journal of Applied Behavior Analysis, 25,* 415–428.

Chaney, C. (1990). Evaluating the whole language approach to language arts: The pros and cons. *Language, Speech, and Hearing Services in School, 21,* 244–249.

Connell, P. (1986). Teaching subjecthood to language-disordered children. *Journal of Speech and Hearing Disorders, 29*, 481–492.

Cooper, J., Moodley, M., & Reynell, J. (1974). Intervention programmes for preschool children with delayed language development: A preliminary report. *British Journal of Disorders of Communication, 9*, 81–91.

Cooper, J., Moodley, M., & Reynell, J. (1979). The developmental language programme. Results from a five year study. *British Journal of Disorders of Communication, 14*, 57–69.

Craig, H.K., & Washington, J.A. (1993). Access behaviors of children with specific language impairment. *Journal of Speech and Hearing Disorders, 36*, 322–337.

Crais, E.R., & Chapman, R.S. (1987). Story recall and inferencing skills in language/learning-disabled and nondisabled children. *Journal of Speech and Hearing Disorders, 52*, 50–55.

Cunningham, A. (1990). Explicit vs. implicit instruction in phonological awareness. *Journal of Experimental Child Psychology, 50*, 429–444.

Dale, P., Notari, A., Crain-Thoreson, C., & Cole, K. (1993, March). *Parent–child storybook reading as an intervention technique for young children with language delays.* Paper presented at the Society for Research in Child Development annual meeting, New Orleans.

Dollaghan, C., & Kaston, N. (1986). A comprehension monitoring program for language-impaired children. *Journal of Speech and Hearing Disorders, 51*, 264–271.

Elbert, M., & Gierut, J. (1986). *Handbook of clinical phonology: Approaches to assessment and treatment.* San Diego: College-Hill Press.

Ellis Weismer, S.E. (1985). Constructive comprehension abilities exhibited by language-disordered children. *Journal of Speech and Hearing Disorders, 28*, 175–184.

Farrar, M.J. (1990). Discourse and the acquisition of grammatical morphemes. *Journal of Child Language, 17*, 607–624.

Fey, M.E. (1986). *Language intervention with young children.* Newton, MA: Allyn & Bacon.

Fey, M.E., & Cleave, P.L. (1990). Efficacy of intervention in speech-language pathology: Early language disorders. *Seminars in Speech and Language, 11*, 165–182.

Fey, M.E., Cleave, P.L., & Long, S.H. (1993, May). *An experimental evaluation of two models of grammar facilitation: Phase II.* Paper presented at the 1993 Symposium on Research in Child Language Disorders, Madison, WI.

Fey, M.E., Cleave, P.L, Long, S.H., & Hughes, D.L. (1993). Two approaches to the facilitation of grammar in language-impaired children: An experimental evaluation. *Journal of Speech and Hearing Research, 36*, 141–157.

Fey, M.E., Cleave, P.L., Ravida, A.I., Long, S.H., Dejmal, A.E., & Easton, D.L. (1994). The effects of grammar facilitation on the phonological performance of children with speech and language impairments. *Journal of Speech and Hearing Research, 37*, 594–607.

Fey, M.E., Long, S.H., & Cleave, P.L. (1994). A reconsideration of IQ criteria in the definition of specific language impairment. In R.V. Watkins & M.L. Rice (Eds.), *Communication and language intervention series: Vol. 4. Specific language impairments in children* (pp. 161–178). Baltimore: Paul H. Brookes Publishing Co.

Fox, B., & Routh, D. (1983). Reading disability, phonemic analysis, and dysphonetic spelling: A follow-up study. *Journal of Clinical Child Psychology, 12*, 28–32.

Friedman, P., & Friedman, K. (1980). Accounting for individual differences when comparing the effectiveness of remedial language teaching methods. *Applied Psycholinguistics, 1*, 151–171.

Fundudis, T., Kolvin, L., & Garside, R.F. (1979). *Speech retarded and deaf children: Their psychological development.* London: Academic Press.

Gallagher, T.M. (1991). Language and social skills: Implications for assessment and intervention with school-age children. In T.M. Gallagher (Ed.), *Pragmatics of language: Clinical practice issues* (pp. 11–41). San Diego: Singular Publishing Group.

Gallagher, T.M., & Craig, H.K. (1984). Pragmatic assessment. Analysis of a highly frequent repeated utterance. *Journal of Speech and Hearing Research, 49,* 368–377.

Gardner, M.F. (1979). *Expressive One-Word Picture Vocabulary Test.* Novato, CA: Academic Therapy Publications.

Gertner, B.L. (1993). *Who do you want to play with? The influence of communicative competence on peer preferences in preschoolers.* Unpublished master's thesis, Department of Speech-Language-Hearing, University of Kansas, Lawrence.

Gillam, R.B. (1994). Whole language principles at work in language intervention. In D. Tibbits (Ed.), *Language intervention: Beyond the primary grades.* Austin, TX: PRO-ED.

Gillam R.B., & Johnston, J.R. (1985). Development of print awareness in language-disordered preschoolers. *Journal of Speech and Hearing Research, 28,* 521–526.

Girolametto, L. (1988). Improving the social-conversational skills of developmentally delayed children: An intervention study. *Journal of Speech and Hearing Disorders, 53,* 156–167.

Goldstein, H., & Cisar, C.L. (1992). Promoting interaction during sociodramatic play: Teaching scripts to typical preschoolers and classmates with disabilities. *Journal of Applied Behavior Analysis, 25,* 265–280.

Goldstein, H., & Gallagher, T.M. (1992). Strategies for promoting the social-communicative competence of young children with specific language impairment. In S. Odom, S.R. McConnell, & M.A. McEvoy (Eds.), *Social competence of young children with disabilities: Issues and strategies for intervention* (pp. 189–213). Baltimore: Paul H. Brookes Publishing Co.

Goldstein, H., Wickstrom, S., Hoyson, M., Jamieson, B., & Odom, S. (1988). Effects of sociodramatic play training on social and communicative interaction. *Education and Treatment of Children, 11,* 97–117.

Hadley, P.A., & Rice, M.L. (1991). Conversational responsiveness of speech- and language-impaired preschoolers. *Journal of Speech and Hearing Research, 34,* 1308–1317.

Hall, P., & Tomblin, J.B. (1978). A follow-up study of children with articulation and language disorders. *Journal of Speech and Hearing Disorders, 43,* 227–241.

Hodgens, J.B., & McCoy, J.F. (1990). Effects of coaching and peer utilization procedures on the withdrawn behavior of preschoolers. *Child and Family Behavior Therapy, 12,* 25–47.

Hodson, B.W., & Paden, E.P. (1991). *Targeting intelligible speech: A phonological approach to remediation* (2nd ed.). Austin, TX: PRO-ED.

Hoff-Ginsberg, E. (1990). Maternal speech and the child's development of syntax: A further look. *Journal of Child Language, 17,* 85–99.

Hoffman, P.R. (1992). Synergistic development of phonetic skill. *Language, Speech, and Hearing Services in Schools, 23,* 254–260.

Hoffman, P.R., Norris, J.A., & Monjure, J. (1990). Comparison of process targeting and whole language treatments for phonologically delayed preschool children. *Language, Speech, and Hearing Services in Schools, 21,* 102–109.

Huntley, R.M.C., Holt, K.S., Butterfill, A., & Latham, C. (1988). A follow-up study of a language intervention programme. *British Journal of Disorders of Communication, 23,* 127–140.

Johnston, J. (1988). Specific language disorders in the child. In N. Lass, L. McReynolds, J. Northern, & D. Yoder (Eds.), *Handbook of speech-language pathology and audiology* (pp. 685–715). Toronto, Ontario, Canada: B.C. Decker.

Kail, R., & Leonard, L.B. (1986). Word-finding abilities in language-impaired children. *ASHA Monographs, 25.*

Kaiser, A., Yoder, P., & Keetz, A. (1992). Evaluating milieu teaching. In S.F. Warren & J. Reichle (Eds.), *Communication and language intervention series: Vol. 1. Causes and effects in communication and language intervention* (pp. 9–47). Baltimore: Paul H. Brookes Publishing Co.

Kamhi, A.G., & Catts, H.W. (1986). Toward an understanding of developmental language and reading disorders, *Journal of Speech and Hearing Disorders, 51,* 337–347.

Kamhi, A.G., & Catts, H.W. (1989). *Reading disabilities: A developmental language perspective.* Boston: Allyn & Bacon.

Kamhi, A.G., Catts, H.W., Mauer, D., Apel, K., & Gentry, B.F. (1988). Phonological and spatial processing abilities in language- and reading-impaired children. *Journal of Speech and Hearing Disorders, 53,* 316–327.

Kamhi, A.G., Lee, R.F., & Nelson, L.K. (1985). Word, syllable, and sound awareness in language-disordered children. *Journal of Speech and Hearing Disorders, 50,* 195–207.

King, R.R., Jones, C., & Lasky, E. (1982). In retrospect: A fifteen-year follow-up report of speech-language-disordered children. *Language, Speech, and Hearing Services in Schools, 13,* 24–32.

Kirchner, D.M. (1991). Reciprocal book reading: A discourse-based intervention strategy for the child with atypical language development. In T.M. Gallagher (Ed.), *Pragmatics of language: Clinical practice issues* (pp. 11–41). San Diego: Singular Publishing Group.

Kirk, S.A., McCarthy, J.J., & Kirk, W.D. (1968). *Illinois Test of Psycholinguistic Abilities.* Urbana: University of Illinois Press.

Ladd, G.W. (1981). Effectiveness of a social learning method for enhancing children's social interaction and peer acceptance. *Child Development, 52,* 171–178.

Ladd, G.W., & Price, J.M. (1987). Predicting children's social and school adjustment following the transition from preschool to kindergarten. *Child Development, 58,* 1168–1189.

Larrivee, L., & Catts, H. (1992, November). *Kindergarten speech-language impairment—primary grade reading disability.* Paper presented at the American Speech-Language-Hearing Association annual convention, San Antonio, TX.

Lee, L. (1974). *Developmental sentence analysis.* Evanston, IL: Northwestern University Press.

Lee L., Koenigsknecht, R., & Mulhern, S. (1975). *Interactive language development teaching.* Evanston, IL: Northwestern University Press.

Leonard, L.B. (1989). Language learnability and specific language impairment in children. *Applied Psycholinguistics, 10,* 179–202.

Leonard, L.B., & Fey, M.E. (1979). The early lexicons of normal and language-disordered children: Developmental and training considerations. In N. Lass (Ed.), *Speech and language: Advances in basic research and practice* (pp. 113–147). New York: Academic Press.

Leonard, L.B., Schwartz, R.G, Chapman, K., Rowan, L.E., Terrell, B., Weiss, A.L., & Messick, C. (1982). Early lexical acquisition in children with specific language impairment. *Journal of Speech and Hearing Disorders, 25,* 554–564.

Leong, C.K. (1989). Productive knowledge of derivational rules in poor readers. *Annals of Dyslexia, 39,* 94–115.

Lie, A. (1991). Effects of a training program for stimulating skills in word analysis in first-grade children. *Reading Research Quarterly, 26,* 235–250.

Lundberg, I. (1988). Preschool prevention of reading failure: Does training in phonological awareness work? In R.L. Masland & M.W. Masland (Eds.), *Pre-school prevention of reading failure* (pp.163–176). Parkton, MD: York Press.

Lundberg, I., Frost, J., & Peterson, O.P. (1988). Effects of an extensive program for stimulating phonological awareness in preschool children. *Reading Research Quarterly, 23,* 263–284.

Magnusson, E., & Naucler, K. (1990). Reading and spelling in language-disordered children—linguistic and metalinguistic prerequisites: Report on a longitudinal study. *Clinical Linguistics and Phonetics, 4,* 49–61.

McEvoy, M.A., Nordquist, V.M., Twardosz, S., Heckaman, K.A., Wehby, J.H., & Denny, R.K. (1988). Promoting autistic children's peer interaction in an integrated early childhood setting using affection activities. *Journal of Applied Behavior Analysis, 21,* 193–200.

Nelson, K.E. (1989). Strategies for first language teaching. In M.L. Rice & R.L. Schiefelbusch (Eds.), *The teachability of language* (pp. 263–310). Baltimore: Paul H. Brookes Publishing Co.

Norris, J., & Damico, J. (1990). Whole language in theory and practice: Implications for language intervention. *Language, Speech, and Hearing Services in Schools, 21,* 212–220.

Norris, J., & Hoffman, P. (1990). Language intervention within naturalistic environments. *Language, Speech, and Hearing Services in Schools, 21,* 72–84.

Norris, J., & Hoffman, P. (1993). *Whole language intervention for school-age children.* San Diego: Singular Publishing Group.

O'Brien, M. (1992). *Promoting successful transition into school: A review of current intervention practices.* (Available from Kansas Early Childhood Research Institute, The University of Kansas, 4132 Haworth hall, Lawrence, KS 66045–2930).

O'Connor, R.E., Jenkins, J.R., Leicester, N., & Slocum, T.A. (1993). Teaching phonological awareness to young children with learning disabilities. *Exceptional Children, 59,* 532–546.

Oden, S., & Asher, S. (1977). Coaching children in social skills for friendship making. *Child Development, 48,* 495–506.

Odom, S.L., & Brown, W.H. (1993). Social interaction skills interventions for young children with disabilities in integrated settings. In C.A. Peck, S.L. Odom, & D.D. Bricker (Eds.), *Integrating young children with disabilities into community programs: Ecological perspectives on research and implementation* (pp. 39–64). Baltimore: Paul H. Brookes Publishing Co.

Padget, S.Y. (1988). Speech- and language-impaired three and four year olds: A five-year follow-up study. In R.L. Masland & M.W. Masland (Eds.), *Pre-school prevention of reading failure* (pp. 52–77). Parkton, MD: York Press.

Paul, R., & Smith, R.L. (1993). Narrative skills in 4-year-olds with normal, impaired, and late-developing language. *Journal of Speech and Hearing Research, 36,* 592–598.

Perfetti, C. (1985). *Reading ability.* New York: Oxford University Press.

Rice, M.L. (1993). "Don't talk to him; he's weird" A social consequences account of language and social interactions. In A.P. Kaiser & D.B. Gray (Eds.), *Communication and language intervention series: Vol. 2. Enhancing children's communication: Research foundations for interventions* (pp. 139–158). Baltimore: Paul H. Brookes Publishing Co.

Rice, M.L., Alexander, A., & Hadley, P.A. (1993). Social biases toward children with speech and language impairments: A correlative causal model of language limitation. *Applied Psycholinguistics, 14,* 473–488.

Rice, M.L., Buhr, J.C., & Nemeth, M. (1990). Fast mapping word-learning abilities of language-delayed preschoolers. *Journal of Speech and Hearing Disorders, 55,* 33–42.

Rice, M.L., Sell, M.A., & Hadley, P.A. (1991). Social interactions of speech and language-impaired preschoolers. *Journal of Speech and Hearing Research, 34,* 1299–1307.

Rizzo, J.M., & Stephens, M.I. (1981). Performance of children with normal and impaired oral language production on a set of auditory comprehension tests. *Journal of Speech and Hearing Disorders, 46,* 150–159.

Saxman, J.H., & Miller, J.F. (1973). Short-term memory and language skills in articulation deficient children. *Journal of Speech and Hearing Research, 16,* 721–730.

Scarborough, H. (in press). On the efficacy of reading to preschoolers. *Developmental Review.*

Schory, M.E. (1990). Whole language and the speech-language pathologist. *Language, Speech, and Hearing Services in Schools, 21,* 206–211.

Schuele, C.M., & van Kleeck, A. (1987). Precursors to literacy: Assessment and intervention. *Topics in Language Disorders, 7,* 32–44.

Schwartz, R.G., Chapman, K., Terrell, B.Y., Prelock, P., & Rowan, L. (1985). Facilitating word combination in language-impaired children through discourse structure. *Journal of Speech and Hearing Disorders, 50,* 31–39.

Shriner, H., Holloway, M.S., & Daniloff, R.G. (1969). The relationship between articulatory deficits and syntax in speech defective children. *Journal of Speech and Hearing Research, 12,* 319–325.

Silva, P.A., Williams, S.M., & McGee, R. (1987). A longitudinal study of children with developmental language delay at age three: Later intelligence, reading and behavior problems. *Developing Medicine and Child Neurology, 29,* 630–640.

Stahl, S.A., & Miller, P.D. (1989). Whole language and language experience approaches for beginning reading: A quantitative research synthesis. *Review of Educational Research, 59,* 87–116.

Stanovich, K. (1988). The right and the wrong places to look for the cognitive locus of reading disability. *Annals of Dyslexia, 38,* 154–180.

Stark, R., Bernstein, L., Condino, R., Bender, M., Tallal, P., & Catts, H. (1984). Four-year follow-up study of language impaired children. *Annals of Dyslexia, 34,* 49–68.

Stark, R.E., & Tallal, P. (1981). Selection of children with specific language deficits. *Journal of Speech and Hearing Disorders, 46,* 114–122.

Tallal, P., Curtiss, S., & Kaplan, R. (1989). *The San Diego longitudinal study: Evaluating the outcomes of preschool impairment in language development.* Washington, DC: National Institute of Neurological and Communicative Disorders and Stroke.

Tannock, R., Girolametto, L., & Siegel, L.S. (1992). Language intervention with children who have developmental delays: Effects of an interactive approach. *American Journal on Mental Retardation, 97,* 145–160.

Tomblin, J.B. (1983). An examination of the concept of disorder in the study of language variation. *Proceedings from the Fourth Wisconsin Symposium on Research in Child Language Disorders* (pp. 81–109). Madison: Department of Communicative Dis-orders, University of Wisconsin—Madison.

Torgesen, J.K., Morgan, S.T., & Davis, C. (1992). Effects of two types of phonological awareness training on word learning in kindergarten children. *Journal of Educational Psychology, 84,* 364–370.

Twardosz, S., Nordquist, V.M., Simon, R., & Botkin, D. (1983). The effect of group affection activities on the interaction of socially isolate children. *Analysis and Intervention in Developmental Disabilities, 3,* 311–338.

Tyler, A., & Nagy, W. (1990). Use of derivational morphology during reading. *Cognition, 36,* 17–34.

van Kleeck, A. (1990). Emergent literacy: Learning about print before learning to read. *Topics in Language Disorders, 10,* 25–45.

van Kleeck, A., & Schuele, C.M. (1987). Precursors to literacy: Normal development. *Topics in Language Disorders, 7,* 13–31.

Wagner, R., & Torgesen, J. (1987). The nature of phonological processing and its causal role in the acquisition of reading skills. *Psychological Bulletin, 101,* 192–212.

Warren, S.F., & Bambara, L.M. (1989). An experimental analysis of milieu language intervention: Teaching the action-object form. *Journal of Speech and Hearing Disorders, 54,* 448–461.

Warrick, N., Rubin, H., & Rowe-Walsh, S. (1993). Phoneme awareness in language-delayed children: Comparative studies and intervention. *Annals of Dyslexia, 43,* 153–173.

Whitehurst, G.J., Falco, F.L., Lonigan, C.J., Fischel, J.E., DeBarsyshe, B.D., Valdez-Menchaca, M.C., & Caulfield, M. (1988). Accelerating language development through book reading. *Developmental Psychology, 24,* 552–559.

Whitehurst, G.J., Fischel, J.E., Caulfield, M., DeBaryshe, B.D., & Valdez-Menchaca, M.C. (1989). Assessment and treatment of early expressive language delay. In P. Aelazo & R. Barr (Eds.), *Challenges to developmental paradigms: Implications for assessment and treatment* (pp. 113–135). Hillsdale, NJ: Lawrence Erlbaum Associates.

Wilcox, J.M., Kouri, T.A., & Caswell, S.B. (1991). Early language intervention: A comparison of classroom and individual treatment. *American Journal of Speech-Language Pathology, 1,* 49–62.

Wilson, B., & Risucci, D. (1988). The early identification of developmental language disorders and the prediction of the acquisition of reading skills. In R.L. Masland & M.W. Masland (Eds.), *Pre-school prevention of reading failure* (pp. 52–77). Parkton, MD: York Press.

2

Curriculum Models
and Language Facilitation
in the Preschool Years

Kevin N. Cole

THE HISTORY OF LANGUAGE INTERVENTION spans a relatively short period. Pioneer work began in the mid-1960s, consisting of the development of behaviorally oriented training models for syntactic and semantic development. Bereiter and Engelmann (1966), and Guess, Sailor, Rutherford, and Baer (1968), for example, identified language training as an appropriate goal for children with disabilities and children at risk for school failure. Since then, remarkable changes in thinking have occurred regarding *how* to facilitate language, *which* aspects of communication to target for intervention, *who* should be involved in the process, and *where* it should be conducted.

Bricker (1993), in a brief history of language intervention, documents patterns of change over the past three decades along these dimensions. Language facilitation has evolved from syntactic and semantic training toward a broader social-communicative competence. It has evolved for highly structured clinical therapy toward intervention within the ecological context where actual communication needs exist. Finally, language facilitation has evolved from a single discipline "pull-out" model (e.g., Gray & Ryan, 1973) toward an interdisciplinary model that includes parents, teachers, speech-language pathologists, and others (e.g., Manolson, 1985).

These changes inevitably have led the process of language intervention into the classroom. The school environment can be an ideal setting to promote language intervention within the framework of these current developments. Working in this environment creates a strong motivation to communicate with teacher and peers. In addition, naturally occurring social interactions and interests of the child in school often can serve as the basis for mapping language. The school environment also can be an ideal setting for an interdisciplinary approach to facilitation of communication skills. While these general characteristics of the classroom help provide opportunities for effective language facilitation, the specific curriculum used, with its framework of goals, activities, materials, and theoretical orientation, is also very likely to influence children's language development.

Curriculum, in the most general definition, is a regular course of study or training within a school. Specific defining characteristics of early school curricula include the content to be taught, the methods of presentation by the teacher, the abilities of the students targeted by the curriculum, and the theoretical model underlying these characteristics. Curriculum models currently used with young children vary substantially along these dimensions. There is ongoing debate, for example, whether a broad developmentally based approach, frequently referred to as developmentally appropriate practice (DAP), is more or less effective than more traditional, behaviorally oriented, early childhood special education (ECSE) practices (Carta, Schwartz, Atwater, & McConnell, 1991). The two fundamental characteristics of DAP models include: 1) using age-appropriate activities, and 2) allowing the child to select activities that follow his or her personal interests (Bredekamp, 1986). In contrast, traditional ECSE models may rely heavily on teacher-selected tasks based on logical didactic progressions that are initiated and directed by the teacher. DAP models also tend to promote child-to-child interactions versus teacher–child interactions, child initiations versus teacher initiations, discovery learning versus a skill-training orientation, skill facilitation disbursed throughout the day during contextual opportunities versus discrete instructional periods, natural consequences of communicative attempts versus secondary reinforcers, and maintenance of a social-communicative context for interaction rather than a didactic context.

It is useful to recognize the similarities between this debate in early childhood special education and a parallel debate specific to language facilitation (Cole & Dale, 1986; Courtright & Courtright, 1979; Prelock & Panagos, 1980; Siegel & Spradlin, 1982) concerning direct versus interactive language facilitation techniques. Many of the characteristics of the divergent curricula used with preschool children may affect language development in ways similar to the direct and interactive language facilitation models that have been examined since the mid-1980s.

Although there is strong advocacy for the sole use of a particular curriculum model with all children (Heshusius, 1991), other possibilities under consideration include the blending of the two broad models for maximum efficiency (Mallory, 1992) as well as an examination of whether each model may be differentially effective with specific subgroups of children (Cole, Dale, & Mills, 1991). Thus, best practices regarding curriculum in the preschool years for all children, including children with delayed language ability, are not yet clearly defined. The purposes of this chapter are: 1) to explore components of curricula that may play a part in a child's language development, 2) to examine existing curricula in light of these components, and 3) to review current research regarding how curricula differentially influence children's language development. This examination includes both broad curriculum models that are designed to address a wide range of developmental domains (e.g., High/Scope [Schweinhart & Hohmann, 1992]) including language, as well as curricula that are designed specifically to facilitate language development (e.g., milieu teaching [Hart & Rogers-Warren, 1978]). It is hoped that this information will lead to more informed selection and modification of curricula and a more effective match between the child with delayed language and the instructional environment.

CURRICULUM VARIABLES
INFLUENCING LANGUAGE FACILITATION

As noted above, curriculum models vary along a variety of dimensions that are likely to affect children's language learning. Variables can be organized into three broad categories including: 1) the environment prescribed by the curriculum, 2) the inclusion of typically developing peers, and 3) the specific instructional methods required by the curriculum. Each of these three dimensions is explored below.

Environmental Factors

Critical features of the classroom environment include the materials available to students, the arrangement of space and activities in the room, and the duration of activities as prescribed by curricula. Each of these three key features is addressed separately.

Materials

A variety of studies have examined the effects of different materials on children's social interactions, and a summary of research presented by Carta, Sainato, and Greenwood (1988) suggests an intuitive pattern in children's play around certain types of materials. It appears that solitary, parallel, or cooperative play can be predicted to some degree on the basis of the materials made available to the child. For example, crayons, art materials, books, and puzzles tended to promote solitary or parallel play, while dolls and housekeeping areas, as well as cooperative games such as checkers and pick-up sticks, tended to result in cooperative play. It is important to note that children played with some materials in a variety of ways, ranging from solitary play to highly cooperative play. All three play levels, for example, occurred with blocks and clay (Rubin, 1977; Shure, 1963; Stoneman, Cantrell, & Hoover-Dempsey, 1983). This suggests that while materials can promote certain types of social interaction, other variables, including the child's developmental level, the social relationship of the children in proximity, and the whims of children, also influence patterns of communication around materials. Additional input may be necessary from the teacher and speech-language pathologist in the form of planned student grouping and modeling of interactions to maximize the effects of materials. In addition, broad changes in theoretical perspective also may be necessary in many school programs in order to make *any* manipulable materials available to children. Schools often emphasize formal instruction in academic skills (Bredekamp, 1986), which can result in classroom arrangements for preschool, kindergarten, and first-grade children that resemble upper-grade classes where there is little direct access to manipulable materials and an emphasis on worksheet tasks. These characteristics are less likely to promote a need to communicate with peers.

Classroom Arrangement

The arrangement of classroom space and the proximity of children to each other within the classroom have an impact on children's attempt at communication, and these features also are dictated or influenced by curricula. For example, small groups of children sitting on rugs without an assigned spot tend to interact among themselves more than students sitting in equidistantly spaced chairs (Krantz & Risley, 1977). Similarly, children tend to play more cooperatively in enclosed spaces than in large open spaces (Carta et al., 1988), suggesting that small, defined centers in classrooms may facilitate child-to-child communication. The conflict that arises for teachers around the issue of classroom arrangement is often one of order versus interaction. Arrangements that facilitate child-to-child interaction also create noise, reduce attention to the teacher, and permit less control by the teacher over the content of the interactions. Curricula that value child directedness tend to promote classroom arrangements that facilitate child-initiated interactions, even at the expense of noise and loss of a high degree of control. In contrast, curricula that stress the importance of maximizing time on task for specifically controlled content are less likely to organize space in a manner that encourages peer-to-peer interaction.

Length of Activities

Another curriculum feature that may influence communicative interaction is the duration of time allotted for child-directed peer interaction. Christie and Wardle (1992) observed typically developing children during both 15- and 30-minute free-play periods. They observed that the 30-minute free-play periods resulted in a higher percentage of cooperative play, including dramatic play where several children adopted roles and acted out stories.

The shorter play periods, in contrast, resulted in a higher percentage of parallel play and unengaged, isolated activity. Although these categories of play are not direct measures of language performance, complexity of play has been positively correlated with communicative ability in typically developing children as well as in children with disabilities (Bates, Thal, Whitesell, Fenson, & Oakes, 1989; Ogura, 1991). In the past, ECSE has deemphasized long periods of child-directed play in favor of teacher-directed instruction time. Odom, Peterson, McConnell, and Ostrosky (1990) found that ECSE classes generally scheduled approximately half the amount of time for peer interaction than did regular early childhood classes. Thus, less opportunity for peer-to-peer language use was provided.

Although the results of the Christie and Wardle (1992) study indicate that increased free-play time will lead to increased practice in language use within a meaningful social context, this interpretation should be made with caution because the study, unfortunately, confounded length of play session with time of day. All short-play periods occurred in the afternoon and all long-play sessions occurred in the morning. It is possible, therefore, that fatigue rather than length of session could account for differences. In addition, all children in the study were typically developing. However, a related study that directly examined language production recently has been conducted with children with developmental delays. Buchanan (1993) explored whether language production increased during the second half of a 40-minute free-play period. Subjects were children between the ages of 3 and 6 years who were assigned randomly to a curriculum using direct language teaching or to a curriculum using a child-directed language instruction approach. Preliminary analyses revealed a trend in which both groups performed similarly during the first half of the free-play session, but children in the child-directed program produced more utterances, longer utterances, and more diverse vocabulary during the second half of the free-play session. Although this information is preliminary, it raises the interesting possibility of an interaction between language facilitation curricula and children's language production during different lengths of time of unstructured play.

Inclusion of Typically Developing Peers

Perhaps no single aspect of preschool curricula has received more attention since the 1970s than the integration of children with disabilities and children who are developing in a typical manner. Curricula have been developed specifically to promote skills within integrated settings (Odom et al., 1988; Osborn, Sherwood, Feuerstein, & Cole, 1993), and a substantial amount of research has been conducted regarding the effects of integration on social, academic, and language development. The impact of integration on language development was anticipated to be positive because of evidence that typically developing children modify their language input to children with less well-developed language skills (Guralnick & Paul-Brown, 1980) and because children with mild disabilities have been shown to use more complex language when speaking to developmentally more advanced children (Guralnick & Paul-Brown, 1986).

Although these studies have demonstrated a positive effect of integration on language production during the short-term experimental condition, there is little evidence that these benefits manifest themselves in the classroom (Odom & McEvoy, 1988). Studies designed to identify differences regarding various aspects of language development for children in integrated or mainstreamed classes found no differences in gains (Cooke, Ruskus, Apolloni, & Peck, 1981; Jenkins, Odom, & Speltz, 1989; Jenkins, Speltz, & Odom, 1985). Although findings of no group advantages for classroom integration are fairly consistent across these studies, the examination of *individual differences* in response to integration has identified intriguing patterns of differential response to segregated and integrated classroom settings. Cole, Mills, Dale, and Jenkins (1991) examined the differential effects of segregated and integrated classes for children with mild to moderate developmental delays ranging in age from 3 to 6 years. Like earlier researchers, they found no group effect for language development. However, they also examined prospectively whether children's performance level at the beginning of intervention differentially influenced the child's ability to benefit from integrated or segregated classrooms. They found that children with relatively higher IQ scores or language scores at pretest made greater gains in language development if they were in integrated classes, while children with relatively lower IQ or language scores at pretest made greater gains in language development if they were in segregated classrooms.

The findings of Cole, Mills, et al. (1991) indicate that children's individual differences may interact with classroom diversity and influence their ability to benefit from intervention. This study examined the effects of two levels of classroom diversity: segregated (12 children with disabilities), and integrated (eight children with disabilities and four children who were developing typically). A later study by Mills (1993) examined three levels of classroom diversity: segregated and integrated levels similar to those described above, and a third level referred to as mainstreaming (five children with disabilities, and nine children who were developing typically). Mills found results similar to the earlier Cole, Mills, et al. (1991) study for the segregated and integrated groups. Surprisingly, the mainstreamed group demonstrated a pattern of individual differences almost identical to the segregated group. The relatively lower functioning children benefited more from segregated and mainstreamed settings and less from integrated settings.

Mills speculated that these unexpected findings might result from a tendency of the larger group of typically developing children in the mainstreamed setting to interact more among themselves than with the lower performing students. This tendency would make the communicative environment in the mainstreamed setting similar to the segregated setting for the children with disabilities. This tendency for typically developing children to prefer to interact among themselves has been noted in earlier studies of mainstreaming (Ispa, 1981; Rogers-Warren, Ruggles, Peterson, & Cooper, 1981). It should be noted that these differential effects accounted for only a small amount of the variance in children's performance. In other words, the individual differences were consistent, but not very large. These results suggest that the performance of children with moderate delays in development should be monitored closely in integrated settings (i.e., settings including more children with disabilities than children who are developing typically) to ensure they do not lag behind the relatively higher functioning children with developmental delays. Similarly, children with mild delays should be monitored closely in mainstreamed settings (i.e, settings with more typically developing children than children with developmental delays) to be sure they receive adequate stimulation.

Instructional Methods

In addition to the broad environmental aspects of curricula that may influence communicative interaction in the classroom setting, a variety of specific instructional methods used by the staff also may influence the effectiveness of language learning in the preschool and kindergarten classroom. These instructional methods include following the child's lead, selection of language goals, and presentation of language instruction at discrete periods during the day in contrast to embedding instruction throughout the daily routines. Each of these areas is addressed below.

Following the Child's Lead

One of the basic principles of DAP-oriented curriculum models is the importance of following the child's focus of interest. This principle stands in sharp contrast to didactically based curricula, which select key exemplars of material to be taught and direct the child's attention to those predetermined stimuli (e.g., Engelmann & Osborn, 1976; Gray & Ryan, 1973). Much of the early empirical support for the importance of following the child's lead came from research with typically developing children. Tomasello and Todd (1983), in an observational study, found that 1-year-old children of mothers who often directed the child's attention in initiating interactions developed vocabulary more slowly than children whose mothers followed the lead of the child in initiating interactions. Tomasello and Farrar (1986) observed that joint attention episodes in mother–child dyads resulted in the production of more utterances and longer conversations by the children. They also noted that the mothers' references to objects while the child was focused on the object were positively correlated to later vocabulary development, and the mothers' references that redirected the child's attention were negatively correlated with later vocabulary development. Tomasello and Farrar (1986) also conducted an experimental examination of the effects of modeling labels when the child attended to the stimulus compared to modeling labels when the child was not attending to any of the stimuli. Consistent with their correlational study, they found that the children's comprehension was significantly better for information presented while the child attended to the stimulus object. A potential drawback to this study noted by Valdez-Menchaca and Whitehurst (1988) is that one of the conditions required that verbal labels were presented only when the child was not attending, which could actually suppress learning. Because adults would be highly unlikely to implement a condition wherein the adult presents information *only* when the child is otherwise occupied, the external validity of the results may be questionable. Valdez-Menchaca and Whitehurst (1988) conducted a similar study using a design that avoided this potential problem. They examined whether typically developing children ranging in age from approximately 2 to 3 years learned Spanish vocabulary better when labels were presented after the child expressed an interest in a toy, or when the labeling was yoked in a matched time sequence. This, to some degree, avoided the problem of presenting labels only when the child was not attending to the toys. Children in the "attending" condition demonstrated significantly better production of Spanish words on posttesting, although both groups performed equally on comprehension measures.

Although early research supporting the practice of following the child's lead did not involve young children with disabilities, the practice is becoming widely prescribed for this group (Mahoney, Robinson, & Powell, 1992). Yoder, Kaiser, Alpert, and Fischer (1993) suggest several rationales regarding why following the child's lead may be an effective technique in facilitating vocabulary development in children. They suggest that children are most attentive and best able to abstract the meaning of speech during joint attention episodes with the adult and that following the child's lead is one of the most effective means of establishing joint attention. Research has been conducted only recently, however, to document the value of following the child's lead for children with disabilities. Mirenda and Donnellan (1986) compared the differential effects of a teacher-directed communicative style with those of a child-directed style for adolescents with autism and adolescents with moderate mental retardation. The teacher-directed method was characterized by teacher selection of topic, teacher initiation of communicative interaction, and structuring the nature of the child's contributions to the topic. The child-directed style, in contrast, was characterized by child selection of topic, child initiation of communicative interaction, and little structuring of the child's contribution to the ongoing conversation. For both groups of children, the child-directed approach resulted in significantly more topic initiations, comments, and questions, while the teacher-directed approach resulted in more topic continuations in response to adult questions and more off-topic comments.

In a related study involving very young (2-year-old) children with severe disabilities, Norris and Hoffman (1990) compared structured, adult-directed instruction to an interactive, child-directed interaction style to determine which method best facilitates production of children's vocalizations, limb movements, and facial or body movements. As in the Mirenda and Donnellan (1986) study, the child-directed style was generally more effective in increasing both type and complexity of communicative interactions in subjects. The structured, adult-initiated method and the interactive, child-initiated methods, however, also included a variety of contrasting variables including type of goals targeted, types of activities undertaken, and types of reinforcers used. Consequently, it is difficult to isolate the influence of this particular aspect of the communicative interactions. A study by Landry and Chapieski (1989) isolated the variable of topic initiator (child-directed or adult-directed) to a greater degree, providing additional evidence that child directedness may be an important element in teaching young children with disabilities. They examined the attention patterns of children with Down syndrome and children who were born preterm and found that the children with Down syndrome were less able to shift their attention to toys in response to their mothers' attempts to redirect their attention.

These results, taken together, suggest that children with developmental delays may be limited in their ability to respond to attention shifts they do not initiate. To examine this possibility directly, Yoder et al. (1993) conducted a study using an alternating treatments design that compared two conditions: "following the child's lead," and "recruiting the child's attention." Subjects were three children with an average age of 43 months with delays in both cognitive and language skills, functioning in Brown's late stage (i.e., MLU=1.5–1.99). For all three children, the teaching of nouns was more efficient when following the child's attentional lead. Following the child's lead resulted in greater generalization of learning across people and materials, and resulted in more productive use of the nouns. This information supports the position held by Mahoney et al. (1992) that curricula for young children that include a strong child-directed component may be more effective in facilitating language skills for children with developmental delays. It should be cautioned, however, that the Yoder et al. (1993) study, like the Tomasello and Farrar (1986) study described above, compared following the child's lead with a condition wherein information was presented only when the child was otherwise engaged. This condition might actually suppress learning according to Valdez-Menchaca and Whitehurst (1988) and does not appear to represent a teaching practice found in even the most highly structured direct teaching curricula. Future research in the area of following the child's lead should include conditions that more closely represent actual teacher-directed practices, or at least temporal yoking of adult-initiated verbal stimuli in the control condition. A finding that following the child's lead is more effective than systematically redirecting the child's attention for all language input is not surprising. This result may unintentionally misrepresent the relative effectiveness of adult input that follows the child's lead and adult input that begins with an adult initiation of topic but does not systematically ignore all expressions of interest by the child.

Selection of Language Goals

The curriculum chosen for use in preschool can influence not only *how* language is facilitated, but also may determine *which* areas of language will be targeted for instruction. Distar Language instruction (Engelmann & Osborn, 1976) for example, targets very specific language goals that are believed to be necessary for school success. This focus on language skills that facilitate academic success, especially in the area of reading, results in the teaching of very specific semantic goals that promote categorization, awareness of similarities and differences, and metacognitive skills. The program also includes syntactic goals that may be important for reading but may not be essential goals for general language development. For example, Distar Language I teaches children to discriminate contexts for use of the articles "a" and "an." Distar Language I was not designed to be a complete language facilitation package for children with delayed language so these constraints in content should not be viewed as programmatic flaws. Nevertheless, this program is a good example of the extent to which language objectives may be predetermined in some curricula.

Curricula that are designed specifically for use with children with language impairments may include specific areas of focus and deemphasize others. The interactive language development program developed by Lee, Koenigsknecht, and Mulhern (1975), for example, focuses primarily on syntax, while the Communication Training Program (Waryas & Stremel-Campbell, 1983) focuses largely on lexical and relational semantics, with some presentation of syntactic instruction.

In all these examples, not only is the area of language to be taught predetermined, but also the specific language forms and sequence of presentation are prescribed. This is in sharp contrast to more child-directed curricula that accommodate goals across the range of language areas (form, content, and use), stress individualized selection of language goals, and often have a flexible order of sequencing of goals based on the child's interests and developmental level (Cole & Dale, 1986; Fey, Catts, & Larrivee, chap. 1, this volume). These characteristics of interactive curricula often are considered to be positive attributes (Mahoney et al., 1992), although they must be juxtaposed with the potential strengths of more structured curricula, including a studied selection of exemplars, careful attention to sequencing to maximize success, and detailed directions to facilitate correct implementation by inexperienced users. Unfortunately, little direct empirical evidence is available to determine the relative advantages of these contrasting methods of goal selection (Fey, 1986; Fey et al., chap. 1, this volume). This is an area where additional research is needed.

Discrete versus Embedded Instruction

The final instructional variable examined is the distribution of language instruction during the school day. Approaches to language intervention in the preschool setting have moved in the direction of teaching during naturally occurring opportunities throughout the day, compared with a massed practice format following the adult's agenda (Prizant & Bailey, 1992). Evidence of the effectiveness of using naturally occurring opportunities is found for children with mild developmental delays (Warren, 1992), children with autism (Hunt & Goetz, 1988), and children with specific language impairment (Warren, McQuarter, & Rogers-Warren, 1984). Research is convincing that language instruction embedded within the daily curriculum is an effective method of facilitating communication. It is less clear, however, whether this method is more effective overall than a massed practice approach such as Distar Language (Engelmann & Osborn, 1976) or the Communication Training Program (Waryas & Stremel-Campbell, 1983), or some combination of the two approaches.

While direct instruction programs, which incorporate discrete periods of massed practice of language skills, have waned in popularity, their relative effectiveness has received little attention until recently. Cole and Dale (1986) examined the relative effectiveness of direct language instruction that incorporated massed practice and interactive language facilitation that provided language stimulation during naturally occurring opportunities throughout the day. Preschool and kindergarten children with language delays were assigned randomly to the two interventions. The authors found no overall differences between the two approaches. Both interventions, however, resulted in significant gains from pretest to posttest on a variety of language measures, several of which were standardized. Gains in standardized scores indicate that improvements for the children receiving direct and interactive interventions were not due to maturation. Later studies by Cole, Dale, and Mills (1991) and Yoder, Kaiser, and Alpert (1991) had similar findings of no overall difference for language facilitation models that varied along a number of characteristics, including massed practice versus embedded facilitation. The variable of distribution of language facilitation (massed practice as opposed to embedded facilitation) is, unfortunately, confounded with other instructional variables such as child versus teacher initiation of interaction and child versus teacher selection of materials in these studies so it is difficult to isolate the specific effect of distribution of instruction.

At this time, we can conclude only that this variable is not sufficient, in itself, to result in significant main effects within the context of the other variables. Given our limited knowledge regarding the relative benefits of the two methods, an approach suggested by Warren and Kaiser (1988) may be the most likely method of ensuring effective intervention. These investigators advise that *some* language facilitation embedded within the classroom milieu be used when a more direct language facilitation approach is implemented because the use of naturally occurring opportunities should result in greater generalization of skills taught.

EXAMPLES OF CURRICULA USED IN PRESCHOOL PROGRAMS

Thus far we have examined individual components of curricula for young children that are likely to influence language learning. Existing curricula, however, often contain varied configurations of these components. Broad curriculum models, as well as curriculum models designed specifically to facilitate language development, may be primarily child directed and interactive, primarily teacher driven and didactically focused, or may include permutations of both models. The Mediated Learning Program (Osborn et al., 1993), for example, which is a broad curriculum for young children with disabilities, includes characteristics of both child-directed and teacher-directed instructional models. It includes predetermined goals and a loose sequence of activities, which are characteristics of more structured programs. The goals of this program, however, are broad, cognitively based targets such as temporal organization and hypothetical thinking. These are more characteristic of child-directed, developmentally based curricula.

Three curricula are described briefly to demonstrate the wide diversity in models and to clarify how models that operate under the same category of developmentally appropriate practices (DAP) may differ.

Prototype Broad Focused Curriculum Models

High/Scope

The High/Scope model (Hohmann, Banet, & Weikert, 1979) is a cognitively oriented curriculum based on the theories of Piaget. It consists of general guidelines and procedures for classroom arrangement, daily routines, and promotion of key experiences including classification, seriation, number concepts, spatial and temporal relations, and language development. The primary focus is on facilitating sensory-motor activities that serve as the basis for cognitive development. Materials are selected to be developmentally appropriate, and the children are allowed choices to help ensure that they are engaged in activities that reflect their personal interests. Guidelines provided to teachers regarding language development strongly stress the promotion of child-to-child communication. The teacher's role is to interpret messages between children that may not be communicated successfully, to attend to the meaning rather than the form of communication attempts, and to restrict the amount of teacher talking in order to allow opportunities for children to initiate or respond. The High/Scope model has been used with at-risk children to a large extent and also is used as the basic curriculum for young children with special needs. It clearly represents a prototype of a DAP model. While the High/Scope model is designed for preschool children, it is important to recognize that the key underlying features of the model are recommended by the National Association for the Education of Young Children (Bredekamp, 1986) for use with children through age 8.

Mediated Learning

Like High/Scope, the Mediated Learning Program (MLP) (Osborn et al., 1993) is a cognitively oriented curriculum. That is, it is designed to facilitate broad abilities such as comparison and classification, rather than specific academic knowledge such as color names or counting. This curriculum also incorporates DAP guidelines by following the child's interests and offering age-appropriate materials and activities. The MLP is described in order to highlight the differences that exist even within theoretically similar curricula because these differences may influence how language is facilitated within the model. The MLP is based on the work of Feuerstein (Feuerstein, Klein, & Tannenbaum, 1991; Feuerstein, Rand, Hoffman, & Miller, 1980), and instructional goals are organized around cognitive processes such as perspective changing, sequencing, and identification of similarities and differences. These processes are thought to be the essential foundation for academic learning. Children are encouraged to adopt a reflective attitude, monitor their own responses, and avoid rapid, impulsive responding. Unlike High/Scope, the teacher plays a role in interpreting the environment. Rather than a focus on child-initiated conversation, the teacher often sets up the environment and highlights critical elements in the environment that lead the child to consideration of one of the cognitive processes to be facilitated. Thus, teacher talk is likely to occur more frequently in the MLP curriculum and teacher–child interactions may be proportionately greater than in a High/Scope model.

The primary difference between the Piagetian-based High/Scope model and the MLP is the emphasis placed on the role of the adult to interpret the environment and to guide the child to perceive salient features of materials or events. The MLP, although primarily a DAP model, allows more teacher-initiated communication, modeling of language, use of tutorial questions (questions to which the teacher knows the answer), and a greater percentage of teacher–child rather than child–child interaction. In addition, the MLP was designed specifically to facilitate integration of children with disabilities and children who are developing typically in the same activities. Activities in the curriculum include suggestions for three levels of conceptual and linguistic complexity of presentation so that children at different ability levels can benefit from activities while in heterogeneous ability groups.

Specific planning to accommodate children with a wide range of abilities is uncommon in a DAP program. Perhaps because DAP models originally were developed for use with typically developing and at-risk children, guidelines for the National Association for the Education of Young Children for developmentally appropriate practices included virtually no reference to the inclusion of young children with special needs even as late as 1987 (Mallory, 1992). This lack of planned adaptation for children with various special needs is one of the primary concerns raised by critics of the current trend toward use of DAP programs for children with disabilities (Carta et al., 1991).

Direct Instruction

In strong contrast to the two DAP models described above, Direct Instruction (DI) (Engelmann & Bruner, 1974; Engelmann & Carnine, 1975; Engelmann & Osborn, 1976) represents a prototype of direct academic instruction. DI is characterized by extensive analysis of skill sequences and very carefully planned communication procedures for the presentation of stimuli. Instruction is explicit and systematic, teacher directed, fast paced, and focused on very specific measurable outcomes (Gersten, Woodward, & Darch, 1986). Student grouping is by ability, so inclusion is not promoted during specific instruction periods. Language, as well as math and other skills, is taught during discrete time periods, using predetermined stimulus materials, specific correction procedures in response to errors, and often incorporating secondary reinforcement systems. As an example of Direct Instruction, a Distar Language lesson might consist of a 20-minute session with the adult modeling a phrase, eliciting a repetition of the phrase on cue with a hand signal, and providing verbal praise and a redeemable token when the child responds correctly. If the child responds in error, a correction sequence might be used in which the adult quickly models the correct answer, repeats the stimulus question, and elicits another response from the child. This model clearly contrasts with DAP curricula along virtually every variable outlined earlier in this chapter.

Examples of Curricula Designed Specifically to Facilitate Communication Development

A range of models also exists for curricula designed specifically to address language development, including hybrids of divergent models. Milieu teaching (Hart & Rogers-Warren, 1978), for example, stresses instruction during naturally occurring opportunities throughout the school day but also uses elicited responding, which is characteristic of direct didactic instruction. Thus, the individual components of curricula reviewed earlier can be combined in a wide variety of ways to form a cohesive curriculum. Several curricula are described below to demonstrate the range of models available and the diverse application of the curriculum components that were described earlier.

Communication Training Program

One language curriculum consistent with a Direct Instruction model is the Communication Training Program (CTP) (Waryas & Stremel-Campbell, 1983). The Communication Training Program is teacher directed, uses a predetermined sequence of goals and objectives, is administered in discrete time periods, and incorporates stimulus pictures to which the child's attention is directed. Targeted language constructs include semantic and syntactic goals. Goals range from comprehension of common nouns to expression of negative forms such as "can't" and "doesn't." In addition, the program contains a well-developed sequence of prerequisite nonverbal goals such as imitating actions and using vocalizations and gestures to make requests. This curriculum is prototypical of the highly structured clinical approaches to language facilitation. Although this type of language development curriculum is becoming less widely used (Bricker, 1993), research comparing the CTP to a more child-directed approach (milieu teaching) indicates that it is as effective overall as the child-directed program and actually may be more effective with children who are functioning close to normal in cognitive ability (Yoder et al., 1991).

The Integrated Preschool Curriculum

A variation of a Direct Instruction curriculum to facilitate communication skills is the Integrated Preschool Curriculum (Odom et al., 1988). The goal of the curriculum is to promote social integration through training in play skills and positive social interaction. This program includes suggested activities and materials to facilitate interaction among children with disabilities and children who are developing typically. The teacher is provided with scripted social skill interventions that include elicited responding and elicited imitation. For example, to facilitate imitative play, the teacher is given ideas for prompts such as, "Look, John is pouring sand in his cup. Can you do that?" The role of the teacher in the interactions, however, is faded over the school year. Goals range from playing independently for a short period of time to playing cooperatively, planning play, and sharing toys. While specific language constructs are not targeted, Jenkins et al. (1989) found that children provided with the scripted social skills intervention performed higher on the Preschool Language Scale (Zimmerman, Steiner, & Pond, 1979) than did children randomly assigned to play groups based on High/Scope guidelines.

Milieu Teaching

On the continuum of Direct Instruction models and DAP models, milieu teaching represents a hybrid that includes characteristics of both approaches (Fey, 1986). Milieu teaching is actually a class of language intervention approaches that include the DAP characteristics of following the child's lead and embedding instruction within natural opportunities that occur throughout the school day. In addition, consequences for children's language use are often functionally related to the response within the social context rather than to secondary reinforcers such as verbal praise or tokens (Kaiser, Yoder, & Keetz, 1992). Direct Instruction characteristics of milieu teaching include the use of explicit prompts to respond. These allow the teacher, to some degree, to determine the type of response the child produces. The prompts can include both elicited responding (e.g., "Tell me where the book is sitting,") and elicited imitation ("Say, 'The book is on the table.'") In addition, the teacher often follows the child's response with an expanded model of the child's utterance. There is substantial evidence that milieu teaching is effective and produces at least some generalizable benefits (Kaiser et al., 1992).

RELATIVE EFFECTIVENESS
OF CONTRASTING CURRICULUM MODELS

The curriculum models described above incorporate the various curriculum components presented earlier in a number of different configurations. This use of different configurations makes prediction of the relative efficacy of the total curriculum packages difficult even if we have information about the effectiveness of the individual components. Fortunately, several studies have compared the relative effectiveness of complete curriculum models as they are applied in school settings. Such studies allow the impact of the models to be examined directly, rather than by inference from our knowledge of the individual components of instruction that comprise the curriculum.

Cole, Dale, and Mills (1991) examined the effects of two highly contrasting curricula for preschool and kindergarten age children: Direct Instruction and Mediated Learning. The authors specifically examined the curriculum effects on language development for the subjects who were diagnosed as having language delays at the beginning of the intervention. The Direct Instruction curriculum consisted of Distar Language I and other Distar materials, as well as use of didactic procedures during teacher–child interactions outside of the small-group Distar teaching sessions. Characteristics of the curriculum, as described earlier, include predetermined language goals in a prescribed sequence, structured reinforcement procedures, and use of elicited imitation and elicited responding. The teacher followed a written script that provides a task such as multiple repetitions of an elicited response consisting of labeling a color (e.g., "This ball is red; what color is this ball?") followed by verbal praise for a correct response. The contrasting curriculum was a preliminary version of the Mediated Learning Program (Osborn & Sherwood, 1988). In contrast to Direct Instruction, the Mediated Learning Program emphasizes the development of broad cognitive abilities rather than specific academic skills. In MLP, the teacher might note an object of interest to the child, such as a paintbrush, and inquire how it is the same as and different from a crayon, then discuss other tools used for writing and drawing that are not in the immediate environment.

The two curricula contrast highly in what and how they teach. However, the overall effectiveness of the two models after 1 year of intervention, as noted earlier, was not significantly different on any language measure. Comparable gains were made by children in both curricula on the Peabody Picture Vocabulary Test–Revised (PPVT–R) (Dunn & Dunn, 1981), the Test of Early Language Development (TELD) (Hresko, Reid, & Hammill, 1981), mean length of utterance (MLU), the Basic Language Concepts Test (Engelmann, Ross, & Bingham, 1982), and the Preschool Language Assessment Instrument (PLAI) (Blank, Rose, & Berlin, 1978). The interaction between the type of program and the children's cognitive and language aptitudes at pretest were examined prospectively, however, and significant disordinal Aptitude X Treatment interactions were found. The direction of the interactions revealed that relatively higher performing students (on an IQ measure and the PLAI at pretest) gained more from   the DI program, whereas relatively lower functioning students gained more from the ML program. Outcome measures included the PPVT–R, MLU, TELD and the PLAI.

A study by Yoder et al. (1991) compared the effects of the Communication Training Program (CTP) (Waryas & Stremel-Campbell, 1983) with milieu teaching (Hart & Rogers-Warren, 1978) and found that there were no main effect differences for preschool children with delayed language. Both programs were equally effective overall. However, milieu teaching was more effective than the Direct Instruction approach for the lower performing children in the study who exhibited ability in the mildly mentally retarded range of cognitive functioning. The results from both of these studies run counter to the conventional wisdom that children who are lower functioning benefit more from high amounts of structure and children who are higher functioning are more equipped to learn from interactive, child-directed instruction (Snow, 1989).

One interpretation of these results is that the more highly structured and scripted programs, such as Distar Language and CTP, are difficult for children who are lower functioning to understand because they are less able to follow the adult's lead (Bloom, Rocissano, & Hood, 1976; Landry & Chapieski, 1989). In contrast, teachers in the Mediated Learning and milieu programs were allowed flexibility to follow the child's lead and respond to the child's communicative attempts. This explanation seems consistent with the findings of Yoder et al. (1993) indicating that children with cognitive delays learn aspects of language more effectively when the teacher follows their lead. Other possible explanations for these findings need to be explored in future research. Perhaps the differences in the outcomes for the contrasting curricula result from the different types of language goals selected as targets for the students who are lower performing and students who are higher performing. It is also possible that the children who are higher functioning may be more able to benefit from teaching strategies that maximize learning and practice time with rapid pacing and frequent responding, although this method of presentation does not allow as much contextual grounding of information or opportunity for generalizing to other settings.

While these results are conceptually interesting, the size of the differences in outcome measures between students who are higher performing and students who are lower performing is not substantial for most instructional purposes. Although the differences are statistically significant, indicating they are unlikely to be due to chance variation alone, they are not large enough to be highly meaningful in an applied program. It also should be noted that the number of statistically significant differences found, while greater than would be expected by chance, were present for only a small portion of the outcome measures examined. Thus, the differences, while intriguing, do not appear to be robust. It seems, however, that individual differences in responses to intervention should be considered in order to optimize language facilitation.

CONCLUSIONS

There is substantial evidence that aspects of the curriculum models used in preschool and kindergarten can influence children's language development significantly. Basic curriculum features such as the time allotted to activities, the arrangement of the classroom, selection of materials, and the degree of integration of typically developing children and children with special needs may all affect children's language development. Because of this influence, speech-language pathologists (SLPs) need to play a strong role as members of the instructional team guiding these decisions. A kindergarten classroom with desks arranged so that all children face the teacher will probably result in little social-communicative interaction and little exploration of the environment. A classroom schedule that provides little time for child-directed activities and unstructured play may limit generalized practice of communication skills. The SLP can provide valuable input regarding the potential benefits of small activity centers with accessible materials for the facilitation of communication skills.

In situations where teachers value child-directed curriculum models but have little experience in mainstreaming children with language disorders, the SLP can help by developing a plan of *specific* language goals to be implemented within ongoing activities. In addition, the SLP can help monitor progress to ensure that intervention is effective and efficient. In some situations, the SLP might advocate for the inclusion of varying degrees of structured language facilitation embedded within the social-communicative context (Wolery, Strain, & Bailey, 1992).

While these two examples may appear contradictory, they reflect our current knowledge regarding the impact of different broad curriculum models as well as our knowledge of curricula designed specifically to facilitate language development. One model is unlikely to be best for all children. We have some indications that children focusing on early language goals can benefit to a greater degree from child-directed approaches, while children who are already using sentences can derive greater gains from more direct, structured approaches. Consideration of the use of both of these tools with awareness and careful monitoring reflects best practices for children with communication needs.

Although this chapter has focused on children in the preschool and kindergarten age ranges, it should be recognized that services to children from birth to 3 and their families, while not yet federally mandated, are facilitated by federal funding support and are increasingly being provided through local education agencies. The role of the SLP in the school system will soon very likely be broadened to include service to infants and toddlers and their families, as well as older preschoolers and school-age students. New frontiers for communication intervention in the school systems likely will include prelinguistic facilitation techniques, such as those evaluated by Warren, Yoder, Gazdag, and Kim (1993), increased parent involvement in intervention (e.g., Manolson, 1985), and a focus on new methods of preventing language disorders as exemplified by the work of Whitehurst and colleagues (e.g., Valdez-Menchaca & Whitehurst, 1992) in which daycare staff and parents are trained in use of specified storybook reading techniques designed to facilitate language development with at-risk children. As local education agencies serve children at increasingly younger ages, language facilitation curricula often become the center of the child's program rather than a peripheral element. Because of this central concern, our need to provide the most appropriate methods matched to the individual needs of the child grows ever more critical.

REFERENCES

Bates, E., Thal, D., Whitesell, K., Fenson, L., & Oakes, L. (1989). Integrating language and gesture in infancy. *Developmental Psychology, 25,* 1006–1019.

Bereiter, C., & Engelmann, S. (1966). *Teaching disadvantaged children in the preschool.* Engelwood Cliffs, NJ.: Prentice Hall.

Blank, M., Rose, S., & Berlin, L. (1978) *Preschool Language Assessment Instrument: The language of learning in practice.* Orlando, FL: Grune & Stratton.

Bloom, L., Rocissano, L., & Hood, L. (1976). Adult–child discourse: Developmental interaction between information processing and linguistic knowledge. *Cognitive Psychology, 8,* 521–552.

Bredekamp, S. (1986). Position statement on developmentally appropriate practice in early childhood programs serving children from birth through age 8. *Young Children, 41,* 4–6.

Bricker, D. (1993). Then, now, and the path between: A brief history of language intervention. In A.P. Kaiser & D.B. Gray (Eds.), *Communication and language intervention series: Vol. 2. Enhancing children's communication: Research foundations for intervention* (pp. 11–31). Baltimore: Paul H. Brookes Publishing Co.

Buchanan, M. (1993). *Effects of duration of play period and instructional approach on the use of language by preschoolers with disabilities during classroom free play.* Unpublished manuscript, University of Washington College of Education, Seattle.

Carta, J.J., Sainato, D.M., & Greenwood, C.R. (1988). Advances in the ecological assessment of classroom instruction for young children with handicaps In S.L. Odom & M.B. Karnes (Eds.), *Early intervention for infants and children with handicaps: An empirical base* (pp. 217–239). Baltimore: Paul H. Brookes Publishing Co.

Carta, J., Schwartz, I., Atwater, J., & McConnell, S. (1991). Developmentally appropriate practice: Appraising its usefulness for young children with disabilities. *Topics in Early Childhood Special Education, 11,* 1–20.

Christie, J., & Wardle, F. (1992). How much time is needed for play? *Young Children, 47,* 28–32.

Cole, K.N., & Dale, P.S. (1986). Direct language instruction and interactive language instruction with language delayed preschool children: A comparison study. *Journal of Speech and Hearing Research, 29,* 206–217.

Cole, K.N., Dale, P.S., & Mills, P.E. (1991). Individual differences in language delayed children's responses to direct and interactive preschool instruction. *Topics in Early Childhood Special Education, 11,* 99–124.

Cole, K.N., Mills, P.E., Dale, P.S., & Jenkins, J.R. (1991). Individual differences in the effects of preschool integration for children with mild and moderate handicaps. *Exceptional Children, 58,* 36–45.

Cooke, T., Ruskus, J., Apolloni, T., & Peck, C. (1981). Handicapped preschool children in the mainstream: Background, outcomes, and clinical suggestions. *Topics in Early Childhood Special Education, 1,* 73–83.

Courtright, J., & Courtright, I. (1979). Imitative modeling as a language intervention strategy: The effects of two mediating variables. *Journal of Speech and Hearing Research, 22,* 389–402.

Dunn, L., & Dunn, L. (1981). *Peabody Picture Vocabulary Test–Revised.* Circle Pines, MN: American Guidance Service.

Engelmann, S., & Bruner, E. (1974). *Distar Reading I and II.* Chicago: Science Research Associates.

Engelmann, S., & Carnine, D. (1975). *Distar Arithmetic I and II.* Chicago: Science Research Associates.

Engelmann, S., & Osborn, J. (1976). *Distar Language I and II.* Chicago: Science Research Associates.

Engelmann, S., Ross, D., & Bingham, V. (1982). *Basic Language Concepts Test.* Tigard, OR: C.C. Publication.

Feuerstein, R., Klein, P., & Tannenbaum, A. (1991). *Mediated Learning Experience: Theoretical, psychosocial, and learning implications.* London: Freund Publishing House.

Feuerstein, R., Rand, Y., Hoffman, M., & Miller, R. (1980). *Instrumental enrichment: Redevelopment of cognitive functions of retarded performers.* Baltimore: University Park Press.

Fey, M. (1986). *Language intervention with young children.* Newton, MA: Allyn & Bacon.

Gersten, R., Woodward, J., & Darch, C. (1986). Direct Instruction: A research based approach to curriculum design and teaching. *Exceptional Children, 53,* 17–31.

Gray, B., & Ryan, B. (1973). *A language program for the nonlanguage child.* Champaign, IL: Research Press.

Guess, D., Sailor, W., Rutherford, G., & Baer, D. (1968). An experimental analysis of linguistic development: The productive use of the plural morpheme. *Journal of Applied Behavioral Analysis, 1,* 297–306.

Guralnick, M., & Paul-Brown, D. (1980). Functional and discourse analysis of nonhandicapped preschool children's speech to handicapped children. *American Journal of Mental Deficiency, 84,* 444–454.

Guralnick, M., & Paul-Brown, D. (1986). Communicative interactions of mildly delayed and normally developing preschool children: Effects of listener's developmental level. *Journal of Speech and Hearing Research, 29,* 2–10.

Hart, B., & Rogers-Warren, A. (1978). A milieu approach to teaching language. In R. Schiefelbusch (Ed.), *Language intervention strategies* (pp. 193–235). Baltimore: University Park Press.

Heshusius, L. (1991). Curriculum-based assessment and direct instruction: Critical reflections of fundamental assumptions. *Exceptional Children, 57,* 315–328.

Hohmann, M., Banet, B., & Weikert, D. (1979). *Young children in action.* Ypsilanti, MI: The High/Scope Press.

Hresko, W., Reid, D., & Hammill, D. (1981). *Test of Early Language Development.* Austin, TX: PRO-ED.

Hunt, P,. & Goetz, L. (1988). Teaching spontaneous communication in natural settings through interrupted behavior chains. *Topics in Language Disorders, 9,* 58–71.

Ispa, J. (1981). Social interactions among teachers, handicapped children, and non-handicapped children in a mainstreamed preschool. *Journal of Applied Developmental Psychology, 1,* 231–250.

Jenkins, J.R., Odom, S., & Speltz, M. (1989). Effects of social integration on preschool children with handicaps. *Exceptional Children, 55,* 420–428.

Jenkins, J.R., Speltz, M., & Odom, S. (1985). Integrating normal and handicapped preschoolers: Effects on child development and social interaction. *Exceptional Children, 52,* 7–17.

Kaiser, A., Yoder, P., & Keetz, A. (1992). Evaluating milieu teaching. In S.F. Warren & J. Reichle (Eds.), *Communication and language intervention series: Vol. 1. Causes and effects in communication and language intervention* (pp. 9–47). Baltimore: Paul H. Brookes Publishing Co.

Krantz, P., & Risley, T., (1977). Behavior ecology in the classroom. In K. O'Leary & S. O'Leary (Eds.), *Classroom management: The successful use of behavior modification* (pp. 349–366). New York: Pergamon.

Landry, S., & Chapieski, M. (1989). Joint attention and infant toy exploration: Effects of Down syndrome and prematurity. *Child Development, 60,* 103–118.

Lee, L., Koenigsknecht, R., & Mulhern, S. (1975). *Interactive language development teaching: The clinical presentation of grammatical structure.* Evanston, IL: Northwestern University Press.

Mahoney, G., Robinson, C., & Powell, A. (1992). Focusing on parent–child interaction: The bridge to developmentally appropriate practices. *Topics in Early Childhood Special Education, 12,* 105–120.

Mallory, B. (1992). Is it always appropriate to be developmental? Convergent models for early intervention practice. *Topics in Early Childhood Special Education, 11,* 1–12.

Manolson, H. (1985). *It takes two to talk: A Hanen early language parent guidebook.* Toronto, Ontario, Canada: Hanen Early Language Resource Center.

Mills, P. (1993). *The effects of levels of integration of cognitive and language development and social behavior of young children with disabilities.* Unpublished doctoral dissertation, University of Washington, Seattle.

Mirenda, P., & Donnellan, A. (1986). Effects of adult interaction style on conversational behavior in students with severe communication problems. *Language, Speech, and Hearing Services in Schools, 17,* 126–141.

Norris, J., & Hoffman, P. (1990). Comparison of adult-initiated vs. child-initiated interaction styles with handicapped prelanguage children. *Language, Speech, and Hearing Services in Schools, 21,* 28–36.

Odom, S., Bender, M., Stein, M., Doran, L., Houden, P., McInnes, M., Gilbert, M., Deklyen, M., Speltz, M., & Jenkins, J.R. (1988). *The Integrated Preschool Curriculum.* Seattle: University of Washington Press.

Odom, S.L., & McEvoy, M.A. (1988). Integration of young handicapped children and normally developing children. In S.L. Odom & M.B. Karnes (Eds.), *Early intervention for infants and children with handicaps: An empirical base* (pp. 241–267). Baltimore: Paul H. Brookes Publishing Co.

Odom, S., Peterson, C., McConnell, S., & Ostrosky, M. (1990). Ecobehavioral analysis of early education/specialized classroom settings and peer social interaction. *Education and Treatment of Children, 13,* 316–330.

Ogura, T. (1991). A longitudinal study of the relationship between early language and play development. *Journal of Child Language, 18,* 273–294.

Osborn, J., & Sherwood, D. (1988). *Mediated Learning Program: Research Draft.* Unpublished manuscript, University of Washington.

Osborn, J., Sherwood, D., Feuerstein, R., & Cole, K. (1993). *Mediated learning program for young children.* Manuscript submitted for publication.

Prelock, P., & Panagos, J. (1980). Mimicry versus imitative production in the speech of the retarded. *Journal of Psycholinguistic Research, 9,* 565–578.

Prizant, B., & Bailey, D. (1992). Facilitating the acquisition and use of communication skills. In D. Bailey & M. Wolery (Eds.), *Teaching infants and preschoolers with disabilities* (2nd ed., pp. 299–361). New York: Merrill/Macmillan.

Rogers-Warren, A., Ruggles, T., Peterson, N., & Cooper, A. (1981). Playing and learning together: Patterns of social interaction in handicapped and non-handicapped children. *Journal of the Division for Early Childhood Special Education, 3,* 56–63.

Rubin, K. (1977). The social and cognitive value of preschool toys and activities. *Canadian Journal and Behavioral Science, 9,* 382–385.

Schweinhart, L., & Hohmann, C. (1992). The High/Scope K–3 Curriculum: A new approach. *Principal, 71,* 16–19.

Shure, M. (1963). The psychological ecology of the nursery school. *Child Development, 34,* 979–992.

Siegel, G., & Spradlin, J. (1982). Language training in natural and clinical environments. *Journal of Speech and Hearing Disorders, 47,* 2–6.

Snow, R. (1989). Aptitude-treatment interaction as a framework for research on individual differences in learning. In P. Ackerman, R. Sternberg, & R. Glaser (Eds.), *Learning and individual differences* (pp. 13–59). New York: W.H. Freeman.

Stoneman, Z., Cantrell, M., & Hoover-Dempsey, K. (1983). The association between play materials and social behavior in a mainstreamed preschool: A naturalistic investigation. *Journal of Applied Developmental Psychology, 4,* 163–174.

Tomasello, M., & Farrar, M. (1986). Joint attention and early language. *Child Development, 57,* 1454–1463.

Tomasello, M., & Todd, J. (1983). Joint attention and lexical acquisition style. *First Language, 4,* 197–211.

Valdez-Menchaca, M., & Whitehurst, G. (1988). The effects of incidental teaching on vocabulary acquisition by young children. *Child Development, 59,* 1451–1459.

Valdez-Menchaca, M., & Whitehurst, G. (1992). Accelerating language development through picture book reading: A systematic extension to Mexican day care. *Developmental Psychology, 28,* 1106–1114.

Warren, S. (1992). Facilitating basic vocabulary acquisition with milieu teaching procedures. *Journal of Early Intervention, 16,* 235–251.

Warren, S.F., & Kaiser, A.P. (1988). Research in early language intervention. In S.L. Odom & M.B. Karnes (Eds.), *Early intervention for infants and children with handicaps: An empirical base* (pp. 89–108). Baltimore: Paul H. Brookes Publishing Co.

Warren, S., McQuarter, R., & Rogers-Warren, A. (1984). The effects of mands and models on the speech of unresponsive language-delayed preschool children. *Journal of Speech and Hearing Disorders, 49,* 43–52.

Warren, S., Yoder, P., Gazdag, G., & Kim, K. (1993). Facilitating prelinguistic communication skills in young children with developmental delay. *Journal of Speech and Hearing Research, 36,* 83–97.

Waryas, C., & Stremel-Campbell, K. (1983). *Communication Training Program.* New York: Teaching Resources.

Wolery, M., Strain, P., & Bailey, D. (1992). Reaching potentials of children with special needs. In S. Bredekamp & T. Rosegrant (Eds.), *Reaching potentials: Appropriate curriculum and assessment for young children* (pp. 92–111). Washington, DC: National Association for the Education of Young Children.

Yoder, P., Kaiser, A., & Alpert, C. (1991). An exploratory study of the interaction between language teaching methods and child characteristics. *Journal of Speech and Hearing Research, 34,* 155–167.

Yoder, P., Kaiser, A., Alpert, C., & Fischer, R. (1993). Following the child's lead when teaching nouns to preschoolers with mental retardation. *Journal of Speech and Hearing Research, 36,* 158–167.

Zimmerman, I., Steiner, V., & Pond, R. (1979). *Preschool Language Scale–Revised.* Columbus, OH: Charles E. Merrill.

PART II

Addressing Basic Intervention Goals with School-Age Children

3

A Rationale for
Naturalistic Speech
Intelligibility Intervention

Stephen Camarata

T HE FIELD OF LANGUAGE INTERVENTION has evolved dramatically since the
1970s, moving from rigorous applications of didactic learning principles to more
recent interventions modeled on natural language acquisition (Camarata &
Nelson, 1992; Camarata, Nelson, & Camarata, in press; Fey, 1986; Hart &
Risley, 1980; Koegel, O'Dell, & Koegel, 1988; Warren & Kaiser, 1986). In contrast, core intervention procedures for remediating speech intelligibility disabilities have not evolved to include naturalistic procedures to any great extent.
Rather, these core intervention procedures have remained primarily didactic
(Camarata, 1993). To be sure, there have been advances and modifications in
speech intelligibility intervention procedures (e.g., Elbert, Powell, & Swartzlander, 1991; Gierut, 1986, 1989, 1990; Hodson, 1986; Weiner, 1981), but didactic intervention procedures, including imitative drill, continue to be integral parts
of most of these programs. The purpose of this chapter is to provide a theoretical argument and preliminary evidence in support of extending naturalistic,
conversation-based procedures to intervention with speech intelligibility disabilities in a manner that parallels recent advances in language intervention procedures. This naturalistic approach has important implications for conducting
intervention in full inclusion and mainstream settings, where imitation-and-drill
procedures are often difficult to implement. It is *not* the intention of this chapter
to suggest that this new approach totally displace existing practice. Rather, the
argument is intended to extend the present scope of speech intelligibility training
to include potentially effective naturalistic conversation procedures.

The preparation of this chapter was supported in part by Award #DC01420 from the National
Institute on Deafness and other Communication Disorders, Award #H023C30070 and Award
#HO23A0052 from the U.S. Department of Education, and an endowment from the Scottish Rite
Foundation of Nashville, TN. The author gratefully acknowledges Marc Fey and Steven Warren for
their insightful reviews of the chapter, and Robert Koegel, Keith Nelson, and Paul Yoder for lively
discussions of theoretical issues.

The first section of this chapter includes a historical perspective on theoretical orientations and intervention procedures for speech disorders. The second section presents a theoretical rationale for viewing speech intelligibility disabilities from a naturalistic perspective. The third section includes a discussion of recent advances in intervention with language disabilities using procedures that parallel those found in natural language learning. The fourth and last section provides a theoretical rationale for integrating speech training into these types of natural language intervention paradigms and includes a presentation of the preliminary studies that support such a model.

HISTORICAL PERSPECTIVE ON
SPEECH INTELLIGIBILITY INTERVENTION

Terminology: Divergent Theoretical Perspectives

It is significant that speech intelligibility training has been, and continues to be, conducted under a number of different names. This is significant because these different names reflect different theoretical orientations as to how analysis and training should be conducted. For example, consider two currently used names of interventions that each have historical significance: articulation training and phonology training. The first, "articulation training," is perhaps the more widely used intervention both from a historical perspective (e.g., Swift, 1918; Van Riper, 1939; 1978) and in terms of current practice (Bernthal & Bankson, 1993). The second, "phonology training." has a venerable history in linguistic circles (e.g., Bloomfield, 1933), but has been applied to speech intelligibility disabilities (cf. "phonological disorders") only since the 1970s (e.g., Ingram, 1976).

Not surprisingly, the terms phonology and articulation have very different connotations with regard to how such disabilities should be viewed. Articulation may be defined as the production of speech sounds, which is accompanied by the skilled, coordinated movements of the speech musculature. In contrast, phonology represents the sounds of the language and the system of rules governing their patterns of change in context.

Thus, intervention with articulation disorders implies that the correct alignment of the tongue, lips, mandible, teeth, and palate is taught in a kind of physical therapy for the articulators. Because articulation is concerned with the motor actions associated with speech production, the focus of intervention is on drill and practice, thought to be required for motor facility and precision, thus improving intelligibility (e.g., Bernthal & Bankson, 1993; Nemoy & Davis, 1954). In contrast, intervention with phonological disorders implies that a specific part of grammar is addressed. In this model, the theoretical focus of intervention is on the rules and representations of sound production (e.g., Hodson & Paden, 1981; Ingram, 1976; Stoel-Gammon & Dunn, 1986). The point is that what one calls the problem reflects one's view of how the disability should be treated, and the terminology applied involves implicit and explicit theoretical assumptions (see Fey, 1992, for similar arguments).

For this reason, this chapter uses the term *speech intelligibility intervention* rather than phonological or articulation intervention. The use of the term speech intelligibility places the emphasis of intervention squarely on the expression of thoughts in a way that can be understood by the listener. Although this may appear to be a relatively minor shift in emphasis, this perspective *explicitly* includes the goal of comprehensible speech, whereas articulation and phonology training *implicitly* assume that comprehensible speech will be produced if the articulatory goals (i.e., precise coordination of the peripheral speech mechanism) and/or the rules and representations (i.e.,the grammar of speech sounds) are learned (Connolly, 1986; Kent, 1993). In practice, there is some question as to the validity of this implicit assumption (e.g., Camarata, 1993), particularly in the areas of generalization and social validity. Because of these concerns, the term speech intelligibility has been used in this chapter.

A Historical Perspective on Intervention

As noted above, although phonology has been studied and applied by linguists and other language specialists for many years, its application in speech intelligibility intervention has extended only since the 1970s (Ingram, 1976). Because of this, the articulation approach has long dominated the intervention literature (cf. Swift, 1918; Van Riper, 1939). Although there is variation in actual technique, the basic intervention model focuses on the direct training of the movements of the various articulators required to produce targeted speech sounds. Procedures include the use of direct imitation and modeling to establish targeted speech sounds, often in isolation; direct prompting; and use of tangible reinforcers. As the student reaches criteria on speech sounds in isolation, intervention then proceeds to the successive levels of sounds in syllables, sounds in words (including the initial, medial, and final position in words), sounds in phrases, and sounds in sentence contexts. At the final level, transfer to spontaneous speech, tangible reinforcers are faded. Many variations on this basic paradigm have been presented in the intervention literature (Bernthal & Bankson, 1993; Nemoy & Davis, 1954; Van Riper, 1939). This type of intervention is typically delivered in intensive one-to-one or small-group, pull-out settings and is often referred to as didactic or analog training because the focus of intervention is on imitation and drill activities.

Although this approach continues to be used, there have been a number of new phonological analysis procedures proposed over the last several decades. Following the publication of *Sound Patterns of English* (Chomsky & Halle, 1968), speech-language pathologists began examining the interrelation between grammar, or linguistic rules, and sound production patterns of children with speech intelligibility disabilities. Thus, the 1970s saw the application of "distinctive features," a classification system of acoustic and articulatory characteristics, to the analysis of speech errors. This application in turn resulted in a shift in the expectations of clinicians in that intervention could be conducted with a subset of sounds that shared a common value for a distinctive feature (e.g., [+ continuant], [+ voice]). Learning was expected to generalize to other sounds in the set without direct training. For example, rather than selecting a single sound (e.g., /s/), which would be expected to improve with intervention, clinicians might select a feature (e.g., [+ continuant]) so that intervention would affect an entire class of sounds. However, this shift focused on the analyses and expected outcomes for intervention rather than on the actual intervention procedures, which remained analog/didactic in nature (e.g., Costello & Onstine, 1976; McReynolds & Bennett, 1972; see Fey, 1992, for a similar argument).

A similar shift in analysis and outcome expectations occurred in the subsequent shift to phonological process analysis, which first appeared in the 1970s and early 1980s (e.g., Hodson & Paden, 1981; Ingram, 1976; Shriberg & Kwiatkowski, 1980). Again, the focus of analysis for describing speech errors essentially shifted to a new set of processes or rules, but the actual intervention procedures remained highly similar to traditional articulatory practices. This point was made eloquently by Shelton (1982) in his critique of Weiner's (1981) minimal contrast approach to intervention:

> However, the treatment delivered also involved [in addition to the minimal contrast/phonological process procedures]: a) instructing the children to say the words satisfactorily, b) providing stimulation with an auditory model, and c) delivering verbal and token reinforcement for correct responses. Aren't these latter three steps rather like the drills that are often used in [traditional] articulation therapy? (p. 336)

This observation can also be made concerning the more recent developments in the analysis of speech errors. These recent developments include generative analyses that are not process-based (Camarata & Gandour, 1984; Gierut, 1989; Gierut, Mi-Hui, & Dinnsen, 1993) and nonlinear models of phonology (Bernhardt, 1992; see Schwartz, 1992). To be sure, there have been significant variations in some aspects of the actual intervention practices. For example, Hodson and Paden (1983) included "auditory bombardment," and "cyclic intervention" in their approach to intervention. Similarly, Weiner (1981) included a word discrimination task and conversation-based procedures designed to draw attention to the child's error patterns. In these procedures, when a child produces a misarticulated word, the clinician might feign misunderstanding to highlight the child's error. For example, if the child says "gill" for "grill," the clinician could indicate that the "gill" cannot be found in the picture—"you said gill, I can't find a gill here." This type of problem-solving activity can be conducted in narrative activities and is designed to increase the child's awareness of his or her speech errors and, in Weiner's procedures, is used in conjunction with traditional drill activities.

In addition, there have been dramatic changes in goal selection and goal attack within phonological, linguistic rule-based approaches (see Elbert & Gierut, 1986; Fey 1992). For example, Gierut (1989) proposed a maximal contrast approach to the remediation of phonological errors. In this model, Gierut argued that intervention with (and acquisition of) forms that are different on a large number of phonetic features may result in increased knowledge of other forms on the phonetic continuum. The actual training is completed on minimal pairs (i.e., words that differ in one phoneme) that include the highest number of contrastive features. For example, the minimal pair "mat-chat" ([mæt] [tʃæt]) contrasts the following features in initial position: voice, nasal, continuant, strident, delayed release, and anterior. In Gierut's model, acquisition of this contrast (m–tʃ) would facilitate acquisition of the subordinate contrasts. As in previous advances in intervention, Gierut evaluated this model using traditional imitation-and-drill procedures. Similarly, Bernhardt (1992) examined the application of nonlinear phonology using auditory awareness training, discrimination, and imitation-and-drill procedures. As in the Gierut study, the focus of the methodology was on the predicted learning (based on nonlinear analyses) within the traditional imitation-and-drill procedures. Thus, although there is a shift in methodology for target selection and expectations for postintervention levels of phonological knowledge, these approaches included prompting, modeling, and reinforcement that are procedurally similar to the approaches they replaced.

One clear exception to these approaches is the whole language approach to phonological intervention (Hoffman, 1990, 1992, 1993; Hoffman, Norris, & Monjure, 1990), which is discussed in more detail in the fourth section of this chapter. Nevertheless, it seems fair to suggest that, despite increased sophistication in the understanding of the ways that speech sounds interact with one another and advances in the technology for analyzing speech errors, current speech intelligibility *procedures* remain rooted in the traditional didactic/analog methodology (see review in Bernthal & Bankson, 1993).

Generalization and Social Validity Issues

The above review indicates that, although there have been advances in theories of speech, these theories often have translated into intervention procedures that share a core analog/didactic basis. This is not necessarily a weakness from an a priori theoretical perspective (see Fey, 1992). Rather, it is an empirical question whether these analog/didactic approaches achieve the desired results; namely, improvements in speech intelligibility that generalize to spontaneous speech and that are noticeable by family members, teachers, peers, and other conversation partners. Such basic aspects of generalization (see the discussions in Fey, 1988; Horner, Dunlap, & Koegel, 1988; Johnston, 1988; McReynolds, 1987; Warren, 1988) and social validity (Horner et al., 1988; Wolf, 1978) are ultimately the most important measures of whether intervention is effective. Because of this, the validity of using analog/didactic intervention typologies as the core of speech intelligibility intervention rests upon the generalization of training goals and the social validity of the procedures. Unfortunately, in studies of speech intelligibility training, generalization is frequently assessed in a very narrow context. Assessment for generalization often includes only probes that resemble the training procedures and materials that often are completed in the intervention setting with the interventionist as the primary interaction partner (often, a one-to-one pull-out setting) (cf. Elbert & McReynolds, 1978; Elbert, Powell, & Swartzlander, 1991; Gierut, 1989; Weiner, 1981). Thus, although these studies have demonstrated generalization to probes, much more extensive generalization data are needed to substantiate the validity of the interventions. This need for more extensive generalization data becomes particularly clear when the development of language intervention procedures is examined. Many analog/didactic language intervention paradigms that resulted in probe generalization were less successful in generating broader kinds of generalization across settings and partners (Leonard, 1981; Siegel & Spradlin, 1985; Spradlin & Siegel, 1982).

Given this state of affairs, it is time to reassess and reevaluate the long-held and fundamental commitment that speech-language pathologists have made to the primary use of analog/didactic intervention procedures. There is a need for critical debate and the systematic, objective evaluation of these intervention procedures and activities. The following sections provide a theoretical rationale for including an intervention approach that employs principles derived from naturalistic conversation interactions and from natural speech and language acquisition. There are several conceptual strands that indicate the promise of such an approach, including those of perceptual models of learning, linguistic models of language that integrate phonology into language, data from studies of normal speech acquisition, and data from populations with disabilities that suggest a co-occurrence and basic integration of speech and language disabilities. Each of these components is discussed in the following section.

A NATURALISTIC PERSPECTIVE ON
SPEECH INTELLIGIBILITY DISABILITIES

Although some have argued that "the entire output of our thinking machine is nothing but patterns of motor coordination" (Sperry, 1952, cited in Kent, 1993, p. 227), it is also true that patterns of motor coordination, at least a far as speech intelligibility is concerned, are nothing without our thinking machine. Thus, speech includes, at minimum, a motor component and a language component. A logical extension of this is that a speech disability may arise from either or both of these origins.

To be sure, a large percentage of children with speech disabilities do display symptoms such as apraxia, dysarthria, delayed gross and fine motor development, and/or evidence of frank neuromuscular impairment (Love, 1992;

Shriberg, Kwiatkowski, Best, Hengst, & Terselie-Weber, 1986). Nevertheless, a strictly articulatory-motor account of speech disabilities would suggest that all, or nearly all, students with speech disabilities should display some kind of motor impairment. Although more sensitive, and as yet untested, technology may in fact reveal very subtle motor disabilities, at this time the data do not indicate that motor involvement accounts for even a plurality of the children with speech disabilities (Shriberg et al., 1986). Thus, other cognitive, linguistic, and/or perceptual factors may be at the root of a large number of speech intelligibility disorders.

Another line of evidence suggesting that language is a crucial component in many speech intelligibility disabilities comes from studies on the co-occurrence of developmental speech and language problems. The data suggest that a large percentage of children with speech disorders also display some form of language disability (e.g., see reviews in Aram & Kamhi, 1982; Bernthal & Bankson, 1993). Although not conclusive because diffuse neurological damage may affect both systems, such a co-occurrence of disabilities is consistent with a model of integrated, parallel learning of speech and language (e.g., Bock,1982; Strand, 1992). Additionally, although some authors have reported that phonological disabilities can occur in isolation (Catts, 1993; Hall & Tomblin, 1978; King, Jones, & Lasky, 1982; Shriberg et al., 1986), there are a number of reports that children with speech disabilities later display learning disabilities as well (Catts, 1989, 1993; Ham, 1958; Hodson, Nomura, & Zappia, 1989; Koppenhaver, Coleman, Kalman, &Yoder, 1991). Clearly, this association between speech disabilities, language impairments, and learning disabilities is consistent with a model that stresses the integration of phonology with other linguistic components.

In normal language acquisition, there is little evidence that children learning language in the ambient environment receive analog/didactic training or drill on individual speech sounds skills from their parents (cf., Brown & Hanlon, 1970; Cross, 1978; Ferguson, 1977; Stoel-Gammon, 1983). Similarly, studies of speech input to children suggest that parents may speak more slowly and articulate more clearly when speaking to young children rather than employ extensive imitation-based strategies (Bernstein-Ratner, 1983; Malsheen, 1980; Stoel-Gammon, 1983). Certainly, in infancy and later, parents imitate the child's productions and the child imitates the parent's productions (Jakobson, 1968). Nevertheless, this imitation is different from the analog/didactic training employed in speech intelligibility intervention in at least two important respects: First, the imitation is naturalistic in that it is largely unprompted. Speidel and Nelson (1989) argued that this form of unprompted imitation is indicative of the child's faculty with the various components of the structures being learned and is often a precursor to advances in learning. In addition, Speidel and Nelson suggest that prompted imitation disrupts the naturalistic flow of the parent–child interaction, may not be directly indicative of the child's current level of competence, and may actually disrupt the learning process. Second, the actual units of imitation are typically much larger than individual sounds, and parents and infants typically imitate syllable strings (Jakobson, 1968), whereas lexical (word-level) imitation is more often observed in preschool children (Speidel & Nelson, 1984). Similarly, Vihman (1992) reported that elicited imitation of isolated speech sounds is a rare occurrence across the many languages that have been studied.

The following example, observed from my own behavior toward my 17-month-old son, is typical of a particular type of speech intelligibility interaction between parent and child. My son approached me and said, "wa doo" [wa du]. I replied, "I don't understand, tell me again." My son then pointed to the refrigerator and repeated, "wa doo." This time, I understood what he was saying and replied, "Oh, want juice, you want juice," and I gave him some juice.

Naturally, this is just one of many such interactions that occur throughout the days, weeks, months, and years of childrearing, and in no way reflected any forethought or meta-strategies on my part. I was simply interacting with him as I normally did (see also the "pig dialogue" [Fey & Gandour, 1982] for a well-documented case of phonological change via naturalistic perceptual feedback during normal language acquisition). These exchanges are examples of a typical kind of interaction and contain many important components of analog teaching methods (i.e., a primary reinforcer in the form of juice). But the most interesting part of these interactions from the perspective of this chapter is not in what was done, but in what *was not* done. First, no imitative prompts were delivered. In both examples, a model only was delivered. Although I have observed parents occasionally deliver an imitative prompt (e.g., "Say juice"), it is significant that many do not. Second, and more important, no modeling or prompting of individual sounds was delivered. That is, I did not say, "Oh, want juice, say (j) [dʒ]." This prompting of individual sounds appears to be unusual in parent–child interactions.

A similar learning platform that relies on parent trainer production is seen in perceptual models of speech acquisition (e.g., Locke, 1980a; 1980b; Yeni-Komshian & Ferguson, 1980) that emphasize: 1) the syllabic and lexical nature of speech input, and 2) the role of feedback, in terms of the parents' model of the correct form that is in immediate contrast to the child's form. This type of learning model has been presented in a concise manner by Nelson (1989) in his discussion of a "rare, event learning mechanism." Nelson based the model on the learning of language structures and provided examples from other behavior categories (e.g., art). The interaction with my son described above illustrates the application of Nelson's naturalistic learning model to speech.

To summarize, one of the theoretical underpinnings for applying analog/didactic intervention to speech intelligibility training has been the implicit assumption that speech disabilities have an underlying motor component that must be addressed in intervention. However, because many children with speech disabilities often do not display independent evidence of motor disabilities, because language and speech disabilities often co-occur, and because speech disabilities can be associated with learning disabilities, it would appear that there may be important parallels between speech disabilities and language disabilities. Finally, the data on natural language acquisition suggest that parents engage in very little overt analog/drill activities with their typically developing children. Instead, parents appear to engage in a more lexically based form of interaction in which feedback to the child includes perceptual modeling of the correct word in a naturalistic conversation context.

These observations of typical development parallel observations from the field of language acquisition and in newly developed naturalistic language intervention procedures. Thus, several independent data sources indicate the importance of examining the potential effectiveness of naturalistic language intervention procedures for speech intelligibility intervention. The following section includes a brief review of the recent advances in language intervention procedures as they pertain to speech intelligibility disabilities.

RECENT ADVANCES IN INTERVENTION WITH LANGUAGE DISABILITIES

The early history of language intervention is remarkably similar to the history of speech intervention summarized above in that training often included extensive use of analog/didactic procedures. The actual sequence and material of this training includes the imitative production of targets following prompts and the extensive application of overt reinforcers (e. g., Gray & Ryan, 1973). These approaches have been effective in establishing production of a wide range of language skills (see reviews in Byrne-Sarricks, 1987; Fey, 1986). However, three basic issues prompted extensive modification of these analog/didactic procedures to include more naturalistic elements. First, researchers found that, although there was a limited type of generalization to highly similar probes, there was less success in obtaining generalization across settings, across behaviors, and across conversation partners (see discussion in Siegel & Spradlin, 1985). Second, although training records often documented progress in targeted behaviors, parents, caregivers, teachers, and/or peers often failed to notice this progress, suggesting a lack of social validity for the intervention. Third, many individuals with severe disabilities such as autism actively resisted participation in analog activities (Koegel, O'Dell, & Koegel, 1988) so that aversive consequences were sometimes required simply to get the child to participate in the training activities. Although individuals with less severe disabilities may display a less than positive attitude toward participation in analog activities (Haley, Camarata, & Nelson, 1994), the reaction from populations with more severe disabilities potentially precludes implementation of the analog procedures (see Koegel, Camarata, & Koegel, in press).

One reaction to these limitations of analog/didactic procedures was to develop interventions that more closely resembled the naturalistic language acquisition model. These procedures ranged from embedding imitative prompts into conversational contexts (e.g., Hart & Risley, 1980; Warren & Kaiser, 1986), and using natural reinforcers (Koegel, O'Dell, & Koegel, 1988), to procedures that included neither imitative prompts nor overt reinforcers (Camarata & Nelson, 1992; Camarata et al., in press; Fey, Cleave, Long, & Hughes, 1993). The parallels between developments in language and phonological intervention support the experimental application of more naturalistic procedures to intervention with speech disabilities to determine whether these positive effects can be observed in the speech domain as well.The following section includes a theoretical model for applying naturalistic conversation-based intervention to speech intelligibility disabilities.

THEORETICAL MODEL FOR NATURALISTIC INTERVENTION WITH SPEECH INTELLIGIBILITY DISORDERS

Nelson (1989) presented a model of a rare event learning mechanism (RELM) discussed earlier to describe the learning of grammatical structures via growth recasts. Recasts are utterances from parents (or clinicians) that include a new linguistic structure embedded within a partial repetition of the child's own prior utterance. For example, if the child said, "Ball roll," a parent recast could be, "Yes, the ball is rolling." Nelson argued that such recasts provide optimal support for learning new grammatical structures if: 1) the parent production immediately follows the child's attempted (but incorrect) target use, and 2) the parent production provides added linguistic information about the way a specific structure is used. Such a recast is called a rare event because, in Nelson's view, parental presentations that combine these elements are relatively rare in parent–child interactions. Nelson's research (Baker & Nelson, 1984; Camarata & Nelson, 1992; Nelson, 1977; Nelson, Camarata, Welsh, Butkowski, & Camarata, 1993) has shown that frequent presentations of growth recasts result in rapid acquisition of new language structures.

The rare event learning mechanism model is potentially applicable to the task of learning phonological targets in conversational contexts. In this case, the basic procedure is identical to that used in learning grammatical targets. The child attempts a phonological target in a conversational context followed by a parental recast. For example, if the child said, "A wion [a lion]," a recast from the parent might be, "Yes, a lion." This response directly parallels a typical recast response for a grammatical target. Nelson (1989) predicted that these kinds of exchanges result in "hot spots" in the child's system in which the child compares a previously stored (incorrect) form with the recently produced (correct) adult form. According to Nelson, these comparisons ultimately may result in a reorganization of the child's system, with the displacement in long-term memory of the incorrect form by the correct form.

Although Nelson (1989) did not discuss the issue directly, a question arises regarding a potential learning hierarchy for different levels of linguistic information (Crystal, 1987). For example, assume that a child produces a reduced form that includes incorrect speech production and omits grammatical morphemes (e.g., "two wion" for "two lions"). If the parent provides recasts that include grammatical morphemes and speech intelligibility models, what forms is the child likely to learn? There are four possibilities: 1) the child could acquire both the grammatical morpheme and the speech form, 2) the child could acquire neither the grammatical morpheme nor the speech form, 3) the child could acquire the grammatical morpheme but not the speech form, or 4) the child could acquire the speech form but not the grammatical morpheme. Studies of acquisition from conversational recasts by typically developing children and by children with disabilities suggest that the possibilities that neither form was acquired and that the child acquired the speech form only are unlikely. These studies also suggested that the acquisition of the grammatical morpheme but not the speech form is likely and often occurs (Baker & Nelson, 1984; Camarata & Nelson, 1992; Camarata et al., in press; Fey, Cleave, Ravida, Long, Dejmal, & Easton, 1994). In addition, the theoretical arguments of Hoffman (1992, 1993) and the results presented by Hoffman et al. (1990) suggest that the acquisition of both forms is possible. However, there are several factors that suggest that simultaneous acquisition of grammatical and speech forms by individuals with disabilities is unlikely.

First, there have been a number of studies that indicate that typically developing children and children with speech and language disabilities have difficulty simultaneously producing increased complexity in speech and grammar (see review in Crystal, 1987). Second, there is evidence that children with speech and language disabilities have difficulty processing grammatical information that is low in phonetic substance (Leonard, MacGregor, & Allen, 1992) and that they have difficulty processing certain aspects of speech information (Tallal, Stark, & Mellits, 1985). This suggests that simultaneous processing of speech and grammatical information and simultaneous production of advanced forms in these domains may be difficult. In combination with the data that indicate that grammatical forms will be processed and produced, the simultaneous recast of grammatical morphemes and speech forms may result only in advances in the grammatical domain (see discussion of Fey et al., 1994, presented below). Although this latter study was not designed to systematically include models of phonological targets, it is assumed that Fey et al. delivered models that not only included grammatical information but also included typical adult sound productions. Because the children in this study displayed speech errors in addition to language impairments, it appears likely that phonological models were coincidentally delivered with the grammatical targets. The above analysis implies that advances in speech-intelligibility will occur if, and only if, the recasted model adds new speech information exclusively. Additional studies are required to test this speculation directly.

Given that many children with disabilities have both speech and language deficits, it is important to determine if simultaneous advances in both domains are possible with intervention. If a specific focus on one domain is required, then the optimal intervals for shifting focus from speech to language (and the reverse) must be determined. Also, speech and language interface directly in the morphological domain. Several specific phonological forms are required to mark certain morphological structures, as in use of [s], [z], [ðz] to mark plural, possessive, third person singular, and contracted copula and auxiliary forms. It would be interesting to determine if naturalistic intervention with these morphological forms resulted in more accurate production of these speech sounds in the phonological systems of children who lacked both the sounds and the morphemes prior to intervention. The following section includes preliminary evidence in support of this theoretical model.

PRELIMINARY EVIDENCE SUPPORTING
NATURALISTIC SPEECH INTELLIGIBILITY INTERVENTION

Preliminary evidence in support of naturalistic speech intelligibility intervention is derived from a recently completed study evaluating whether specific sounds could be trained using naturalistic intervention procedures (Camarata, 1993). The study included two children (ages 3;10 and 4;3 at the onset of treatment) with speech disabilities. Both subjects fell significantly below expected levels on standardized articulation assessments and on phonological analysis of spontaneous speech and language samples, but both children's spontaneous speech was partially intelligible to family members and to speech clinicians working with them. One child had been identified as having a language impairment by standardized testing and language sample analysis, whereas the other child scored within the normal range on these assessments. Because both children passed audiometric screening and also passed an oral-motor screening exam, they met the definition of phonological disorders of unknown etiology (Shriberg et al., 1986).

Speech intelligibility in both children was targeted using the procedures described above in the example of interaction with my son. Incorrect productions were responded to with an immediate correct model at the word or phrase level. Specifically, when a word was attempted that included an incorrect production of the targeted sound, the clinician responded positively to the semantic content of the production and then delivered a correct model. For example, if the child said, "This is a wion [lion]," and the target sounds included [1], the clinician responded, "Yes, a lion, it's a lion." No imitative prompts or direct motor training were provided at any time. The materials included toys, books, and games that were appropriate for the child's age level and selected by the clinician to ensure that many opportunities would be available for production of the targets. In the above example using [1], toys included lions, Lego building blocks, toy lips, Lincoln Log toys, and alphabet books (including large sections on [1]).

The hypothesis in this study was that the naturalistic intervention procedures would prove highly effective in generating rapid transfer and generalization for those speech sounds where some evidence of productivity was available (i.e., the child could produce the sound correctly in some contexts but not others). It was also hypothesized that the intervention would prove less effective for those sounds that were never produced correctly in any context. The results of the study were promising in that dramatic gains were observed in generalization of both kinds of sounds during intervention. That is, as predicted, sounds with some prior evidence of productivity were acquired within only a few sessions. In addition, although there was a longer latency period, extending to 10 weeks for some sounds, the sounds for which there was no prior evidence of productivity also were learned. Furthermore, for both sound types, the productions immediately generalized to spontaneous speech. There was positive evidence of social validity because parents and other relatives reported improvements in overall intelligibility following intervention. Naturally, this outcome could have resulted from fortuitous timing rather than from the intervention, but the application of a multiple baseline single-subject design across subjects and across behaviors minimized this threat to the validity of the study. At the least, this initial study suggests that further testing of the model with larger subject pools and diverse populations is warranted.

Potential Applications of Naturalistic Speech Intelligibility Training

Perhaps the most promising aspect of this intervention model of naturalistic speech intelligibility training is that, theoretically, it would unify speech intelligibility intervention and language intervention. This, in turn, could result in implementing speech intervention in a much less restrictive environment than is currently practiced. In addition, naturalistic procedures could be adapted to and incorporated into recent advances in phonological theory. For example, intervention based upon phonological process theory could be conducted by targeting one or more elements within the process and monitoring any changes in untargeted sounds thought to be included in the process. If the process of "stopping" (Edwards, 1992; Elbert, 1992; Hodson, 1986; Ingram, 1976; Shriberg & Kwiatkowski, 1980) were targeted, one could target a subset of those sounds undergoing the process (e.g., [f], [ʃ]) and monitor whether associated sounds (e.g., [s], [z], [v]) also change. In this way, the intervention design would be identical to that in studies that use imitation-and-drill to examine phonological process treatment (e.g., Elbert, 1992; Elbert, Dinnsen, & Powell, 1984; Powell & Elbert, 1984). Similarly, the conversation-based intervention could be applied to other emerging phonological intervention models. For example, in maximal contrast intervention (Gierut, 1989), contrastive elements could be targeted by using key minimal pairs in the intervention context (i.e., meat-seat, moo-Sue, mow-sew) to establish a productive contrast within Gierut's maximal learning framework. As with phonological processes, predicted untreated acquisitions would be monitored as well (see Gierut, 1989, 13–14).

In the beginning of this chapter, it was noted that the purpose of the chapter was not to totally displace existing analog/didactic interventions. Rather, the purpose has been to argue for extending the scope of practice to include naturalistic procedures. I speculate that the outcome of such interventions will parallel what often has been observed in the language intervention literature: a consistent advantage for naturalistic procedures (Camarata & Nelson, 1992; Camarata et al., in press), but some degree of effectiveness for analog/didactic intervention evident within certain populations (e.g., individuals with cerebral palsy) and perhaps at certain developmental levels (see Yoder, Kaiser, & Alpert, 1991). However, these speculations should not preclude direct experimental testing. Recall that the original speculation presented in this chapter was that the naturalistic procedures would not be highly effective for speech sounds for which there was no evidence of productivity. Experimental testing of this hypothesis revealed, at least within that study (Camarata, 1993), that the hypothesis was not correct.

Finally, there is no a priori rationale for maintaining "pure" versions of either intervention. Perhaps some hybrid (see Fey, 1986), akin to incidental teaching of language goals, which includes imitation in naturalistic contexts, will prove most effective for remediating speech intelligibility disabilities.

Comparison to Whole Language

As noted above, there has been at least one other naturalistic approach presented in the recent literature on speech intelligibility disabilities. This approach, presented under the rubric of whole language intervention (Hoffman, 1990; 1992; 1993; Hoffman et al., 1990), includes naturalistic interaction and an absence of imitative prompts and/or tangible reinforcers. As such, there are a number of important similarities between the naturalistic procedures described previously in this chapter and the whole language approach. However, a fundamental difference in these procedures concerns the posited importance of a direct focus on speech intelligibility targets. Although I agree wholeheartedly with the argument that phonological knowledge can be learned within a naturalistic conversational context (see Hoffman, 1990, p. 242; Hoffman, 1993, p. 143; Hoffman et al., 1990, p. 103). Hoffman also asserted that advances in speech will result from a focus on nonspeech language tasks such as narrative skills and syntax:

> Concurrently, articulation may become clearer as the addition of more syntactic constructions, morphological forms, and lexical entries requires that these forms be contrasted via more complex syllable shapes and a more complete phonemic inventory. Thus, at every moment of active processing, each level may be refined by assimilations and accommodations at all other levels. (Hoffman et al., 1990, p. 108)

This position is in direct contrast to the hypothesis that learning in a naturalistic context requires adult models that include specific elements that are missing from the child's form (Nelson, 1989). That is, the intervention model developed by Nelson (1989) and tested by Camarata and Nelson (1992) and Camarata et al.

(in press), posits that target acquisition will occur when there are multiple relevant, salient, and challenging presentations (within a naturalistic context) of specific language forms. Whole language procedures, however, predict that more general language interaction with the child will result in improvements in speech intelligibility.

In Hoffman et al. (1990), two children with speech intelligibility disabilities were examined. Cluster reduction was targeted in one child using a minimal pairs approach, which included traditional imitation procedures (e.g., clinician models, prompts and reinforcers) in addition to perceptual training (see Hoffman et al., 1990, p. 103). The other child received intervention using a whole language approach. The whole language intervention procedures included story retelling and conversational interaction with the clinician, but included no direct intervention with speech intelligibility (see Fey et al., chap. 1, this volume, for more detail on the Hoffman et al. [1990] procedures). Hoffman et al. reported gains in phonology for both children including increases in the score of the child receiving whole language intervention on the Templin-Darley Screening Test of Articulation (Templin & Darley, 1969), number of correct clusters, and overall percentage of consonants produced correctly, and a decrease in the number of reduced clusters. The child receiving the phonological intervention consistently demonstrated slightly higher gains in these measures (see Hoffman et al., 1990, Table 4, p. 104).

Hoffman et al. (1990) also measured language abilities in terms of performance on a standardized test and in terms of a number of language structures produced in narratives (e.g., complex sentence use, verb tense errors, pronoun errors). They reported that the child receiving whole language intervention made larger gains on these measures. This suggests that language intervention can result in incidental advances in phonology as well. However, several additional factors must be examined when interpreting this outcome. First, as Hoffman et al. (1990) noted, "The increases in phonological performance were consistently greater for the child treated via the phonological [analog/didactic] approach (S2), than for the child taught using the whole language approach (S1), by relatively small amounts" (p. 107). Because the matched child receiving analog/didactic intervention made improvements in both speech and language, and because a pre- and posttest design was employed to measure gains (see Schwartz & Camarata, 1985), it is possible that gains were attributable in part to maturational factors rather than to intervention effects (note that a third child, a triplet of the two participants in the study, had typically developing speech and language skills; see also Fey et al., 1994).

The second factor to be considered is that both children were highly variable in pre- and posttest language measures. For example, the child receiving whole language intervention used from 0% to 45% complex sentences in the preintervention samples and used from 41% to 50% complex sentences in the postintervention samples. In contrast, the child receiving phonological intervention used from 4% to 20% complex sentences in preintervention samples and used from 12% to 26% in postintervention samples. One could argue (as in Hoffman et al., 1990) that relative improvement in complex sentence use occurred for the child receiving whole language intervention. Another perspective is that gains in the highest scores at preintervention when compared to postintervention (the highest percentage reflecting the child's "true" complex sentence capabilities) were quite similar (5% gain for whole language intervention compared with 6% for phonological intervention; see Hoffman et al., 1990, Table 5).

In addition, it should be noted that postintervention measures were conducted using a task (telling "The Three Bears") that was similar to training conditions for whole language intervention. Finally, the reported increases in the standardized test (spoken language quotient, Test of Language Development–Primary [Newcomer & Hammill, 1982] were higher for the child receiving whole language intervention, but preintervention differences and variation in subjects (e.g., lower vocabulary skills for the child receiving phonological intervention) may also account, in part, for the results. Thus, the results presented by Hoffman et al., 1990, are intriguing because: 1) positive results were reported for application of a conversation-based intervention, 2) simultaneous gains were reported in speech and language, and 3) gains were reported in speech that were incidental to language teaching. Therefore, the study should be replicated while controlling for the factors discussed above.

The theoretical position of Nelson (1989) and the findings of Camarata and Nelson (1992) predict that whole language procedures that lack a specific focus on speech intelligibility would not be effective. This is because learning in this model, particularly learning by children with disabilities, requires that the target forms be made salient and occur relatively frequently. It is assumed that target salience is enhanced when a child's production that includes a speech error is followed immediately by a clinician/teacher/parent model that includes accurate presentation of the targeted sounds. However, it is expected that such interactions will occur at a relatively low frequency in any naturalistic interaction. Therefore, to ensure the child's recognition of the target and comparison to, and modification of, his or her own production, high concentration of such interactions may be required.

Furthermore, the errors in speech production that children with disabilities make may result in modifications of the adult response that extend beyond the processing capabilities of the child. For example, in the case of a child going to the refrigerator and saying "wa doo," an alternative naturalistic response could be an expansion of the child's utterance such as, "Oh, you want some juice in your cup." In this case, it is possible that the child will attend to the added grammatical and lexical elements in the adult model, rather than the phonetic details, because the meaningful components of the model are in direct competition with the speech intelligibility components (see discussion in MacWhinney, 1989).

Because the primary purpose of any interaction is to convey meaning, any additional meaningful units presented to the child by the adult model may be more salient than the speech intelligibility information. Thus, the model predicts the greatest effects when meaning (and grammar) are held relatively constant.

This hypothesis is consistent with the report by Whitehurst, Fischel, Arnold, and Lonigan (1992), who reported that treating children with expressive language delay with home-based language intervention did not reduce the subsequent incidence of phonological problems.

The results of the recent study by Fey et al. (1994) are consistent with this position. Fey et al. reported that a naturalistic intervention focusing on grammar in a group of 30 preschoolers with grammatical impairments had no incidental effects on the subjects' phonologies. Specifically, grammatical expression improved, whereas the phonological targets (which did not receive direct intervention) did not. Fey et al. concluded that: "Despite a close relationship between the development of grammar and phonology, language intervention approaches...should address phonological problems directly if significant effects on phonology are to be expected" (p. 594). Although Fey and colleagues did not argue for application of naturalist procedures to phonological intervention, their results are consistent with the expectation that a direct focus on speech intelligibility may be required within an intervention. Such a focus generally is not included in whole language approaches (Hoffman et al., 1990). Additional studies are required to determine whether procedures with a specific focus on speech intelligibility or whether whole language procedures are the most effective in facilitating children's speech production skills.

REFERENCES

Aram, D., & Kamhi, A. (1982). Perspectives on the relationship between phonological and language disorders. *Seminars in Speech, Language, and Hearing, 3,* 101–114.

Baker, N.D., & Nelson, K.E. (1984). Recasting and related conversational techniques for triggering syntactic advances by young children. *First Language, 5,* 3–22.

Bernhardt, B. (1992). The application of nonlinear phonological theory to intervention with one phonologically disordered child. *Clinical Linguistics and Phonetics, 6,* 259–281.

Bernstein-Ratner, N. (1983, November). *Increased vowel precision in the absence of increased vowel duration.* Paper presented at the American Speech-Language-Hearing Association annual convention, Cincinatti, OH.

Bernthal, J., & Bankson, N. (1993). *Articulation disorders.* Englewood Cliffs, NJ: Prentice Hall.

Bloomfield, L. (1933). *Language.* New York: Holt, Rhinehart & Winston.

Bock, K. (1982). Toward a cognitive psychology of syntax: Information processing contributions to sentence processing. *Psychological Review, 89,* 1–47.

Brown, R., & Hanlon, C. (1970). Derivational complexity and the order of acquisition in child's speech. In J. Hayes (Ed.), *Cognition and the development of language* (pp. 11–54). New York: John Wiley & Sons.

Byrne-Sarricks, M. (1987). Treatment of language disorders in children: A review of experimental studies. In H. Wintz (Ed.), *Human communication and its disorders: A review* (pp. 167–201). Norwood, NJ: Ablex.

Camarata, S. (1993). The application of naturalistic conversation training to speech production in children with speech disabilities. *Journal of Applied Behavior Analysis, 26,* 173–182.

Camarata, S., & Gandour, J. (1984). On describing idiosyncratic phonologic systems. *Journal of Speech and Hearing Disorders, 49,* 262–266.

Camarata, S., & Nelson, K.E. (1992). Treatment efficiency as a function of target selection in the remediation of child language disorders. *Clinical Linguistics and Phonetics, 6,* 167–178.

Camarata, S., Nelson, K.E., & Camarata, M. (in press). A comparison of conversation-based to imitation-based procedures for training grammatical structures in specifically language impaired children. *Journal of Speech and Hearing Research.*

Catts, H. (1989). Speech production deficits in development dyslexia. *Journal of Speech and Hearing Disorders, 54,* 422–428.

Catts, H. (1993). The relationship between speech-language impairments and reading disabilities. *Journal of Speech and Hearing Research, 36,* 948–958.

Chomsky, N., & Halle, M. (1968). *Sound patterns of English.* New York: Harper & Row.

Connolly, J. (1986). Intelligibility: A linguistic view. *British Journal of Disorders of Communication, 21,* 371–376.

Costello, J., & Onstine, J. (1976). The modification of multiple articulation errors based upon distinctive feature theory. *Journal of Speech and Hearing Disorders, 41,* 199–215.

Cross, T. (1978). Mothers' speech and its association with rate of linguistic development in young children. In N. Waterson & C. Snow (Eds.), *The development of communication* (pp. 189–206). New York: John Wiley & Sons.

Crystal, D. (1987). Towards a bucket theory of language disability: Taking account of interaction between linguistic levels. *Clinical Linguistics and Phonetics, 1,* 7–21.

Edwards, M. (1992). In support of phonological processes. *Language, Speech, and Hearing Services in Schools, 23,* 233–240.

Elbert, M. (1992). Consideration of error types: A response to Fey. *Language, Speech, and Hearing Services in Schools, 23,* 241–246.

Elbert, M., Dinnsen, D., & Powell, T. (1984). On the prediction of phonologic generalization learning patterns. *Journal of Speech and Hearing Disorders, 49,* 309–317.

Elbert, M., & Gierut, J. (1986). *Handbook of clinical phonology.* London: Taylor & Francis.

Elbert, M., & McReynolds, L. (1978). An experimental analysis of misarticulating children's generalization. *Journal of Speech and Hearing Research, 21,* 136–149.

Elbert, M., Powell, T., & Swartzlander, P. (1991). Toward a technology of generalization: How many exemplars are sufficient? *Journal of Speech and Hearing Research, 34,* 81–87.

Ferguson, C. (1977). Baby talk as simplified register. In C. Snow & C. Ferguson (Eds.), *Language input and acquisition.* Cambridge, MA: Cambridge University Press.

Fey, M. (1986). *Language intervention with young children.* Boston: Allyn & Bacon.

Fey, M. (1988). Generalization issues facing language interventionists. *Language, Speech, and Hearing Services in Schools, 19,* 242–281.

Fey, M. (1992). Articulation and phonology: Inextricable constructs in speech pathology. *Language, Speech, and Hearing Services in Schools, 23,* 225–232.

Fey, M., Cleave, P., Long, S., & Hughes, D. (1993). Two approaches to the facilitation of grammar in children with language impairment: An experimental evaluation. *Journal of Speech and Hearing Research, 36,* 141–157.

Fey, M., Cleave, P., Ravida, A., Long, S., Dejmal, A., & Easton, D. (1994). The ef-fects of grammar facilitation on the phonological performance of children with speech and language impairments. *Journal of Speech and Hearing Research, 37,* 594–607.

Fey, M., & Gandour, J. (1982). The pig dialogue: Phonological systems in transition. *Journal of Child Language, 9,* 517–520.

Gierut, J. (1986). On the assessment of productive phonological knowledge. *Journal of the National Student Speech Language Hearing Association, 14,* 83–100.

Gierut, J. (1989). Maximal opposition approach to phonological treatment. *Journal of Speech and Hearing Disorders, 54,* 9–19.

Gierut, J. (1990). Differential learning of phonological oppositions. *Journal of Speech and Hearing Research, 33,* 540–549.

Gierut, J., Mi-Hui, C., & Dinnsen, D. (1993). Geometric accounts of consonant-vowel interactions in developing systems. *Clinical Linguistics and Phonetics, 7,* 219–236.

Gray, B., & Ryan, B. (1973). *A language program for the nonlanguage child.* Champaign, IL: Research Press.

Haley, K., Camarata, S., & Nelson, K.E. (1994). Social valence in children with specific language impairment during imitation-based and conversation-based intervention. *Journal of Speech and Hearing Research, 37,* 378–388.

Hall, P., & Tomblin, B. (1978). A follow-up study of children with articulation and language disorders. *Journal of Speech and Hearing Disorders, 43,* 227–241.

Ham, R. (1958). Relationship between misspelling and misarticulation. *Journal of Speech and Hearing Disorders, 23,* 294–297.

Hart, B., & Risley, T. (1980). In vivo language intervention: Unanticipated general effects. *Journal of Applied Behavior Analysis, 11,* 407–432.

Hodson, B. (1986). *The assessment of phonological processes.* Danville, IL: Interstate.

Hodson, B., Nomura, C., & Zappia, M. (1989). Phonological disorders: Impact on academic performance? *Seminars in Speech and Language, 10,* 252–259.

Hodson, B., & Paden, E. (1981). Phonological processes which characterize unintelligible and intelligible speech in early childhood. *Journal of Speech and Hearing Disorders, 46,* 369–373.

Hodson, B., & Paden, E. (1983). *Targeting intelligible speech.* San Diego: College-Hill.

Hoffman, P. (1990). Spelling, phonology, and the speech-language pathologist: A whole language perspective. *Language, Speech, and Hearing Services in Schools, 21,* 238–243.

Hoffman, P. (1992). Synergistic development of phonetic skill. *Language, Speech, and Hearing Services in Schools, 23,* 254–260.

Hoffman, P. (1993). A whole language treatment perspective for phonological disorder. *Seminars in Speech and Language, 14,* 142–152.

Hoffman, P., Norris, J., & Monjure, J. (1990). Comparison of process targeting and whole language treatments for phonologically delayed preschool children. *Language, Speech, and Hearing Services in Schools, 21,* 102–109.

Horner, R., Dunlap, G., & Koegel, R. (Eds.). (1988). *Generalization and maintenance: Life-style changes in applied settings.* Baltimore: Paul H. Brookes Publishing Co.

Ingram, D. (1976). *Phonological disability in children.* New York: Elsevier/North Holland.

Ingram, D. (1989). *First language acquisition.* Cambridge: Cambridge University Press.

Jakobson, R. (1968). *Child language, aphasia, and phonological universals.* The Hague: Mouton.

Johnston, J. (1988). Generalization: The nature of change. *Language, Speech, and Hearing Services in Schools, 19,* 314–329.

Kent, R. (1993). Speech intelligibility and communicative competence in children. In A. Kaiser & D. Gray (Eds.), *Communication and language intervention series: Vol. 2. Enhancing children's communication* (pp. 223–237). Baltimore: Paul H. Brookes Publishing Co.

King, R., Jones, C., & Lasky, E. (1982). In retrospect: A fifteen year follow-up report of speech-language disordered children. *Language, Speech, and Hearing Services in Schools, 13,* 24–33.

Koegel, R., Camarata, S., & Koegel, L. (in press). Aggression and noncompliance: Behavior modification through naturalistic language remediation. In J. Matson (Ed.), *Autism in children and adults: Etiology assessment and interventions.* Sycamore, IL: Sycamore Press.

Koegel, R., O'Dell, M., & Dunlap, G. (1988). Producing speech use in nonverbal autistic children by reinforcing attempts. *Journal of Autism and Developmental Disorders, 18,* 525–538.

Koegel, R., O'Dell, M., & Koegel, L. (1988). A natural language teaching paradigm. *Journal of Autism and Developmental Disorders, 17,* 187–199.

Koppenhaver, D., Coleman, P., Kalman, S., & Yoder, P. (1991). The implications of emergent literary research for children with developmental disabilities. *American Journal of Speech-Language Pathology, 1,* 38–44.

Leonard, L. (1981). Facilitating linguistic skills in children with specific language impairment. *Applied Psycholinguistics, 2,* 89–118.

Leonard, L., McGregor, K., & Allen, G. (1992). Grammatical morphology and speech perception in children with specific language impairment. *Journal of Speech and Hearing Research, 35,* 1076–1085.

Locke, J. (1980a). The inference of speech perception in the phonologically disordered child: I. *Journal of Speech and Hearing Disorders, 45,* 431–444.

Locke, J. (1980b). The inference of speech perception in the phonologically disordered child: II. *Journal of Speech and Hearing Disorders, 45,* 445–468.

Love, R. (1992). *Childhood motor speech disability.* New York: Macmillan.

MacWhinney, B. (1989). The teachability of language. In M. Rice & R. Schiefelbusch (Eds.), *The teachability of language* (pp. 63–104). Baltimore: Paul H. Brookes Publishing Co.

Malsheen, B. (1980). Two hypotheses for phonetic clarification in the speech of mothers to children. In G. Yeni-Komshian & C. Ferguson (Eds.), *Child phonology* (Vol. 2). New York: Academic Press.

McReynolds, L. (1987). A perspective on articulation generalization. *Seminars in Speech and Language, 8,* 217–240.

McReynolds, L., & Bennett, S. (1972). Distinctive feature generalization in articulation training. *Journal of Speech and Hearing Disorders, 37,* 462–470.

Nelson, K.E. (1977). Facilitating children's syntax acquisition. *Developmental Psychology, 13,* 101–107.

Nelson, K.E. (1989). Strategies for first language teaching. In M. Rice & R. Schiefelbusch (Eds.), *The teachability of language* (pp. 263–310). Baltimore: Paul H. Brookes Publishing Co.

Nelson, K., Camarata, S., Welsh, J., Butkowski, L., & Camarata, M. (1993). *Effects of imitative and conversational recasting treatment of the acquisition of grammar in children with specific language impairment and younger language matched-children.* Manuscript submitted for publication.

Nemoy, E., & Davis, S. (1954). *Correction of defective consonant sounds.* Magnolia, MA: Expression Company.

Newcomer, P., & Hammill, D. (1982). *Test of language development–primary.* Austin, TX: PRO-ED.

Oller, D. (1981). Infant vocalizations: Explorations and reflexivity. In R. Stark (Ed.), *Language behavior in infancy and early childhood* (pp. 85–103). New York: Elsevier/North Holland.

Powell, T., & Elbert, M. (1984). Generalization following the remediation of early and late developing consonant clusters. *Journal of Speech and Hearing Disorders, 49,* 211–218.

Schwartz, R. (1992). Nonlinear phonology as a framework for phonological acquisition. In R. Chapman (Ed.), *Processes in language acquisition and disorders* (pp. 108–124). St. Louis, MO: Mosby-Yearbook.

Schwartz, R., & Camarata, S. (1985). Examining relationships between input and language development: Some statistical issues. *Journal of Child Language, 12,* 199–207.

Shelton, R. (1982). Response to Weiner. *Journal of Speech and Hearing Disorders, 47,* 336.

Shriberg, L. (1993). Four new speech and prosody-voice measures for genetics research and other studies in developmental phonological disorders. *Journal of Speech and Hearing Research, 36,* 105–140.

Shriberg, L., & Kwiatkowski, J. (1980). *Natural process analysis.* New York: John Wiley & Sons.

Shriberg, L., Kwiatkowski, J., Best, S., Hengst, J., & Terselie-Weber, B. (1986). Characteristics of children with phonological disorders of unknown origin. *Journal of Speech and Hearing Research, 51,* 140–160.

Siegel, G., & Spradlin, J. (1985). Therapy and research. *Journal of Speech and Hearing Disorders, 50,* 226–230.

Speidel, G., & Nelson, K. (1984). *The many faces of imitation in language learning.* New York: Springer-Verlag.

Sperry, R. (1952). Neurology and the mind-brain problem. *American Scientists, 40,* 291–312.

Spradlin, J., & Siegel, G. (1982). Language training in natural and clinical environments. *Journal of Speech and Hearing Disorders, 47,* 2–6.

Stoel-Gammon, C. (1983, November). *Variations of style in mother's speech to young children.* Presented at the American Speech-Language-Hearing Association annual convention, Cincinnati, OH.

Stoel-Gammon, C., & Dunn, C. (1986). *Normal and disordered phonology in children.* Austin, TX: PRO-ED.

Strand, E. (1992). The integration of speech motor control and language formulation in process models of acquisition. In R. Chapman (Ed.), *Processes in language acquisition and disorders.* St. Louis, MO: Mosby-Yearbook.

Swift, W. (1918). *Speech defects in school children.* Cambridge, MA: Riverside Press.

Tallal, P., Stark, R., & Mellits, D. (1985). Identification of language impaired children on the basis of rapid perception and production skills. *Brain and Language, 25,* 314–322.

Templin, M., & Darley, F. (1969). *The Templin-Darley Screening Tests of Articulation.* Iowa City, IA: University of Iowa Press.

Van Riper, C. (1939). *Speech correction.* Englewood Cliffs, NJ: Prentice Hall.

Van Riper, C. (1978). *Speech correction* (6th ed.). Englewood Cliffs, NJ: Prentice Hall.

Vihman, M. (1992). *Patterns of phonological acquisition: Cross-linguistic evidence.* Paper presented at the annual Midwest City Phonology Conference, Champaign IL.

Warren, S. (1988). A behavioral approach to generalization. *Language, Speech, and Hearing Services in Schools,* 19, 292–303.

Warren, S., & Kaiser, A. (1986). Incidental language teaching: A critical review. *Journal of Speech and Hearing Disorders, 51,* 291–299.

Weiner, F. (1981). Treatment of phonological disability using the method of meaningful minimal contrast: Two case studies. *Journal of Speech and Hearing Disorders, 46,* 97–103.

Whitehurst, G., Fischel, J., Arnold, D., & Lonigan, C. (1992). Evaluating outcomes with children with expressive language delay. In S.F. Warren & J. Reichle (Eds.), *Communication and language intervention series: Vol. 2. Causes and effects in communication and language intervention* (pp. 277–314). Baltimore: Paul H. Brookes Publishing Co.

Wolf, M.M. (1978). The case for subjective measurement or how applied behavior analysis is finding its heart. *Journal of Applied Behavior Analysis, 11,* 203–214.

Yeni-Komshian, G., & Ferguson, C. (1980). *Child phonology: Vol. 2. Perception.* New York: Academic Press.

Yoder, P.J., Kaiser, A.P., & Alpert, C.L. (1991). An exploratory study of the interaction between language teaching methods and child characteristics. *Journal of Speech and Hearing Research, 34,* 155–167.

4

Intervention for Word-Finding Deficits in Children

Karla K. McGregor and Laurence B. Leonard

Many children with impaired language or learning have word-finding deficits. In discourse, these children show frequent word substitution errors that may be semantically based (e.g., daisy for rose) or phonologically based (e.g., rouge for rose) as well as circumlocutions (e.g., it's red and it smells good), fillers (e.g., uhm, well), and nonspecific words (e.g., flower-thing). In single word–naming activities, their performance may be slow and/or inaccurate. Words that occur infrequently are more difficult to find (German, 1979; Leonard, Nippold, Kail, & Hale, 1983). Yet, comprehension of the problematic words as demonstrated by recognition in picture-pointing tasks is good (e.g., the child can point to a rose when shown pictures of roses, daisies, tulips, and violets). The purpose of this chapter is to discuss the nature of impaired word finding. In particular, the status of word-finding problems as part of broader language and learning deficits is explored. In addition, some ways that children with word-finding problems might be assisted are suggested. These issues are further examined in two clinical case studies included at the end of the chapter.

THE NATURE OF WORD-FINDING DEFICITS

An adequate understanding of word-finding deficits requires consideration of both word finding itself as well as the relationship between word finding and language ability in general. These are discussed in turn.

Storage and Retrieval Processes

In current models of memory, word knowledge is represented as a network in which similar entries are linked (e.g., Kail & Bisanz, 1982). In parallel-access network models (e.g., Marslen-Wilson, 1989; McClelland & Rumelhart, 1986; Morton, 1970), multiple related entries are activated during word finding. Connected entries, or nodes, may be associated by category membership (e.g., cat and dog), functional properties (e.g., knife and scissors) and physical characteristics (e.g., fire and sun). This type of association helps to explain why substitution errors of children with word-finding problems are often semantically related to their targets (e.g., daisy for rose). In some models of the lexicon, input and output representations of phonological information about words are connected through the semantic component (e.g., Caramazza, 1988). This connection helps to explain why phonological errors sometimes occur in which the child appears to have accessed the correct semantic representation but not the correct phonological schema (e.g., rouge for rose).

We come to "know" very frequently experienced words better than infrequently experienced words. In terms of a memory model, we might say that nodes encoding frequently encountered words become well elaborated (i.e., a lot of information about those words is stored) and tightly linked and organized to related nodes in the lexicon. The greater the number and strength of links between nodes, the more alternative retrieval routes exist and the easier the memory process (Kail, 1990). In fact, access to highly prototypical or scripted exemplars becomes automatic (Rabinowitz, 1991). This explains why high-frequency words are more quickly found than low-frequency words.

There has been considerable debate about whether memory failure is the result of alterations in stored information, the retrievability of that stored information, or both (for a review, see Howe & Brainerd, 1989). In retrieval accounts, forgetting is caused by failure to access permanently stored information. Retrieval can be inhibited by cues that are substantially different than those at encoding or by interference from activation of entries that are related to the target (Miller, Kasprow, & Schactman, 1986). In storage accounts, something about the representation itself makes it difficult to find information—either the original encoding was weak (i.e., not much information about the word has been stored), or inaccurate, or it has faded because of disuse.

In an analysis of the word finding of children with language impairments, Leonard et al. (1983) discussed two possible sources of word-finding difficulty: a breakdown in storage or a breakdown in retrieval. Further experiments involving tasks such as memory scanning, repeated free recall, and confrontation naming indicated storage rather than retrieval-based naming deficits (Kail & Leonard, 1986). According to Kail and Leonard (1986), children with language impairments learn words later than their typically developing peers; therefore, their word knowledge is less extensive. This is presumably because nodes corresponding to words in long-term storage are weaker and links between nodes are fewer and weaker. Similarly, Segal (1989, in Segal & Wolf, 1993) posited that the word-finding problems of children with dyslexia may reflect subtle problems of storage, such as a lack of knowledge regarding multiple word meanings. In sum, storage limitations involving poorly elaborated and integrated semantic and/or phonological representations may underlie word-finding deficits in children.

Kail and Leonard (1986) acknowledged that children with language impairments may not always use retrieval strategies flawlessly either. In addition, Denckla and Rudel (1976a) suggested that the naming problems of children with dyslexia are retrieval based because they know the problematic words at some level. Does this mean that retrieval-based word-finding deficits constitute discrete disorders separable from broader language and learning problems? Not necessarily: Certain retrieval strategies may involve metalinguistic, syntagmatic, or paradigmatic word knowledge that is deficient in children with language and learning impairments. Furthermore, if children do not have rich word representations stored in memory, then fewer details of the word are available to assist retrieval.

In any case, determining whether or not word-finding problems are retrieval based is problematic. It is common practice in studies of naming to ensure that children have a recognition knowledge of words that are difficult to find (i.e., they can point to the item in a picture array although their naming of the item is slow or errorful). However, recognition of problematic words does not effectively eliminate storage-elaboration problems as a source of the word-finding difficulty and prove that these difficulties are retrieval based. Kail and Leonard's (1986) conception of elaborated knowledge involves knowing the word in many ways and at many levels. A child may recognize a word in an array and still not have elaborate knowledge of that word.

Word-Finding Deficits as Part of More Global Language Problems

The traditional definition of a word-finding deficit—difficulty generating words that are seemingly comprehended—does not address the issue of whether the word-finding problems are discrete deficits or part of a more general problem with language. Two types of information suggest that the latter is more likely. First, simply on logical grounds, it is apparent that the limitations of storage discussed in the previous section go beyond lexical knowledge per se. For example, knowledge of the verb "donate" includes understanding that it can be used in the prepositional phrase construction, as in "Let's donate the money to the Art Fund," but not in the double object construction, as in "Let's donate the Art Fund the money." Similarly, knowledge of the word "asparagus" includes knowing its multisyllabic nature and stress pattern. It follows that children with limited ability to learn syntax and phonology would be at a disadvantage in the area of word finding as well.

Empirical data also suggest that word-finding problems are likely to coexist with other language difficulties. Word-finding problems have been reported in several different groups of children who are at risk for language deficits in general, including those with brain damage (Campbell & Dollaghan, 1990; Dennis, 1980, 1992; Dennis & Barnes, 1992; Dennis, Hendrick, Hoffman & Humphreys, 1987; Hough, DeMarco, & Pabst, 1992; Stark & McGregor, 1993; Wing, 1990a), learning disabilities (German, 1984; Wiig & Semel, 1975, 1984), dyslexia (Denckla & Rudel, 1976a, 1976b; Felton, Naylor, & Wood, 1990; Segal & Wolf, 1993; Wolf & Obregon 1992; Wolff, Michel, & Ovrut, 1990), specific language impairments (Anderson, 1965; Fried-Oken, 1984; Kail, Hale, Leonard,

& Nippold, 1984; Leonard et al., 1983; Rubin & Liberman, 1983; Schwartz & Solot, 1980), and fluency disorders (Telser, 1971). These difficulties in speed and/or accuracy of word finding generally co-occur with deficits in related language abilities such as object description (Ewing-Cobbs, Levin, Eisenberg, & Fletcher, 1987; Levin & Eisenberg, 1979), knowing alternate and figurative meanings (Dennis & Barnes, 1990); and fast mapping (i.e., constructing a semantic and phonological representation of a word on the basis of a single exposure to it) (Dollaghan, 1987; Rice, Buhr, & Nemeth, 1990). Furthermore, many children with these language and learning impairments present with imprecise or incomplete discourse (Dennis & Barnes, 1990; German, 1987). The ability to express exact meanings in discourse draws strongly on a rich knowledge of words and the range of situations in which they can be used as well as implementation of this knowledge in real time.

Deficits in word finding are certainly not reported for all children in each of these groups cited as at risk for language and learning disorders. It could be that the children without reported word-finding deficits have adequate word-finding skills. However, it is just as likely that these children's limitations in word finding are simply less dramatic than their problems with other aspects of language. However, just as some children may have no significant problem with word finding, it also seems to be rare that a child with word-finding problems has, at some point, no other documented deficit in language ability. In fact, we are not aware of any such individual.

WORD FINDING AS THE FOCUS OF INTERVENTION

Because word-finding deficits are seen primarily in children who are otherwise at risk for language disorders, it is reasonable to ask whether word-finding skills warrant special attention. This question is best addressed by considering the educational implications of word-finding problems.

Educational Implications

A great motivation for helping children to overcome their word-finding problems is that these deficits are likely to affect academic achievement (Schwartz & Solot, 1980). Activities such as oral recitation; confrontation naming; confrontation dialogue; spelling; filling in blanks; writing on a particular topic; and supplying synonyms, antonyms, and homonyms may be challenging for the child with word-finding problems. In addition, exams and tests with time limitations may be especially difficult. Wiig and Semel (1984) noted that formal language and academic tasks impose stricter constraints on what is acceptable language than spontaneous conversation. Word-finding errors, therefore, may be most debilitating in the classroom.

One further concern with regard to test-taking situations is the word retrieval demands of cognitive measures. Snyder and Godley (1992) pointed out that word-finding deficits may negatively affect performance on some IQ measures. For example, the Stanford-Binet Intelligence Scale (Terman & Merrill, 1973) and the Slossen Intelligence Test for Children and Adults (Slossen, 1977) require specific word-retrieval responses. Speech-language pathologists may work with school psychologists to select nonverbal IQ measures for these children and to consider the potential effects of their word-finding deficits when interpreting performance on cognitive assessments.

Poor word-finding skills also have negative consequences for narrative construction, a frequent classroom activity. German (1987) elicited narratives from 14 7- to 12-year-old children with language impairments and their typically developing peers matched for age, receptive vocabulary level, and IQ. The children with language impairments had documented word-finding problems in single-word naming. In the narratives, these children showed two distinct profiles. Thirty-five percent of them were less productive (i.e., produced shorter stories) than their peers. German (1992b) described this as a difficulty in retrieving narrative schemata. Fifty-seven percent of the children with language impairments told stories of equal length to their peers but manifested word-finding behaviors such as repetitions, reformulations, and substitutions significantly more often. German and Simon (1991) found that children with word-finding problems showed a particularly high frequency of insertion of comments about their word finding (e.g., "that's a hard one to remember") in narrative productions. Because writing, telling, and retelling stories may be difficult for children with word-finding problems, narratives should be considered as contexts for assessment and remediation.

Finally, word-finding deficits negatively affect reading development. Naming and reading are thought to be interactive processes requiring both semantic and phonological information (Wolf, 1984). Poor readers have poorer naming skills than average readers (Catts, 1989). In fact, theorists have proposed that good speed and automaticity of word finding is crucial to skilled reading because the attentional capacity needed for processing is made available when names are found quickly (LaBerge & Samuels, 1974; Perfetti, 1985). Speed of word naming correlates with both accuracy and comprehension of written text (Perfetti, 1985). Furthermore, the speed and accuracy of kindergarten children on some word-retrieval tasks is predictive of their later reading skill in grades one through four. Wolf and Obregon (1992) found that from grade two, naming speed for graphemes (numbers and letters) predicted skill in lower-level processes such as word recognition. However, performance on confrontation naming predicted skill in more complex processes such as reading comprehension in grades three and four. The relations between reading, vocabulary skill, and word finding are complex, but there is abundant evidence that children with word-finding deficits are at increased risk for reading difficulty.

In fact, the consistency with which children with dyslexia show word-finding difficulties is strong evidence for the tight link between naming and reading skills. These children exhibit word-finding problems characterized by slow naming speed, although there are naming errors as well (Denckla & Rudel, 1976a, 1976b; Wolff et al., 1990). Problems in the speed of word finding in primary-grade children with dyslexia persist into middle childhood and even into adulthood (Felton et al., 1990; Wolf & Obregon, 1992). The naming speed problems of children with dyslexia appear to be part of a generalized deficit in automatic verbal responding to any visual stimuli, including not only words and letters but also pictured objects, colors, and digits (Bowers & Swanson, 1991; Denckla & Rudel, 1976b).

Wolf and Segal (1992) argued that naming-speed deficits are a causal factor in the poor reading skills of children with dyslexia. Specifically, they claimed that "slower letter- and word-naming speeds directly impede decoding and word-recognition processes" (p. 61), resulting in decreased automaticity in the processing of orthographic patterns. However, these authors recognize, along with Stanovich (1986), that reading problems and receptive vocabulary development exist in a reciprocal relation. Poor reading negatively affects vocabulary growth, and vocabulary deficits further impede reading ability. Therefore, although children with dyslexia show poor naming primarily as a result of word-finding deficits, receptive vocabulary problems may also contribute to poor naming, especially in older readers. Further research is needed to clarify the complicated relation between word-finding deficits, oral language impairments and reading impairments.

Nature of Intervention

Given the communicative and academic impact of word-finding deficits, intervention is warranted. In the following sections, we review the available literature in order to demonstrate the management decisions made by clinical investigators interested in effective word-finding interventions. These decisions concern the types of words to be taught, the proper setting for intervention, the types of activities employed, and the manner in which outcomes are measured.

Target Words

Experimental intervention designs employing statistical comparisons require a high degree of control in training word targets. For this reason, most word-finding intervention studies have included targets that are balanced for frequency of occurrence and word length. These words must be pictured in a consistent manner. Therefore, object words, because they are easily depicted, are chosen most often. These practices may not be the most appropriate guides to choosing target words in true clinical settings. Because of the potential academic impact of poor word finding, it is sensible to choose target word types that benefit the child in the classroom.

German (1992a, 1992b) suggested that target words for school-age children should coincide with current classroom themes and that random word lists are not appropriate. Segal and Wolf (1993) chose age-appropriate words from their students' readers. For each child, they grouped the words according to his or her level of knowledge (unknown, acquainted, or established). These groupings may be useful when determining intervention strategies.

For children of all ages, choosing target words organized around themes and interests may be beneficial. Haynes (1992) chose words that were relevant to the interests of the individual child: "water life" for a boy who had a pond in his yard and "hotels" for a boy whose mother was a new hotel employee. Organizing intervention around themes also can provide easier ways to elaborate words by comparing and contrasting words related by the theme. These words need not be object names but could include relevant actions and attributes also. In addition, thematically related words could be woven together more easily into discourse or narrative, if that is a goal.

Another important factor in choosing targets is the type of word that the child finds problematic. Although one could choose to work only on the specific words observed to be difficult, the inconsistency of word-finding problems makes this strategy challenging. However, patterns in the problematic words can sometimes be discerned. For example, Harris (1992) reported on a child whose word finding was worst with characters' names, thereby interrupting the flow of his narrative productions. Looking for patterns in problematic word types and targeting only these types may make intervention more efficient and also may lead to greater generalization of intervention effects. However, this idea has not been tested empirically.

Intervention Setting

Interventions may be adapted to individuals, small groups, and classroom settings. The best interventions may cross these boundaries to allow the child to practice in a variety of settings, thereby facilitating generalization. For the most part, the majority of intervention studies have fallen short of this ideal because they involved only one-to-one work (Casby, 1992; Haynes, 1992; McGregor & Leonard, 1989) or small group work (Wing, 1990b; Wright, 1993). Intervention that does not take place in the classroom should at least involve a bridge to the classroom. Teacher and students should be aware of compensatory strategies that are helpful for participation in the classroom. Classroom activities may be modified to facilitate word finding. For example, German (1992a, 1992b, 1993) suggested that language specialists work with both students and teachers to facilitate word finding in routine classroom discussions and in test-taking situations through use of cueing strategies, multiple choice formats, additional response time, and review and rehearsal of notes.

Activities

Two main approaches to remediation of word-finding problems have received most attention: increasing storage elaboration and increasing retrieval strategies.

Activities that clearly fall within the domain of elaboration are those that help the child to learn new information about target words. Activities that focus on retrieval allow the child to practice using already known information to guide his or her access to word retrieval. Of course, the amount and type of information that is already known by one child may not be known by another. Hence, category labels have been used in elaboration training for some children who presumably were not able to identify category labels prior to intervention (Wing, 1990b) and in retrieval training for others who could identify category labels prior to intervention (McGregor & Leonard, 1989). Relevant information about target words also can involve semantic characteristics such as multiple meanings (Haynes, 1992; McGregor & Leonard, 1989; Wing, 1990b; Wright, 1993); phonological characteristics such as first sound and number of syllables (McGregor & Leonard, 1989; Wing, 1990b; Wright, 1993); imagery characteristics such as visual and auditory representations (Wing, 1990b); kinesthetic and tactile characteristics such as size, texture, and movements (Johnson & Myklebust, 1967); and syntactic characteristics such as privilege of occurrence (Casby, 1992).

McGregor and Leonard (1989) compared the effectiveness of elaboration and retrieval activities as interventions for children with language impairments with word-finding problems. Elaboration training involved teaching semantic and phonological characteristics of target words. The child never had to produce the target word during elaboration. Retrieval training involved using known semantic and/or phonological information to retrieve words. For example, the clinician explained that it is sometimes helpful to think of the first sound of a word when trying to remember it. The first sound of a group of words was then identified and the child was asked to name each word. Words that were trained in both the elaboration and retrieval conditions were more accurate at posttest and maintenance test than those that were trained with either elaboration or retrieval alone.

Wright (1993) used a combined elaboration and retrieval training approach involving both semantic and phonological information with four children, ages 7;2–8;8, with severe language impairments. These children not only improved their accuracy of naming on trained words but also on control words that were untrained. Wright proposed that the children had extracted strategies that they then applied to new words. However, she did not note any increases in word-finding accuracy outside of confrontation naming tasks.

Wing (1990b) incorporated both storage elaboration and retrieval activities in her intervention with two groups of 6-year-old children with language impairments. One group received intervention involving semantic information about the target words in primarily storage-based activities, the other received intervention focused on phonological information and imagery in primarily retrieval-based activities. Generalization to untrained targets on the Test of Word Finding (German, 1989) was found for the phonological imagery-trained group but not for the semantic-trained group. It is not clear whether the generalization is attributable to the fact that this group practiced phonological and imagery information or to the fact that they practiced it in a retrieval context.

Elaboration and retrieval activities also can improve speed of word finding. In a pilot study involving 30 children with dyslexia, Segal and Wolf (1993) used rapid naming drills, practice with word-retrieval strategies such as innovative word coining, phonological cueing, and imagery. They also used language exercises such as word association, multiple meanings, and relating words to personal experiences as methods of increasing the automaticity of retrieval rate and accuracy in these children. Their stated intervention purpose was to increase flexibility, fluency, and accuracy as well as strategies for richness, suggesting both an elaboration and retrieval approach.

Casby (1992) tested an intervention focused on increasing elaboration only, but in very rich ways and at multiple levels. The intervention was based on levels-of-processing (Craik & Lockhart, 1972). Briefly, Craik and Lockart (1972) proposed a "levels-of-processing" model of semantic memory that is compatible with the idea that poor elaboration of the words stored underlies word-finding deficits. According to the model, to process a word at a semantic-syntactic level is to process it deeply. Deep processing leads to greater elaboration and stronger encoding. In a number of studies, Craik and Lockhart demonstrated that typical adults and children showed better recall when stimuli were processed at a deep level than when stimuli were processed at a shallow (acoustic-phonetic) level. Using this framework, Casby (1992) tested a word-finding intervention for an 11-year-old boy whose language impairment was a result of an occlusive cerebrovascular disease. The goal of the intervention was to facilitate deep processing to establish richer and more elaborate information about the meaning of a word, its semantic relations with other words, and its syntactic privileges of occurrence. Activities involved using target words in sentences and making conceptual or categorical statements about target words. This child did show decreases in naming latency and errors as a result of the intervention but showed little generalization to untrained words. Casby pointed out that storage activities alone may not generalize well because only trained words have been elaborated.

Additional investigators have suggested that for any individual child it may be appropriate to focus primarily on either elaboration or retrieval. If probing indicates extensive knowledge of troublesome target words, retrieval practice may be the most effective and efficient intervention. This approach was advocated by German (1992a, 1992b) for children in her studies who had retrieval problems only. Furthermore, the stage of intervention has implications for choosing an elaboration or retrieval focus. Nippold (1992) advocated an emphasis on retrieval activities once elaborative word learning has been accomplished. The potential for generalization of phonological imagery-based retrieval strategies to untrained words as demonstrated by Wing (1990b) illustrates the relevance of retrieval practice to effective word-finding intervention. However, determining which word-finding problems are retrieval based and which are storage based continues to be difficult even in experimental settings. The safest clinical practice at this time may be to include both a storage and a retrieval focus in word-finding interventions.

Common to each of the intervention studies reviewed above is an emphasis on training prior to, or in prevention of, episodes of word-finding difficulty. Another approach is to practice and implement cues to help children through actual instances of word-finding difficulty. Rubin, Bernstein, and Katz (1989) compared the utility of semantic cues (superordinate category, location, or function of the object) and phonological cues (the first syllable of the word) provided to 15 good and 15 poor first-grade readers during word-finding problems on the Boston Naming Test (Kaplan, Goodglass, & Weintraub, 1983). For both groups, phonological cues were more helpful than semantic cues. Specifically, the group of poor readers corrected 48% of their word-finding errors when provided with phonetic cues only but they corrected only 7% of their errors when given semantic cues only. Rubin et al. (1989) hypothesized that phonological cues are helpful because they allow the child to find the correct representation, fill in parts of incomplete representations, or initiate phonological processing. Other investigators have emphasized the effectiveness of a broad range of cues including associative semantic cues (e.g., antonyms, synonyms, category names), phonological cues (e.g., initial sound, rhyming word, number of syllables), graphemic cues (e.g., first letter), gestures (i.e., acting out the word), and imagery (i.e., picturing the word in your mind) (German 1979, 1982, 1992a; Wiig & Semel 1984). Providing cues may help children to express themselves accurately in conversations and classroom activities. In addition, the clinician can teach children to take responsibility for self-cueing after effective cues are identified and practiced (German, 1992a, 1992b).

Measuring Outcome

Determining the outcome of word-finding intervention generally has been accomplished by measuring reduction in latency of response and number of errors in confrontation-naming tasks. It is best to measure the latency of a single response in milliseconds, a feat difficult in clinical settings. However, there is a clinically applicable modification that has proven useful. The pictures of words in a single intervention set are displayed in front of the child. Timing with a digital stopwatch begins when the child names the first picture and ends after naming of the last picture. In this way, naming times for an intervention set of consistent size can be determined to 1/100 of a second. With repeated probes, the clinician can track decreases in naming time. This procedure has been used reliably in the study of speed of word finding (Casby, 1992; Denckla & Rudel, 1976a).

Tracking the decrease in errors is a straightforward process. One modification included in some studies is a maintenance probe in which the number of errors on target naming is determined some time after intervention has been completed, usually 1 month, in order to see if the beneficial effect of the intervention is lasting (Haynes, 1992; McGregor & Leonard, 1989; Wright, 1993). Furthermore, it may be worthwhile to track decreases in errors within spontaneous discourse. Although the utility of diagnosis and intervention within discourse contexts has been demonstrated (German, 1992; German & Simon, 1991), analysis of quality of discourse as an outcome measure has not been studied empirically. However, one obvious approach would be to compare pre-intervention and post-intervention spontaneous language samples. Also, more structured tasks such as story retelling could be used to monitor the use of specific words in connected discourse. Finally, in addition to tracking the number of errors, some investigators have looked for change in type of error. For example, Harris (1992) noted an increase in self-corrections during oral reading, an indication of increased self-monitoring on the part of the child.

Efficacy of Intervention

Overall, the studies reviewed above demonstrate that we can help children to improve accuracy and speed of naming; that is, we can help them to improve on the kinds of word-finding tasks typically used to test word-finding deficits. Whether children who receive such training become more able in conversations, narration, or reading activities is unclear. There are few intervention studies that have analyzed improvements in both naming and discourse levels. In addition, we have little evidence that improved naming skill positively affects reading. One exception is Beck, Perfetti, and McKeown (1982) who implemented a vocabulary instruction program for one fourth-grade class in an effort to improve their lexical access and reading comprehension. The program was designed to "bring about the deep and fluent level of word knowledge seen as necessary to enhance processing" (p. 509). Tasks included defining, sentence generation, classification, oral and written production, and timed games. Both accuracy and speed of recall of single words and recall of text improved relative to a control class who received what was described only as a "textbook curriculum." Also, Harris (1992) described intervention for a child with language and reading impairments whom she saw in three settings: individually, in a small group of four children, and in a mainstreamed classroom setting. Over a 3-month period, the child learned to identify the initial sounds of words and began to use this information to help him find words during classroom reading activities. More intervention studies that promote and measure generalization in a variety of contexts and skill domains are necessary to evaluate the effectiveness of various approaches.

Given that many children's word-finding problems seem related to general limitations in lexical knowledge, a broad-based approach to language intervention might seen to be the most appropriate. However, if the focus of intervention is too broad, the benefit to word-finding ability may be minimized. The literature reviewed above suggests that word-finding interventions should be sufficiently focused to provide some critical experiences. For example, intervention should enhance both phonological and semantic mapping as these skills are deficient in many children at risk for word-finding problems. New information about words should be presented during intervention so that elaborateness of lexical storage may be increased. In addition, the intervention should include naming practice in an effort to improve automaticity by strengthening retrieval routes. Furthermore, because word knowledge involves not only semantic and phonological information but syntactic information such as privilege of occurrence, practice in discourse and narrative contexts should be part of word-finding interventions. Finally, interventions should involve many settings in an effort to promote generalization and to provide opportunities to encode words in a variety of contexts.

CASE STUDIES

Following is a description of the nature of and intervention with word-finding deficits in two boys, Kevin and Bob. (These names are fictitious.) These children participated in intervention programs that met many of the objectives stated above, although in some ways the programs were far from ideal. Detailed descriptions of these boys and their interventions are potentially useful for a number of reasons. First, the descriptions exemplify the fact that word-finding deficits occur as part of broader impairments; in these individuals word-finding problems occurred along with impairments in language and fluency. Second, observations of the children at preschool provide demonstrations of two different and rather subtle ways that word-finding deficits may be manifested in the classroom. Third, these case studies illustrate ways that intervention decisions follow from a theoretical perspective and a detailed word-finding profile. And finally, these case studies point to areas where research is needed.

Background of Kevin and Bob

Kevin (age 5;0) and Bob (age 4;9) both were diagnosed as having mild to moderate expressive delays in morphology, syntax, and fluency at the age of 3 years. Kevin had a phonological impairment as well. Both children had receptive skills that were within the normal range. A few months after entering intervention programs for their fluency and language problems, both children were suspected of having word-finding problems and were given the Word Latency Test (Rutherford & Telser, 1971). They evidenced numerous semantic substitutions (e.g., hand for finger, cake for pie) and latencies ranging from 3 to 4 seconds in duration.

Pre-intervention Testing

A detailed analysis of Kevin's and Bob's word finding, word knowledge, and verbal memory skills was completed. Some of the results appear in Table 1.

The Token Test for Children (DiSimoni, 1978) was administered to assess memory for sequential verbal information. Whereas Kevin scored within the

Table 1. Kevin's and Bob's scores on measures of expressive vocabulary and verbal memory

Test	Kevin's score	Bob's score
Expressive One-Word Picture Vacubulary Test–Revised (Gardner, 1990)		
(M = 100, SD = 15)	128	130
Token Test for Children (DiSimoni, 1978)		
(M = 500, SD = 5)	500	490
Sound Mimicry Subtest of the Goldman-Fristoe-Woodcock Auditory Skills Test Battery (Goldman, Fristoe, & Woodcock, 1974)		
(M = 50, SD = 10)	46	46

normal range for his age, Bob did not. Both Kevin and Bob scored age appropriately on the sound mimicry subtest of the Goldman-Fristoe-Woodcock Auditory Skills Test Battery (Goldman, Fristoe, & Woodcock, 1974). However, neither boy repeated the three syllable stimuli on the test correctly.

On the first administration of the Expressive One-Word Picture Vocabulary Test–Revised (EOWPVT-R; Gardner, 1990), the boys scored one to two standard deviations above the mean. The scores demonstrate that the boys did have appropriate levels of expressive vocabulary development; however, their access to words was variable. When the EOWPVT-R was administered repeatedly and cues were given for words that were in error, as recommended by Fried-Oken (1987), both children demonstrated inaccurate word finding. Their substitutions were primarily semantic, either superordinates (e.g., tool for wrench) or coordinates (e.g., square for rectangle). However, some phonological errors also were noted, especially on multisyllabic words (e.g., mometer for thermometer). Kevin used both phonological (first-sound) and semantic (category or function) cues to aid his retrieval. Bob benefited when given phonological cues, but not when given semantic cues, to aid retrieval. Subsequent probes indicated that Kevin could supply information regarding initial sound, category, and function of target words independently, but Bob could not give either semantic or phonological information.

Semantic and phonological substitution errors also occurred in the spontaneous discourse of both children. Nouns, both object labels and proper names, were most often problematic.

In story telling and retelling activities, neither Kevin nor Bob showed use of an emergent story grammar other than an appropriate sequential ordering of events. In addition, both boys frequently used pronouns without appropriately established referents in their narratives.

In summary, these two boys showed many similarities in their word-finding profiles. Both showed inconsistent word finding of nouns in single-word naming and spontaneous discourse although their receptive and expressive vocabularies were age appropriate. Both showed primarily semantic word-finding errors with some phonological errors on multisyllabic word targets. Finally, both exhibited some signs that retrieval of narrative schemata might be impaired, although such skills are just emerging in typically developing children at their ages.

In contrast, there were some potentially important differences between the two. Kevin knew more about the words he wanted to find, and he could use both semantic and phonemic cues to guide his retrieval. Bob had trouble using semantic cues to guide retrieval, but he was helped by phonological cues.

Word Finding in the Classroom

Both Kevin and Bob were enrolled in half-day regular preschool programs. Kevin's classroom schedule involved alternating free-play and organized activities. During free play, he was observed to repeat words when trying to gain attention in large groups, but he nevertheless initiated discourse in large- and small-group settings frequently. He did not make any specific word-finding substitution errors during observation of free play.

Kevin's teacher chose and scripted organized classroom activities. There were definite rules to follow such as where to sit, how to get permission to speak, and how to take a turn. The observed activity involved finding words that started with the "letter of the week." Kevin enjoyed participating in this activity and, according to his teacher, generally was better than his classmates at these word games. Kevin's teacher also reported that his occasional word-finding errors were self-corrected if she repeated the word in a questioning tone.

Bob's classroom was less adult directed. Children were encouraged to initiate their own activities. Bob tended to choose one-to-one interactions with either an adult or another male child. During the observation, he listened to a story on tape with another boy. Other children chose to participate in pretend play, crafts, dramatic play, and snack time. Bob did join a small group for a few minutes, in which there was a discussion about the meaning of the word "goon" that was in one of their songs. The teachers encouraged the children to draw what they thought a goon was. Bob listened but did not participate.

Gym period involved an organized game that was chosen and explained by a designated game leader of the day. The game leader provided very convoluted and incoherent directions and several children asked questions to clarify their roles. Bob did not ask questions and when the game began chose not to participate.

Although specific instances of word-finding difficulty were not noted during the observation, Bob most often interacted nonverbally. In particular, he avoided communication in large groups. Observation of the classroom and an interview with his teacher revealed a rich language and preliteracy classroom focus. The alphabet was posted in addition to written schedules and lists of children's responsibilities, such as whose turn it was to bring a snack. Children kept notebooks in which stories they narrated to their teachers were written. Bob's teacher reported his interest in print and in the story notebooks in particular.

In summary, although they exhibited rather similar histories and profiles of word-finding errors, Kevin's and Bob's word-finding problems were manifested in subtle and different ways in the classroom. Kevin initiated discourse and participated successfully in oral naming activities. He was interested in sounds and letters. His difficulty with word finding was manifested by increased word repetitions and occasional word substitutions that he self-corrected when cued. His ability to self-correct is interesting in light of our probe data indicating that he had a rather advanced word knowledge (even of problematic targets) when compared with Bob. Also, the structure provided in his classroom was probably beneficial to him. Furthermore, the emphasis on oral language learning was most likely advantageous.

Bob was less of a risk taker when it came to communicating in the classroom. He appeared to compensate for his word-finding problem by withdrawing, especially in large groups. Bob might not have been able to participate successfully in oral language activities in his classroom because they were complex and unstructured. In one-to-one situations, he was more successful. Furthermore, he enjoyed print, making up stories with his teacher, and listening to stories on tape. These interests were positive, and they may illustrate the modes of communication with which he was most comfortable.

Recommendations to Kevin's teachers included continued self-correction cueing. In addition, helping him negotiate initiation and turn-taking in groups was suggested. It was recommended to Bob's teachers that they aid his participation during group discussions by providing more structure. Examples included asking multiple-choice questions, negotiating turns for him, and cueing words and statements. It was also suggested that when Bob was the game leader, the teacher might help him choose a game that was familiar (rather than one he made up) so that he would be better able to concentrate on the form of the directions and so that the teacher could cue when necessary. Finally, teachers from both classrooms were encouraged to continue their emphasis on early literacy activities, which both children found enjoyable.

Word-Finding Intervention

An intervention plan was developed based on the profiles of these boys. We wanted to ensure that the children continued to benefit from a combined storage and retrieval approach. Previously, the boys' word-finding interventions were focused on building semantic representations. Activities included comparing within and across semantic categories and listing critical attributes and functions. This information was elaborated in discussions, games, and craft activities with each child and then used to cue retrieval during naming practice. Recently, we have incorporated phonological information into the children's intervention protocols. Our motivation for including this information stemmed from the fact that both children experienced difficulty with finding the syllable shapes of multisyllabic words. A detailed explanation of the phonological intervention is presented in McGregor (in press). In general, the phonological component of intervention involved information about the initial sound and the number of syllables in target words. During elaboration training, each child identified the initial sound in the target word with the help of the clinician. Also, cards with numbers on them were used as a visual cue to aid each child as he tapped out the number of syllables in the target words. During retrieval training, initial sounds and numbers of syllables were provided as cues during instances of word-finding breakdown in rapid naming exercises. Although the children were only 4 and 5 years old, they were highly successful at learning to identify sounds and syllables. Such activities may be implemented even more readily with school-age children.

In addition, we have introduced both boys to a basic story grammar to aid in the establishment and retrieval of narrative schemata and to provide a discourse context for word-finding intervention. In the initial stage of work on narrative construction, each child was helped to order and describe sequential cards depicting a simple story. The child was prompted toward more elaborate and cohesive stories by following the clinician's models. The clinician cued narrative devices such as setting statements, identification of characters, and use of temporal coordination.

Both children have been successful in reducing the numbers of errors in confrontation naming. Also, types of errors have changed; more self-corrections were evidenced after the phonological intervention was introduced. Kevin demonstrated generalization of a strategy, that is, he was observed to tap out syllables when he was having difficulty naming untrained words. Unfortunately, he did so inconsistently, and it was difficult to discern clear patterns of generalization to untrained words for either boy. However, it is noteworthy that when Kevin used trained strategies on trained words, his errors were reduced.

Finally, the intent of the storytelling practice was to help the children learn a basic narrative schemata that they could further elaborate. A logical next step would involve weaving target words from the single-word storage and retrieval activities into these narrative frames. Such activities may promote generalization to untrained contexts. This remains to be investigated empirically.

CONCLUSIONS AND SUMMARY

Research into intervention with word-finding problems in the preschool and school years has just begun. Theoretically sound interventions are being proposed and tested. To date, there has been a focus on elaboration and retrieval training. Semantic and phonological information is typically included although some interventions have involved the use of imagery and deep (semantic-syntactic) processing. These interventions lead to a reduction in latency and errors in naming, providing preliminary evidence for the efficacy of such approaches. However, further refinements in word-finding interventions are warranted. If word-finding problems are symptomatic of broader language and learning deficits, as we have proposed, then we should provide interventions to enhance word-finding skills while also addressing other problems, recognizing that one deficiency potentially contributes to another. It is unlikely that naming drills in which words are neither elaborated nor practiced in connected discourse will improve word finding beyond confrontation-naming tasks. It is also unlikely, in our view, that a broad-based language intervention aimed at improving some other linguistic domain such as phonology or syntax will substantially improve word finding. What we may move toward is a word-finding intervention that gives a child a range of experiences to enhance elaboration and retrieval of target word types in a variety of tasks and settings.

Greater recognition of the importance of examination and treatment of word finding in discourse contexts may lead to better word-finding intervention. We need to know whether word-finding interventions that are focused on improved naming have a beneficial effect on connected discourse and, conversely, whether discourse-based interventions lead to improvements in naming. If we find that discourse activities are effective intervention contexts for word-finding deficits, then the storage and retrieval model will need to be expanded in order to account for such results. Potentially, these effects could be explained within the current model as increasing storage elaboration. Alternatively, models of discourse might be modified to include word-finding processes. In any case, models of word finding can be refined and enhanced by good intervention research.

Further research is also needed to establish the link, if any, between word-finding interventions and improved reading abilities. Existing theoretical models of reading (e.g., LaBerge & Samuels, 1974; Perfetti, 1985) lead us to propose that gains in speed of word and letter access should facilitate progress in reading. This is a fruitful area for research, not only for the population with dyslexia, but also for all students with language impairments who are at risk for reading difficulties.

Because the impact of word-finding deficits on communication and academic performance is potentially great, more effective intervention in the preschool and school years is imperative. Continued research on effective word-finding interventions ultimately may lead to a better understanding of memory and the lexicon and, most important, to our improved ability to help children who experience word-finding deficits. In the meantime, clinicians should continue to deliver theoretically motivated interventions derived from careful pre-intervention profiles. Because word-finding profiles vary across populations and across individuals, interventions that are theoretically sound *and* tailored to the needs of the individual are most likely to be beneficial.

REFERENCES

Anderson, J.D. (1965). Initiatory delay in congenital aphasoid conditions. *Cerebral Palsy Journal, 26,* 9–12.

Beck, I., Perfetti, C., & McKeown, M. (1982). Effects of long-term vocabulary instruction on lexical access and reading comprehension. *Journal of Educational Psychology, 74,* 506–521.

Bowers, P.G., & Swanson, L.B. (1991). Naming speed deficits in reading disability: Multiple measures of a singular process. *Journal of Experimental Child Psychology, 51,* 195–219.

Campbell, T.F., & Dollaghan, C.A. (1990). Expressive language recovery in severely brain-injured children and adolescents. *Journal of Speech and Hearing Disorders, 55,* 567–581.

Caramazza, A. (1988). Some aspects of language processing revealed through the analysis of acquired aphasia: The lexical system. *Annual Review of Neurosciences, 11,* 395–421.

Casby, M.W. (1992). An intervention approach for naming problems in children. *American Journal of Speech-Language Pathology, 1,* 35–42.

Catts, H. (1989). Phonological processing deficits and reading disabilities. In A.G. Kamhi & H.W. Catts (Eds.), *Reading disabilities: A developmental language perspective* (pp. 101–132). Newton, MA: Allyn & Bacon.

Craik, F., & Lockhart, R. (1972). Levels of processing: A framework for memory research. *Journal of Verbal Learning and Verbal Behavior, 11,* 671–684.

Denckla, M.B., & Rudel, R.G. (1976a). Naming of object drawings by dyslexic and other learning disabled children. *Brain and Language, 3,* 1–15.

Denckla, M.B., & Rudel, R.G. (1976b). Rapid automatized naming (RAN): Dyslexia differentiated from other learning disabilities. *Neuropsychologia, 14,* 471–479.

Dennis, M. (1980). Language acquisition in a single hemisphere: Semantic organization. In D. Caplan (Ed.), *Biological studies of mental processes* (pp. 159–185). Cambridge, MA: MIT Press.

Dennis, M. (1992). Word finding in children and adolescents with a history of brain injury. *Topics in Language Disorders, 13,* 66–82.

Dennis, M., & Barnes, M.A. (1990). Knowing the meaning, getting the point, bridging the gap, and carrying the message: Aspects of discourse following closed head injury in childhood and adolescence. *Brain and Language, 39,* 428–446.

Dennis, M., & Barnes, M.A. (1992). Discourse in children with early hydrocephalus and in normally developing age peers. *Canadian Psychology, 33,* 435. (Abstract)

Dennis, M., Hendrick, E.B., Hoffman, H.J, & Humphreys, R.P. (1987). Language of hydrocephalic children and adolescents. *Journal of Clinical and Experimental Neuropsychology, 9,* 593–621.

DiSimoni, F. (1978). *Token Test for Children.* Allen, TX: DLM Teaching Resources.

Dollaghan, C.A. (1987). Fast mapping in normal and language-impaired children. *Journal of Speech and Hearing Disorders, 52,* 218–222.

Ewing-Cobbs, L., Levin, H.S., Eisenberg, H.M., & Fletcher, J.M. (1987). Language functions following closed-head injury in children and adolescents. *Journal of Clinical and Experimental Neuropsychology, 9,* 575–592.

Felton, R.H., Naylor, C.E., & Wood, F.B. (1990). Neuropsychological profile of adult dyslexics. *Brain and Language, 39,* 485–497.

Fried-Oken, M. (1984). *The development of naming skills in normal and language deficient children.* Unpublished doctoral dissertation, Boston University.

Fried-Oken, M. (1987). Qualitative examination of children's naming skills through test adaptations. *Language, Speech, and Hearing Services in Schools, 18,* 206–216.

Gardner, M.F. (1990). *Expressive One-Word Picture Vocabulary Test–Revised.* Novato, CA: Academic Therapy Publications.

German, D.J. (1979). Word-finding skills in children with learning disabilities. *Journal of Learning Disabilities, 12,* 43–48.

German, D.J. (1982). Word-finding substitutions in children with learning disabilities. *Language, Speech, and Hearing Services in Schools, 13,* 223–230.

German, D.J. (1984). Diagnosis of word-finding disorders in children with learning disabilities. *Journal of Learning Disabilities, 17,* 353–358.

German, D.J. (1987). Spontaneous language profiles of children with word-finding problems. *Language, Speech, and Hearing Services in Schools, 18,* 217–230.

German, D.J. (1989). *Test of Word Finding.* Allen, TX: DLM Teaching Resources.

German, D.J. (1992a, November). *Remediation, compensatory programming, and self-advocacy instruction for word finding disorders.* Paper presented at the American Speech-Language-Hearing Association annual convention, San Antonio, TX.

German, D.J. (1992b). Word-finding intervention for children and adolescents. *Topics in Language Disorders, 13,* 33–50.

German, D.J. (1993). *Word Finding Intervention Program.* Tucson, AZ: Communication Skill Builders.

German, D.J., & Simon, E. (1991). Analysis of children's word-finding skills in discourse. *Journal of Speech and Hearing Research, 34,* 309–316.

Goldman, R., Fristoe, M., & Woodcock, R.W. (1974). *Goldman-Fristoe-Woodcock Auditory Skills Test Battery.* Circle Pines, MN: American Guidance Service.

Harris, J. (1992). I can read it with my eyes shut: A case-study of reading difficulty in a language-impaired child. *Child Language Teaching and Therapy, 8,* 314–326.

Haynes, C. (1992). Vocabulary deficit—one problem or many? *Child Language Teaching and Therapy, 8,* 1–17.

Hough, M.S., DeMarco, S., & Pabst, M.J. (1992, November). *Word finding in adults and children with right hemisphere dysfunction.* Paper presented at the American Speech-Language-Hearing Association annual convention, San Antonio, TX.

Howe, M.L., & Brainerd, C.J. (1989). Development of children's long-term retention. *Developmental Review, 9,* 301–340.

Johnson, D.J., & Myklebust, H.R. (1967). *Learning disabilities: Educational principles and practices.* New York: Grune & Stratton.

Kail, R. (1990). *The development of memory in children* (3rd ed.). New York: W.H. Freeman.

Kail, R., & Bisanz, J. (1982). Information processing and cognitive development. In H.W. Reese (Ed.), *Advances in child development and behavior* (Vol. 17, pp. 45–81). New York: Academic Press.

Kail, R., Hale, C.A., Leonard, L.B., & Nippold, M.A. (1984). Lexical storage and retrieval in language-impaired children. *Applied Psycholinguistics, 5,* 37–49.

Kail, R., & Leonard, L.B. (1986). Word-finding abilities in language-impaired children. *ASHA Monographs, 25.*

Kaplan, E., Goodglass, H., & Weintraub, N. (1983). *The Boston Naming Test.* Philadelphia: Lea & Febiger.

LaBerge, D., & Samuels, S.J. (1974). Toward a theory of automatic information processing in reading. *Cognitive Psychology, 6,* 293–323.

Leonard, L., Nippold, M., Kail, R., & Hale, C. (1983). Picture naming in language-impaired children. *Journal of Speech and Hearing Research, 26,* 609–615.

Levin, H.S., & Eisenberg, H.M. (1979). Neuropsychological outcome of closed head injury in children and adolescents. *Child's Brain, 5,* 281–292.

Marslen-Wilson, W.D. (Ed.). (1989). *Lexical representation and process.* Cambridge, MA: MIT Press.

McClelland, J., & Rumelhart, D. (1986). *Parallel distributed processing: Explorations in the microstructure of cognition* (Vols. 1 and 2). Cambridge, MA: MIT Press.

McGregor, K.K. (in press). The use of phonological information in a word-finding treatment for children. *Journal of Speech and Hearing Research.*

McGregor, K.K., & Leonard, L.B. (1989). Facilitating word-finding skills of language-impaired children. *Journal of Speech and Hearing Disorders, 54,* 141–147.

Miller, R.R., Kasprow, W.J., & Schactman, T.R. (1986). Retrieval variability: Sources and consequences. *American Journal of Psychology, 99,* 145–218.

Morton, J. (1970). A functional model of human memory. In D.A. Norman (Ed.), *Models of human memory* (pp. 203–254). New York: Academic Press.

Nippold, M.A (1992). The nature of normal and disordered word finding in children and adolescents. *Topics in Language Disorders, 13,* 1–14.

Perfetti, C.A. (1985). *Reading ability.* New York: Oxford University Press.

Rabinowitz, M. (1991). Semantic and strategic processing: Independent roles in determining memory performance. *American Journal of Psychology, 104,* 427–437.

Rice, M., Buhr, J., & Nemeth, M. (1990). Fast mapping word learning abilities of language delayed pre-schoolers. *Journal of Speech and Hearing Disorders, 55,* 33–42.

Rubin, H., Bernstein, S., & Katz, R.G. (1989). Effect of cues on object naming in first-grade good and poor readers. *Annals of Dyslexia, 39,* 116–124.

Rubin, H., & Liberman, I. (1983). Exploring the oral and written language errors made by language disabled children. *Annals of Dyslexia, 33,* 111–120.

Rutherford, D., & Telser, E. (1971). *Word Latency Test.* Paper presented to the Association for Children and Adults with Learning Disabilities, Chicago.

Schwartz, E., & Solot, C. (1980). Response patterns characteristic of verbal expressive disorders. *Language, Speech, and Hearing Services in Schools, 11,* 139–144.

Segal, D., & Wolf, M. (1993). Automaticity, word-retrieval, and vocabulary development in reading disabled children. In L. Meltzer (Ed.), *Strategy assessment and instruction for students with learning disabilities: From theory to practice* (pp. 141–165). Austin, TX: PRO-ED.

Slossen, R.L. (1977). *Slossen Intelligence Test for Children and Adults.* East Aurora, NY: Slossen Educational Publications.

Snyder, L.S., & Godley, D. (1992). Assessment of word-finding disorders in children and adolescents. *Topics in Language Disorders, 13,* 15–32.

Stanovich, K.E. (1986). "Matthew effects" in reading: Some consequences of individual differences in the acquisition of literacy. *Reading Research Quarterly, 4,* 360–407.

Stark, R.E., & McGregor, K.K. (1993). *Follow-up study of a right- and a left-hemispherectomized child: Implications for developmental language disorder.* Unpublished manuscript.

Telser, E. (1971). *An assessment of word-finding skills in stuttering and non-stuttering children.* Unpublished doctoral dissertation, Northwestern University, Evanston, IL.

Terman, L., & Merrill, M. (1973). *Stanford-Binet Intelligence Scale.* Boston: Houghton Mifflin.

Wiig, E., & Semel, E.M. (1975). Productive language abilities in learning disabled adolescents. *Journal of Learning Disabilities, 8,* 578–586.

Wiig, E.H., & Semel, E.M. (1984). *Language assessment and intervention for the learning disabled* (2nd ed.). Columbus, OH: Charles E Merrill.

Wing, C.S. (1990a). Defective infant formulas and expressive language problems: A case study. *Language, Speech, and Hearing Services in Schools, 21,* 22–27.

Wing, C.S. (1990b). A preliminary investigation of generalization to untrained words following two treatments of children's word-finding problems. *Language, Speech, and Hearing Services in Schools, 21,* 151–156.

Wolf, M. (1984). Naming, reading, and the dyslexias: A longitudinal overview. *Annals of Dyslexia, 34,* 87–115.

Wolf, M., & Obregon, M. (1992). Early naming deficits, developmental dyslexia, and a specific deficit hypothesis. *Brain and Language, 42,* 219–247.

Wolf, M., & Segal, D. (1992). Word finding and reading in the developmental dyslexias. *Topics in Language Disorders, 13,* 51–65.

Wolff, P.H., Michel, G.F., & Ovrut, M. (1990). Rate variables and automatized naming in developmental dyslexia. *Brain and Language, 39,* 556–575.

Wright, S.H. (1993). Teaching word-finding strategies to severely language-impaired children. *European Journal of Disorders of Communication, 28,* 165–175.

5

Syntax for School-Age Children

A Discourse Perspective

Cheryl M. Scott

CHILDREN IN NEED OF LANGUAGE intervention in their elementary school years present many challenges to regular and special educators and to clinicians. One challenge lies in defining the construct of language impairment (LI), particularly specific language impairment (SLI) (Aram, Morris, & Hall, 1993; Leonard, 1991). Children with developmental language problems not attributable to identifiable cognitive, sensory, or behavioral disabilities are a heterogeneous group (Fletcher, 1992; Miller, 1991). Experienced language clinicians would find it hard to identify two children with the exact same profile of linguistic strengths and weaknesses. Some children have difficulty with both comprehension and production, while others' problems congregate only in production processes. Some children's language-learning problems encompass semantic, syntactic, and phonological systems, whereas other children's difficulties are only measurable in one component. As children learn written language, individual patterns of difficulty in word identification, comprehension, composition, and spelling become evident. This heterogeneity has spurred researchers to propose several different classification schemes for language disorder subtypes (e.g., Bloom & Lahey, 1978; Fey, 1986; Fletcher, 1992; Miller, 1991; Nation & Aram, 1977). The fact that no one system has been widely adopted by language researchers or clinicians to date underscores the complexity of the problem.

A second challenge for language interventionists stems from the conceptual complexities inherent in the topic of language. With its multiple *units* (e.g., phonemes, morphemes, words, phrases, clauses, sentences, discourse), *modes* (spoken, written, sign), *genres* (conversation, narration, description, persuasion), and *interactions* among units, modes, and genres, language presents a formidable conceptual puzzle when it fails to function well in children. To bring some manageability to the task, language clinicians for many years have applied a component model of language in describing and remediating impairments. Syntax, the grammatical component of language, has occupied a central role. But there are problems with isolating syntax from meaning and discourse; this chapter stresses syntactic and discourse interactions.

A third challenge results from our limited knowledge base regarding language impairment in general, and syntax in particular, in older children. Language clinicians who work with preschool children with language impairments share a relatively well-defined theoretical and descriptive body of knowledge about syntax. Syntax metrics (e.g., MLU) are commonly employed in assessment, and syntactic structures (e.g., grammatical morphemes) are commonly targeted in intervention. In contrast, the role of syntax as an organizational tool for intervention work with school-age children throughout the elementary years is less apparent.

The main purpose of this chapter is to outline parameters of a body of knowledge about syntax in school-age children with and without language problems and to use these parameters as a basis for intervention applications. The first section outlines the domain of syntax from a discourse perspective. Discourse constraints are shown to motivate the use of several syntactic structures. In their elementary school years between kindergarten and sixth grade, children encounter many forms of planned spoken and written discourse not found in the social interaction and story contexts of their preschool years. For the sake of assessment and intervention relevance, it is important to examine syntactic structures typical of school discourse, namely written discourse of all kinds, and informational (expository) genres. The second section surveys developmental evidence of discourse-motivated syntactic structure, with an emphasis on forms specific to writing and expository discourse. A third section summarizes research on syntactic problems in school-age children with language impairments. Although there are conflicting findings, children with language impairments gain general proficiency with most high-frequency syntactic structures found in conversational and narrative discourse (Fletcher, 1992). Lower frequency structures more characteristic of informational and written discourse, while not absent in the language of children with language impairments, are produced less often when compared to children developing typically (Scott & Klutsenbaker, 1989). In the final section, literature that suggests interventions for children's problems with language structure are reviewed. Although there are few intervention efficacy studies specific to the topic of language structure, issues and information from the first three sections of the chapter offer some direction for the design of intervention applications and efficacy research, and these are explored. Throughout the chapter, the children of central interest are those meeting basic exclusionary criteria (e.g., Stark & Tallal, 1981) for SLI. The chapter is concerned with syntactic capabilities evident in children's self-generated discourse, both spoken and written. Evidence from comprehension studies, although central to the broad topic of learning language form, are not addressed.

THE DOMAIN OF SYNTAX

Language professionals probably would agree that syntax is a set of rules for combining words into sentences. For most sentences, it is relatively easy to find agreement among trained and untrained speakers on whether a sentence is "grammatical"; that is, whether it conforms to an internalized set of rules that are conventional for a community of speakers. Children have mastered many of these rules by the age of 5 (McNeill, 1966; Rees, 1974). The final form sentences take, however, depends upon many factors including situational context (e.g., audience) and discourse context (previous sentences and planned future sentences). For example, a speaker would be likely to say, "Kate turned off the light," if the light were new or emphasized information, "Kate turned the light off," if "the light" had already been mentioned at some previous point (Celce-Murcia, 1991), and, "Kate turned it off," if reference to the light were sufficiently recent and established (Halliday & Hasan, 1976). Whether a family member or casual acquaintance is being addressed could account for the alternative forms "Jack will get here at noon," and "My cousin Jack on my Dad's side of the family will...." Celce-Murcia (1990) offers an overview of several categories of grammar-discourse interactions including tense-aspect-modality, word order, subordination/complementation, and topic/theme. Whereas sentential syntax is learned at an early age, a large part of later grammatical growth involves learning to apply *discourse-motivated syntactic options* according to subtle but important semantic/pragmatic distinctions.

Additional discourse parameters also affect syntactic form. Major among these are mode (spoken or written delivery) and genre or discourse type (e.g., narration, description, argument, procedure). The following discussion presents an overview of several form–mode and form–genre interactions that are particularly salient for elementary school–age children because of their representation in the school curriculum and/or their developmental significance. Comprehensive reviews of structural differences among various types of spoken and written discourse are available in several sources including the work of Biber (1986, 1988, 1992), Chafe (1982, 1991), and Halliday (1985, 1987).

Spoken and Written Form

Biber (1986), in his review of literature on spoken and written syntactic structure, noted that written language is often characterized as syntactically more complex than spoken language. Halliday (1985, 1987), however, held that it is the *type* of complexity, not complexity per se, that distinguishes spoken and written language. Spoken language is complex via strings of clauses joined by coordinating and subordinating conjunctions and complementary clauses. The complexity in written language is found in nominalized forms and in complex noun phrases with premodification and postmodifying phrases and clauses. Halliday (1985) illustrated this distinction with the following example contrasting spoken and written versions of the same information (p. 81):

Spoken: Because the technology has improved, it's less risky than it used to be when you install them at the same time, and it doesn't cost so much either.

Written: Improvements in technology have reduced the risks and high costs associated with simultaneous installation.

Information in the spoken version is coded in five clauses connected with the conjunctions *because, than, when,* and *and.* In contrast, the written sentence is a single clause in which information coded in predicate form in the spoken version is recoded within complex noun phrases. Halliday (1985, 1987) characterizes this distinction between the spoken and written mode as a *linear* (strings of clauses) versus a *hierarchical* (nominal embedding) code.

It seems a simple matter to analyze spoken and written discourse in order to confirm Halliday's (1987) hypothesis, but in reality such attempts are complicated by the fact that effects of mode alone (whether spoken or written) are difficult to separate from effects of genre (the type of discourse). Spoken language most frequently serves to maintain social relationships (i.e., social conversations, telling personal stories), while written language more commonly serves for the transmission of information (Brown & Yule, 1983). In order to isolate the effects of mode, then, it would be necessary to study written and spoken versions of the same genre. When this sort of study has been done, Halliday's account of spoken and written form differences has generally been supported (cf. Beaman, 1984, for adult spoken and written narratives, and Scott & Klutsenbaker, 1989, for spoken and written narratives and descriptions, produced by 11-, 14-, and 21-year-olds). To illustrate, in summarizing a narrative video, a 14-year-old in a study by Scott and Klutsenbaker (1989) spoke, "Finally his Mom talked to his Dad and they let him go down there," but wrote, "After a discussion they agree." In this example, information coded in subject-predicate form ("his Mom talked to his Dad") is expressed nominally ("a discussion"). A similar recoding occurs between the spoken form, "And he went to the big city to see if a fisherman would take him," and the written version, "he went to the city to ask about a fishing place," produced by an 11-year-old in the same study.

Halliday and others claim that the temporal constraints inherent in online language formulation required for speaking encourage a linear code, while writing, with its more relaxed time frame, allows for greater application of recursive embedding characteristic of a hierarchical code. In addition, the temporal constraints of spoken language bring about a severely restricted set of complex forms, according to recent work by Biber (1992), whereas written texts show a much greater variety of complex forms. This difference in variety is important when intervention applications are discussed in the final section of this chapter.

Genre Effects on Form

Genre is generally understood as distinguishing types of discourse according to function or purpose. Stories are told for different reasons than are directions, explanations, arguments, and opinions and contain different content. It follows that form, or syntax, varies as well and that certain structures are characteristic of certain types of discourse (Hatch, 1992).

The list of potential genres of interest for school-age children is long, but researchers have concentrated on narrative, opinion, and several expository

SYNTAX: A DISCOURSE PERSPECTIVE / 111

(informational) subtypes including description, explanation, and direction (cf. Brown, Anderson, Shillcock, & Yule, 1984; Neville, 1988)—types that play an important role in school settings (Scott, 1994; Westby, 1994). Longacre (1983) pointed out two basic differences between narrative and informational discourse that help to explain syntactic characteristics of each type. Whereas narratives are agent-focused (i.e., about people doing things) and chronologically based (temporally organized), informational discourse is not agent-focused (about objects and ideas) and is logically based (organizational structures of several types including main and supporting arguments, problem–solution, cause–effect, compare–contrast, topical). Narratives, consequently, contain high frequencies of names and pronouns as grammatical subjects (Jane...she), simple past tense verbs, sometimes alternating with perfect forms to distinguish background information (*wandered* through the forest, *had walked* for 3 days), temporal connectives (the next day, that afternoon), and relative clauses (once there was a little pony who lived on a farm with a bunch of other ponies). Syntactic consequences of object/idea grammatical subjects and logical organization schemes found in informational discourse include present tense, present progressive, attributive adjectives, passives, nominalization, and pre- and postmodification of nouns (two plants growing side by side).

Differences at the sentence level have implications for overall syntactic complexity. When a variety of narrative and informational texts written by adults are compared, narrative discourse has shorter sentences (13.8 words on average) and fewer clauses per sentence (2.4 clauses) than informational discourse (21.0 words and 2.8 clauses (Francis & Kucera, 1982).

Limitations of Conversational Language
Samples as Measures of Syntax in School-Age Children

One of the most common ways of determining the status of a child's syntactic knowledge is to analyze free speech samples, usually utterances produced by the child within a conversational, or perhaps a storytelling, context. The most common global quantitative measure of syntactic level is average sentence length, in morphemes or words. Additionally, specific structures can be counted, and are sometimes weighted, to arrive at a developmental stage placement or level (e.g., Crystal, Fletcher, & Garman, 1976, 1990; Lee, 1974; Miller, 1981; Scarborough, 1990). For the most part, consecutive sentences uttered by the child are analyzed as isolated units. This scenario—the syntactic analysis of consecutive utterances in spoken language samples—continues to play a very central role in the assessment of children with language impairment at both preschool and school-age levels (Hux, Morris-Friehe, & Sanger, 1993), in determining effects of intervention, and in research on the construct of specific language impairment itself (cf. Aram et al., 1993).

Unfortunately, such language sample procedures, developed largely with preschool children, provide only limited information about discourse-motivated syntactic capabilities of school-age children. One problem is that such procedures neglect form–function relationships beyond the level of the sentence and are thus insensitive to children's discourse-based syntactic knowledge. A clinician may sum certain structures across sentences and determine the proportional frequency of grammatically correct instances, but this tells us nothing about whether these forms were *appropriate choices,* as discussed above, given the discourse context. A count of pronouns, for example, would be unrevealing unless accompanied by information about appropriateness (i.e., established antecedents). Likewise, tallies of subordinate clauses would be uninteresting if information on variety and discourse appropriateness were not included.

A second problem with preschool language sample methods is the restricted range of sample types. Hux et al. (1993) found that school-based clinicians usually collect language samples in a conversational setting with an adult; however, this form of discourse is not typical of school discourse contexts (Brown et al., 1984; Scott, 1994). Because syntactic forms are genre-specific, restricting samples to conversational contexts provides little opportunity for the use of forms important in academic discourse such as spoken explanation, argument, and written language. A final issue is the developmental mismatch that exists when language sampling protocols developed for preschool children are used with older children. To illustrate, the Language Analysis, Remediation, and Screening Procedure (LARSP) (Crystal et al., 1990) is based on studies of language acquisition through age 5; the protocol would fail to capture important grammatical growth beyond that age.

SYNTACTIC GROWTH IN ELEMENTARY SCHOOL YEARS

A discourse-motivated view of syntax, as discussed in the preceding section, prompts language clinicians to look in different places and ask different questions about school-age children's syntactic knowledge than is characteristic of preschool language analysis. We become interested in the form of children's writing and the extent to which writing is structurally different from speaking. We are interested in children's syntactic capabilities for the types of spoken and written discourse important in school settings (e.g., information-related talk, as discussed by Brown et al., 1984, and expository writing as well as narrative writing). Later developing metalinguistic awareness is also of great interest; for example, children's notions about what constitutes a sentence and their knowledge of multiple ways of communicating similar information (e.g., syntactic paraphrase). Explicit knowledge about syntactic structure is important because curricula throughout the elementary years increasingly depend upon and tap into children's developing notions about structure.

Development of Written Form
Studies of the structural development of children's writing can be grouped into two broad types. One group of studies can be characterized as large-scale,

cross-sectional structural surveys (e.g., Hunt, 1965, 1970; Loban, 1976; O'Donnell, Griffin, & Norris, 1967). In this research, writing done in school has been analyzed quantitatively for average sentence length, extent of subordination, and frequency of syntactic structures, in particular, types of dependent clauses. Typically, analysis has been broad-based and discourse–form relationships were not explored. Nonetheless, the data show that the structural complexity of writing increases rather dramatically from mid- to late elementary years and beyond, with longer sentences, more extensive subordination, and higher frequencies of later developing forms. Table 1 lists structures cited in these studies as markers of grammatical development in writing. Perera (1984, 1986a, 1986b) and Scott (1988, 1989) have reviewed this material in detail. It is important to note that the youngest children in these survey studies were third

Table 1. Structures cited as markers of grammatical development in writing

Complex noun phrases (NP)

Postmodification of head noun via prepositional phrases and nonfinite clauses:

a boy named Yanis...

a little girl with braids running down the road...

a plant in the desert by the oasis...

Postmodification of head nouns via relative clauses, particularly nouns used as grammatical subjects:

The first dance I ever went to was...

The fisherman who came to his rescue convinced the others...

Complex NPs used as grammatical subjects

Appositives

Mrs. Smith, my first grade teacher,...

Desert creatures, like scorpions,...

Nonrestrictive relative clauses

Harold, whose army had just marched across England, was...

Adverbial fronting

Every Sunday we have waffles for breakfast.

In the early evening you can always see him.

When it finally rains, the plants bloom.

Adverbial fronting with subject/verb inversion

There stood a little tiger cub...

On the other side of the mountain was a small cabin.

Nonfinite adverbial clauses

Hoping to catch him, she hurried.

They are on their own *after hatching.*

Verb phrase expansion via tense, aspect, and modal auxiliaries

Could have been talked into...

Will not be coming.

Coordinated NPs, predicates, and series constructions

Animals found in the desert such as badgers, snakes, lizards...

Many mice and other rodents will be...

(mean age 8;8 in O'Donnell et al., 1967) and fourth graders (Hunt, 1965, 1970; Loban, 1976); in other words, children capable of writing at the text level. Comparable studies of grammar in earlier stages of writing have not been undertaken.

Other studies have asked more specific questions about particular structures in children's writing; for example, questions about complex noun phrases, relative clauses, nonfinite and verbless adverbial clauses, word order alterations (Perera, 1986b), and interrupting constructions (Yerril, 1977, as cited in Perera, 1986b) such as appositives, nonrestrictive relative clauses, and prepositional phrases (the point of interruptions for such structures is frequently between the subject and verb). According to Perera (1986b), these forms are particularly sensitive indicators of grammatical maturity specific to the written mode. A fine-grained grammatical analysis is required to demonstrate such sensitivity, however. To illustrate, it is only in their role as *subject* modifiers that complex noun phrases and relative clauses are developmentally significant in writing when compared with speaking. Children use complex noun phrases and relative clauses in other grammatical roles (e.g., direct objects) in both speaking and writing from an early age.

One of the central questions in writing development is the extent to which early written form grows out of spoken form. To what extent does a spoken language grammar "drive" the hand? When children first begin to write at the text level (i.e., several sentences on a common topic), which typically occurs in the second grade, written form is similar to spoken form (Kroll, 1981; Perera, 1986a). Children may be capable of greater syntactic complexity in speaking than in writing (Loban, 1976) because so much of their energy in writing is taken up with forming letters and spelling words (but see contrary evidence in a study by Lehnert, 1982, in a first-grade classroom where writing was emphasized). Almost from the beginning, however, and definitely by mid-elementary years, children's writing becomes uniquely "written" in structure. Even young children's writing shows far fewer, if any, examples of spoken forms such as "you know," "well," "and all," and recapitulatory pronouns (Jane, she...) (Perera, 1986a). Typically by age 9 and sometimes earlier, children's writing shows evidence of syntactic forms that would be unusual in any but the most literate forms of speaking, forms such as fronted adverbials, complex noun phrases with extensive pre- and postmodification of the head noun, subordinate clauses with nonfinite verbs (i.e., verbs lacking tense and number marking), and passive voice. Table 2 provides examples of such forms from the writings of children between the ages of 7 and 12. It is hard to imagine children speaking these sentences, and, in fact, Perera (1986b) provides evidence that such structures are almost exclusively written. The fact that the writing of many children looks written from an early age, largely without explicit instruction, has implications for teaching language to school children, as explored in the final section of this chapter.

Table 2. Writing examples illustrating children's knowledge of "written" grammar

1. *At lunchtime when their frined came* they were verey surprised to see them there. (Phrasal and clausal adverbial fronting; age 7; narrative; Kress, 1982, p. 72)

2. On Friday 1st July we all got in the bus and waved to Miss Martyn. *We're off I thought,* there was lots of merry talk in the bus. (Inverted order of main/subordinate clause for thematic reasons; age 8; narrative; Kress, 1982, p. 61)

3. There are also *seven Eagle fethers on a background* and *a blue sky with the name of our State, Oklahoma, in white* (Extensive pre- and postmodification of nouns, appositive construction; age 9; informational; author's files) 1983

4. The first thing *I wanted to do* was learn to swim. (Subject relative clause; age 9; (Narrative) Handscombe, 1967, cited by Perera, 1986a, p. 511)

5. When Anna woke up Christmas morning she ran downstairs to see all her presents. It was finally Christmas morning and no one was up yet. *Mysteriously* one present at the back was moving. (Fronted manner adverbial; age 10; narrative; author's files)

6. She was so excited that she shook the grab-bag puppy box *forgetting what was in it.* (Nonfinite subordinate clause; age 10; narrative; author's files, 1989)

7. The Red Salander is a coral red lizard with black spots on it's back. They live in southern New York west to Ohio and south to central Georgia. They *can be found* near clear, cool springs and streams. (Passive voice; age 10; informational; author's file, 1987)

8. *The crew of a modern jet airliner* must have *all the information they need* at their fingertips, so *a great amount of work* goes into designing *the best possible light deck control panels.* (Extensive pre- and postmodification of head nouns in NPs; age 12; informational; Kress, 1982, p. 66)

Specific structures of interest appear in italics and are identified in the parentheses, followed by age of writer, type of discourse (genre), and reference citation.

Development of Genre-Specific Form

Syntactic structures produced by children when they speak or write flow from the genre-specific intentions (e.g., to argue, inform, describe, tell a story) inherent in the particular discourse type as well as sentence-specific propositions within the discourse. It is necessary, therefore, to ask questions about syntax development couched within questions about genre development. Most normative data on spoken syntax development in preschool and elementary school–age children has come from the analysis of conversation and/or narrative discourse (Scott, 1988). Likewise, much of the data on written syntax development is based on narrative writing (e.g., O'Donnell et al., 1967). The data must be interpreted accordingly. Conversational and narrative contexts provide limited opportunities for the occurrence of forms characteristic of informational discourse that, in school, takes the form of written language much of the time. A case in point is the discourse-specific form of grammatical subjects. Because grammatical subjects in conversation and in narration are most often person names and pronouns, which do not accept phrasal expansion, noun phrase (NP) elaboration and modification forms are rare. For example, an 11-year-old writes, "One day *Yanis* was taking the sheep to the meadow and a lamb went wild. *It* ran up the mountain. When *he* got to the top *he* saw..." (Scott & Klutsenbaker, 1989).

Elaborated NPs would be expected with a much higher frequency in informational, logically structured discourse where subjects are more likely to be objects or abstract ideas, often grammatically expanded for listeners and readers, as in the following example of a fifth grader's writing for the classroom newspaper: "At a 95-minute news conference, retired Admiral Thomas Davis said that *Peary's claims about finding the North Pole* were supported by scientific means." (author's file).

Of the many types of discourse produced by children, developmental investigation has centered on the broad categories of narrative and non-narrative (informational) discourse, most frequently in the written mode. Indeed, Kress (1982) found it difficult to separate genre and mode (writing) development and stated that genre "is a necessary and integral part of the achievement of writing; the two are inextricably interwoven" (p. 99). Currently, there exists a debate about the onset and status of informational discourse. Some researchers have found relatively sophisticated informational writing earlier than others.

It is well known that most children can tell and some can write stories in the early elementary years (Westby, 1989). Informational writing is thought to lag behind narrative writing (Scott, 1989, 1994). The literature contains occasional comparisons of narrative and informational writing from the same child, which appear to support the developmental primacy of narrative writing. One manifestation of this primacy is in terms of productivity; narratives are frequently much longer than informational texts (cf. Kress, 1982, pp.100–101). Cognitive differences are sometimes invoked to explain the earlier development of narratives. Whereas narratives mirror reality for children in terms of time-based experiences, informational and factual discourse expresses very different cognitive structures. Kress (1982) illustrates this point in references to the following factual text written by a 12-year-old:

Beaked Whales
(1) The Beaked Whales live out in mid-ocean, where the tasty squid are found. (2) Squid, it seems, provide most of their meals. (3) Men do not know much about their family because even the scientists who study whales have seen very few Beaked Whales. (4) Generally members of this family have long, narrow snouts, or "beaks".... (11) It is unusual in colour, so if you should see one, you should be able to recognize it.... (15) you may possibly see one.... (p. 113)

Kress details how in several seemingly innocuous syntactic choices this child has demonstrated sophisticated cognitive strategies. These include: 1) universal present, coded in present tense verbs, indicating understanding that actions/events happen at all times (e.g., live, provide, know, study); 2) universal agents, coded in the general pronoun *you,* indicating understanding that events happen irrespective of particular participants (sentences 11 and 15); and 3) absent agents, coded with agentless passives, indicating understanding that specific agents are immaterial (e.g., where the tasty squid *are found*).

Thus, informational writing reflects a very different cognitive perspective, one in which the self is no longer central and objects and ideas become the focus of attention.

Although acknowledging the cognitive and linguistic demands of informational discourse, several researchers have found evidence of informational writing with considerable hierarchical text structure by the third grade. In a study of 100 pieces of first- through third-grade nonnarrative writing, Newkirk (1987) found that 49% of the third-grade pieces were classified as paragraphs (defined as a series of at least three topically related clauses). This compared with a 15% rate for first graders. Langer (1985, 1986) has reported that third graders are also capable of producing internally structured informational text, in both spoken and written versions, although text structure becomes more elaborate in older grades.

The challenges inherent in informational writing, however, should not be underestimated. In a large scale cross-sectional study of Scottish school-age children, Neville (1988) found improvement in content, language, and style of informational writing (description, directions, explanation) between the ages of 8 and 11. Thereafter, however, progress slowed, *particularly in sentence formation as revealed in punctuation*. Neville (1988) found many students at ages 13–14 who struggled with surface form although they showed evidence of having a sufficient store of ideas for their writing. Additional detail on the development of modality and genre-specific discourse can be found in Scott (1994).

Compared to studies of genre development in written language, particularly informational discourse, research into school-age children's spoken discourse is undeveloped, especially in the U.S. In Britain, spoken discourse characteristic of academic settings (e.g., narration, direction, explanation, description, argument), referred to as "oracy," has received more attention in language research. Neville's (1988) national study of Scottish school-age children (ages 8–9, 10–11, and 13–14) revealed that spoken informational discourse was more difficult than narrative discourse on a recount task, as revealed by ratings of content and language/style. Moreover, there was less improvement with age on spoken tasks than on written tasks. Of particular interest for language clinicians was the finding that some of the poorest writers were nevertheless able to deliver spoken recounts of comparable material using good sentence structure. Unfortunately for purposes of this chapter, syntactic form was not a focus in Neville's work and figured into her analysis system only as global ratings of sentence structure.

To summarize, by the mid-elementary grades, children can produce both narrative and informational discourse in spoken and written form. Development of both content and form continues throughout elementary and secondary grades, albeit at an apparently slower pace in the spoken mode. Both genre and mode exert considerable influence on syntactic form. To underscore the significance of genre effects on syntax, compare Texts 1 and 2 in Figure 1. These texts are part of a corpus of spoken and written versions of narrative and informational discourse (Scott & Klutsenbaker, 1989). Children in this study watched narrative and informational (descriptive) videos and then produced both spoken and written summaries. Text 1 is a written summary of the narrative video produced by an 11-year-old fifth grader. Text 2 is a written summary of a descriptive video produced by the same child. Comparative quantitative data for the two texts are shown in Table 3. Sentences in the informational text are substantially longer with greater subordination. Noun phrases in the informational text are also longer (see lines 12–16, Text 2) as would be expected when objects (plants) and abstract ideas (e.g., *chance,* line 29, Text 2) are subjects. Universal present tense in the informational text contrasts with past tense in the narrative. Series constructions, exemplars (e.g., *like*) are found in Text 2, as well as syntactic parallelism (lines 17–19). Clearly, our knowledge of this child's discourse-motivated syntactic skill is broadened by the availability of informational as well as narrative data.

Children's Explicit Knowledge of Syntax

An important piece of the developmental picture for school-age children involves their explicit, conscious knowledge of syntactic structure. Children's conscious awareness of syntax is increasingly tapped in schoolwork as they progress through elementary school. Perusal of a recently published fourth grade language arts textbook (Haley-James & Stewig, 1993) revealed that children were asked to manipulate syntactic structure in a variety of ways, including the following:

Distinguishing between sentences and nonsentences
Segmenting sentences into subjects and predicates
Forming compound sentences from simple sentences
Correcting run-on sentences
Finding nouns in sentences
Forming noun plurals and possessives
Forming compound phrases from simple sentences

Not all language educators agree that children benefit from the types of grammar exercises presented in such textbooks, a point that is explored further in the final section of this chapter. (See also Gilliam, McFadden, & van Kleeck, chap. 6, this volume.) Few would disagree, however, that one of the most central types of syntactic awareness for school-age children is awareness of the sentence as a linguistic unit, particularly as that awareness relates to the development of written form. It seems logical to assume that explicit awareness of several types of syntactic units (phrases, for example) would somehow stem from or relate to sentence awareness. Bauers and Pettit (1990) investigated sentence awareness by asking children the question, "Is that a sentence?" about several different types of picture/statements. The children, who ranged in age from 4 to 8 years of age, were also asked to justify their response: "What makes you think it is (not) a sentence?" Some picture/statements were grammatically well-formed and conformed to a truth criterion (e.g., "The boy is rowing a boat," represented an accu-

TEXT 1

1. This third story is about
2. this kid named Yanis they
3. lived on a island yanises
4. fiamly was all farmers yanis
5. was a dedicated farmer
6. one day yanis was
7. taking the sheep to the
8. meadow and a lamb went
9. wild it ran up the
10. mountian when he got to
11. the top he saw the sea
12. for the first time the
13. sea that surrounded his island
14. From then on yanis, dreamed
15. of being a fisherman his father
16. noticed that yanis was not
17. himself yanis told his
18. father his dream his father
19. took him to the elder
20. of the town the elder
21. said to try new jobs first
22. he tried baking the water
23. they baked with made
24. him think of the sea.
25. Then he shoe making the
26. leather made him think
27. of a sail on a ship. Last
28. he tried woodworking the wood

29. made him think of building
30. a ship. Finaly his dad let
31. yanis go his dad thought
32. yanis would find out
33. how hard it is to be
34. a fisherman then come
35. home to be a farmer. Yanis
36. traveled for two days
37. then came to the town on
38. the coast. He told kids
39. what he was going to do
40. they laughed at him. But a
41. woman took pitty on yanis
42. and took yanis to her home
43. the woman told yanis he
44. would have to work to
45. stay there anymore. Yanis
46. looked for a job but he
47. could not find one they
48. made fun of him. He made
49. a fishing pole. One day he
50. met a man named Crostos
51. and he thought him the way
52. to fish. One day a fisher-
53. man got real sick Crostos
54. talked the fisherman into
55. taking yanis the fisherman
56. found out yanis was a
57. good fisherman and they
58. hired him.

TEXT 2

1. In the mountians the air
2. goes down the side of the
3. mountian and gets hot and
4. forms a desert. The desert
5. has one main tree called
6. the soursos tree opens up
7. when it rains and traps the
8. water so it can live off the
9. water later. The desert has
10. bushes mainly cactuses there
11. are many kinds of coctuses.
12. There are alot of animals who
13. live in the desert like turtles,
14. rabbits, wild boars, scorpians, spiders,
15. desert foxes, many kinds of insects,
16. and lots of lizards. The
17. animals look for food in the
18. day and look for caves or
19. dig holes at night. In the cool
20. soil a foot down in the soil
21. it can be 25° cooler in the
22. hole than outside. But animals
23. like the badger and the hog
24. nosed skunk know just where
25. to find them. They dig
26. them out of the ground
27. then eat them. When it rains
28. in the desert there is uasaly
29. a good chance of flash
30. flooding becaus the soil is
31. so dry and hot that it
32. cant take in very much water
33. There are rivers in the deser
34. uasaly there are oasis next to
35. the river an oasis a place
36. where bushes and trees grow.

Figure 1. Two written texts by an 11-year-old fifth grader. Text 1 is a written narrative; Text 2 is a written descriptive text.

Table 3.   Comparison of quantitative measures obtained for two written summaries produced by an 11-year-old fifth grader

Measure	Text 1: narrative	Text 2: descriptive
Total words	292	187
Total T-units	37	15
Words/T-unit	7.89	12.46
Clauses/T-unit (subordination)	1.68	1.93
Noun phrase words/total words	.59	.64
Words/noun phrase	1.76	2.73

Adapted from Scott & Klutsenbaker (1989).

rate description of an accompanying picture). Other statements were inaccurate
with regard to the picture, but were nevertheless grammatically well formed. In
addition, some statements were not grammatical, having either word-order or
omission errors but were accurate descriptions (structure criterion, e.g., "a boy
and a girl"), and still others were designed to evoke sense criterion justification
(e.g., "The boat is talking under the water"). Although a majority of all children
(75%–100%, depending on age) said that grammatically correct statements were
sentences, the younger children frequently used truth criteria to justify their decision (50%–64%). Although the youngest children identified grammatically
incorrect statements as sentences, by the age of 8, most children rejected such
sentences. Still, one half of the 8-year-olds used a sense criterion rather than a
grammatical criterion for their decision. Thus, although most children by age 8
accurately assign sentence status to statements based on surface grammaticality,
at the same time they frequently rationalize their decision based on meaning
rather than form.

Another approach to studying metalinguistic awareness of sentence and
phrasal constituents comes from analyzing children's punctuation strategies. In a
comparison of first- and third-grade writers' self-generated, text-level writing,
Cordeiro (1988) found that older children were only slightly more accurate in
placing periods at the end of sentences (53% for third graders compared with
46% for first graders). Errors of commission (i.e., periods placed where none are
called for), however, differed according to age. Younger children used periods in
a wide variety of ways, for example as spacers between syllables and words, or
to mark the end of a line or page. Only 54 of 965 (5.6%) total errors fell at syntactic boundary points within the sentence. By the third grade, however, 161 of
174 (92.5%) total errors were syntactically motivated (e.g., the marker separated
phrases or clauses). Adverbials, either phrasal or clausal, were the syntactic unit
most often improperly isolated by the use of errant periods. Punctuation errors
apparently persist for many children. In Neville's study of Scottish children
(Neville, 1988), 18% of the children ages 13–14 still made more than 10 errors
in 10 lines of their own text-level writing.

Kress (1982) believes that it is *through* text-level writing that children
"work out" what a sentence is grammatically. Speaking cannot teach children

about sentences because sentences are not units of speaking, according to Kress. Sentences eventually may become units of speaking, but only after their establishment as units in writing. Like Halliday (1985, 1987), Kress (1982) considers the clause (or clause-like units) to be the primary unit of spoken language, these being linked together with conjunctions or by simple juxtaposition. Early "sentences" in the writing of children are topically, rather than grammatically, motivated; successive sentences in a narrative, for example, each stand for a time-ordered event, or story grammar element, and could be given a title. Kress (1982) offers many examples to illustrate his point, but one from the author's files (1983) is also a good illustration. Figure 2 is a fictional narrative written by a child of 7 years and 10 months. The child's punctuation, spelling, and linage have been preserved. Using the child's end-sentence punctuation (either a period or a capital letter), the text has been divided into nine "sentences." Study of the placement of these markers clearly illustrates their textual, rather than grammat-

TEXT 3

(1) Once there was a little horse who lived on a farm with a whole bunch of other horses. (2) he was happy he could run jump and kick as he pleased and he just was as playfull as a pony could be. (3) but one day when the pasture gate was left open he and his horses family and the others ran out they walked for miles until they came to a grassland whe they could play. (4) but this little pony thought being here was no better than being in the pasture he was so dreamy that little horse he used to be wild almost. (5) One day he told a nearby horse his problem he told that all he wanted was to be in paradice paidice he laughed no such thing he said I've got to go tell the others then all the others broke out PARADICE! ha ha ha realy he sniffeld well Ill just find it myself (6) So he set of for the road the other horses still laughing not even payhing atation to his walking away. (7) When he hit the road then he cam by a town called brookland it was very small but he pouynded and kicked on doors but all he got was some door slams but then he got to a house he kicked as hard as his stubby legs could kick and someone came rushing to the door it was a little boy his dad came rushing after him and he said Dad can I keep him his dad said well we have the stuff you need to take care of a horse so you can. (8) The little boy took very good care of him he bushed him, peted him, kept him warm and sometims he even sleped with him. (9) the little horse thought no such thing as Paradise he laughed thats what they think.

(1) Setting, where the pony lives

(2) Setting, why the pony is happy

(3) Initiating event – escaping to another place

(4) Internal reaction – the pony's reaction, different from the rest

(5) Response plan – plan to find paradise meets with ridicule

(6) Attempt – starting off to find paradise

(7) Action and consequence – the pony finds the boy

(8) End-state – the pony gets good care

(9) Reaction, affect – the pony has the last laugh

Figure 2. Fictional narrative written by a child age 7 years, 10 months. Using the child's end-of-sentence punctuation, the text has been divided into "sentences," which are numbered from 1 to 9 above.

ical, motivation. Each sentence corresponds to a story grammar element and can be given a topical title. Eventually, as children write longer texts, paragraphs take over as the major topical units, and children develop a true sense of the sentence as a grammatical, rather than topical, unit.

Information summarized in this section indicates that children have learned a considerable amount about literate textual and sentence structure in their early school years. Evidence can be found in terms of a gradual but steady increase in the length and complexity of spoken utterances and written sentences and in the increasingly frequent appearance of structures typical of written discourse and informational genres. The process of learning to write helps children carve out an explicit awareness of syntactic units such as phrases, clauses, and sentences—an awareness which is thought to feed back into the production of the literate forms needed in more planned, informational types of spoken discourse. The next section discusses the extent and nature of syntactic difficulty that many children with language impairments have. Rarely, however, has syntax been explored from a discourse perspective, as advocated in this chapter, and many questions about discourse and sentence-level interactions remain unanswered.

SYNTAX PROBLEMS IN SCHOOL-AGE
CHILDREN WITH LANGUAGE IMPAIRMENTS

What evidence is there that school-age children with language impairments have difficulty with the syntactic component of language and what is the nature of that difficulty? Answers represent relatively uncharted territory, especially when compared with results from syntax studies in preschool children with language impairments. Normative information about syntax ("ages and stages") is not available for school-age children to the same extent as it is for preschool children, with the result that the normative standard of comparison is less assured. In fact, an ages and stages approach to linguistic development may not be a useful approach in school-age children due to the protracted, gradual nature of linguistic growth in this period (Scott, 1988). Issues raised in the introductory section of this chapter also complicate the search for answers. Challenges presented include the construct of specific language impairment itself, the heterogeneity of children with language impairments, and the multidimensional and interactional nature of language components. Increasingly, the literature on children with language impairments contains articles and position papers addressing operational definitions of language impairments, especially for research purposes, methodological concerns regarding control groups in research (i.e., language matches), eligibility for school programs, and overlap with other groups including learning disability, reading disorders, and low achievers (American Speech-Language-Hearing Association [ASHA], 1982; Lahey, 1990; McCauley & Demetras, 1990; Plante, Swisher, Kiernan, & Restrepo, 1993). Interpretation and generalization problems in research concerning school-age children with language impairments remain formidable.

In light of the need for a discourse-motivated account of syntax, as discussed in the first section, research into school-age syntactic ability faces additional obstacles. The majority of investigations have sampled spoken conversational and narrative discourse, leaving informational and written forms of discourse relatively unexplored. Furthermore, many of the syntactic forms of interest in school-age children are by nature lower frequency forms, even in informational discourse. In order to study such forms as they occur spontaneously, lengthy and repeated discourse samples are required for a comprehensive analysis.

As a final caveat, it should be noted that ostensible problems with syntax— ostensible in the sense that studying a transcript of speaking or writing would reveal obvious grammatical forms—are not characteristic of all school-age children with language impairments. Although much validation work remains to be done, researchers have proposed several subtypes free of grammatical complications (cf. Fletcher, 1992; Leadholm & Miller, 1992, Miller, 1991). Children in such groups may have an assortment of word-finding, rate, dysfluency, and semantic referencing difficulties, but surface syntactic form and complexity level appear to be intact.

Given these challenges, it is not surprising that there have been relatively few studies of spoken and written syntax in school-age children with language impairments. This section summarizes available descriptions of syntax and explores possible explanations for those findings.

Syntactic Abilities: Description

Because school-age children with language impairments were once preschool children with language impairments, it seems reasonable to ask what we might expect based on syntactic descriptions available from the younger children. We know, for example, that preschool children with language impairments use fewer complex sentences (i.e., two or more clauses) than their age-matched controls and that they have difficulty with grammatical morphemes (Leonard, 1992), particularly those marking verbs (Bliss, 1989). The lack of complexity, noun and verb phrase expansion, and omission of obligatory grammatical markers results in utterances that are shorter than those produced by age-matched controls. Most errors are errors of omission, not commission (i.e., omissions of obligatory forms rather than added forms that result in agrammatic utterances). Word order is usually preserved.

Problems of this nature persist into the school-age years. Structures that appear less frequently in the spoken and written output of children with language impairments include complex sentences (usually defined as sentences containing a main clause plus one or more dependent clauses), and noun phrase and verb phrase expansions (Fletcher, 1992; Gillam & Johnston, 1992; Skarakis-Doyle & Mentis, 1991; Tyack, 1981).

The sentence complexity of school-age children with language impairments has received some attention. Gillam and Johnston (1992) explored both spoken and written narratives in 10 school-age children with language impairments (ages 9;0–11;7) and three groups of typically achieving children matched for age, language, and reading ability. Compared to age- and language-matched subjects, subjects with language impairments used fewer complex sentences in spoken and written narratives, and group differences were even more pronounced in the written mode.[1] (Complex sentences were defined as sentences containing a main clause and one or more additional coordinating, subordinating, complementing, or relative clauses.) In fact, there was a complete reversal of the effect of mode (speaking or writing) on complexity. Whereas age- and language-matched subjects used more complexity when they wrote, subjects with language impairments used more complexity when they spoke. One of the most interesting results in Gillam and Johnston's work came from their analysis of the particular types of complexity that contributed to these differences. The major differentiator between children with language impairments and those matched for age was for *combined* complex sentences (i.e., sentences that contained more than one form of dependent clause; for example, a sentence with a relative clause and an adverbial clause). Whereas age-matched children used combined complex sentences frequently in spoken (28% of all sentences) and written texts (18%), less than 2% of the sentences of children with language impairments contained more than one dependent clause. In addition, language-matched subjects produced more combined complex sentences than the children with language impairments (6% in both spoken and written narratives).

The extent to which sentence complexity and grammatical errors interact was also explored by Gillam and Johnston (1992). The authors' definition of complex sentences in the findings discussed above required that the sentence be grammatically correct. When incorrect complex sentences (46% of all complex spoken sentences and 78% of all complex written sentences) were added to correct complex sentences, the children with language impairments, like their age and language peers, produced more complex written than spoken sentences. Gillam and Johnston did not discuss the types of errors that occurred on complex sentences, but the extent of error, particularly in complex written sentences (78%), was dramatic when compared with control subjects (5% spoken and 7% written for age-matched subjects; 11% and 10% for language-matched subjects).

---

[1]The unit of analysis used by Gillam and Johnston (1992) was actually a T-unit (Hunt, 1965), with a T-unit (terminable unit) defined as one main clause with any attached dependent clauses. Comparison of data across studies is complicated by the fact that researchers have used different methods of segmenting transcripts. For example, data on percent of complex sentences from the Gillam and Johnston study cannot be compared with data from Roth and Spekman (1989) because Roth and Spekman segmented transcripts using Lee's (1974) criteria. The use of Lee's criteria would result in many two-clause sentences coordinated with *and,* whereas the T-unit criterion counts these as separate units, except in cases where the second clause coreferential subject is deleted. For example, *he went to the store and bought some soda* would be one T-unit, but *his Mother took him to the store/ and she paid for the soda* would be two T-units. Use of Lee's criteria would result in a substantially higher percentage of complex sentences, particularly in narrative discourse where many clauses begin with *and.* A comparison of these data in the two studies bears this out.

Roth and Spekman's (1989) findings also bear on sentence complexity and error. Spoken narratives produced by 93 children who either had learning disabilities or who were typically achieving (ages 8;0–13;11) were recorded and compared on 67 syntactic variables. The only significant difference occurred in the percent of correct complex sentences. Children who were typically achieving produced a slightly higher, but nonetheless significantly different, percentage of correct complex sentences (a 6% difference). Roth and Spekman concluded that their groups were essentially comparable in terms of sentence-level syntax revealed in narrative discourse. Their findings, however, may be attributable to ceiling effects inherent in their narrative task. Asking children of that age (8–14) to "make up a story" may not be sufficiently engaging. If comparisons had been made in other types of discourse, for example, informational discourse, differences between groups might have been observed.

Additional information on the development of sentence complexity via subordination operations is available in several case study reports of school-age children with language impairments. Tyack (1981) described a 10-year-old girl with language impairment who used 28% complex sentences in a 100-utterance picture description language sample; however, many of these were noted to be "incorrectly formed" (p. 51). There were only two relative clauses, and adverbial clauses were restricted to *because*. Moreover, the child confused *because* and *so* semantically. This child was described as having difficulty comprehending oral instructions and in reading comprehension although her decoding skills were good.

Skarakis-Doyle and Mentis (1991) followed a child with language impairment from age 10 to 12;6 (MLU 4.5–5.5), examining a cumulative transcript of 759 total utterances. Results are reported in considerable detail. In terms of the number of complex sentences attempted in conversation, the child was inferior to age-matched subjects, but similar to children matched on language measures. However, many more sentences of the child with a language impairment contained errors of word omission, substitution, constituent disagreement, or word order than was the case for the younger control subjects. Also, compared to control subjects, more sentences were dyadic, meaning that the complexity depended on successive utterances of the child's or on a sequence with his interlocutor (e.g., Adult: "Where would you put it?" Child: "In my room but its carpet."). This dyadic strategy was given a positive interpretation by Skarakis-Doyle and Mentis, who concluded that the child had arrived at a unique solution to his problem of coding complex information relations.

Donahue (1984) conducted one of the few studies designed to test whether children could understand and use syntactic devices tied to a particular discourse constraint. Specifically, she asked whether children with learning disabilities would be as adept as age-matched controls in the use of syntactic devices that mark given information compared with new information. Syntactic structures targeted in the stimulus items included passive, cleft (it is the boy who is riding the horse), pseudocleft (the one who is riding the horse is a boy), and contrastive stress (the boy is riding the horse). On the production task, children with learning disabilities were as effective as age-matched controls in marking the given versus new contrast, but used syntactically simpler forms (active sentences and contrastive stress) more frequently than complex forms (cleft, pseudocleft, and passive sentences).

Syntactic difficulties also have been observed in the writing of school-age children with language impairments. Studies have concentrated on mid- to late elementary students, since few children with language impairment are writing regularly at the text level before that time. As discussed above, error rates in writing are higher than in speaking (Gillam & Johnston, 1992). Compared to age-matched students, structural problems in the writing of students who are low-achieving or who have learning disabilities or language impairments include shorter T-units (Hunt, 1970; Loban, 1976), fewer complex sentences (Hunt, 1970; Loban, 1976), difficulty with inflectional suffixes (Rubin, Patterson, & Kantor, 1991), and fewer adverbial clauses of concession (e.g., *even though he had a chance,* he didn't go to the game) and nonfinite verbs (Loban, 1976). Newcomer and Barenbaum (1991) reviewed 18 investigations of writing ability (12 narrative, 6 expository) in upper elementary school-age children with learning disabilities. Across these studies, T-unit length (see footnote 1) was the most frequently used global measure of syntax. The measure did not distinguish reliably children with learning disabilities from age-matched controls. The authors explained the lack of sensitivity of the T-unit to the fact that less mature structures have the potential to lengthen sentences just as much as more mature structures. A frequent finding across studies was higher rates of grammatical and punctuation errors for children with learning disabilities. In the previous section, metalinguistic awareness of sentences as units, as revealed in punctuation ability, was cited as an important part of linguistic growth in school-age children. Indeed, the persistence and frequency of punctuation errors in children with language impairments may signify problems at a deeper linguistic level than is implied when punctuation difficulties are described as problems with surface "mechanics."

This review of the grammatical abilities of school-age children with language impairments reveals that sentence complexity via embedding and subordination operations is a particularly vulnerable syntactic area. When errors occur, they occur more frequently in complex sentences, and they also are exacerbated in the written mode. Inflectional morphology, a problem for most preschool children with language impairments, remains problematic for school-age writers (Rubin et al., 1991). Many school-age children with language impairments are capable of producing an essentially "normal" syntactic code in unplanned conversational contexts and in constrained narrative contexts (Roth & Spekman, 1989), although they may display other word-finding and fluency problems (Fletcher, 1992; Miller, 1991). Few investigations of syntactic capabilities in more taxing forms of informational discourse have been undertaken.

The findings described above agree well with findings of syntactic ability in more controlled elicitation conditions. Curtiss, Katz, and Tallal (1992) examined the evolution of 29 linguistic structures longitudinally in a set of picture-pointing (receptive) and sentence completion (expressive) tasks for 28 children with language impairments, beginning at age 4, for 5 years. Curtiss and her colleagues were interested especially in the question of syntactic delay versus deviance, and their procedures and stimuli were designed to analyze a large set of structures *and the relationship between structures* by examining violations from an expected sequence of acquisition. Such violations would have provided evidence for deviance. Curtiss et al. (1992) found very few violations overall, and there were as many outliers in their language-matched control sample as there were in the group of children with language impairments. They concluded that the children with language impairments were constructing a similar grammar in a similar way as children without language impairments.

Studies reviewed here also underscore the Scarborough and Dobrich (1990) finding of "illusory" recovery in children with language impairments at ages 5–7. By the age of 5, children had acquired enough language and spoke it "correctly" enough that they were no longer considered to have language impairments. Linguistic problems again surfaced, however, when these children encountered curricula of the mid-elementary years with its emphasis on extended, more complex informational discourse. The syntactic problems encountered by school-age children with language impairments appear to be problems of degree rather than kind.

Syntactic Adjustments for Discourse Mode and Genre

The second section of the chapter reviewed children's developing abilities in tailoring structure to discourse mode and genre, as well as their increasing conscious awareness of phrases and sentences. Some researchers have investigated the productions of school-age children with language impairments from a perspective of discourse sensitivity. Topics include comparisons of spoken and written structure, comparisons of structure for different discourse types, and analysis of forms used for specific types of discourse functions (e.g., coding given as opposed to new information).

Gillam and Johnston (1992), as reported above, compared spoken and written form and content in narratives produced by children with language impairments (ages 9;0–11;7) in response to picture stimuli. Group differences in mode relationships were not found for the amount of form (average sentence length and number of sentences per story), or for the amount and organization of language content. As indicated previously, group differences were found for the percentage of complex sentences, with children with language impairments producing fewer such sentences when writing, and age-matched children producing a higher percentage in writing. Children with language impairments also produced the highest percentage of grammatically unacceptable sentences, particularly in the written mode. Writing, it appears, had a damping effect on the ability of children with language impairments to construct grammatically well-formed complex sentences. Gillam and Johnston (1992) interpreted their results as support for the continuing syntactic difficulties experienced by school-age children with language impairments, difficulties that appear to be exacerbated by the process of writing.

Findings reported by Scott and Klutsenbaker (1989) support the idea that writing places an extra burden on children with language impairments in formulating complex sentences. They compared spoken and written versions of four narrative and informational summaries (two of each), produced by an 11-year-old child with a language impairment and an age-matched control. In three of four comparisons, written summaries of the child with the language impairment contained proportionally fewer complex sentences than spoken summaries. The reverse was true for the control subject; in three of four comparisons, the written version contained a higher percentage of complex sentences. In the fourth comparison, a narrative written text was less complex than the spoken text.

Writing may not be an obstacle to sentence complexity and grammaticality for all children with language impairments, however. Both age and severity of impairment could affect results. If students' conscious awareness of written form develops with increased writing experience, then the relaxed time constraints associated with writing might be advantageous. The author has worked clinically with adolescent students with language impairments whose written language compared favorably with spoken versions on sentence length and complexity measures. The child with a severe impairment studied longitudinally by Skarakis-Doyle and Mentis (1991) produced more complex sentences as well as a greater variety in written narratives than in spoken conversation (see Skarakis-Doyle, 1985). It should be noted, however, that the effects of mode and genre cannot be separated when comparing written narratives with spoken conversation.

The effects of genre on the output of seven children with language impairments (ages 9;0–11;1) were investigated by MacLachlan and Chapman (1988). The two variables of interest were frequency of communication breakdowns and utterance length. Genre was found to exert a greater influence on the number of communication breakdowns (i.e., stalls, repairs, abandoned utterances) for the group with language impairments when compared with both language- and age-matched groups. Although all subjects were less fluent when producing narratives, the discrepancy between the discourse types was considerably more pronounced for the children with language impairments. Only the older children (those with language impairments and their age-matched controls) produced longer utterances in the narrative condition; the difference in utterance length between narrative and conversation was greater for the children with language impairments, although not statistically significant. Results were interpreted to suggest a close relationship between utterance length and frequency of communication breakdown for children with language impairments.

Accounting for Syntax Findings

Information reviewed above suggests that explanations for the persistence of syntactic difficulties in certain school-age children with language impairments may need to shift in focus from representational to processing accounts. In a representational (knowledge-based) account, children are thought to lack the rule for a particular syntactic form; in a processing account, the child "knows" about the form but has difficulty deploying that knowledge in real time (Fletcher, 1992). The fact that children with language impairments almost always produce *some* exemplars of *most* syntactic structures, and that these structures are mastered at the same developmental point relative to other forms (Curtiss et al., 1992, as discussed above), underscores potential processing explanations for structural differences between children with and without language impairments. As Curtiss and Tallal (1991) point out, "The result is less performance for the same amount of representational knowledge" (p. 208).

A processing account of structural difficulties fits well with results from studies that have compared syntactic capabilities across mode and genre. Gillam and Johnston's (1992) finding that the error rate of children with language impairments increases substantially in complex sentences, and dramatically in complex written sentences compared to complex spoken sentences, could be explained by the additional processing demands of writing as opposed to speaking. Such demands include spelling, forming letters, deciding about punctuation—demands that perhaps overshadow the benefits gained from a more relaxed time frame of writing compared with speaking. Additional findings reviewed above that support a processing account include the decrease in sentence complexity in writing compared to speaking (Scott & Klutsenbaker, 1989) and an increase in communication breakdown in narrative compared to conversational speaking (MacLachlan & Chapman, 1988).

Another potential contributor to syntactic difficulties is the fact that many higher level structures that figure prominently in mode and genre adjustments are, by nature, low-frequency structures (e.g., relative clauses modifying grammatical subjects, nonfinite subordinate clauses, cleft sentences).[2] If the essence of later language development is learning to apply discourse-motivated grammatical *options,* as hypothesized in this chapter, it follows that some low-frequency literate forms may not be viable options for children with language impairments who have more limited resources, or at least that the forms will take

---

[2] The fact that a structure occurs less frequently in the language does not diminish its importance. If, for example, there were only one cleft sentence and one nonrestrictive relative clause in an informational passage of five paragraphs, those two structures have nevertheless made an important contribution to setting the literate tone of that passage. Likewise, it would be odd if every sentence in a text contained five clauses; rather, it is the variety of sentence lengths—some short and some long—that makes writing more interesting. Thus, the child who does not develop the ability to use the occasional nonrestrictive relative clause or the occasional five-clause sentence is at a disadvantage for the full development of literate language style.

longer to learn. For example, a child with a language impairment, like a younger child without an impairment, may code a logical relation via a simpler juxtaposition system (i.e., put the related clauses next to one another and let the listener or reader figure out the relationship) rather than coding the same relation via a complex sentence with an explicit adverbial subordinate conjunction. It is of some interest that frequency of occurrence of syntactic structures has figured in theoretical accounts of preschool children's syntactic difficulties (Dromi, Leonard, & Shteiman, 1993; Leonard, 1992).

The nature of the more limited resources supporting syntactic development in certain children with language impairments remains elusive. A straightforward limited capacity processor, where increases in the complexity of one component of the linguistic system forces complexity reductions in other components, was not supported in an investigation by Masterson and Kamhi (1992). These investigators studied syntactic, phonological, and fluency interactions in imitated and spontaneous speech of children with language impairments, with reading impairments, and typically developing (ages 6;0–9;0). Contrary to expectations, they found similar patterns of interaction across groups, a finding which calls into question simple capacity processing explanations for difficulties of children with language impairments. The question is far from settled, however, because group differences may have occurred on different tasks using different measures of complexity.

INTERVENTION APPLICATIONS

Language clinicians and educators interested in the place of syntax and grammar instruction for school-age children with language impairments will find a rich store of information about discourse–grammar connections, spurred by the recent research in discourse analysis as discussed at the outset of this chapter. Information also is available on the development of higher level syntax in school-age children, as well as the types of problems encountered by children with language impairments, although much work remains to be done. Unfortunately, clinicians can find less information on specific goals and procedures, and almost no information on the effectiveness of teaching syntax to children with language impairments. There are, nonetheless, several sources of information that can be tapped by clinicians who believe that syntax has a place in language intervention with school-age children. One source is in the field of English as a second language (ESL), where effectiveness issues surrounding grammar teaching have a long history of debate (cf. Celce-Murcia, 1991; Chafe, 1991; Garrett, 1986). Likewise, there are relevant discussions and research in the education and learning disabilities fields. The discussion below draws from those sources as well as from research presented thus far in outlining applications and directions for the teaching of syntax to school-age children with language impairments. It should be noted, however, that very few clinical or pedagogical studies that speak directly to efficacy have been reported.

There is a range of choices that clinicians and teachers of language might make in the teaching of syntax to school-age children. Two important choices are whether to use direct or indirect (meaning-based) approaches, and the mode for teaching (spoken or written or combinations) (see Fey, Catts, & Larrivee, chap. 1, this volume; Gillam et al., chap. 6, this volume). Some clinicians might take the approach that syntax should not be taught directly out of context devoid of broader discourse meaning. A direct approach to teaching syntax usually means that children are presented with lists of sentences designed to heighten awareness of a particular form. For example, they might be asked to distinguish between active and passive sentences, underline relatives clauses in sentences, or fill in verb forms that signal appropriate subject–verb agreement. In an indirect approach, children are exposed to types of discourse thought to facilitate particular types of grammatical growth. If children need to learn about noun phrase expansion, for example, they would be exposed to informational written discourse where such forms are prominent. An approach between these two extremes might involve using language at the discourse level, but in a more carefully engineered or focused manner. A child might be asked to retell a narrative specifically written to emphasize relative clauses needed to provide background information on multiple characters (e.g., one son who lived at home, and a daughter who was away at school). Decisions about the mode of instruction are also important. How clinicians manage the listening, speaking, reading, and writing requirements of the intervention program can be expected to affect outcome. A written structural exercise such as sentence combining, for example, can affect reading comprehension (Wilkinson & Patty, 1993). Although a structural goal may pertain to speaking, having the child locate a structure in written material and/or practice writing the structure may be an effective way to bring about a change in spoken language.

Indirect Approaches: Discourse Environments that Facilitate Syntactic Growth

Information presented in previous sections has characterized the essence of later language development as learning to apply discourse-motivated syntactic choices. Most children, with reasonable exposure, learn when to exercise grammatical choices and do so with very little, if any, formal instruction (Kress, 1982). Earlier in the chapter, for example, it was shown that forms characteristic of the written mode (e.g., there stood a little tiger cub) are found in children's writing at the age of 8. The discourse environment, then, is a critical element of grammatical growth for all children, including those with language impairments. Acquainting children with a variety of text types at earlier ages is a theme increasingly visible in educational language literature. Children should hear informational language as well as stories, should read books and materials other than stories, and should be expected to speak and write several types of discourse (Freeman, 1991; Neville, 1988).

Language curricula in schools increasingly reflect a discourse perspective and interest in form–function interactions. Perera (1992) has documented the importance afforded to discourse variety in the National Curriculum in English adopted recently in England and Wales. The curriculum dictates that children be exposed to and given practice in producing a wider variety of text types than has been typical of classrooms in the past. There are clearly stated levels of attainment in speaking and listening, and reading and writing. For example, the writing goals and programs of study for children age 5–8 specify:

> Pupils should undertake a range of chronological writing including some at least of diaries, stories, letters, accounts of tasks they have done and of personal experiences, records of observations they have made, e.g. in a science or design activity, and instructions, e.g. recipes. [They should also] undertake a range of non-chronological writing which includes... some at least of lists, captions, labels, invitations, greeting cards, notices, posters... plans and diagrams, descriptions, e.g. of a person or place, and notes for an activity, e.g. in science or designing and making. (Cox, 1991, cited in Perera, 1992, p. 186)

According to Perera (1992), this degree of attention to text variety in the curriculum applies not only to the early years of schooling but holds throughout, to age 16 and beyond. She cites two major justifications for the emphasis on text variety. One is the need to handle a variety of texts in everyday life. The second is the realization that "different varieties of language have characteristically different linguistic features; this applies to vocabulary, to sentence syntax and to the overall organization of the discourse" (p. 186). This point has been a major theme of the present chapter.

The findings of several researchers support an earlier emphasis on and need for informational discourse in elementary school curricula. Newkirk (1987), who found evidence that third graders were capable of writing informational text in ordered paragraphs, wrote that the elementary years need not be a time when "narrative must do for all" (p. 142). Neville (1988) called for more attention to informational text based on her finding that such text was difficult for children at every stage, but particularly so at the ages of 8–9 years. Recalling informational text was more difficult regardless of whether the children heard or read the material or whether they spoke or wrote their responses. Language clinicians are frequently better acquainted with programs that teach narrative text than with those geared to informational discourse. Sources on informational text activities for school children include Freeman (1991), Graves (1991), and Painter and Martin (1986).

The timing of this emphasis on text variety may be important. Neville's (1988) large-scale study of the listening, reading, speaking, and writing abilities of Scottish children cited earlier revealed that children between the ages of 8 and 12 changed rapidly, "moving really into a different 'ball-game' as far as skills of *literacy* are concerned" (p. 205). This growth curve slowed considerably, however, from ages 12 to 14. Whether the leveling-off should be attributed to developmental factors or less-than-optimal English teaching in secondary schools is open to question according to Neville. Leveling-off effects also have been reported by Rubin et al. (1991), specifically for morphological knowledge, as demonstrated in both cloze tasks and spontaneous text-level writing. Adults with low literacy skills in their study did no better than normal second grade children, calling into question whether continued exposure alone will be sufficient for continued structural growth.

The fact that school-age children with language impairments may need interventions that are more direct should not diminish the importance of making an adequate variety of text types available within natural contexts. Children with language impairments should hear informational as well as narrative text read aloud and they should be encouraged to write in a full range of genres. Speaking turns should be manipulated to encourage more monologues and extended turns of all types, including personal narratives, descriptions, procedures, and opinions.

Direct Approaches in Syntax Teaching

At the other end of the continuum are procedures that focus on particular forms, usually at the sentence level. An example of a direct procedure is the program devised by Tyack (1981) to teach sentence complexity (i.e., coordinate and subordinate clauses) to a 10-year-old with language and learning disabilities. In one program, the child responded to pictures and the written cue *because* with *clause 1 + because + clause 2* sentences. In another, the child was taught to cross out the co-referential subject in the second clause (e.g., Sam found a cat/ Sam took it home) and then write the coordinated second clause with appropriate subject deletion (e.g., Sam found a cat and [took it home]). Tyack reported that after 6 months of intervention, the frequency of complex sentences generated in a picture description task increased from 28% to 62%. Tyack did not report further details of the child's intervention (e.g., number of sessions, stimuli per session, or other activities).

Other examples of sentence-level, decontextualized grammar exercises can be found in elementary level language arts textbooks and in syntax workbooks marketed in special education catalogs. What these sources have in common is that forms are taught in sets of isolated sentences. Table 4 shows examples of such exercises.

Target structures found in these exercises are typically not those listed in Table 1 as characteristic of written language development in school-age children. Rather, targets are simpler structures, for example, simple subjects and predicates and parts of speech (e.g., nouns, verbs, adjectives, adverbs). Practice sentences are usually short, even in late elementary-level texts. It is difficult to see how children make connections between the types of sentences found in these exercises and those they themselves say, write, hear, and read, which are frequently longer and considerably more complex. To this author's knowledge,

Table 4. Examples of sentence-level grammar teaching exercises found in fourth-grade language arts textbooks

Subjects and predicates

For each sentence, write "subject" if the subject is underlined or "predicate" if the predicate is underlined.

1. The dog was lost for a week. (subject)
2. The family went to Disneyland. (predicate)

Adjectives

Find the adjective that describes the underlined noun. Does it tell what kind or how many?

1. Five people lost their homes in the huge fire. (five: how many; huge: what kind)
2. The friendly dog followed the boy home. (friendly: what kind)

Singular and plural nouns

Write the correct noun to complete the sentence and label it as singular or plural.

1. My father owns a hardware (store, stores). (store: singular)
2. My dog likes to chase (stick, sticks). (sticks: plural)

Adapted from Haley-James & Stewig (1993) and Ragno, Toth, & Gray (1993).

the efficacy of using grammatical exercises of this type with children in regular or special education classrooms has not be demonstrated.

In contrast, one type of direct syntax teaching activity for which there is a substantial database in regular education is sentence combining. In a sentence-combining (SC) exercise, two or more simple (one-clause) sentences are combined into a longer, more complex sentence. An educational application of transformational grammar (cf. Mellon, 1969), SC exercises require deletion, insertion, addition, and rearrangement operations. Table 5 provides examples of several different types of complex sentences formed from application of SC operations. Examples A and B are based on two simple sentences; example C is formed by combining three sentences. The last example (D) illustrates that a short text can be created from a sentence-combining exercise. SC exercises can be written in cued or uncued versions.

The rationale for SC was that children would gain insight into the control of sentence complexity, which they could then apply in online text-level writing (Hunt, 1965; Mellon, 1969; O'Hare, 1973). It was reasoned that children have knowledge of sentence complexity that they fail to apply in writing; SC exercises were thought to facilitate more routine application of that knowledge. Numerous studies have demonstrated that SC training is effective in increasing sentence complexity in the compositions of elementary-age and older students (Neville & Searls, 1985). More recently studies have looked into the effects of SC on reading comprehension where positive results have also been demonstrated (cf. Wilkinson & Patty, 1993).

Although research on SC has been limited to students in regular education programs, it seems reasonable to predict that school-age children with language impairments could benefit from this direct approach. The procedure devised by Tyack (1981) and described earlier used a variation of a SC format and met with

Table 5. Examples of sentence-combining formats

A. Cued
The dance will be held on Saturday. (how)
The students volunteer to clean up. (if)
The dance will be held on Saturday if the students volunteer to clean up.

B. Uncued
John was a good dancer.
John was a good ballplayer.
John was a good dancer and ballplayer.

C. Cued
He hit the home run. (when)
The crowd went crazy. (,)
The crowd poured onto the field. (and)
When he hit the home run, the crowd went crazy and poured onto the field.

D. Uncued (Neville & Searls, 1985, p. 47)
A land lies in central Asia.
The land is large.
The land is barren.
The land is called the Gobi.
Winters are harsh.
There are winter winds.
They are from the north.
The summers are short.
They are hot.
They are dry.
A large, barren land called the Gobi lies in central Asia. Winters are harsh with winds from
   the north. The short summers are hot and dry.

some success in increasing spoken language complexity in a 10-year-old child with a language impairment. Sources that outline SC activities adapted to spoken language and lower level language ability include Combs (1977), Perron (1976), and Reutzel (1986). Gerber (1993) provided examples of SC formats that result in complex sentences containing relative clauses and adverbial clauses of time, contrast, and condition.

Several task formats in addition to sentence combining are useful in direct approaches to syntax instruction. Wiig and Semel (1984) provide examples of formats including cloze, completion, paraphrase, and sentence formulation with key words. Many of the examples in Wiig and Semel's book (1984) are shown with structures appropriate for younger children. New exercises using higher level forms would need to be constructed for many school-age children with language impairments. Scott and Rush (1985) detailed how task formats can be used to teach higher level adverbial conjuncts (e.g., however, in addition, therefore).

Discourse-Based Approaches in Syntax Teaching

Discourse-based approaches to the teaching of syntax share certain features with both direct and indirect methods. Similar to indirect approaches, training takes place largely at the discourse level, using real texts of high interest to children. In common with direct approaches, however, children's attention is directed in an explicit way to particular structures and certain grammatical features.

Structures targeted in a discourse-based approach are those that play important roles in school-age children's academic and social discourse (Mentis, 1993; Scott, 1994). Structures listed in Table 1, for example, would be appropriate for children with language impairments when the focus is on academic discourse. Similar to focused stimulation approaches with preschool children (Fey, 1986), discourse-based intervention strives to make particular forms "more salient" for children. One way to do this is to introduce discourse examples that favor target forms. For example, descriptive informational texts contain higher frequencies of complex NPs with pre- and postmodifications because traits and locations of objects are important. In historical texts it is important to provide relevant background context; nonrestrictive relative clauses serve this purpose (e.g., Harold, whose army had just marched across England, was....).

A variety of recognition/awareness and production activities could be used within a discourse-based approach. In general, the clinician models the behavior and then gradually elicits participation and increasing independence on the part of the child (e.g., "Most of the time we will find these connective words at the beginning of the sentence, such as this word *also,* but sometimes they can be stuck in the middle or come at the end," or, "I'm going to see if the writer used any relative clauses to tell us more about the subject, but first I have to underline the subject."). Highlighting, underlining, and tallying target structures in real texts, in the author's clinical experience, is interesting to most school-age children. Texts that increase interest include the children's own speaking or writing, a sibling or parent's writing, comic and cartoon books, well-known books that children have either read themselves or that have been read to them, transcripts of TV programs, greeting cards, and the children's school textbooks. Several of the task formats discussed above as direct approaches are adaptable to discourse-level production activities. Cloze, completion, and paraphrase formats, in particular, are useful.

In addition to awareness of specific structures characteristic of academic texts, children can be taught to judge the overall level of syntactic complexity of a text. One way to do this is to help children identify simple and complex sentences, where complex sentences are defined as those that have two separate verbs (clauses). If children can find verbs in sentences, they can do this task. This gives children a way to conceptualize sentence complexity within texts they write ("I used five complex sentences in my story of 10 sentences. That's better than the last one I wrote.") and read ("No wonder I had trouble with that passage, almost every sentence was complex.").

An ESL Perspective

Within the ESL language teaching literature, discourse-based grammatical approaches have been proposed recently as a compromise in the debate on grammar instruction (Celce-Murcia, 1991; Garrett, 1986). Teaching methods in ESL before the 1980s could be considered direct in that grammar was taught as a sentence-level phenomenon, without regard for wider meaning or discourse context. Proponents of contrasting communicative approaches to language teaching, which dominated in the 1980s, rejected explicit teaching of grammar on the grounds that knowledge gained in such exercises is not "usable" in online communication, spoken or written. Grammatical competence was thought to be implicit and learned through exposure to language input. Lower level grammar would "take care of itself" when higher level meaning and function were emphasized (Celce-Murcia, 1991, p. 145). Chafe (1991), however, pointed out that the poor results from grammar instruction may have been because grammar was taught in irrelevant ways. If students were taught to make more direct connections between grammar and context, Chafe predicted, results would be different.

As an illustration of the difference between direct sentence-level and discourse-based approaches for ESL learners, Celce-Murcia (1991) compared procedures in several ESL textbooks used to teach the passive voice. The direct texts used sentence-level exercises with completion and rewrite formats. In the discourse-based text, the passive voice was taught in a unit on technology that began with an extended text for reading comprehension. Next came awareness activities at the text level, followed by sentence-level exercises related to the text and topic. Finally, speaking and writing assignments on technology encouraged the use of appropriate passive and active forms.

The dialogue in the ESL literature would appear to have some application in language teaching for school-age children with language impairments. Almost by definition, school-age children with language impairments who have syntax difficulties are children for whom lower level grammar has not "taken care of itself," assuming reasonable exposure to academic and social discourse. More explicit direct and/or discourse-based approaches to language instruction appear to be in order.

Syntax Teaching and Mode: An Integrated Approach

Mode considerations are important in instruction. Clinicians and teachers of school-age children with language impairments can take advantage of cross-modal procedures that are not available to younger children who do not read or write. Speaking can be "captured" in written form for analysis. Following the text by reading while listening at the same time makes structures more explicit. Perera (1992) observed that some grammatical forms may first be acquired through experience with reading and writing. Only later are these forms transferred to related spoken forms of discourse. For example, a child originally might learn about appositive structures (which restate and/or elaborate nouns) through reading or writing and later come to use appositives in spoken contexts where they are appropriate. As discussed previously, writing, although not necessarily more complex per se than speaking, usually contains a greater *variety* of complex sentences (Biber, 1992). Reading and writing, then, are seen not only as skills to be learned but as *agents* in continuing language development processes. It is unlikely that clinicians working with school-age children with language impairments can teach syntax without concerning themselves with written language.

Clinicians who incorporate written language in their intervention programs for syntax will benefit from studying writing programs that emphasize conscious awareness of text structure and metacognitive strategies (e.g., Englert et al., 1988; Seidenberg, 1989). Children are motivated to write in order to convey particular meanings for particular reasons, not to produce impressive syntax. Clinicians need to be able to provide scaffolding for the production of well-organized text concurrently with well-formed text. A well-organized text is one that conforms to top-level text structure expectations for a specific narrative or informational genre. A well-formed text would contain syntactic structures that supported the cohesion, elaboration, thematic, and propositional requirements of the genre. Newcomer and Barenbaum (1991) reviewed 11 studies on the effectiveness of writing intervention for students with learning disabilities; of these, 8 studies used subjects between the third and sixth grade. Training procedures in most studies centered on teaching writing strategies (e.g., self-directed prompts). The studies present a picture of improvement in writing fluency, coherence, and overall quality. Although syntax was not measured directly, it is likely that syntactic improvements occurred concurrently. Text-level and sentence-level instruction can be effectively coordinated (e.g., Scott & Davidson, 1991).

CONCLUSIONS AND SUMMARY

Language clinicians interested in syntactic contributions to language impairments of school-age children find themselves at an interesting but precarious crossroad. Developments within the field of discourse analysis have highlighted numerous ways in which sentential syntax reflects textual, genre, and mode parameters. As exposure to written and informational language in school accumulates, children learn to comprehend and produce varieties of language that differ structurally from the conversational and narrative discourse of their preschool years.

The elementary-school years provide children with many opportunities to learn about a variety of types of discourse. Children are capable of producing informational written text by the third grade (Newkirk, 1987). Whether informational or narrative, children's writing looks uniquely "written" from a structural standpoint almost as soon as they write at the text level. Several researchers stress that it is through the act of text-level writing that children develop conscious awareness of syntactic units such as phrases and sentences (Cordeiro, 1988; Kress, 1982). Likewise it is in writing that children first produce some of the low-frequency forms characteristic of literate language—forms that will later transfer to literate spoken language (Perera, 1992). The upper elementary–school grades appear to be a particularly active period for developing the syntactically complex forms characteristic of written and informational language (Loban, 1976; Neville, 1988; O'Donnell et al., 1967), but learning continues for many years to come.

Children with language impairments, however, produce higher level syntactic structures less frequently than their age-matched peers. Their output contains more errors, particularly when they attempt complex sentences with two or more clauses and when they write (Gillam & Johnston, 1992). The fact that punctuation errors persist in the writing of children with learning disabilities (Newcomer & Barenbaum, 1991) suggests that conscious awareness of phrasal, clausal, and sentence constituents is less developed than that of children without learning difficulties.

Information in this chapter should be helpful in designing intervention programs. Clinicians should have a better idea of specific structures to target as well as the types of discourse most likely to facilitate the learning of those structures. It is unlikely that school-age children with language impairments benefit from procedures that target simple phrases, clauses, and sentences. Complex sentences with two or more clauses and expanded noun and verb phrases are more appropriate structural targets. Clinicians would seem to have a powerful ally in writing, where higher level structures can be "captured" for awareness activities.

With the advent of whole language approaches in schools and communication-based approaches in second-language teaching, clinicians might conclude that more direct approaches to the teaching of linguistic form are ill-advised. Such a conclusion seems premature in light of the lack of efficacy research with school-age children with language impairments (see Gillam et al., chap. 6, this volume). As outlined above, syntax can be taught more or less directly; a broad array of approaches await study. What seems clear is that knowledge of the discourse-motivated nature of later learned forms is helpful in designing such studies.

REFERENCES

American Speech-Language-Hearing Association. (1982, November). Position statement on language learning disorders. *Asha, 937–945.*

Aram, D., Morris, R., & Hall, N. (1993). Clinical and research congruence in identifying children with specific language impairment. *Journal of Speech and Hearing Research, 36,* 580–591.

Bauers, A., & Pettit, D. (1990). Exploring young children's language awareness. *Child Language Teaching and Therapy, 6,* 279–304.

Beaman, K. (1984). Coordination and subordination revisited: Syntactic complexity in spoken and written narrative discourse. In D. Tannen (Ed.), *Coherence in spoken and written discourse* (pp. 45–80). Norwood, NJ: Ablex.

Biber, D. (1986). Spoken and written textual dimensions in English: Resolving the contradictory findings. *Language, 62,* 384–414.

Biber, D. (1988). *Variation across speech and writing.* New York: Cambridge University Press.

Biber, D. (1992). On the complexity of discourse complexity: A multidimensional analysis. *Discourse Processes, 15,* 133–163.

Bliss, L. (1989). Selected syntactic usage of language-impaired children. *Journal of Communication Disorders, 22,* 277–289.

Bloom, L., & Lahey, M. (1978). *Language development and language disorders.* New York: John Wiley & Sons.

Brown, G., Anderson, A., Shillcock, R., & Yule, G. (1984). *Teaching talk: Strategies for production and assessment.* New York: Cambridge University Press.

Brown, G., & Yule, G. (1983). *Teaching spoken language.* New York: Cambridge University Press.

Celce-Murcia, M. (1991). Discourse analysis and grammar instruction. *Annual Review of Applied Linguistics, 11,* 135–151.

Chafe, W. (1982). Integration and involvement in speaking, writing, and oral literature. In D. Tannen (Ed.), *Spoken and written language: Exploring orality and literacy* (pp. 35–53). Norwood, NJ: Ablex.

Chafe, W. (1991). Grammatical subjects in speaking and writing. *Text, 11,* 45–72.

Combs, W. (1977). Sentence-combining practice aids reading comprehension. *Journal of Reading, 21,* 18–24.

Cordeiro, P. (1988). Children's punctuation: An analysis of errors in period placement. *Research in the Teaching of English, 22,* 62–75.

Cox, B. (1991). *Cox on Cox.* London: Hodder & Stroughton.

Crystal, D., Fletcher, P., & Garman, M. (1990). *The grammatical analysis of language disability: A procedure for assessment and remediation* (2nd ed.). London: Whurr Publishers.

Curtiss, S., Katz, W., & Tallal, P. (1992). Delay versus deviance in the language acquisition of language-impaired children. *Journal of Speech and Hearing Research, 35,* 373–383.

Curtiss, S., & Tallal, P. (1991). On the nature of the impairment in language-impaired children. In J. Miller (Ed.), *Research on child language disorders: A decade of progress* (pp. 189–210). Austin, TX: PRO-ED.

Donahue, M. (1984). Learning disabled children's comprehension and production of syntactic devices for marking given versus new information. *Applied Psycholinguistics, 5,* 101–116.

Dromi, E., Leonard, L., & Shteiman, M. (1993). The grammatical morphology of Hebrew-speaking children with specific language impairment: Some competing hypotheses. *Journal of Speech and Hearing Research, 36,* 760–771.

Englert, C., Raphael, T., Anderson,, L., Anthony, H., Fear, K., & Gregg, S. (1988). A case for writing intervention: Strategies for writing informational text. *Learning Disabilities Focus, 3,* 98–113.

Fey, M.F. (1986). *Language intervention with young children.* Newton, MA: Allyn & Bacon.

Fletcher, P. (1992). Sub-groups in school-age language impaired children. In P. Fletcher (Ed.), *Specific speech and language disorders in children* (pp. 152–182). San Diego: Singular Publishing Group.

Francis, W.N., & Kucera, H. (1982). *Frequency of analysis of English usage: Lexicon and grammar.* Boston: Houghton Mifflin.

Freeman, E. (1991). Informational books: Models for student report writing. *Language Arts, 68,* 470–473.

Garrett, N. (1986). The problem with grammar: What kind can the language learner use? *Modern Language Journal, 70,* 133–148.

Gerber, A. (1993). *Language-related learning disabilities: Their nature and treatment.* Baltimore: Paul H. Brookes Publishing Co.

Gillam, R., & Johnston, J. (1992). Spoken and written language relationships in language/learning impaired and normally achieving school-age children. *Journal of Speech and Hearing Research, 35,* 1303–1315.

Graves, D. (1991). *Investigative nonfiction.* Portsmouth, NH: Heinemann.

Haley-James, S., & Stewig, J. (1993). *English.* Boston: Houghton Mifflin.

Halliday, M.A.K. (1985). *Spoken and written language.* Oxford: Oxford University Press.

Halliday, M.A.K. (1987). Spoken and written modes of meaning. In R. Horowitz & S.J. Samuels (Eds.), *Comprehending oral and written language* (pp. 55–82). San Diego: Academic Press.

Halliday, M.A.K., & Hasan, R. (1976). *Cohesion in English.* London: Longman.

Handscombe, R.J. (1967). *The written language of nine- and ten-year-old children.* (Report No. 24–28). London: The Nuffield Foundation.

Hatch, E. (1992). *Discourse and language education.* New York: Cambridge University Press.

Hunt, K. (1965). *Grammatical structures written at three grade levels.* Champaign, IL: National Council of Teachers of English.

Hunt, K. (1970). Syntactic maturity in school children and adults. *Monographs of the Society for Research in Child Development, 35,* (1, Serial No. 134).

Hux, K., Morris-Friehe, M., & Sanger, D.D. (1993). Language sampling practices: A survey of nine states. *Language, Speech, and Hearing Services in Schools, 24,* 84–91.

Kroll, B. (1981). Developmental relationships between speaking and writing. In B. Krill & B. Vann (Eds.), *Exploring speaking-writing relations: Connections and contrasts* (pp. 32–54). Urbana, IL: National Council of Teachers of English.

Kress, G. (1982). *Learning to write.* London: Routledge & Kegan Paul.

Lahey, M. (1990). Who shall be called language disordered? Some reflections and one perspective. *Journal of Speech and Hearing Disorders, 55,* 612–620.

Langer, S. (1985). Children's sense of genre: A study of performance on parallel reading and writing tasks. *Written Communication, 2,* 157–187.

Langer, S. (1986). Reading, writing, and understanding: An analysis of the construction of meaning. *Written Communication, 3,* 219–267.

Leadholm, B.J., & Miller, J.F. (1992). *Language sample analysis: The Wisconsin Guide.* Madison: Wisconsin Department of Public Instruction.

Lee, L. (1974). *Developmental sentence analysis: A grammatical assessment procedure for speech and language clinicians.* Evanston, IL: Northwestern University Press.

Lehnert, L. (1982). A comparison of syntactic structures in first-graders' oral and written language. *Reading Horizons, 22,* 258–262.

Leonard, L. (1991). Language impairment as a clinical category. *Language, Speech, and Hearing Services in School, 22,* 66–68.

Leonard, L. (1992). Specific language impairment in three languages. In P. Fletcher & D. Hall (Eds.), *Specific speech and language disorders in children: Correlates, characteristics, and outcomes* (pp. 118–126). San Diego: Singular Publishing Group.

Loban, W. (1976). *Language development: Kindergarten through grade twelve.* Champaign, IL: National Council of Teachers of English.

Longacre, R.E. (1983). *The grammar of discourse.* New York: Plenum.

MacLachlan, B., & Chapman, R. (1988). Communication breakdowns in normal and language-learning disabled children's conversation and narration. *Journal of Speech and Hearing Disorders, 53,* 2–7.

Masterson, J., & Kamhi, A. (1992). Linguistic trade-offs in school-age children with and without language disorders. *Journal of Speech and Hearing Research, 35,* 1064–1075.

McCauley, R., & Demetras, M. (1990). The identification of language impairment in the selection of specifically language-impaired subjects. *Journal of Speech and Hearing Disorders, 55,* 468–475.

McNeill, D. (1966). The creation of language by children. In J. Lyons & J. Wales (Eds.), *Psycholinguistic papers* (pp. 99–132). Edinburgh: Edinburgh University Press.

Mellon, J. (1969) *Transformational sentence-combining.* Urbana, IL: National Council of Teachers of English.

Mentis, M. (1993, November). *Discourse problems and their relationships to syntax and semantics.* Paper presented at the American Speech-Language-Hearing Association annual convention, Anaheim, CA.

Miller, J. (1981). *Assessing language production in children.* Baltimore: University Park Press.

Miller, J. (1991). Quantifying productive language disorders. In J. Miller (Ed.), *Research on child language disorders: A decade of progress* (pp. 211–220). Austin, TX: PRO-ED.

Nation, J., & Aram, D.M. (1977). *Diagnosis of speech and language disorders.* St. Louis: C.V. Mosby.

Neville, D.D., & Searls, E.F. (1985). The effect of sentence-combining and kernel-identification training on the syntactic component of reading comprehension. *Research in the Teaching of English, 19,* 37–60.

Neville, M. (1988). *Assessing and teaching language: Literacy and oracy in schools.* London: Macmillan Education.

Newcomer, P., & Barenbaum, E. (1991). The written composing ability of children with learning disabilities: A review of the literature from 1980 to 1990. *Journal of Learning Disabilities, 24,* 578–593.

Newkirk, T. (1987). The non-narrative writing of young children. *Research in the Teaching of English, 21,* 121–144.

O'Donnell, R., Griffin, W., & Norris, R. (1967). *Syntax of kindergarten and elementary school children: A transformational analysis.* Champaign, IL: National Council of Teachers of English.

O'Hare, F. (1973). *Sentence combining.* Urbana, IL: National Council of Teachers of English.

Painter, C., & Martin, J. (1986). *Writing to mean: Teaching genres across the curriculum.* Sydney: Applied Linguistics Association of Australia.

Perera, K. (1984). *Children's writing and reading.* London: Blackwell.

Perera, K. (1986a). Grammatical differentiation between speech and writing in children aged 8 to 12. In A. Wilkinson (Ed.), *The writing of writing* (pp. 90–108). New York: Open University Press.

Perera, K. (1986b). Language acquisition and writing. In P. Fletcher & M. Garman (Eds.), *Language acquisition* (2nd ed., pp. 494–533). New York: Cambridge University Press.

Perera, K. (1992). Reading and writing skills in the National Curriculum. In P. Fletcher & D. Hall (Eds.), *Specific speech and language disorders in children: Correlates, characteristics and outcomes* (pp. 183–193). San Diego: Singular Publishing Group.

Perron, J. (1976). Beginning writing: It's all in the mind. *Language Arts, 53,* 652–657.

Plante, E., Swisher, L., Kiernan, B., & Restrepo, M. (1993). Language matches: Illuminating or confounding? *Journal of Speech and Hearing Research, 36,* 772–776.

Ragno, N., Toth, M., & Gray, B. (1993). *World of language.* Morristown, NJ: Silver Burdett Ginn.

Rees, N. (1974). The speech pathologist and the reading process. *Asha, 16,* 255–258.

Reutzel, D.R. (1986). The reading basal: A sentence combining composing book. *The Reading Teacher, 39,* 194–199.

Roth, F., & Spekman, N.J. (1989). The oral syntactic proficiency of learning disabled students: A spontaneous story sampling analysis. *Journal of Speech and Hearing Research, 32*, 67–77.

Rubin, H., Patterson, P., & Kantor, M. (1991). Morphological development and writing ability in children and adults. *Language, Speech, and Hearing Services in Schools, 22*, 228–235.

Scarborough, H.S. (1990). Index of productive syntax. *Applied Psycholinguistics, 11*, 1–22.

Scarborough, H.S., & Dobrich, W. (1990). Development of children with early language delay. *Journal of Speech and Hearing Research, 33*, 70–83.

Scott, C. (1988). Spoken and written syntax. In M. Nippold (Ed.), *Later language development: Ages nine through nineteen* (pp. 49–95). San Diego: College-Hill Press.

Scott, C. (1989). Learning to write: Context, form, and process. In A. Kamhi & H. Catts (Eds.), *Reading disabilities: A developmental language perspective* (pp. 261–302). Boston: College-Hill Press.

Scott, C. (1994). A discourse continuum for school-age students: Impact of modality and genre. In G. Wallach & K. Butler (Eds.), *Language learning disabilities in school-age children and adolescents: Some underlying principles and applications.* (pp. 219–252) Columbus, OH: Merrill Macmillan.

Scott, C., & Davidson, A. (1991, November). *Supported writing projects with LLD students: Process and products.* Paper presented at American Speech-Language-Hearing Association annual convention, Atlanta, GA.

Scott, C., & Klutsenbaker, K. (1989, November). *Comparing spoken and written summaries: Text structure and surface form.* Paper presented at the American Speech-Language-Hearing Association annual convention, St. Louis, MO.

Scott, C., & Rush, D. (1985). Teaching adverbial connectivity: Implications from current research. *Child Language Teaching and Therapy, 1*, 264–280.

Seidenberg, P. (1989). Relating text-processing research to reading and writing instruction for learning disabled students. *LD Focus, 5*, 4–12.

Skarakis-Doyle, E. (1985, November). *Complex sentences in a language disordered preadolescent: Language production.* Paper presented at the American Speech-Language-Hearing Association annual convention, Washington, D.C.

Skarakis-Doyle, E., & Mentis, M. (1991). A discourse approach to language disorders: Investigating complex sentence production. In T.M. Gallagher (Ed.), *Pragmatics of language: Clinical practice issues* (pp. 283–305). San Diego: Singular Publishing Group.

Stark, R., & Tallal, P. (1981). Selection of children with specific language deficits. *Journal of Speech and Hearing Disorders, 46*, 114–122.

Tyack, D. (1981). Teaching complex sentences. *Language, Speech, and Hearing Services in Schools, 12*, 49–56.

Westby, C. (1989). Assessing and remediating text comprehension problems. In A. Kamhi & H. Catts (Eds.), *Reading disabilities: A developmental language perspective* (pp. 199–259). Boston: College-Hill Press.

Westby, C. (1994). Communication refinement in school age and adolescence. In W.O. Haynes & B.B. Shulman (Eds.), *Communication development: Foundations, processes, and clinical applications* (pp. 341–383). Englewood Cliffs, NJ: Prentice Hall.

Wiig, E., & Semel, E. (1984). *Language assessment and intervention for the learning disabled.* Columbus, OH: Charles E. Merrill.

Wilkinson, P., & Patty, D. (1993). The effects of sentence combining on reading comprehension of fourth grade students. *Research in the Training of English, 27*, 104–125.

Yerrill, K. (1977). *A consideration of the later development of children's syntax in speech and writing: A study of parenthetical, appositional, and related items.* Unpublished doctoral thesis, University of Newcastle-upon-Tyne, UK.

6

Improving Narrative Abilities

Whole Language and Language Skills Approaches

Ron Gillam, Teresa U. McFadden, and Anne van Kleeck

A̅s THE BASICS OF LANGUAGE development at the sentence level have become better understood, efforts have turned to describing children's ability to communicate by connecting sentences together. One approach to studying these larger linguistic units, or texts, has been to focus on children's narratives—their real or imaginary reports of "what happened" (Lahey, 1988, p. 267). To date, we have learned a great deal about the course of typical and atypical narrative development, and we have begun to propose clinical procedures for fostering narration in children with language disorders.

As is often the case for language intervention in general, most suggestions for fostering the narrative abilities of children with language disorders have not been tested empirically. The study reported in this chapter provides a preliminary attempt to break this pattern by comparing the impact that two approaches to facilitating narrative skills had on the production of children's spoken and written narratives. One of these interventions had a meaning emphasis; we refer to it as the whole language approach. The other intervention had a form emphasis and is referred to as the language skills approach.

Prior to reporting on this study, we discuss: 1) why educators need to be concerned with the narrative development of children with language disorders, 2) the rationale underlying the two different approaches that were compared, and 3) what different kinds of measures of narration can tell us about the nature of typical and atypical development. After we summarize the findings of our investigation, we conclude the chapter with a discussion of the potential educational implications of our results and our thoughts about directions for future research.

Preparation of this chapter was partially supported by a grant from the National Institute on Deafness and Other Communication Disorders (1K08 DC00086-01) to the first author. Special thanks to Kathy Hauswirth and Ilene Morford,who worked with the first author in collaborative speech-language/learning disabilities resource rooms, and to the students and teachers at East and West Elementary Schools in Douglas, Wyoming.

WHY IS NARRATIVE DEVELOPMENT IMPORTANT?

It has been shown that narrative abilities affect children's performance in such classroom activities as show-and-tell, sharing time, and storytelling (e.g., Hicks, 1991; Michaels, 1981). While these kinds of activities may be important, the need to consider the narrative skills of children with language delays extends far beyond helping them tell better stories or provide better descriptions during show-and-tell contexts. Narrative skills may affect academic success in a more pervasive manner by providing a critical bridge to print literacy.

Learning to read and write involves figuring out how sounds relate to letters, how letters relate to words, and how letter shapes are produced and combined to represent words and sentences. However, literacy development goes beyond mastering the mechanics of speech-to-print relationships. Literacy entails the construction of personal and communal meanings through reading and writing. Enjoying and writing stories is one major catalyst for reading and writing instruction, and learners need to have a basic knowledge of the conceptual organization and linguistic conventions that are involved in narration if they are to become successful readers and writers.

Narrative development may affect academic success at an even more basic level. Scholars in a number of disciplines have proposed that narratives form the foundation of human thinking. Howard (1991), for example, claimed that "when we think, we do so by fitting story themes to the experience we wish to understand" (p. 189). In a similar vein, Bruner (1986) suggested that narrative is pervasive in daily thought and dominates over paradigmatic, scientific thought styles.

Finally, narratives are important to children's social development because they are an integral aspect of conversation in mainstream culture. As Deese (1983) noted, by having at its core the telling of experience, narration encompasses much of our daily social interaction. A study by Preece (1987) supported the important role of narration in children's social interactions. In this study, three children between the ages of 5 and 7 regularly produced narrative forms in conversations that were recorded during an 18-month observation period.

For a variety of culural, experiential, and developmental reasons, some students have less knowledge than others of the language forms and organizational devices that are typical of narrative discourse. Children with language disorders, for example, frequently present deficiencies in understanding and/or using the sentence-level form–content interactions that serve as the basis for both conversational and literary discourse. These deficiencies place children with language disorders at an immediate disadvantage upon entering the formal educational setting. The language-intensive nature of what is to be learned, as well as the means for teaching it, practically ensures that their speaking and listening difficulties will become involved in cause-and-effect relationships with reading and writing difficulties. Furthermore, it seems logical to suggest that problems in spoken and written narration might reflect an underlying difficulty with using narration in the service of thought, a basic problem that could have a profound impact on numerous aspects of academic achievement and social acceptance.

TWO APPROACHES TO LANGUAGE EDUCATION AND THEIR IMPACT ON NARRATIVE DEVELOPMENT

How should we facilitate the development of narrative skills in children with language disorders? Do these children need more experience with producing meaningful narratives, or do they need to be systematically taught the language skills that underlie narration? This is an important pedagogical issue that mirrors questions about the differential effects of teaching methods for early reading instruction. In reading instruction, there is a raging controversy about the relative benefits of literacy education that emphasizes reading for meaning as children are immersed in literacy (a whole language approach) versus literacy education that involves direct instruction in the formal skills that are believed to underlie reading (a code emphasis or phonics approach). As with the reading pedagogy controversy, there are compelling rationales for both whole language (experiential/ meaning emphasis) and language skills (direct instruction/form emphasis) approaches to language education.

Rationale for the Whole Language Approach

Whole language is a philosophy of education that seeks to promote simultaneous development in areas of curriculum that are traditionally taught separately. Whole language education is predicated on two main assumptions. The first assumption is that interrelating speaking, reading, writing, and listening activities around a common theme benefits the development of language form and content in all communicative modalities (e.g., Goodman, 1986; Harste, Woodward, & Burke, 1984; Newman, 1985). The second assumption is that learning processes such as engagement, demonstration, creation, experimentation, inquiry, imagination, and reflection are critical aspects of educational experiences (Harste et al., 1984; Rich, 1985; Watson, 1989). In a meaning-oriented curriculum, students choose among books and activities, explore multiple interpretations of stories, take responsibility for their own pace of learning, self-monitor their performance, critically examine each other's writing, and share their work with a variety of audiences.

In traditional curricula, children often are expected to work quietly by themselves or to participate in teacher-led discussions that feature a great deal of teacher talk and relatively little child talk. Whole language curricula, in contrast, operate from the premise that children develop various language abilities best by using language. As such, lots of child talk is encouraged. Children listen to and read stories and engage in extensive discussions about them. They also enact and retell stories.

Together with discussion, narratives are the major currency of the whole language approach, and they are used in the service of real communicative situations. Narrative development itself is very likely to be enhanced along with the other aspects of language and literacy development that whole language curricula are designed to support. In this approach, it is assumed that when activities are meaningful and relevant to children they will be motivated to communicate, and they will seek out the needed language forms to do so. Therefore, their need to convey meaning in narratives serves as the catalyst for developing the forms necessary for adequate text construction.

In the whole language approach used in our study, children were immersed in narratives by being read aloud to frequently, by reading to each other, by engaging in extensive discussions before and after stories were read, by enacting stories, by writing stories, and by using children's literature as a basis for creative expression in other media such as art, music, and dance. The narratives they practiced in a variety of spoken contexts served as the basis for their written compositions.

The uses of language that are promoted in whole language approaches—particularly the focus on having classroom conversations about children's literature—gain further support from the research on narrative development (Martinez & Teale, 1989; McCabe & Peterson, 1991; Teale, 1984; Wells, 1986). This research indicates that conversations in general, and conversations about books in particular, are important contexts for narrative development. At the most fundamental level, oral conversations are the earliest form of texts. In addition, personal event narratives are fostered in social conversations, and imaginative narratives are fostered in conversations surrounding books. We examine each of these research areas in more detail.

First, it is in the context of early conversations that mainstream culture children learn the essence of text construction, which is that contributions should be semantically related. Shugar (1978), in fact, discusses how dyadic interactions between mother and children create text. In other words, children first learn to relate sequential sentences semantically by connecting them to the sentences of others in conversations. They participate in dyadically constructed texts before they produce them independently as "single authors" (Heath, 1983; McCabe, 1991; McCabe & Peterson, 1991). This process makes conversational development a critical step in the development of all types of textual language, including narratives. Indeed, numerous researchers have demonstrated the need for social interaction in the development of narrative abilities (e.g., Hudson & Shapiro, 1991; Preece, 1987; Rubin & Wolf, 1979; Sachs, 1980; Snow & Goldfield, 1981; Vygotsky, 1978).

The second area of relevant research indicates that oral conversations are the first context in which mainstream culture children learn to produce personal narratives that report past experiences.[1] Early on, a parent may prompt the child to report an event that they both experienced to a third party who was not present. So, Dad may say, "Tell your Mom what we saw at the grocery store." If the child falters, Dad will often prompt and add information to the child's tale in a variety of ways. Indeed, whether they were present at the event being reported or not, parents often assist their children in producing personal narratives, thereby compensating for the children's immature memories, linguistic abilities, and listener adaptation skills (e.g., McCabe & Peterson, 1991; Sachs, 1983; van Kleeck & Swofford-Berg, 1981). The scaffolding that is provided by adult assistance is gradually withdrawn as children develop sophisticated language forms necessary for embedding increasingly complex narratives into their own conversations.

The third research finding supporting the use of a whole language approach in narrative intervention is that, at an early age, mainstream culture children are exposed to imaginative narratives in oral conversations about pictures and storybooks (Heath, 1982; Scollon & Scollon, 1981; Snow, 1983; van Kleeck, Hamilton, & McMahon, 1992; Wells, 1986).[2] In interactive storybook reading, both the adult "reader" and the child "listener" question and comment freely on information presented in the text and pictures of a book. As in other types of conversation, dialogue surrounding books occurs as adults and children participate jointly in "the construction of a complex text" (Martinez & Teale, 1989, p. 126).

Adult scaffolding in interactive book reading marks "the relevant categories of information" (Snow & Goldfield, 1981, p. 132) that children eventually need to include in their own imaginative narratives, such as settings, characters, problems, motivations for actions, and resolutions. Also, adults model ways that narrators can express, react to, and evaluate these relevant categories of information. As children mature in their ability to process forms that convey larger chunks of semantically related information and, thus, need less help in comprehending extended texts, adults read longer sections of books and expect children to sit and listen (e.g., Heath, 1980; Teale, 1984). There is some evidence that children with language disorders learn about the relative differences between spoken and written language from listening to stories (Gillam & Johnston, 1992).

Proponents of whole language approaches stress the commonalties of narratives in spoken and written modalities. Both spoken and written narratives are composed of connected sentences. Additionally, narratives in both modes use language that is decontextualized (Harste et al., 1984; Westby, 1984). Because the narrator's job is to create context with words rather than with actions and surroundings, information presented in spoken and written narratives must be made

---

[1]Westby (1989b) reviews work showing that personal narratives rarely occur in the Mexican-American, Chinese-American, and African-American communities that have been studied. However, reporting what has happened to others is frequent in these groups, and these reports undoubtedly play the same role in narrative development as personal narratives.

[2]Mexican-American and Chinese-American families tend to read or tell stories about people and historical events, while storybooks have been nearly absent in African-American working-class households in studies reviewed by Westby (1989b).

explicit if the narrator is to adapt appropriately to the listener or the reader. Thus, learning to get and give meaning via language alone, rather than from a combination of language and the shared nonlinguistic context, likely has roots in early experiences with listening to and telling personal and imagined stories.

Rationale for the Language Skills Approach

Children with language disorders frequently present problems with language form at the basic level of sentence formulation. Thus, it should come as no surprise that they present problems with many of the skills that are involved in creating cohesive and coherent narratives. For this reason, it is possible that direct instruction in the "nuts and bolts" of narrative construction—basic skills underlying listening, speaking, reading, and writing—might be the most efficacious way to facilitate the development of narration in these children.

In a language skills curriculum, educators systematically teach the subskills that are believed to enable students to comprehend stories (through listening or reading) and to produce stories (through speaking or writing). Language skills education is founded on the assumption that explicitly teaching the discrete skills that comprise a task is more effective than implicitly teaching these skills as they happen to arise. Proponents of language skills approaches to education believe that literacy processes such as letter knowledge, phonemic segmentation, graphophonic analysis, sound blending, and spelling are best taught by separately concentrating on specific aspects of listening, speaking, reading, and writing.

Language skills instruction typically involves procedures such as task analysis, subskill teaching, and mastery learning. A didactic style of teaching is used in which teachers and speech-language pathologists (SLPs) specify instructional objectives, teach the steps that lead to specific skills, and provide numerous opportunities for children to practice the skills that have been taught. Teacher talk tends to consist of explanations and questions; student talk tends to consist of responses to questions and requests for clarification. Conversations between students are not a routine aspect of language skills curricula.

Interactional models of cognitive processing often are used as theoretical support for language skills approaches. These models of cognition posit higher-level meaning structures that exchange information with lower-level perceptual structures during the cognitive activities that are involved in listening, speaking, reading, and writing.

For example, interactional theories of reading (Adams, 1989; Just & Carpenter, 1980; McClelland, 1986; Stanovich, 1984) suggest that successful reading involves a number of levels of knowledge (visual feature, letter, word, syntax, and semantics) that simultaneously affect each other. However, these simultaneous interactions are not believed to occur until children are capable of reading independently. In order for that to happen, it is thought that they must first learn phonological decoding skills, which are believed to depend on phonological awareness skills (Stanovich, 1986). In support of this theory of development and the language skills approach to education, research reported by Ball and Blachman (1991), Ehri and Wilce (1985), and Lundberg, Frost, and Peterson (1988) indicates that teaching students how to perform phonological awareness tasks influences positively the development of word identification abilities (see also Fey, Catts, & Larrivee, chap. 1, this volume). However, word identification abilities are only a small subset of the abilities that underlie fluent reading.

According to the language skills model, speech-language pathologists and other educators who want to improve the narrative abilities of children with language disorders should teach the skills that underlie narration directly. The approach to language skills education reported in our study involved explicit instruction on such skills as phonological analysis and synthesis, sound-letter correspondences (phonics), vocabulary, grammar, reading comprehension, spelling, and writing mechanics. Children worked on spoken language abilities (e.g., comprehension, production, and appropriate use of vocabulary and grammar) with a speech-language pathologist. In separate activities in a separate room, children worked on the basics of literacy (e.g., graphophonic analysis, reading comprehension, spelling, writing conventions) with a resource room teacher. Students were given the opportunity to integrate these skills in meaning-based tasks that were designed to tap text comprehension (e.g., answering questions about short reading passages) and production (e.g., writing paragraphs and short stories). However, in nearly all other teaching activities, the meaning of narratives was subordinate to the focus on form.

There are numerous political differences between the philosophies that underlie whole language and language skills approaches to education, and proponents on both sides have trumpeted these differences in their battles for public support. We have neither the inclination nor the space to delve into that subject. In addition, we do not discuss the variety of theories and educational practices that fall within the general categories of whole language and language skills models.

We have tried to show that there are good reasons why educators might decide to use either a whole language or a language skills approach to language education, and we have argued that both approaches could result in improved narrative abilities in children with language disorders. Having explained the foundations for the two approaches to language education that are compared in our study, we now turn to a discussion of the types of measures that have been used to evaluate spoken and written narratives in previous research.

MEASURING NARRATIVE ABILITIES

Researchers and clinicians who are interested in extra-sentential language (narratives, discussions, conversations, and explanations) employ assessment measures that are sensitive to textual language development. There are a variety of measurement approaches that emphasize different aspects of narration. Three types of measures, story grammar analysis, form analysis, and cohesion analysis, are used frequently to evaluate the narratives of children with and without language disorders. Three other types of measures, high point, stanza and refrain, and holistic scoring, are less well known and generally have not been used in evaluating the narratives of children with language disorders. The following section briefly describes each of these approaches, how they have contributed to our understanding of normal development, and how they have been used to evaluate narratives produced by children with language disorders.

Story Grammar Analysis

Story grammar analysis (Mandler & Johnson, 1977; Peterson & McCabe, 1983; Stein & Glenn, 1979) and plot analysis (Botvin & Sutton-Smith, 1977; Gillam & Johnston, 1992) provide information about the episodic organization and causal relations of propositions in a text. These analyses examine how narrators weave a variety of content elements (e.g., characters, initiating events, internal responses, reactions) into episodes. These analyses are oriented toward what has been described as the universal content of narratives: the protagonist's goals and their expression, the protagonist's efforts to achieve these goals, and the outcomes of such efforts (Mandler, Scribner, Cole, & DeForest, 1980).

Narratives develop from a succession of thematically united utterances to stories with sequences of events that follow a familiar chronology (Applebee, 1978; Peterson & McCabe, 1983; Sutton-Smith, 1986). Children's earliest personal narratives and stories (which usually emerge by age 2½) show no episodic organization and carry little in the way of comprehensible referential information. Botvin and Sutton-Smith (1977) found that these earliest narratives consisted of disorganized, associatively connected events that were related to particular themes. Utterances describing these events were primarily composed of juxtaposed nouns.

After 3 years of age, however, the referential component of narratives becomes more apparent. Syntactic and semantic development, together with development of knowledge about episode structure, makes childrens' narratives much more understandable to adults. In mature story forms, referential information is presented in one or more episodes that contain complicating or disequilibrating events and goal-directed resolutions.

Stories that contain causal relations and problems that are resolved emerge in the later preschool years and are clearly established by 8 years of age (Botvin & Sutton-Smith, 1977; Peterson & McCabe, 1983). The ability to produce stories and personal narratives with complete and embedded episodes continues to develop through the age of 14 years (Roth & Spekman, 1986).

Story grammar analysis and plot analysis have been used to compare narratives produced by children with and without language disorders. An early narrative recall study by Graybeal (1981) showed that children with language disorders recalled less than their age-matched peers, but showed no differences in accuracy, organization, or temporal ordering. Hierarchical story grammar relations and coherent story progression have been documented in narratives produced by children with language disorders, but their episodes are shorter and less elaborate, setting and character information is reduced, and less attention is given to attempts, plans, and internal responses (Gillam, 1989; Gillam & Johnston, 1992; Liles, 1985; Merritt & Liles, 1987; Roth & Spekman, 1986, 1989).

Form Analysis and Cohesion Analysis

Form analysis and cohesion analysis have been collapsed into one section because of the overlapping nature of grammar and cohesion and their mutual attention to such aspects of language as conjunction and pronoun use. The use of cohesion in English is best described in the seminal work of Halliday and Hasan (1976). Cohesion involves both sentence structures and word choices and their relationship to preceding and succeeding utterances (endophorphic reference) or nonlinguistic context (exophoric reference). Halliday and Hasan define four types of cohesion: conjunction cohesion (e.g., forms such as and, then, and but, and adverbials such as next, therefore), reference cohesion (e.g., pronouns, demonstratives), lexical and structural parallelism (e.g., repetition of a word) and ellipsis (i.e., omission of an item retrievable from elsewhere in the text). Successful use of cohesion involves the use of a variety of references that are placed strategically in order to convey the author's meaning clearly and unambiguously.

There have been numerous studies of textual cohesion devices in children's narratives (e.g., Bennett-Kastor, 1981, 1984; Karmiloff-Smith, 1981; Klecan-Aker & Hedrick, 1985; Martin, 1983). A recurrent finding in these studies has been the developmental move from exophoric or context-dependent cohesion (e.g., a child points in order to clarify the referent for the listener) to endorphic or "within the text" reference (e.g., the entire burden for clarifying the referent is in the language). As would be expected, the development of discourse cohesion recapitulates the order of logical relations found in sentence development (moving from additive to temporal to causal logical relations).

By 8 years of age, children can provide generally clear and coherent narratives (Pelligrini, Galdo, & Rubin, 1984), but sophistication in the use of cohesion continues to develop through adolescence (Klecan-Aker & Hedrick, 1985; Yde & Spoelders, 1985). Development involves increases in the frequency and variety of forms and the distance between cohesive ties (Bennett-Kastor, 1984) as well as further reductions in ambiguity (Klecan-Aker & Hedrick, 1985).

Compared to their chronological age peers, many children who have language disorders have been shown to have difficulties with grammar, repairs, and the use of cohesive devices in narrative contexts (Gillam & Johnston, 1992; Liles, 1985, 1987; Liles & Purcell, 1987; MacLachlan & Chapman, 1988; Purcell & Liles, 1992; Scott, chap. 5, this volume). Stories produced by children with language disorders often contain fewer words and sentences (Gillam & Johnston, 1992; Liles, 1985; Merritt & Liles, 1987; Roth & Spekman, 1986,

1989) than those of their peers. There may be fewer complex sentences and more mazes (false starts, repetitions, or reformulations), and their sentences are more likely to contain grammatical errors than sentences contained in stories produced by typically achieving children of the same age. These difficulties may be exacerbated by the demands of creating coherent, episodic structure. Errors occur more often at interepisodic junctions where children must coordinate two episodes (Liles, 1987).

Why Go Beyond Story Grammar Analysis, Form Analysis, and Cohesion Analysis?

Story grammar, form, and cohesion analyses have provided valuable insights into the narrative abilities of typically developing children and children with language-learning impairments. However, narratives are more than descriptions of settings and episodes with cohesively linked and grammatically well-formed sequences of propositions. Narratives are produced in context, for present or implied audiences (Bakhtin, 1986). Narratives also are produced with perspective or voice (Labov, 1972; Polanyi, 1989). The art of narrative—the achievement of suspense, mystery, curiosity, and emotional involvement—is realized through skillful manipulation of language and textual organization (Brewer, 1985). How are charm, interest, clarity, vigor, honesty, appropriateness, freshness, subtlety, or depth analyzed? Three approaches that consider some of these aspects of narrative and that generally have not been explored in the field of child language disorders are high point analysis (Labov, 1972), stanza and refrain analysis (Gee, 1991), and holistic scoring (Diederich, 1974; Myers, 1980). These diverse approaches to narratives provide additional and different insights into the nature of a child's story.

High Point Analysis

High point analysis was developed by Labov (1972) and further refined by Kernan (1977) through the examination of the narratives of both African-American and European-American children and adolescents. High point analysis focuses on the point of the tale (i.e., how clever, brave, or clumsy the protagonist was) and how this point is transmitted to the listener through the structure and content of the narrative. Narrative is seen as a performance in which the narrator focuses on the artistic form of the story, its climax (or "high point"), and the maintenance of audience comprehension and interest.

Components such as introductions, abstracts, evaluations, and codas (summing up) are used to separate the narrative from the ongoing discourse, to indicate climactic moments, and to transmit personal meaning. Components such as orientations, complications, and resolutions are similar to the settings, disequilibriums, and resolutions of story grammar analyses, but differ in the sensitivity to the intentions of the speaker and the needs of the listener (e.g., "My brother

Tom said..." provides setting information but would be considered unnecessary orientation information if the child were speaking to her mother). Paralinguistic (e.g., gesture and stress) and contextual features (e.g., who the audience is) are considered in addition to linguistic production. Because of the emphasis on personal meaningfulness, these approaches have been applied more often to personal than fictional narratives (but they can be used for either type).

Prior to the age of 3, children produce stories that are characterized by distinct prosody and rhyme. Applebee (1978) and Sutton-Smith (1986) have described stories such as the example below as "verse stories."

> Tessie May come
> Come round here
> Come dum
> Da-dum, da-dum
> da-dum
> (Sutton-Smith, 1986, p. 4)

Because young children often appear to be carried along by the poetic power of their performance, they may have little control over the form that their verse stories take. With age and experience, event sequences and character dialogue gradually take the place of prosody as the major integrator of performance (Sutton-Smith, 1986). Nevertheless, stories that are produced during make-believe play often are accompanied by a singsong cadence that is typical of verse stories (Giffin, 1984).

Awareness of audience is an important factor in the development of narrative performance. Three-year-old children do not show clear awareness of listener needs, do not tie their narratives into ongoing conversation, and do not provide introductions or codas (Umiker-Sebeok, 1977). They do, however, provide evaluative information that conveys how they feel about the events they are talking about (e.g., "And I was scared to come in."). Between 3 and 4 years of age, listener awareness improves significantly, as indicated by the use of introductions and orientations and better integration of stories into conversation.

By 6 years of age, most children tell personal narratives that conform to Labov's (1972) description of what makes a good story (Peterson & McCabe, 1983). Six-year-olds provide complicating action, problems that are evaluated in some way, resolutions, and, sometimes, endings (the components of a classic plot). Furthermore, 6-year-olds appear to be aware of audience needs because they appropriately orient their listeners to who, what, where, and when events in their personal narratives take place.

Development between ages 7 and 14 is marked by an increasing concern for the successful transmission of the point of the tale in relationship to the needs of the audience (Kernan, 1977; Labov, 1972). Evaluation is conveyed increasingly through implicit (e.g., "I said, 'Oh my God, here it is!' ") rather than explicit (e.g., "It was really quite terrific!") messages. Changes in performance aspects of narrative occur into adulthood (Labov, 1972). Specifically, adults develop the ability to contrast actual events with other potential but unrealized events (e.g., "That child knew more than I did. If I had not listened to him, I would have been lost for hours."). These contrasts often involve the kinds of complex syntactic constructions that increase in frequency and sophistication of use between the ages of 10 years and adulthood (Labov, 1972).

Sleight and Prinz (1985) applied some aspects of high point analysis to the narratives of children with and without language-learning disorders. In examining the use of abstracts, orientations, and codas, the researchers found lower rates of use of some types of orientations among children with language-learning disorders. Liles and Purcell (1987) examined the ability of children with language disorders to modify their narratives to suit audiences that were either naive or informed. The typically achieving group, unlike the group with language disorders, increased the number of complete episodes for their naive listeners. Liles (1987) suggested that this difference was due to the inability of the children with language disorders to produce more complex stories rather than their lack of awareness of listener needs. Evidence for this conclusion came from these children's increase in the number of clauses and the use of personal reference as a cohesive marker with naive listeners. Further support for this explanation comes from Liles and Purcell (1987). These investigators found that both a control group and a group of children with language disorders repaired errors of meaning more often than errors of grammar when they repaired verbal errors in their narratives.

Stanza and Refrain Analysis

Gee provides another analysis approach, referred to as stanza and refrain analysis. This method focuses on the rhythm and pattern of stories (Gee, 1991; Hicks, 1991; Silliman, Aurilio, & Nitzberg, 1992). Utterances are grouped into lines, stanzas, and refrains to show the patterns and artistry involved in narrative production. Significant themes as well as cultural patterns of storytelling emerge when narratives are analyzed in this way. Gee's method has been applied to both European-American and African-American narratives, and it is well-suited to poetic styles of storytelling. Although this method has not been used to compare the narratives of children with and without language disorders, Silliman et al. (1992) provided a cogent example of the new insights made possible by this approach by showing the poetic command of narrative achieved by an African-American student. His story appeared to be highly deficient and disorganized from a story grammar perspective, but it appeared to be quite sophisticated from a stanza and refrain perspective. Thus narrative success can occur on one or more different levels that are not necessarily interrelated.

Holistic Scoring

Holistic scoring arose out of a need to provide a reliable way of evaluating the overall quality of written compositions (Diederich, 1974) and is frequently used in regular education. In holistic scoring, raters assign a single score to a narrative that indicates the rater's overall impression of its quality. Judgments are based on comparisons between the narrative and stories of predetermined quality. The details of carrying out holistic scoring vary across authors (e.g., Diederich, 1974; Kirby & Liner, 1981; Myers, 1980), but the essential aspects involve forming initial impressions of stories, selecting prototypes (called anchors), collaborating with a group of raters on descriptions (called rubrics), and rating a group of stories. By focusing on general impressions formed from thinking about stories as wholes and by attempting to describe aspects of stories that are considered to be strong or weak, educators can arrive at new insights into a learner's conceptual and language processes, as well as into their understanding of what makes a good story.

To date, holistic scoring has not been reported in studies of narrative production by children with language disorders. However, this analysis shows considerable potential as a reliable means of qualitative assessment and as a way to evaluate progress. An application of this procedure is given later in this chapter.

Telling versus Writing Narratives

The content and form of narratives are affected by the mode of expression. The immediacy of speaking and the permanency of writing make for different narrative styles. Written narratives are associated with a decontextualized, explicit, and formal style of language while spoken narratives are more contextualized, implicit, and casual. Additionally, written narratives are integrated with a smooth delivery (if read) and with large idea units while spoken narratives contain more fragmentation with pauses, fillers, repetitions, and rephrasings.

Even spoken and written narratives elicited in school settings, which might be expected to take on the more formal characteristics of written language, show these differences in organization and structure (Chafe & Danielewicz, 1987). In their study of elementary school–age children, Gillam and Johnston (1992) found that spoken narratives contained longer sentences and more connectives than written narratives. However, linkages between problems and resolutions within episodes were more likely to be left unspecified in children's spoken, as compared to written, narratives. Gillam and Johnston reported that this led to diffusely organized spoken texts, with organizational strengths occurring at the sentence level (i.e., better clausal cohesion). The organizational strengths of written narratives, with a higher proportion of linked episode components, primarily occurred at the textual level (i.e., better story coherence and more elaborate plots).

The development of written narratives appears to follow the same general pattern as the development of spoken narratives. Just as with spoken narratives, children produce written narratives that contain action and incomplete episodes before they begin to create complete episodes (Freedman, 1987; Guthrie, 1984). There is a lag, however, in comparison to spoken language. Freedman reports that only half of the grade-five students in his study achieved the level of plot-development in written narratives that all of the 7-year-olds in the Botvin and Sutton-Smith (1977) study achieved orally.

The development of written narration continues throughout the school years, with the percentage of stories that include at least one episode increasing through the twelfth grade. During adolescence, children's speaking and writing become increasingly differentiated as written narratives become longer, more coherent, and better organized in comparison to spoken narratives (Daiute, 1989; Kroll, 1981; Perera, 1984).

Only one study (Gillam & Johnston, 1992) has evaluated relationships between spoken and written narratives of children with language disorders. These researchers assessed the cognitive, linguistic, and literacy factors underlying spoken and written narration of children between the ages of 9 and 12 with language disorders and three groups of typically achieving children. The children with language disorders were significantly weaker than age-, language-, and reading-matched controls in the use of complex linguistic forms in both spoken and written narratives. The children with language disorders also presented more grammatical errors in both modalities, with an especially high proportion of errors in their written stories.

Gillam and Johnston argued that factors specific to the writing process (e.g., mechanical, cognitive, or some combination of the two) probably underlie differences in the ways school-age children organize the form and content of their spoken and written stories. Further, they demonstrated that relationships between spoken and written language in children with language disorders are similar to those found in typically achieving children. Like typically achieving children and adults, children with language disorders used more subordinated and embedded clauses in their writing than in their speech. However, they made more errors on these kinds of constructions than they did on simple or coordinated clauses, a fact that at first glance made their written language look less competent than their spoken language.

Summary

Narration is clearly a revealing linguistic arena. The complexities of dealing simultaneously with lexical choices, sentential relations, and textual organization present important challenges for children with language disorders, challenges that must be addressed in order for these students to meet the increasingly demanding linguistic requirements of academic curricula in the later elementary grades.

Knowing that narration involves the integration of language form and meaning in complex ways, it is reasonable to question whether efforts to facilitate narrative development should emphasize form or meaning. The inclination might be to answer, "Both," and it is clearly the case that increasing knowledge and use of developmentally appropriate form–content interactions is the ultimate goal of most language intervention programs (Fey, 1986). However, few intervention procedures place equal emphasis on both form and meaning, and such a broad approach might initially overwhelm children who experience language-learning problems. It seems that many of the language intervention approaches that have been proposed in the literature begin with a form emphasis or a meaning emphasis and work toward form–content interactions. Is the best initial catalyst for narrative development, then, a focus on form or meaning? The following study was designed as a preliminary investigation into this issue.

NARRATIVES OF STUDENTS WHO RECEIVED
WHOLE LANGUAGE OR LANGUAGE SKILLS INTERVENTION

To evaluate the effects that form-focused and meaning-focused language intervention have on the development of narration, we compared postintervention spoken and written narratives produced by two matched groups of students with language disorders. One group had attended a combined speech-language/learning disability classroom that utilized a whole language approach to language intervention. Language intervention consistent with whole language tenets has been discussed extensively in the recent literature (Gillam, 1991, in press; Norris & Damico, 1990; Norris & Hoffman, 1993; Westby & Costlow, 1991). This language intervention is essentially a meaning-focused enterprise. The other group of students with language disorders had received form-focused direct instruction in basic spoken and written language skills. Goals from the students' individualized education programs (IEPs) are compared in Table 1.

Subjects

Eight children with language disorders between the ages of 9 and 12 years ($M=$ 10;10) participated in the study (Table 2). All of these children presented normal nonverbal cognitive abilities (quotients above 90) as measured by the Test of Nonverbal Intelligence (Brown, Sherbenou, & Johnsen, 1982) together with depressed language abilities (quotients below 85) as indicated by performance on the Detroit Tests of Learning Aptitude–2 (Hammill, 1985). In addition, all eight children had been diagnosed as having learning disabilities by school district child study teams using the criteria of their state (1.5 SD or greater discrepancy between intellectual ability and academic achievement).

The eight subjects represented a subset of the total students in each intervention setting and were selected because they were reasonably well matched for age, verbal intelligence, reading, and writing abilities 2 years prior to data collection and for nonverbal intelligence and degree of language disorder at the time of data collection (Table 2). Four subjects had received all of their special education assistance in a whole language setting for a period of no less than 2 consecutive years (whole language group). The other four students had attended language skills programs for an equivalent period (language skills group).

Table 1. Examples of IEP goals for subjects who received whole language or language skills instruction

Spoken language instruction

Whole language: Brandon will tell fictional stories that contain two or more complete episodes. (Productive criterion: noted on 5 separate occasions)

Language skills: Kelli will provide multiple pieces of personal information (including first and last name, address, age, school, grade, birthdate, brothers, sisters, pets) in response to questioning by at least two different adults (clinician, teacher, parent) with no prompting.

Writing instruction

Whole language: Brandon will make sentence- and text-level changes to original stories after conferring with a peer and a teacher (productive criterion: noted on three separate occasions).

Language skills: Kelli will write sentences using correct capitalization and punctuation where necessary with 90%–100% accuracy.

Reading comprehension instruction

Whole language: Brandon will contribute information about settings, characters, motivations, problems, and solutions from stories that he reads during book discussions. (Knowledge will be demonstrated in each category on two separate occasions.)

Language skills: Kelli will sequence sentences to create a story. Given five sentences, Kelli will number each sentence in correct sequence with 90%–100% accuracy.

Word analysis instruction

Whole language: Brandon will use knowledge of word order relationships, meaning relationships, phonics, graphic construction, and textual relations to predict words that he has indicated that he is unsure of. (Productive criterion: 80% accuracy observed on three separate occasions)

Language skills: Kelli will be able to identify the vowel diphthongs *au, aw, oi, ou, ow,* and *oy.* Given 20 groups of three words each, Kelli will select the vowel diphthongs in each group that have the same sound with 85%–100% accuracy.

Spelling instruction

Whole language: Brandon will circle words he believes may be misspelled in original writing pieces, look them up in the dictionary, and correct them if necessary. (Productive criterion: 90% of his misspellings will be corrected in three separate stories).

Language skills: Kelli will be able to do daily assignments within his third-grade spelling text with 85%–100% accuracy.

Unfortunately, it was not possible to match students on number of hours spent in special services programs each week. Students in the language skills group spent, on average, nearly 10 hours per week in resource room settings (4 hours more than students in the whole language group). The students in the whole language group averaged resource room assistance for approximately 2 hours on 3 days each week, a total of 6 hours.

Children's literature was used as the principal reading material in most of the classrooms in the school with the whole language resource room. Some teachers used basal texts as supplemental material, but basal readers and workbooks were not used as sole reading materials in any of the regular classrooms attended by the subjects in this study. All classrooms reserved time each day for sustained silent reading, sustained silent writing, and reading aloud. Staff mem-

Table 2. Mean values for subjects who received whole language or language skills instruction

| | Age in years[a] | Instruction hours[b] | Pre-intervention measures | | | | Postintervention measures |
			W-J[c] Reading	W-J[d] Writing	Verbal IQ[e]	TONI[f]	DTLA–2 quotient[g]
Whole Language	10;9	6*	453.8	455.2	83.5	101	74
Language Skills	10;11	9.7	467.5	454	87.8	108	77.5

[a]Chronological age at time of data collection.

[b]Instruction hours = number of hours per week in whole language or language skills programs as indicated on student's IEP (*excludes resource room hours for math assistance).

[c]W-J Reading = reading cluster score on the Woodcock-Johnson Psycho-Educational Achievement Battery (Woodcock & Johnson, 1977).

[d]W-J Writing = written language cluster score on the Woodcock-Johnson Psycho-Educational Achievement Battery.

[e]Verbal IQ = quotient from the verbal scale of the Wechsler Intelligence Scale for Children-Revised (WISC-R, Wechsler, 1974).

[f]TONI = quotient on the Test of Nonverbal Intelligence (TONI) (Brown, Sherbenou, & Johnsen, 1982).

[g]DTLA–2 quotient = verbal cluster quotient from the Detroit Tests of Learning Aptitude–2 (DTLA–2, Hammill, 1985).

bers were involved in teacher teams, which met regularly to develop integrated curriculum ideas.

A basal reading program with a phonics emphasis was used in all the classrooms that the language skills students attended, and the principal stressed the "back to basics" aspects of the school's curriculum. This is not to say that students in this school did not engage in meaningful reading or writing. It means only that instruction in language skills was emphasized more than generalized language arts experiences. One teacher explained the school's philosophy in this way: "We believe that students who have a firm background in phonics, written mechanics, and spelling will grow up to be better readers and writers."

Procedures

Whole Language Education

The first author collaborated with two learning disabilities resource room teachers in developing and implementing a meaning-based language intervention strategy to promote the development of interpersonal and academic communication. Children's literature served as the principal means for demonstrating lexical, sentential, and textual aspects language. In this whole language approach, language intervention activities took the form of literature responses in which students were encouraged to "revalue" (Goodman, 1986) themselves as language learners. Numerous aspects of this curriculum were designed to be consistent with whole language educational tenets and practices (see Gillam, 1994; Norris, 1993; Norris & Damico, 1990; Norris & Hoffman, 1993; Watson, 1989).

Book Selection To begin the sequence, teachers or students selected a book that demonstrated particular concepts (e.g., time or causality), content–

form interactions (e.g., adverbial clauses or causal subordination), or textual conventions (e.g., episode coordination or embedding) that had been targeted for intervention for a number of the students. When students selected demonstration books, they were empowered as learners because they were making important contributions to the classroom curriculum. When teachers selected demonstration books, their selection decisions were driven by their knowledge of the interests and needs of the students.

The use of predictable books has been advocated for facilitating reading development with beginning readers and with children who are at risk for learning problems (Heald-Taylor, 1987a, 1987b; Rhodes & Dudley-Marling, 1988). These books enable young readers to access the language, content, and sequence of a story quickly because they contain highly predictable features such as rhythm and rhyme, repeated or cumulative textual patterns, logical sequences, familiar scripts, and/or supportive illustrations.

Mirra Ginsburg's (1974) book, *Mushroom in the Rain,* is a predictable book that was used to demonstrate embedded episode structures. In this story, an ant crawls under a tiny mushroom to escape the rain. As it continues to rain, a mouse, then a butterfly, then a bird ask the ant to share his shelter. The animals even help a rabbit escape from a fox by making room for him under the mushroom. When the storm ends, the ant wonders how they all could fit under a mushroom that was once barely large enough for just himself. A helpful frog poses a question that leads the animals—and the reader—to the answer. This story contains a "rabbit escapes from fox" episode embedded within one of a series of "animals seek and find shelter during the rain" episodes that are embedded within a larger "mushroom growing during the rain" episode.

Pre-discussion Before reading the book, questions that promoted the activation of story-related schemata were presented to and discussed with the whole class. Students developed a list of predictions and questions about the book's content as they talked about the title, author, and illustrations. Examples of group discussion questions for *Mushroom in the Rain* include: "What do you think animals do when it rains?" "What are mushrooms?" "Would a mushroom make a very good shelter from the rain?" "What animals might be able to stay dry by getting under a mushroom?" "Is rain good for plants?" "Why?"

Read Aloud A predictable book was read aloud to the group at the conclusion of the schemata activation discussion. After a teacher read through the book, choral reading was used as an entry point for individual and paired reading experiences.

Each time students read or heard a book again, they increased their familiarity with the story structure and the language of the text. Greater familiarity with the book and its language increased the likelihood that students would incorporate the content and language into their literature-response activities. When multiple copies of books were available, students were free to refer to the books, take them home, take them to their regular classrooms, or read them with someone else in the group.

Book Discussion   After stories were read aloud two or more times, teachers held a postreading book discussion. The group reviewed and evaluated their pre-reading predictions and answered text interpretation questions posed by the teacher. Students were encouraged to refer to the original stories as frequently as they needed to formulate answers to questions such as the following (adapted from Goodman, Watson, & Burke, 1987):

1. Who were the characters in the story?
2. What do we know about each character?
3. What happened?
4. What was (were) the problem(s) in the story?
5. How was (were) the problem(s) solved?
6. Why do you think the author wrote this book? What was he or she trying to do with this story?
7. Have you ever read or heard any other stories like this one?

Discussion questions were also developed using Bloom's taxonomy of educational objectives (Bloom, 1956; Wilson, Lanza, & Barton, 1988). Examples of *Mushroom in the Rain* questions that conform to the six levels of the taxonomy are:

1. Knowledge: What animal was running away from the fox?
2. Comprehension: Why were all of the animals able to fit under the mushroom when it was barely large enough for just the ant at the beginning of the story?
3. Application: What would have happened if the fox had asked to get under the mushroom too?
4. Analysis: How does the end of the story relate to the beginning?
5. Synthesis: If the mushroom had not been there, what could the animals have done to get out of the rain?
6. Evaluation: Would you recommend this book to a friend? Why or why not?

Oral Re-creation   Following the book discussion, students and teachers collaborated in enacting the story with toys and props. For *Mushroom in the Rain,* a number of animal figures were spread out on a table and the children individually or in teams designed props (different sizes of mushrooms) to use while presenting the original story or their own versions. Teachers even brought a watering can to make a realistic rain storm.

Enactments provided opportunities for students to use vocabulary and language structures from the demonstration books in slightly altered contexts. For example, a teacher might begin an enactment by saying, "One day an ant was walking out in the woods when it started to rain. He saw a tiny mushroom and squeezed in under it. John, what happened next?" Students were free to create their own events or replicate episodes from the book. In keeping with the intention to value all language products, students were not required to reproduce the book's text exactly. Teachers cared more about the meanings that the children were expressing than the form of their utterances.

Alternate Communication Systems   Students and teachers elaborated and refined their understanding of a story by creating plays, songs, games, pictures, collages, or puppet shows. Although speaking, reading, and writing are the principal modalities for communication, art, music, drama, and dance also should be valued because they can contribute to realizing and communicating new meanings. Some of the children with language impairments in these collaborative classrooms possessed distinct artistic talents. When students shared pictures they had drawn, games they had made, or songs they had composed, they had opportunities to think of ways to verbally encode complex ideas that had been generated and conveyed across a variety of modalities.

For example, two students collaborated in designing a *Mushroom in the Rain* board game in which animal playing pieces moved along a path toward sunlight. Along the way, they encountered predators, a variety of shelters, and other animals in need. The authors of this game wrote a set of rules for players to follow. They also had a number of opportunities to explain their game to other students in the school who were interested in playing it.

Authorship Sequence   Students dictated or wrote books that were derivatives of the demonstration books. Gillam (1994) has described a sequence for creating, revising, and sharing student-authored books. Students in the collaborative resource room wrote individually or worked together in writing teams. They began by deciding on a topic and by generating a semantic map (a graphic network depicting the ideas contained in a story and their relationships). Younger or less confident writers were encouraged to create "parallel" books that used sentence forms and/or text structures that appeared in the demonstration books. Because textual patterns were readily available in the original books, the creation of parallel books decreased the task demands involved in authoring completely original stories.

As students transformed their semantic maps into stories, they were advised to use invented spellings and to concentrate on getting their meaning on paper. Errors in language form and writing mechanics were ignored until stories were relatively complete. Teachers used growth-relevant recasts such as expansions and expatiations (Camarata & Nelson, 1992; Nelson, 1989, 1991) during writing conferences with students as a means of calling attention to and revising form and content errors.

Students conferred with each other and with teachers before publishing their books as final products. Conferring about their writing was an especially important context for the students' language development. Discussions primarily concerned meanings that students had worked hard to get onto paper. When teachers and students made style and grammar changes collaboratively, examples of alternative language forms were provided in a context that naturally focused students' attention on the meanings they wanted to convey and the forms that best expressed their intentions. When students wrote text modifications above or to the side of their original sentences, they compared various forms of communicating their ideas in a deliberate manner. Rewriting their papers after conferring with their teacher provided students with yet another opportunity to consider differences between their original language and the alternatives that arose during editing conferences.

Once students were satisfied with their stories, they entered their text into a computer, cut up the printouts, pasted their finished type onto blank book pages, created illustrations, then bound the book with tagboard backing and wallpaper covers. Students read their finished books aloud to each other, shared them with kindergarteners and first graders, and then took them home or cataloged them into the room library. Sharing the stories brought closure to the writing process in a very positive manner.

Intertextual Ties   Beaugrande (1984) referred to the process of using knowledge of one text to inform comprehension of another text as "intertextuality." As readers construct meanings, they make connections between the text at hand and previously encountered books, movies, stories, and experiences. Short (1985) demonstrated that comprehension is enhanced when classroom environments facilitate intertextuality. As a variety of stories are experienced and discussed, children reorganize their knowledge and construct new interpretations of previously encountered books. This knowledge, in turn, provides the foundation for comprehension of books yet to be experienced.

In the whole language curriculum, when students had made progress writing their own stories, they read and discussed books that were similar to the original demonstration book. For example, in the *Mushroom in the Rain* sequence, one intertextuality discussion focused on *The Mitten* by Alvin Tresselt (1964). In this retelling of an old Ukrainian folktale, a young boy who is gathering firewood drops his mitten in the snow. In turn, a mouse, a frog, an owl, a rabbit, and a fox find shelter from the cold in the mitten. Later, a wolf, a boar, and even a bear manage to squeeze in. As a cricket climbs in, the mitten breaks. Later, the boy returns to find his mitten torn to pieces and cannot imagine what could have happened to it.

Students discussed similarities and differences between *The Mitten* and *Mushroom in the Rain*, and teachers listed their ideas on a large chart. Nearly everyone saw the similarities related to escaping from the weather and making room where it seemed as if there could not be any. The discussion began with the obvious contrast between snow and rain and the fact that the fox joined the other animals in *The Mitten* but not in *Mushroom in the Rain*. One student raised the issue of predators and their prey, and other students debated whether the smaller animals in *The Mitten* would have trusted the larger animals not to eat them. When it became clear that nearly everyone thought *Mushroom in the Rain* was believable while *The Mitten* was not, the discussion turned to ways to change *The Mitten*. At this point, students moved from story comprehension to text generation because the discussion forced them to interpret the story from an author's perspective. This important shift in thought style emerged naturally as students thought about and discussed intertextual ties.

Language Skills Education

Students who attended the language skills classrooms completed skill exercises in workbooks, sequenced reading and spelling programs, and ditto packets. Workbook-based skill exercises involved such activities as combining two or three independent clauses to form a single complex sentence, correcting ungrammatical sentences, and adding proper punctuation to sentences. One of the sequenced reading programs that many of the students completed required students to read two or three short passages and to answer multiple choice questions about each passage. Questions usually concerned character actions, sequences of events, and main ideas. Students checked their responses with an answer key and recorded their scores on a form located in their personal files. If 90% of the questions for a given passage were answered correctly, they could advance to the next level in the program. If they answered less than 90% of the questions about a passage correctly, they would have to repeat the assignment the following day.

Each day, students in the language skills room read to the teacher from assigned books (often a basal reader that was used in their classroom) and completed spelling lessons in a spelling workbook. They also wrote sentences that were dictated by the teacher two or three times each week. Their written sentences were graded for completeness, spelling, capitalization, and punctuation. Once or twice each week, students in the language skills group wrote paragraphs or short stories on story-starter worksheets. Their stories were corrected by the teachers and graded according to students' use of grammatically acceptable sentences, appropriate written language conventions, and accurate spelling.

Students in the language skills program also worked on phonic decoding skills each day. Decoding lessons were conducted in small groups of two or three students. The teacher introduced one or two specific sound–symbol relationships during each session. She demonstrated the sound–symbol relationships by listing possible spelling variations, then students would completed a group decoding drill in which they read words presented on flashcards. Finally, students were given individual seat-work assignments on ditto pages that were meant to reinforce the lesson.

Students in the language skills group met with the speech-language pathologist at their school once or twice each week for 30-minute sessions. These students' language goals primarily focused on phonological analysis, vocabulary grammar, and sequencing abilities. Tasks such as identifying the beginning and ending sounds in spoken words, counting out syllables, and blending sequences of sounds to create words were employed to increase phonological analysis abilities. Vocabulary improvement activities included listening to and repeating word definitions, providing opposites, and completing sentences that had some words deleted (a cloze procedure). To improve syntax, the SLP corrected grammatically incorrect utterances and modeled sentences for students to imitate. In activities similar to those of Interactive Language Development Teaching (Lee, Koenigsknecht, & Mulhern, 1975), the SLP read stories that contained multiple examples of certain target forms. She then asked questions designed to elicit the target forms. Tasks, such as placing pictures in correct temporal order and retelling short stories, were used to facilitate sequencing abilities. Use of a basal reading series that focused on surface level rote retention and practice assignments that focused on writing from dictation, phonological analysis, sentence imitation, and sentence sequencing were educational experiences that were directed at improving specific skills related to formal aspects of language.

Typically, between three and five students attended the language skills resource room at any one time. Spoken language intervention was conducted in a separate room. The SLP and resource room teacher reported that they rarely planned language activities together. As the resource room teacher said, "I assume that she knows what she is doing, and she assumes that I know what I'm doing."

Collecting Narratives

Samples of spoken and written narratives were obtained according to procedures established by Gillam and Johnston (1992). Students were asked to create two spoken and two written stories about pictures they selected from sets of three color photographs of various action and nature scenes. Picture sets were changed for each narrative to prevent students from telling or writing the same story twice. This procedure fostered ownership while ensuring that the story creation setting remained the same for all.

Language Analysis Following Gillam and Johnston (1992), content and form aspects of the student narratives were analyzed at sentential and textual levels of discourse. In this analysis system, the "content" component pertained to conceptual (semantic) structures and the "form" component pertained to linguistic (syntactic) structures. Three measures of language content were calculated. *Propositions per T-unit* measured the number of idea units expressed in sentences. *Number of dyads* (problem resolution pairs) measured the number of episodes contained in stories (the minimum requirement for an episode was that a problem got resolved). *Percent of embedded dyads* measured the complexity of story organization (more complex stories should contain a higher proportion of embedded problem resolution pairs). Three measures of language form also were calculated: *Morphemes per T-unit* measured the length of sentences, *percent of acceptable T-units* measured the grammatical acceptability of sentences, and *percent of marked relationships* measured the use of connectives to join clauses.

It is likely that the content measures and the form measures are correlated to some degree. For example, stories that contained fewer than one dyad could not contain embedded dyads, and omission of obligatory markers in spoken or written sentences would influence both morphemes per T-unit and percent of acceptable T-units. Gillam (1989) and Gillam and Johnston (1992) provide further explanations of these measures and the nature of their intercorrelations.

Results

Figures 1 and 2 depict the group differences for measures of language in spoken and written narratives. Means and standard deviations for the three content measures and three form measures are provided in Table 3. Results for the three content measures revealed that the spoken stories produced by the whole language students contained a greater number of ideas per T-unit, a greater number of episodes (determined by the number of dyads), and a greater number of embedded dyads than stories produced by the language skills students. Results for the written narratives were less consistent. The written stories of the whole language students contained a higher proportion of embedded dyads but fewer propositions per T-unit than the stories of the language skills students. There was little difference, however, in the number of problem resolution pairs in written stories produced by students in the two groups.

On measures of language form, the values of the language skills students were higher than the values of the whole language students for morphemes per T-unit, percent of acceptable T-units, and percent of marked relationships for both spoken and written stories. In comparison with the whole language students, the language skills students produced longer sentences that were more likely to be grammatically acceptable. In addition, the language skills students used more connectives to explicate relationships between clauses in their spoken and written stories than did the whole language students. Consistent with earlier findings for typically achieving 10-year-olds (Gillam, 1989), spoken values exceeded written values for both the language skills and the whole language groups.

It is assumed that higher scores on these analyses would indicate "better" narratives. However, quality is a difficult concept to dissect and quantify. The measures that were used to assess specific form and content variables might be

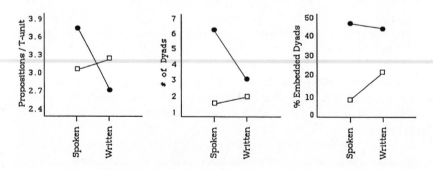

Figure 1. Measures of language content for spoken and written narratives produced by students in the whole language group and in the language skills group. (Black circles = whole language group, white squares = language skills group.)

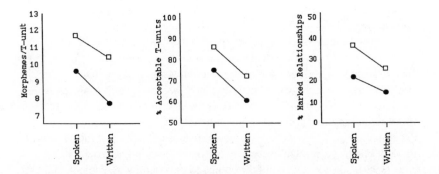

Figure 2. Measures of language form for spoken and written narratives produced by students in the whole language group and in the language skills group. (Black circles = whole language group, white squares = language skills group.)

expected to favor the students in the language skills group because, like the form-oriented curriculum that they experienced daily, these measures concerned discrete, countable components of spoken and written narratives (Isaacson, 1991; Parker, Tindal, & Hasbrouck, 1991). A more holistic evaluation that results in a single judgment of narrative quality (Myers, 1980) would incorporate hard to quantify factors such as clarity, expansiveness, charm, and creativity into the analysis, and might be expected to favor the students in the whole language group. In holistic scoring, quality is established through absolute judgments of what is desirable by the scorer and relative comparisons between stories.

The 32 narratives collected for this study (two spoken and two written stories from each of the eight students) were submitted to an adaptation of the holistic scoring procedure described by Diederich (1974) and Myers (1980). The investigators coded the transcripts of the stories to enable blind scoring and read

Table 3. Means and standard deviations for the content and form measures

Measure	Whole language students		Language skills students	
	Mean	SD	Mean	SD
Propositions per T-unit (spoken)	3.76	1.02	3.09	.54
Propositions per T-unit (written)	2.71	1.12	3.23	1.23
Number of dyads (spoken)	6.25	2.68	1.5	1.29
Number of dyads (written)	3.0	2.16	2.0	2.44
Percent embedded dyads (spoken)	48.0	34.47	8.25	16.5
Percent embedded dyads (written)	47.0	37.76	21.5	31.12
Morphemes per T-unit (spoken)	9.78	2.34	11.73	1.07
Morphemes per T-unit (written)	7.9	2.36	10.45	2.51
Percent acceptable T-units (spoken)	76.25	8.61	86.87	10.85
Percent acceptable T-units (written)	59.75	6.75	72.82	13.93
Percent marked relationships (spoken)	22.24	13.18	37.96	25.86
Percent marked relationships (written)	14.93	13.87	25.95	20.15

each story. The narratives were then rank ordered and categorized. Four quality categories were distinguishable (with *1* representing the worst stories and *4* representing the best stories) in this set of 23 narratives. Tentative descriptions (referred to as rubrics) were devised, and prototypical stories (referred to as anchors) were selected for each of the four categories. A graduate student in speech-language pathology then independently assigned scores to the entire set of narratives. Finally, the two scorers reviewed their placements and reached a consensus on any disagreements and rubrics. The final rubrics and anchors appear in Table 4. There were disagreements on scores for 5 of the 32 stories, with only one disagreement exceeding a 1-point margin. Diederich (1974) and Myers (1980) consider a 1-point difference to be essential agreement, and aim for an essential agreement rate of 90%–95%. Under these conditions, agreement between the two raters in this study reached 97%. The two scorers reached a consensus on all five disagreements after a short discussion.

Figure 3 depicts the percent of each group's spoken and written stories that were assigned to the four quality categories. To be rated as a good narrative (a score of 4), a story had to contain one or more episodes that captivated the raters or entertained them with ironic twists, exciting climaxes, or interesting morals. Basic narratives, those containing one or more episodes that did not captivate the readers, received a rating of 3. Texts with organizational difficulties received a rating of 2. Three types of difficulties were present in this set of stories: bare-bones narratives with major omissions, no elaboration, or little captivation; confusing narratives with considerable elaboration that verged on being a description; or good descriptions that went beyond surface-level details. Texts that consisted of unelaborated lists of features (i.e., poorly elaborated settings only), received a rating of 1.

Fifty percent of the spoken narratives of the whole language group and 25% of their written narratives were judged to be good stories. Stories that were produced by students in the language skills group did not fare as well. None of their spoken stories and only 12.5% of their written stories received good ratings.

The two groups of subjects evidenced different general trends. Students in the whole language group tended to tell stories that were either basic or elaborated narratives (ratings of 3 and 4), but tended to write stories that contained considerable organizational problems (ratings of 2). Students in the language skills group tended to tell stories that contained considerable organizational problems (ratings of 2). Their written stories were nearly equally distributed in the poor narrative (rated as 1), organizational difficulties (rated as 2), and basic narrative (rated as 3) categories.

Discussion

In interpreting these results, it is best to remember that this is a preliminary, posttest-only comparison of spoken and written stories produced by students

Table 4.   Rubrics for the four holistic scoring categories

Score	Features
4.	A good story with a climax or an ending twist or other captivating features. Syntax, vocabulary, and cohesion errors may be present that occasionally affect flow but not idea expression.

Example

One day there was a duck. She had some eggs. And she never ever left the eggs. And she almost starved to death. She couldn't get off her eggs because she didn't want no animals to get them while she went for food. Then one day she, her four cracks opened at the same time. The little, there was little chickies. She hurried up the, went to eat some food. The chickies followed her too. But they couldn't walk very good. But they fell down and kept falling down. Then she getting back and putting them in their wings. Then she brought them there. And she fed the chickies and her. And then after they got finished eating they went back home. Then they got some more fur. And then they went for a swim the next day after they got finished eating. Then they went swimming after a while. They swimmed for a long long time. But one didn't know how to swim. Then she heard it and came back and picked it up on her, and picked it up and put it in her fur. Then she took it out of her fur. And then she setted it on the water and hanged on to it by the neck and to teach it how to swim. And then she went back home and then ate and then played for awhile like hide-and-go-seek and kind of like jumping. And they're trying to learn how to fly like their mother. The mother named them, one quackie, one no swimming, doesn't know how to swim, and one fuzzy, and one scardy.

3.	This writing or telling constitutes a story, but may lack or be unsuccessful in achieving the captivating aspects of good stories. Some elaboration is present, but language limitations may affect expression of ideas.

Example

My dad and me, we went to the ocean. We borrowed a boat from a friend. And we went and fish. And we went out in the middle of the ocean. We stop our lines in water for about 2 minutes. And I got a bite. And I jump up and got my pole. And I yelled, I got a bite. And my dad came. And he said, start reeling it in. It was a salmon. My dad said, "It is time to go home." So we went home. And the engine fell out. And we pulled the engine all the way to the shore. And when we got there a friend said, "What happened." We was come back. The engine fell out.

2.	Two patterns are possible, and both contain considerable linguistic difficulties. 1) A barebones narrative with no elaboration or captivation. If some elaboration is present, the narrative has some other major gap such as no ending.

Example

Once upon a time there was a waterhill. And one day these people came, five them. One was name Bobby. And a girl is Misty. A girl name is Christina and Jill. They went down the waterhill. It was fun. Let's go again. So they did. And then Misty got hurt. Her hair got caught on a stick. The stick broke. Then they left, went home.

2) A confusing narrative with considerable elaboration verging on description, or a good description that goes beyond surface details but with no narration.

Example

The boy is behind, in front of the trees. He's got a gun. He's gonna kill an animal. His name is John. He's got a handkerchief over his mouth. He's looking for animals, for coyotes and birds, and guarding his home with his friend behind him. Whatever that is. He's got a necklace on the shape of a money. He looks mad. The boy's got a handkerchief over his mouth because it stinks. He'll run out of bullets. He's going raccoon hunting and birds and for raccoons birds and squirrels. And

(continued)

Table 4. (*continued*)

Score	Features
	he's gonna kill snakes. His necklace has got the money shape and is dirty on the ground. He's protecting his family by intruders, to kill the intruders if they try to get in. He is sort of hiding so that nobody will see him. Bad people, lions, tigers, cheetahs are are bad people. His friend's helping him protect one part. And he's protecting the other part so that way nobody, nothing or nobody gets into his family's house. They live out in the forest with trees that has a tunnel. And the marking on the trees shows where they go in. He's strong. And his friend's strong. They are mean to the animals. They catch fish for food, get bananas to eat from the trees, coconuts. He's got a hound dog for hunting. Then their mom, then their mom comes home. They ask what's anybody's got in. They tell them, no. But we caught some fish. They have a river around the forest where their house is. Their house is on the inside with the trees on the outside. It's a very far ways from town. And they eat fish for separate dinner and breakfast. It's almost two minutes now? Finish up. His friend goes home. His mom's not home yet. So he comes back over, stays with his friend because John's friends mom told him to stay over at his friend's house until she got back and to check if she's back or not. His mom's nice. The moms are friends. And the dads work together. And they live right beside each other in the house. The end.
1.	A poor description without narration that consists of a list of features with no elaboration.
	Example
	This guy is playing music with bunches of drums. He's at a music place. And he's singing to people. And he's playing the drums. He has black marks on his face. And he's wearing a Indian coat. The coat is white. He's got a beard. And he has a watch. There is a lot of lights in that place he is in.

who received two different types of language education. Some overlap might be expected in group performance in a study with only four subjects in each group, and this was indeed the case. There were no measures in which all four students in one group performed either higher or lower than all four students in the other group. Nonetheless, we believe the trends in the data are clinically and theoretically interesting and are consistent enough to merit attention.

In this admittedly small sample of spoken and written narratives, students from whole language and language skills classrooms presented different patterns of relationships between form and content properties of spoken and written narratives. These different patterns occurred despite the fact that their general language skills, as measured by the DTLA–2, were quite similar. Unfortunately, we cannot be entirely certain that the students' narrative abilities didn't differ somewhat from the outset. We know only that students performed at similar levels on the reading and writing clusters of Woodcock-Johnson Psycho-Educational Battery, Part Two: Tests of Achievement and on the Verbal section of the WISC–R 2 years before the data for this study were collected. However, it is interesting that the differences in the narrative abilities of two groups of students were quite consistent with the emphases of the educational programs to which they were exposed.

The four students who received form-oriented direct instruction in language skills produced spoken and written narratives that earned higher values on

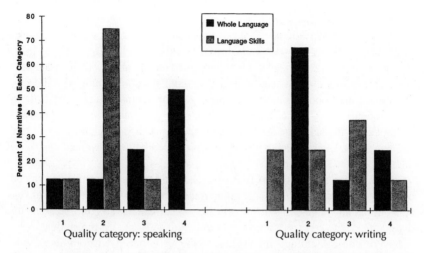

Figure 3. Holistic analysis of spoken and written narratives produced by students in the whole language group and in the language skills group. (Black bars = whole language group, gray bars = language skills group.)

form measures. Spoken narratives produced by students in the whole language group tended to receive higher values on content measures and on holistic judgments of quality. Consistent differences did not emerge for measures of the content of written narratives.

These preliminary results imply that the type of educational environments to which children are exposed may have predictable ramifications for their learning. The children in the whole language group were involved in a literacy-based collaborative intervention program that emphasized language content to a greater extent than language form. Following their participation in the program, the students told narratives that earned higher language content scores but lower language form scores. Because of their educational experiences, they may have perceived that good stories require good ideas—lots of propositional content and lots of story structure. The children in the language skills group may have perceived that form is what makes a good story—lots of long and grammatically complex sentences.

It is also possible that children in the whole language group had the ability to produce well-formed grammatical structures, but could include these only at the expense of semantic detail. Conversely, the children in the language skills group might have been able to produce longer, more semantically complex stories, but only at the expense of form. Thus, a compromise of sorts may have been operating independently of, or in concert with, different perceptions of what characterizes a good story that were held by students in each group.

In either case, the results of this preliminary study of spoken and written narration are somewhat problematic for proponents of both the language skills and the whole language approaches to language education. The finding that the spoken narratives of students in the language skills group were content-poor in comparison to narratives produced by students from the whole language group suggests that an educational emphasis on subskills related to written language form may not be sufficient in and of itself to aid in developing narrative skills. Failure to focus on language content may yield technically more accurate sentences, but stories that are generally weak and uninteresting. Traditional didactic instruction that focuses on written language form seems to have very little to offer students in the way of helping to create richer narratives in spoken or written modes. If the language skills teachers had focused on language content to a greater extent, their students might have produced better organized and more interesting stories.

The language–form properties of spoken and written narratives produced by students in the whole language group did not compare well with those of students in the language skills group. Furthermore, there appeared to be a greater dissociation between spoken and written language forms for the students who received whole language intervention when compared with students who received language skills intervention.

Whole language education is founded on the assumption that interrelating speaking, reading, writing, and listening activities around a common theme (content) benefits the development of both language form and content in reading, writing, and spoken language. The findings reported above do not readily support this hypothesis. The whole language program certainly affected the content of the student's spoken narratives in a positive manner. Relative to the students in the language skills group, however, emphasis on spoken language content did not appear to positively affect spoken language form, written language form, or written language content.

CONCLUSION

Possible Curricular Alternatives

Given the preliminary nature of these data, we are not in a position to make definitive statements about the best approach for facilitating narrative development in children with language disorders. However, SLPs and other educators do not have the luxury of waiting until the best data are obtained before deciding what to pursue in language intervention. Given this circumstance, we can offer some tentative suggestions.

Because narration affects mental, social, and academic functioning, it is certainly an important aspect of spoken and written discourse that deserves attention in language assessment and intervention. We believe that narratives provide interesting, meaningful, and linguistically complete means for demonstrating ways that concepts, vocabulary, sentence structures, and scripts are woven together to create coherent, cohesive, and informative texts. Intervention that focuses on narrative comprehension and production in the context of listening to, reading, talking about, and writing stories should have benefits for the development of interpersonal communication and cognitive/academic communication in children with language disorders.

Because we value the production of interesting and meaningful stories, we would not abandon a narrative-based approach to language education in favor of a language skills curriculum. At the same time, we recognize the potential limitations of the whole language approach for developing language form. Therefore, we would recommend a hybrid version of these two intervention paradigms (see Fey et al., chap. 1, this volume, for a discussion of hybrid approaches). Our revised approach would begin and end with meaningful texts, but it would encourage educators to focus on specific aspects of form when there is a pragmatically relevant reason for doing so. For example, a SLP may decide to discuss causal constructions with a student during a writing conference about a story in which the student consistently expressed causal relationships in grammatically unacceptable ways.

This approach would be in accord with some whole language theorists who advocate specific instruction on language forms in the context of general exploration of language content (e.g., Graves, 1983; Newman & Church, 1990; Norris & Hoffman, 1993). However, it is antithetical to other whole language theorists who do not believe meaning should be interrupted to focus on form (e.g., Edelsky, 1991; Harste et al., 1984; McKenzie, 1991). Our findings lend empirical support to more moderate variants of the whole language philosophy. Choosing between intervention approaches becomes a question of what is paramount, and we believe the content of language should be paramount. Form, nevertheless, is also critical.

It seems clear that SLPs should attend to specific language-form issues. While we could teach the formal properties of sentences through imitation or dictated writing experiences directly, this approach would not support the creation and use of newly learned forms in creating whole texts. A better approach might involve increased attention to editing processes. That is, when students have generated some content that is meaningful to them and that, as authors, they are invested in, educators could focus their attention on a variety of forms that could be used for expressing meaningful, self-generated content. This kind of instruction could occur in mini-lessons (Calkins, 1983). In the mini-lesson format, students and teachers focus on a subset of form issues that arise from the student's spoken or written storytelling. For example, after listening to a group of students tell their versions of a class experience, we realized that many were expressing ideas about causality but were having trouble with causal structures. We concocted a version of a story that contained many of the problematic causal structures that we had heard in the children's stories, gave copies of the transcript to all the students, and projected the transcript on an overhead screen. After reading through the story twice, we led the group in a discussion of a variety of grammatically acceptable options for restating the ideas that were expressed. We wrote the best options over the text on the overhead, had the students correct their personal copies, and had the group re-read the story aloud.

This approach is consistent in the following respects with Johnston's (1985) view of the critical principles in language intervention: We knew that a focus on causal structures was developmentally appropriate for these students because they were producing other kinds of subordinated clauses, and they had occasional success expressing causal relationships during conversations. The approach we used matched these children's cognitive styles because the demonstration story was developed in response to the kinds of stories they had been telling and writing. Our instructional methods served to focus the children's attention on a critical aspect of storytelling (the means for expressing causality) in a manner that incorporated listening, reading, speaking, and writing. Finally, our lesson was functional for two reasons. First, it involved an ability, storytelling, that played a major role in students' social and academic lives. Second, our lesson helped to clarify a form–content relationship that might well be important in the generation of other stories.

As we have shown, the content-oriented methods used in the whole language curriculum do proffer opportunities for increasing skills in language form. With more concentration on language form during authoring activities (e.g., through the use of instructional activities such as mini-lessons), such a curriculum could create a natural language context for demonstrating how texts are constructed. Students would generate their own stories, and SLPs and other educators would help them work through any difficulties they might have with content–form interactions. Such a program would immerse students in narratives; it would involve numerous natural opportunities for discussion of the form and content properties of the language of narration, and it would use narration as a basis for creative expression in other modes (art, music, dance). We believe this kind of intervention would have a positive influence on the development of both interpersonal communication and cognitive/academic communication in children with language disorders.

Research Issues

Given the paucity of current intervention research and the preliminary nature of the study reported here, it would be ideal if this investigation were replicated with a larger number of students. An extended replication should involve the collection of specific pre-intervention information about narrative abilities and should include measures of narrative comprehension and production.

In research designed to compare the relative effectiveness of experiential and meaning-oriented language interventions with those that are instructional and form oriented, decisions about which language measures to employ could be shaped by the examiner's theoretical orientations. Holistic measures might be expected to favor whole language approaches, whereas discrete measures might be expected to favor language skills approaches. We have shown that the theories that underlie these two approaches to language education are quite different, as are their goals and expected outcomes. When measures that are sensitive to the learning outcomes of both intervention approaches are employed, investigators

and educators will have the information necessary to compare the strengths and
weaknesses of each strategy objectively.

REFERENCES

Adams, M.J. (1989). *Beginning to read: Thinking and learning about print.* Cambridge, MA: MIT Press.
Applebee, A.N. (1978). *The child's concept of story: Ages two to seventeen.* Chicago: University of Chicago Press.
Bakhtin, M.M. (1986). *Speech genres and other late essays.* Austin: University of Texas Press.
Ball, E.W., & Blachman, B.A. (1991). Does phoneme awareness training in kindergarten make a difference in early word recognition and developmental spelling? *Reading Research Quarterly, 26,* 49–66.
Beaugrande, R. (1984). *Text production: Toward a science of composition.* Norwood, NJ: Ablex.
Bennett-Kastor, T.L. (1981). Noun phrases and coherence in child narratives. *Journal of Child Language, 10,* 135–149..
Bennett-Kastor, T.L. (1984). Cohesion and predication in child narrative. *Journal of Child Language, 13,* 353–370.
Bloom, B. (Ed.). (1956). *Taxonomy of educational objectives handbook I: Cognitive domain.* New York: McKay.
Botvin, G.J., & Sutton-Smith, B. (1977). The development of structural complexity in children's fantasy narratives. *Developmental Psychology, 13,* 377–388.
Brewer, W.R. (1985). The story schema: Universal and culture-specific properties. In D.R. Olson, N. Torrance, & A. Hildyard (Eds.), *Literacy, language, and learning: The nature and consequences of reading and writing* (pp. 167–194). Cambridge, UK: Cambridge University Press.
Brown, L., Sherbenou, R., & Johnsen, S. (1982). *Test of nonverbal intelligence.* Austin, TX: PRO-ED.
Bruner, J. (1986). *Actual minds, possible worlds.* Cambridge, MA: Harvard University Press.
Calkins, L.M. (1983). *Lessons from a child: On the teaching and learning of writing.* Portsmouth, NH: Heinemann.
Camarata, S., & Nelson, K.E. (1992) Treatment efficiency as a function of target selection in the remediation of child language disorders. *Clinical Linguistics and Phonetics, 6,* 167–178.
Chafe, W.L., & Danielewicz, J. (1987). Properties of spoken and written language. In R. Horowitz & S.J. Samuels (Eds.), *Comprehending oral and written language* (pp. 61–93). Orlando, FL: Academic Press.
Daiute, C. (1989). Play as thought: Thinking strategies of young writers. *Harvard Educational Review, 59*(11), 1–23.
Deese, J. (1983). Foreword. In C. Peterson & A. McCabe, *Developmental psycholinguistics: Three ways of looking at a child's narrative* (pp. xiii–xxxi). New York: Plenum.
Diederich, P.B. (1974). *Measuring growth in English.* Champaign, IL: National Council of Teachers of English.
Edelsky, C. (1991). Authentic reading/writing versus reading/writing exercises. In K. Goodman, L.B. Bird, & Y. Goodman (Eds.), *The whole language catalog* (p. 72). Santa Rosa, CA: American School Publishers.
Ehri, L., & Wilce, L. (1985). Movement into reading: Is the first stage of printed word learning visual or phonetic? *Reading Research Quarterly, 20,* 163–179.

Fey, M.E. (1986). *Language intervention with young children.* Newton, MA: Allyn & Bacon.

Freedman, A. (1987). Development in story writing. *Applied Psycholinguistics, 8,* 153–170.

Gee, J.P. (1991). Memory and myth: A perspective on narrative. In E. McCabe & C. Peterson (Eds.), *Developing narrative structure* (pp. 1–26). Hillsdale, NJ: Lawrence Erlbaum Associates.

Giffin, H. (1984). The coordination of meaning in the creation of a shared make-believe reality. In I. Bretherton (Ed.), *Symbolic play: The development of social worlds* (pp. 73–100). Orlando, FL: Academic Press.

Gillam, R. (1989). *An investigation of interrelationships between spoken and written language in language/learning-impaired and normally achieving school-age children* (Doctoral dissertation, Indiana University, Bloomington.).

Gillam, R. (1991). A personal paradigm shift. In K. Goodman, Y. Goodman, & L. Bird (Eds.), *The whole language catalog* (p. 56). Santa Rosa, CA: American School Publishers.

Gillam, R. (1994). Whole language principles at work in language intervention. In D. Tibbits & H. Winitz (Eds.), *Language intervention: Beyond the primary grades.* Austin, TX: PRO-ED.

Gillam, R., & Johnston, J.R. (1992). Spoken and written language relationship in language/learning-impaired and normally achieving school-age children. *Journal of Speech and Hearing Research, 35,* 1303–1315.

Ginsburg, M. (1974). *Mushroom in the rain.* New York: Macmillan.

Goodman, K. (1986). *What's whole in whole language?* Portsmouth, NH: Heinemann.

Goodman, Y., Watson, D., & Burke, C. (1987). *Reading miscue inventory: Alternative procedures.* New York: Richard C. Owen.

Graves, D. (1983). *Writing: Teachers and children at work.* Portsmouth, NH: Heineman.

Graybeal, C.M, (1981). Memory for stories in language-impaired children. *Applied Psycholinguistics, 2,* 269–283.

Guthrie, J.T. (1984). Writing connections. *Reading Teacher, 37,* 540–542.

Halliday, M.A.K. (1975). *Learning how to mean: Explorations in the development of language.* London: Edward Arnold.

Halliday, M.A.K., & Hasan, R. (1976). *Cohesion in English.* London: Longman.

Hammill, D. (1985). *Detroit Tests of Learning Aptitude–2.* Austin, TX: PRO-ED.

Harste, J., Woodward, J., & Burke, C. (1984). *Language stories and literacy lessons.* Portsmouth, NH: Heinemann.

Heald-Taylor, G. (1987a, March). How to use predictable books for K–2 language arts instruction. *The Reading Teacher, 23–30.*

Heald-Taylor, G. (1987b, October). Predictable literature selections and activities for language arts. *The Reading Teacher, 6–12.*

Heath, S.B. (1980). The functions and uses of literacy. *Journal of Communication, 30,* 123–133.

Heath, S.B. (1982). What no bedtime story means: Narrative skills at home and at school. *Language in Society, 11,* 49–76.

Heath, S.B. (1983). *Ways with words: Language, life, and work in communities and classrooms.* Cambridge, UK: Cambridge University Press.

Hicks, D. (1991). Kinds of narrative: Genre skills among first graders from two communities. In A. McCabe & C. Peterson (Eds.), *Developing narrative structure* (pp. 137–154). Hillsdale, NJ: Lawrence Erlbaum Associates.

Howard, G. (1991). Culture tales: A narrative aproach to therapy in cross-cultural psycholgy and psychotherapy. *American Psychologist, 40,* 187–197.

Hudson, J., & Shapiro, L. (1991). From knowing to telling: The development of children's scripts, stories, and personal narratives. In A. McCabe & C. Peters (Eds.), *Developing narrative structure* (pp. 83–136). Hillsdale, NJ: Lawrence Erlbaum Associates.

Isaacson, S. (1991). Assessing written language skills. In C.S. Simon (Ed.), *Communication skills and classroom success* (pp. 224–239). Eau Claire, WI: Thinking Publications.

Johnston, J. (1985). Fit, focus and functionality: An essay on early language intervention. *Child Language Teaching and Therapy, 1,* 125–134.

Just, M.A., & Carpenter, P.A. (1980). A theory of reading: From eye fixations to comprehension. *Psychological Review, 4,* 329–354.

Karmiloff-Smith, A. (1981). The grammatical marking of thematic structure in the development of language productions. In W. Deutsch (Ed.), *The child's construction of language* (pp. 121–147). New York: Academic Press.

Kernan, K.T. (1977). Semantic and expressive elaboration in children's narratives. In S. Ervin-Tripp & C. Mitchell-Kernan (Eds.), *Child discourse* (pp. 91–102). New York: Academic Press.

Kirby, D., & Liner, T. (1981). *Inside out: Developmental strategies for teaching writing.* Montclair, NJ: Boynton-Cook.

Klecan-Aker, J.S., & Hedrick, D.L. (1985). A study of the syntactic language skills of normal middle school children. *Language, Speech, and Hearing Services in Schools, 16,* 2–7.

Kroll, B. (1981). Developmental relationships between speaking and writing. In B. Kroll & R. Vann (Eds.), *Exploring speaking-writing relationships: Connections and contrasts* (pp. 32–54). Champaign, IL: National Council of Teachers of English.

Labov, W. (1972). *Language in the inner city.* Philadelphia: University of Pennsylvania Press.

Lahey, M. (1988). *Language disorders and language development.* New York: Macmillan.

Lee, L., Koenigsknecht, R., & Mulhern, S. (1975). *Interactive language development teaching.* Evanston, IL: Northwestern University Press.

Liles, B.Z. (1985). Cohesion in the narratives of normal and language disordered children. *Journal of Speech and Hearing Research, 28,* 123–133.

Liles, B.Z. (1987). Episode organization and cohesive conjunctives in narratives of children with and without language disorders. *Journal of Speech and Hearing Research, 30,* 185–196.

Liles, B.Z., & Purcell, S. (1987). Departures in the spoken narratives of normal and language-disordered children. *Applied Pyscholinguistics, 8,* 185–202.

Lundberg, I., Frost, J., & Peterson, O. (1988). Effects of an extensive program for stimulating phonological awareness in preschool children. *Reading Research Quarterly, 23,* 363–384.

MacLachlan, B., & Chapman, R. (1988). Communication breakdowns in normal and language learning-disabled children's conversation and narration. *Journal of Speech and Hearing Disorders, 53,* 2–7.

Mandler, J.M., & Johnson, N.S. (1977). Remembrance of things parsed: Story structure and recall. *Cognitive Psychology, 9,* 111–151.

Mandler, J.M., Scribner, S., Cole, M., & DeForest, M. (1980). Cross-cultural invariance in story recall. *Child Development, 51,* 19–26.

Martin, J.R. (1983). The development of register. In J. Fine & R.O. Freedle (Eds.), *Developmental issues in discourse* (pp. 1–39). Norwood, NJ: Ablex.

Martinez, M., & Teale, W. (1989). Classroom storybook reading: The creation of texts and learning opportunities. *Theory in Practice, 28*(2), 126–135.

McCabe, A. (1991). Preface: Structure as a way of understanding. In A. McCabe & C. Peterson (Eds.), *Developing narrative structure* (pp. 217–254). Hillsdale, NJ: Lawrence Erlbaum Associates.

McCabe, A., & Peterson, C. (1991). Getting the story: A longitudinal study of parental styles in eliciting narratives and developing narrative skills. In A. McCabe & C. Peterson (Eds.), *Developing narrative structure* (pp. 217–254). Hillsdale, NJ: Lawrence Erlbaum Associates.

McClelland, J.L. (1986). The programmable blackboard madel of reading. In J. McClelland & D. Rumelhart (Eds.), *Parallel distributed processing: Explorations in the microstructure of cognition: Vol. 2. Psychological and biological models* (pp. 121–169). Cambridge MA: MIT press.

McKenzie, M. (1991). "But wait! Everything was upside down! In K. Goodman, L.B. Bird, & Y. Goodman (Eds.), *The whole language catalog* (p. 234). Santa Rosa, CA: American School Publishers.

Merritt, D.D., & Liles, B.Z. (1987). Story grammar ability in children with and without language disorder: Story generation, story retelling, and story comprehension. *Journal of Speech and Hearing Research, 30,* 539–552.

Michaels, S.J. (1981). "Sharing time:" Children's narrative styles and differential access to literacy. *Language and Society, 10,* 443–487.

Myers, M. (1980). *A procedure for writing assessment and holistic scoring.* Urbana, IL: National Council of Teachers of English.

Nelson, K.E. (1989). Strategies for first language teaching. In M. Rice & R. Schiefelbusch (Eds.), *The teachability of language* (pp. 263–310). Baltimore: Paul H. Brookes Publishing Co.

Nelson, K.E. (1991). On differentiated language-learning models and differentiated interventions. In N. Krasnegor, D. Rumbaugh, R. Schiefelbusch, & M. Studdert-Kennedy (Eds.), *Biological and behavioral determinants of language development* (pp. 399–429). Hillsdale, NJ: Lawrence Erlbaum Associates.

Newman, J. (Ed.). (1985). *Whole language: Theory in use.* Portsmouth, NH: Heinemann.

Newman, J.M., & Church, S.M. (1990). Myths of whole language. *The Reading Teacher, 44,* 20–26.

Norris, J. (1993). Some questions and answers about whole language. *American Journal of Speech-Language Pathology, 1*(4), 11–14.

Norris, J., & Damico, J. (1990). Whole language in theory and practice: Implications for language intervention. *Language, Speech, and Hearing Services in Schools, 21,* 212–220.

Norris, J., & Hoffman, P. (1993). *Whole language intervention for school age children.* San Diego: Singular Publishing Group.

Parker, R., Tindal, G., & Hasbrouck, J. (1991). Progress monitoring with objective measures of writing performance for students with mild disabilities. *Exceptional Children, 57,* 61–73.

Pelligrini, A., Galdo, L., & Rubin, D. (1984). Context in text: The development of oral and written language in two genres. *Child Development 55,* 1549–1555.

Perera, K. (1984). *Children writing and reading.* London: Blackwell.

Peterson, C., & McCabe, A. (1983). *Developmental psycholinguistics: Three ways of looking at a child's narrative.* New York: Plenum.

Polanyi, L. (1989). *Telling the American story: A structural and cultural analysis of conversational storytelling.* Cambridge, MA: MIT Press.

Preece, A. (1987). The range of narrative forms conversationally produced by young children. *Journal of Child Language, 14,* 353–373.

Purcell, S.L., & Liles, B. (1992). Cohesion repairs in the narratives of normal-language and language-disordered school age children. *Journal of Speech and Hearing Research, 35,* 354–362.

Rhodes, L., & Dudley-Marling, C. (1988). *Readers and writers with a difference.* Portsmouth, NH: Heinemann.

Rich, S.J. (1985). Restoring power to teachers: The impact of "whole language." *Language Arts, 62,* 717–724.

Roth, F.P. (1986). Oral narrative abilities of learning-disabled students. *Topics in Language Disorders, 7*(1), 21–30.

Roth, F.P., & Spekman, N.J. (1986). Narrative discourse: Spontaneously generated stories of learning-disabled and normally achieving students. *Journal of Speech and Hearing Disorders, 51,* 8–23.

Roth, F.P., & Spekman, N.J. (1989). The oral syntactic proficiency of learning disabled students: A spontaneous story sampling analysis. *Journal of Speech and Hearing Research, 32,* 67–77.

Rubin, S., & Wolf, D. (1979). The development of maybe: The evolution of social roles into narrative roles. *New Directions in Child development, 6,* 15–28.

Sachs, J. (1980). The role of adult-child play in language development. *New Directions in Child Development, 9,* 33–48.

Sachs, J. (1983). Talking about the there and then: The emergence of deplaced reference in parent-child discourse. In K.E. Nelson (Ed.), *Children's language* (pp. 1–28). Hillsdale NJ: Lawrence Erlbaum Associates.

Scollon, R., & Scollon, S.B.K. (1981). *Narrative, literacy and face in interethnic communication.* Norwood, NJ: Ablex.

Scott, C., & Rush D. (1985). Teaching adverbal connectivity: Implications from current research. *Child Language Teaching and Therapy, 1,* 264–280.

Short, K. (1985). *Literacy as a collaborative experience.* Unpublished doctoral dissertation, Indiana University, Bloomington.

Shugar, G. (1978). Text analysis as an approach to the study of early linguistic operations. In N. Waterson & C. Snow (Eds.), *The development of communication* (pp. 227–251). Chichester, UK: John Wiley & Sons.

Silliman, E. R., Aurilio, P.K., & Nitzberg, L.A. (1992, November). *Oral versus literate styles of storytelling: Three approaches to assessment.* Paper presented at the American Speech-Language-Hearing Association annual convention, San Antonio, TX.

Sleight, C.C., & Prinz, P.M. (1985). Use of abstracts, orientations, and codas in narration by language-disordered and nondisordered children. *Journal of Speech and Hearing Disorders, 50,* 361–371.

Snow C.E. (1983). Literacy and language: Relationships during the preschool years. *Harvard Educational Review, 53,* 165–189.

Snow, C.E., & Goldfield, B. (1981). Building stories: The emergence of information structures from conversation. In D. Tannen (Ed.), *Analyzing discourse; Text and talk* (pp. 127–141). Washington, DC: Georgetown University Press.

Stanovich, K.E. (1984). The interactive-compensatory model of reading: A confluence of developmental, experimental, and educational psychology. *Remedial and Special Education, 5,* 11–19.

Stanovich, K.E. (1986). "Matthew effects" in reading: Some consequences of individual differences in the acquisition of literacy. *Reading Research Quarterly, 21,* 360–406.

Stein, N.L., & Glenn, C.G. (1979). An analysis of story comprehension in elementary school children. In R. Freedle (Ed.), *New directions in discourse processing* (Vol. 2, pp. 53–120). Norwood, NJ: Ablex.

Sutton-Smith, B. (1986). The development of fictional narrative performances. *Topics in Language Disorders, 7*(1), 1–10.

Teale, W. (1984). Reading to young children: Its significance for literacy development. In H. Goleman, A. Oberg, & F. Smith (Eds.), *Awakening to literacy* (pp. 110–121). Portsmouth, NH: Heinemann.

Tresselt, A. (1964). *The mitten*. New York: Scholastic

Umiker-Sebeok, D.J. (1977). Preschool children's intraconversational narratives. *Journal of Child Language, 6,* 91–109.

van Kleeck, A., Hamilton, L., & McMahon, C. (1992, November). *Mothers' and fathers' book reading strategies with preschoolers.* Paper presented at the American Speech-Language-Hearing Association annual convention, San Antonio, TX.

van Kleeck, A., & Swofford-Berg, S. (1981). *Maternal strategies for eliciting the reportative function in young children.* Unpublished manuscript, University of Texas at Austin.

Vygotsky, L.S. (1978). *Mind in society: The development of higher psychological processes.* Cambridge, MA: Harvard University Press.

Watson, D. (1989). Defining and describing whole language. *The Elementary School Journal, 90,* 129–141.

Wechsler, D. (1974). *Manual of the Wechsler Intelligence Scale for Children–Revised.* New York: Psychological Corporation.

Wells, G. (1986). *The meaning makers: Children learning language and using language to learn.* Portsmouth, NH: Heinemann.

Westby, C. (1984). Development of narrative abilities. In G. Wallach & K. Butler (Eds.), *Language-learning disabilities in school-age children* (pp. 103–127). Baltimore: Williams & Wilkens.

Westby, C. (1989a). Assessing and remediating text comprehension problems. In A. Kamhi & H. Catts (Eds.), *Reading disabilities: A developmental language perspective* (pp. 199–259). Boston. College-Hill Press.

Westby, C. (1989b, November). *Cultural variations in storytelling.* Paper presented at the American Speech-Language-Hearing Association annual convention, St. Louis, MO.

Westby, C., & Costlow, L. (1991). Implementing a whole language program in a special education class. *Topics in Language Disorders, 11*(3), 69–84.

Wilson, C., Lanza, J., & Barton, J. (1988). Developing higher level thinking skills through questioning techniques in the speech and language setting. *Language, Speech, and Hearing Services in Schools, 19,* 428–431.

Woodcock, R.W., & Johnson, M.B. (1977). *Woodcock-Johnson Psycho-Educational Battery, Part Two: Tests of Achievement.* Allen, TX: DLM Teaching Resources.

Yde, P., & Spoelders, M. (1985). Text cohesion: An exploratory study with beginning writers. *Applied Psycholinguistics, 6,* 407–416.

7

Conversational Intervention with Children with Specific Language Impairment

Bonnie Brinton and Martin Fujiki

ONE OF THE MAJOR OUTCOMES of the "pragmatic revolution" (Duchan, 1984) has been an emphasis on the importance of communication in the context of social interaction. This emphasis has resulted in a great deal of research during the 1980s and 1990s on the pragmatic skills of children with specific language impairment (SLI). The focal point of much of this work has been the ability of children with SLI to participate effectively in conversation. However, despite increased attention, our knowledge of the conversational abilities of children with SLI is still incomplete. Several major questions remain: What aspects of conversation present children with SLI with the greatest difficulties? Can these problems be alleviated by intervention? If these problems can be addressed effectively, what will be the impact of this improvement on quality of life? Answers to these questions depend, in part, on how one views language impairment and language intervention.

Traditionally, language impairment has been viewed as a gap between a child's actual and expected functioning considering chronological age or cognitive level (Fey, 1986). This perspective is important in that aspects of language are still developing in school-age children (e.g., Nippold, 1988), and problems in acquisition must be referenced against some developmental expectation. However, it is also critical to consider the broader implications of language impairment. For example, Tomblin (1983) suggested that impairment is present when a current or predicted language behavior places a child "at some level of risk for disvalue in one or more domains of life function" (p. 105). This view of language impairment can be expanded to define a deficit according to its impact

The authors are indebted to dedicated student clinicians, including Lee Robinson and Barbara Taylor, for their work with C.D. We would also like to acknowledge support from the undergraduate research trainee program, College of Education, Brigham Young University. Most of all we would like to thank C.D. and his family for their faith in us and their cooperation with this project.

on an individual's quality of life. Although quality of life is difficult to quantify, for the school-age child it is heavily influenced by social relationships, academic achievement, and independent functioning. Judgment of the nature and severity of language impairment should take into account the effect of communicative skills on each of these areas. In addition, one measure of the efficacy of intervention should be the extent to which it ultimately results in some improvement in behaviors important to quality of life.

This chapter first examines the conversational skills of children with SLI. Questions of efficacy with respect to intervention with conversation are then addressed. We then present a detailed case study focusing on the efficacy of language intervention with the communication problems of one child with SLI. For this individual, considerations of quality of life motivated an intervention program that took place in a conversational context and focused on interactional and structural goals. In this chapter, we employ a broad definition of conversation similar to that suggested by Nelson (1993), defining conversation as naturally occurring verbal interaction between two or more speakers. Thus, conversation may take place in a variety of contexts (e.g., the home, classroom), with a range of conversational partners (e.g., family, peers, teachers).

THE NATURE OF CONVERSATIONAL LANGUAGE IMPAIRMENT

It has been argued that conversation provides an excellent context for various types of language learning during the preschool and elementary school years (e.g., Blank, Rose, & Berlin, 1978; Nelson, 1989; Silliman & Cherry Wilkinson, 1991; Speidel, 1987). Conversational skills also play an important role in the formation and maintenance of social relationships for school-age children (e.g., Asher & Renshaw, 1981; Black & Hazen, 1990; Dodge, Pettit, McClaskey, & Brown, 1986; Gottman, 1983; Hazen & Black, 1989). Given these two factors, it seems reasonable that conversational problems would limit a child's access to contexts in which linguistic and social skills are displayed and practiced, and thereby have the potential to threaten development in both areas. However, the nature of conversational language impairment remains elusive. Describing the conversational abilities of children with SLI has been a main thrust of "pragmatic" research in recent years.

A basic issue is whether children with SLI have difficulty with conversational skills. As illustrated in the review to follow, the answer to this question must be qualified. Many (but not all) children with SLI have difficulty with many (but not all) aspects of conversational behavior. For some of these children, conversational difficulty is relatively subtle; for others, it is a primary concern.

As with most areas of research, the methods used by researchers to study conversation dictate the types of questions that may be asked and answered and the extent to which results may be generalized. McTear and Conti-Ramsden (1992) noted that three different types of designs have been applied to the study of the pragmatic abilities (including conversation) of children with SLI: group designs, case studies, and large-scale group comparisons using pragmatic protocols (e.g., Prutting & Kirchner, 1987). In the following section, we sample the literature on the conversational skills of children with SLI, focusing on studies using group designs and case studies. Our primary purpose is to illustrate the contributions and limitations of these different methodological procedures to the understanding of conversational language impairment. More general reviews of this literature may be found in Craig (1991) and McTear and Conti-Ramsden (1992).

STUDIES OF CONVERSATIONAL SKILLS OF CHILDREN WITH SLI

Group Designs

Group designs frequently have been used to compare the conversational skills of children with SLI to those of language age–matched (LA) and/or chronological age–matched (CA) peers. The purpose of comparing children with SLI to their CA peers is to focus on differences in behaviors of children considered similar in cognitive level but different in structural language ability. This comparison is important to those researchers and clinicians who are concerned with the functional and social ramifications of language impairment. If children with SLI do not employ specific conversational behaviors as effectively as the CA peers who are typically their classmates, they are at a disadvantage in social contexts in which conversations play an important role (e.g., Craig & Washington, 1993; Hadley & Rice, 1991).

The purpose of comparing children with SLI to LA peers is to focus on differences in the behavior of children considered to be at a similar language level but differing in rate of language development. Theoretically, studies using this design should illuminate the relationship of structural language performance and conversational skill. For example, if children with SLI perform more poorly on a conversational task than children matched for structural language level, this would suggest that the pragmatic difficulty exceeds the structural deficit. Alternatively, if children with SLI perform similarly to their LA peers, it would suggest that deficits in conversational performance are in line with structural problems. The LA–SLI comparison is particularly important to researchers who have a modular view of language development and/or who consider pragmatic difficulties as the likely fallout of inadequate structural abilities.

The results of group studies taken as a whole have been equivocal. Children with SLI have displayed a wide variety of proficiency on different aspects of conversation. Results have ranged from performance below that of their LA peers to performance similar to that of their CA peers. A sampling of the literature on two general aspects of performance, conversational assertiveness and responsiveness (Fey, 1986), illustrates this variability.

Studies Supporting the Notion of Conversational Impairment

With regard to assertiveness, Conti-Ramsden and Friel-Patti (1983) examined the conversations of mother–child dyads of children with SLI (chronological age range 3;6–5;4 years) and peers without impairments matched for mean length of utterance (MLU). Although the dyads did not differ in the number of conversational turns produced, the subjects without impairments produced a significantly greater number of initiations than the children with SLI. Snyder (1978) found that children with SLI (ages 1;8–2;6 years) produced imperative and declarative performatives. However, unlike their LA peers without impairments, they tended to use nonlinguistic means to do so. Craig and Evans (1989) found that children with SLI (ages 8;8–13;11 years) were less effective at obtaining a turn by interrupting than either their CA or LA peers. These authors suggested that this difficulty might be related to problems projecting ahead to transition relevance points in conversation where a speaking turn might be available.

Several investigations have yielded data suggesting that children with SLI may be less responsive to the conversational bids of others when compared with their peers. For example, Brinton and Fujiki (1982) found that dyads of children with SLI between the ages of 5;6 and 6;0 years were less responsive to choice questions, product questions, and requests for clarification than dyads of CA peers. Whereas typically developing subjects frequently responded appropriately, subjects with SLI often ignored or responded inappropriately to these requests.

Rosinski-McClendon and Newhoff (1987) introduced various conversational probes into naturalistic interactions with children with SLI with expressive impairments (ages 4;1–5;9 years). One of these probes was a syntactically simple question focusing on a point under discussion or an object of attention. Subjects with SLI were less responsive to these probes from an adult than LA peers matched on the basis of MLU. Gallagher and Darnton (1978) examined the ability of children with SLI In Brown's stages I, II, and III to revise their utterances in response to a request for clarification. These data were then compared to the responses of typically developing children at a similar language level (Gallagher, 1977). Both groups revised their utterances in response to the requests for clarification. However, response strategies used by the subjects with SLI did not vary across development stages as did the response strategies of the LA subjects. The profile of response patterns produced by the group with SLI was not characteristic of the typically developing subjects at any stage.

Brinton, Fujiki, Winkler, and Loeb (1986) studied the ability of children with SLI with expressive deficits (groups of 5-, 7-, and 9-year-olds) to respond to stacked sequences of requests for clarification (Huh? What? I didn't understand that) during a picture description task. Children with SLI produced a greater number of inappropriate responses than typically developing subjects as the clarification request sequence progressed. Brinton, Fujiki, and Sonnenberg (1988) extended this work by examining the ability of children demonstrating both expressive and receptive deficits (ages 7;6–11;1 years) to respond to stacked requests for clarification in naturalistic conversation with an adult. Although all of the subjects seemed to appreciate the need to respond, children with SLI produced more inappropriate responses than either LA or CA peers. Typically developing subjects also used sophisticated repair strategies more frequently than did the subjects with SLI.

Studies Questioning the Notion of Conversational Impairment

In contrast to the research discussed above are studies in which children with SLI performed much the same as their LA and CA peers on various aspects of conversational assertiveness and responsiveness. For example, Fey and Leonard (1984) examined the conversational assertiveness of children with SLI (ages 4;7–6;2 years) in interactions with an adult, a CA peer, and a LA peer. The children with SLI performed much the same as their CA peers on most measures (e.g., contingent queries, questions, imperatives). There was also some evidence that these children were more conversationally skilled on many of the measures examined than were their LA peers.

In a study discussed previously, Rosinski-McClendon and Newhoff (1987) found that children with SLI (Ages 4;1–5;9 years) did not differ from LA peers on two specific probes of topic manipulation designed to examine conversational assertiveness (maintaining a topic after asking the examiner a question and getting no response and maintaining a topic after the examiner had changed the topic). Rowan, Leonard, Chapman, and Weiss (1983) examined the production of imperative and declarative presuppositions in children with SLI (ages 2;8–4;2 years) at the single-word level of language development. Unlike the Snyder (1978) study previously discussed, differences were not observed between SLI and LA groups in the frequency of use of either of these functions.

Regarding responsiveness, Leonard (1986) compared the conversational replies of subjects with expressive SLI (ages 2;10–3;6 years) with typically developing children matched on expressive language age. All children were observed in adult–child interactions. Subjects with SLI produced both a greater range of replies and a higher frequency of replies to questions and statements than the linguistically typical subjects.

In work cited previously, Craig and Evans (1989) compared the response patterns of children with SLI to those of their CA and LA peers in adult–child interaction. Child utterances produced within 2 seconds of an adult utterance were examined to determine if they were semantically contingent on the adult utterance. Differences between groups were not significant. Craig and Evans (1993) replicated these findings in comparisons between children with expressive SLI, children with expressive-receptive SLI, CA peers, and LA peers in adult–child interactions.

Potential Explanations

There are several potential explanations for these disparate findings. First of all, a number of factors contribute to both conversational assertiveness and responsiveness. It might be expected that children with SLI would do well on some conversational parameters and not as well on others, with certain skills more prone to breakdown. However, other explanations also merit consideration. For example, McTear and Conti-Ramsden (1992) suggested several potential problems in the use of group designs to study pragmatic language impairment, including: 1) the assumption that children with pragmatic impairment form a homogeneous group, 2) the manner in which children with SLI are matched with their linguistically typical peers, and 3) a lack of precision in the way in which pragmatic behaviors are examined.

The use of a group design assumes that subjects with SLI perform in a homogeneous manner. However, this assumption may be problematic. As has been observed by Fey (1986) and Fey and Leonard (1983), children with SLI may demonstrate differing conversational profiles. Some children with seriously impaired language form and content may be active conversationalists, interacting relatively well despite their structural problems. There are also children with relatively good structural skills who have difficulty interacting appropriately. For example, Adams and Bishop studied a group of 57 children with SLI between the ages of 8 and 12 years and identified 14 of them as having a semantic-pragmatic disorder (Adams & Bishop, 1989; Bishop & Adams, 1989). The language of these children was characterized by a range of behaviors, including relatively good structural skills, verbosity, perseveration, circumlocutions, difficulty taking turns and maintaining topics, and problems with comprehension. (For other examples of children with good structural skills and poor interactional skills, see Blank, Gessner, & Esposito, 1979; Fujiki & Brinton, 1991; McTear, 1985a.) Grouping children with varying communicative profiles may influence the results of a study, as the wide range in individual performance may mask control and experimental group differences.

On a related note, there is recent evidence suggesting that the extent of the child's general deficits in the areas of production and comprehension may be associated with conversational ability. In the Craig and Evans (1989) study mentioned previously, four of five subjects with SLI produced relatively consistent patterns of performance. These four subjects displayed deficits of both production and comprehension. The remaining subject performed much more like children in the CA and LA groups. This child had impaired expressive skills paired with relatively good receptive skills.

Craig and Evans (1993) investigated this notion further, contrasting the conversational performance of children with expressive SLI (ages 7;1–10;1 years) and expressive-receptive SLI (ages 8;3–9;10 years) with the performance of LA and CA peers. Subjects with expressive-receptive SLI profiles were less effective at obtaining a turn by interrupting than the expressive SLI, CA, or LA groups. The two groups with SLI also differed on several other (but not all) aspects of turn-taking and cohesion. These findings suggest that subjects with expressive deficits may perform differently in conversation than subjects with both expressive and receptive involvement.

The second issue of concern is the manner in which children with SLI are matched with their linguistically typical peers. A variety of methods have been used to match children with SLI to children at the same language level who have typically developing language skills. As McTear and Conti-Ramsden (1992) observed, general measures such as MLU have often been used for this purpose. However, such measures may or may not be appropriate, depending upon the child's level of development. The use of a structural measure such as MLU also assumes that conversational development is tied to grammatical development. McTear and Conti-Ramsden question this assumption, as do other authors (e.g., Johnston, 1985; McTear, 1985b).

In addition to issues raised by McTear and Conti-Ramsden, recently Plante, Swisher, Kiernan, and Restrepo (1993) pointed out several limitations in designs employing language-age matching. Among these, the authors note that, because language is a multidimensional skill, it is difficult to obtain a true match. Additionally, LA peers are typically several years younger than the children with SLI with whom they are matched. This almost certainly introduces cognitive, social, and emotional differences into the design. However, results are rarely interpreted with respect to these factors.

The final point of discussion has to do with the lack of precision in the way in which pragmatic behaviors are examined. McTear and Conti-Ramsden (1992) pointed out that it is particularly important to consider not only how behaviors are used, but also the "nature of the behaviors and the circumstances under which they are produced" (p. 59). Consider a study conducted by Craig and Gallagher (1986), which presented a detailed analysis of responses to comments by a child referred to as Clark, a 4;3-year-old with deficits in language production but relatively normal comprehension. Clark was observed in interactions with two CA and two LA peers. Clark's frequency of responding was variable, influenced by the behavior of the child with whom he was interacting. For example, Clark's rate of responding increased with: 1) an increase in his conversational partner's other-directed turns, 2) the occurrence of a particular discourse pattern (comment or contingent query by Clark followed by associated comment by partner), and 3) a shared referent within the previously noted discourse pattern. The production of responses to comments by the CA and LA peers was not influenced by these factors in dyadic interactions with either a same-age or different-age partner. As this study illustrates, simple analysis (in this case, frequency of appropriate responding) may present a superficial picture of abilities.

Certainly, the disparity of findings on the conversational performance of children with SLI cannot be attributed completely to a lack of detailed study. However, it is possible that in some cases a more sophisticated analysis might reveal a clearer picture of performance.

Case Studies

One way to extend our understanding of conversational impairment, and at the same time address some of the problems described above, is through the use of detailed case studies. Although this type of work carries its own set of limitations, such research can provide a useful supplement to the group design by allowing the detailed examination of an individual subject (McTear & Conti-Ramsden, 1992).

Several case studies of children with SLI have documented specific conversational problems apparently unrelated to deficits in language structure. For example, McTear (1985a) reported the case of a 10-year-old boy with relatively good structural skills who had difficulty interacting in conversation because he was highly nonassertive. Conversely, Fujiki and Brinton (1991) described the case of a 9;11-year-old boy who was highly assertive and minimally responsive in conversation. Conti-Ramsden and Gunn (1986) followed a child with SLI from age 3 to 6 years. This child responded long before he initiated utterances in conversation. Additionally, he produced utterances that labeled or described long before he produced requests.

In one of the few available studies that has examined the influence of a child's impaired language skills on quality of life, Tomblin and Liljegreen (1985) presented the case of Marcia, a 12-year-old girl with SLI. Informal observation by persons in Marcia's social environment revealed that a principal problem was her high rate of nonresponsiveness. Marcia frequently did not respond to the requests or comments of others, and when she did reply, the response was often minimal. Further assessment revealed that this problem did not stem from a lack of comprehension of the propositional content of questions, or from a failure to understand the illocutionary force behind question forms. Rather, Marcia's nonresponsiveness appeared to be linked to topic manipulation. She was capable of interacting on topics that she had initiated but was nonresponsive to topics initiated by others.

As noted previously, case studies are also subject to a range of limitations. For example, they report the case of a unique individual and may not be generalizable to other subjects. Additionally, unless they are longitudinal in nature, case studies only present a picture of an individual for a brief moment in time (McTear & Conti-Ramsden, 1992). However, they do provide a means of examining the behavior of an individual child in great detail, revealing patterns of performance that might otherwise be impossible to detect.

IS INTERVENTION WITH CONVERSATIONAL LANGUAGE IMPAIRMENT EFFICACIOUS?

If conversational problems form an important component of language impairment, the efficacy of intervening with these problems is a critical issue. Unfortunately, the available research on children with SLI typically has not progressed beyond the point of identifying conversational impairment. Intervention studies are rare. However, it is illuminating to consider a body of literature related to the language intervention mainstream. A number of researchers working with individuals with developmental disabilities have designed intervention programs to improve social skills and interactions. To achieve these goals, these investigators often have targeted specific conversational behaviors such as entering an interaction, responding to questions, asking questions, developing appropriate topics, providing acknowledgment, and complimenting conversational partners. Typically, multiple baseline designs have been employed. With some exceptions (Roessler & Lewis, 1984; Rychtaric & Bornstein, 1979), these studies suggest that specific conversational behaviors can be established with intervention and generalized across certain contexts and time. Considering some of these studies illustrates the general direction of this work.

Schloss and Wood (1990) found that verbal prompting coupled with a self-monitoring technique was effective in increasing the ability of two adults with mental retardation to ask and answer certain types of question in conversation. Noted increases in some targeted behaviors were still observed 6 months following training. Wildman, Wildman, and Kelly (1986) used instructions, modeling, and behavioral rehearsal to train seven adults with mental retardation to ask questions, limit self-disclosing comments, and compliment partners. Gains observed with intervention were maintained 3 months later. Chadsey-Rusch, Karlan, Riva, and Rusch (1984) taught three adults with retardation to ask questions of a conversational partner. The training package consisted of instructions, modeling, and rehearsal. Additionally, verbal prompts were used during conversation ("It's your turn to ask me a question." [p. 220]). Judges' ratings of subjects' conversational abilities increased from interactions in baseline to interactions in intervention. Kelly, Furman, Phillips, Hathorn, and Wilson (1979) used modeling, coaching, and rehearsal to teach two youths with mental retardation to respond to questions, ask questions, and invite their conversational partners to participate in an interaction. Subjects demonstrated the targeted behaviors post-intervention, and some maintenance into free-play situations was noted.

Other studies have examined the effects of intervention on topic manipulation in conversation. For example, Bradlyn et al., (1983) employed instruction, modeling, behavioral rehearsal, and feedback to train five youths with mental retardation to initiate topics of high interest (as well as self-disclosing statements and acknowledgments). Following intervention, targeted skills were observed in the subjects' conversations with peers with mental retardation and in interactions with peers without mental retardation. Skills were maintained when three of the subjects were seen again 5 months later. Hunt, Alwell, Goetz, and Sailor (1990) taught 3 youths with severe mental retardation to initiate and develop topics using communication books. In this study, subjects were taught to pair verbal contributions with pointing to a picture in a communication book using a prompt-fade strategy. In addition, peer partners without mental retardation were instructed to respond to comments and to add questions. All three subjects generalized targeted behaviors to conversational contexts not included in training.

Although most of these intervention studies have concentrated on adolescents and adults, there is also research focusing on the effects of such programs on the conversational skills of children with developmental disabilities. Nelson, Gibson, and Cutting (1973) used a combination of modeling, instructions, and social reinforcement to teach a 7-year-old boy with mental retardation to use grammatically correct questions, smile appropriately, and develop appropriate topics in conversation. All behaviors increased following training, and increases in smiling and questioning were evident 3 1/2 months post. Haring, Roger, Lee, Breen, and Gaylord-Ross (1986) used cues and imitation of conversational bids to teach three 10- to 13-year-old students with mental retardation to manipulate topic and found that training generalized to naturalistic contexts. Charlop and Milstein (1989) used modeling, rehearsal, and tangible reinforcement to teach three 6- to 8-year-old children with autism to participate in scripted conversations. Fifteen months after training, subjects maintained the new scripts with various topics. Hunt, Alwell, and Goetz (1991) found that three 6- to 10-year-old children with severe developmental disabilities increased turn initiation in conversations using a communication book with peers without disabilities. Subjects were taught to pair contributions with pictures in their books. However, the procedure was effective only if the peer also were trained to elicit turns with questions.

This evidence suggests that conversational behaviors have been facilitated using a variety of intervention techniques with adults and children with developmental disabilities. Although the results of the studies described above are encouraging, there are still major questions to be answered concerning the generalization of behaviors targeted in intervention. Behaviors such as those addressed are fully functional only when they can be employed appropriately in a wide variety of dynamic contexts. The studies described above generally were not designed to consider this type of impact.

Little research is available investigating the efficacy of similar conversational intervention with children with SLI. Two important exceptions include Bedrosian and Willis (1987) and Dollaghan and Kaston (1986). Bedrosian and Willis described an intervention program for a 5-year-old boy with expressive language impairment. The intervention involved instruction, modeling, and feedback to target the initiation of memory-related (past) and future-related topics within naturalistic conversations. Procedures included encouraging the child to discuss previous activities as well as structuring activities that the child could discuss after completion. After a 6-month intervention period, increases were noted in the initiation of past and future topics, and a significant increase in level of syntactic development was evident as well. Dollaghan and Kaston (1986) trained four 5- to 8-year-old children with SLI to request clarification of inadequate messages. Intervention consisted of phases focusing on active listening, detection, and reaction to various types of inadequate messages. Procedures included instruction, practice, role playing, and referential communication activities. Subjects demonstrated dramatically increased levels of requesting clarification of trouble sources in audiotaped tasks. Gains were maintained 3–6 weeks after intervention was completed.

Studies drawn from the literature on individuals with developmental disabilities combined with work such as that of Bedrosian and Willis (1987) and Dollaghan and Kaston (1986) suggest that addressing specific conversational behaviors can be a viable intervention endeavor. It appears that behaviors such as requesting, responding to questions, and manipulating topics appropriately in conversation respond to various intervention methods. What is not so evident, however, is the degree to which new behaviors generalize and the extent to which new behaviors enrich a child's life.

EDUCATIONAL IMPLICATIONS

Language impairment in school-age children should be viewed not only according to gaps between expected and observed skills on language-based tasks, but also according to how specific behaviors influence the child's quality of life. Although an elusive concept, quality of life for most school-age children is influenced by the ability to function in conversation, among other factors. Conversational interaction provides a way of forging and maintaining social relationships, participating in preacademic, academic and literacy experiences, and functioning independently in daily living.

Conversational impairment is an issue for many children traditionally identified with SLI on the basis of structural deficits. These children may demonstrate conversational impairment associated with or exceeding structural difficulty. Conversational problems often have devastating effects on a child's social and academic life. Intervention programs designed to enhance conversational skills are important for many children with SLI.

The remaining portion of this chapter is devoted to a description of a case study for a child referred to as C.D. This case illustrates a conversational approach to intervention employed with a child demonstrating specific language impairment. Selected conversational behaviors were emphasized to improve communication in order to enhance C.D.'s quality of life.

CASE STUDY: C.D.

Background Information

C.D. was the fourth of five children of middle-class white parents.[1] C.D.'s developmental and medical histories were generally unremarkable with the exception of his speech and language development. At 4 years and 5 months, C.D. was

---

[1]This is an actual case study presented with permission. Names and identifying information have been changed to protect confidentiality.

diagnosed with language impairment at a large children's medical center. Soon after this evaluation, C.D. was enrolled in a special education preschool class through his public school district.

Evaluation Plan

C.D. was enrolled in our clinic for language intervention at age 5;1 years. On first impression, C.D. seemed to be an active communicator. Although structural language difficulties were evident, C.D. participated in conversations and activities willingly. He played with his siblings and children in the neighborhood and was outgoing and pleasant in conversation. Despite these strengths, several concerns emerged from initial screening (see Screening Checklist for Children with Language Impairment [Brinton & Fujiki, 1994]):

1. C.D. frequently responded to questions with single word or stereotypic answers.
2. C.D. frequently changed topics in response to questions.
3. C.D. did not always contribute substantive comments to topics introduced by others.
4. Adults who interacted with C.D. reported they did an inordinate amount of work to make the interaction successful.
5. Aspects of form–content interactions interfered with communication.

To address the areas of concern highlighted by the screening, an in-depth assessment was conducted. That assessment included:

1. A battery of formal test measures
2. Naturalistic language sampling—two 30-minute spontaneous language samples were collected, one with C.D. and his mother, and one with C.D. and a familiar peer. Interesting materials were provided, but no attempt was made to structure the interactions.
3. Structured language sampling—a 30-minute interaction between C.D. and a clinician—was also collected. This interaction was largely naturalistic. However, the clinician inserted various probes to examine specific conversational abilities.

Evaluation Results

The results of the formal testing are presented in Table 1. As indicated, C.D.'s language and cognitive scores confirmed the diagnosis of expressive and receptive language impairment.

Several structural parameters were analyzed from the data obtained in the three language samples. A semantic-syntactic analysis (Lahey, 1988) was performed on the child-peer sample, and C.D.'s language was productive at stage 5. Analysis of grammatical morphemes in all three samples suggested that C.D. produced most early developing forms (Brown's stages I through V) appropri-

Table 1. Results of formal testing measures for C.D.

Test	Age at administration	Standard score	Test mean	SD
PPVT[a]	4;9	64	100	15
CELF[b]	5;1	59 total	100	15
		70 receptive	100	15
		50 expressive	100	15
Subtests				
Linguistic concepts	5;1	5	10	3
Sentence structure	5;1	3	10	3
Oral directions	5;1	8	10	3
Word structure	5;1	3	10	3
Formulated sentences	5;1	4	10	3
Recalling sentences	5;1	3	10	3
EOWPVT[c]	5;1	25th %tile		
WPPSI-R[d]	4;5	85 full-scale IQ	100	15
		105 perf. IQ		
		69 verbal IQ		

[a]Peabody Picture Vocabulary Test–Revised (Dunn & Dunn, 1981).
[b]Clinical Evaluation of Language Function–Revised (Semel, Wiig, & Secord, 1987).
[c]Expressive One-Word Picture Vocabulary Test (Gardner, 1979).
[d]Wechsler Preschool Primary Scale of Intelligence–Revised (Wechsler, 1989). (The WPPSI-R was administered during C.D.'s assessment at the children's medical center.)

ately 50% (or more) in obligatory contexts. However, C.D.'s production of complex sentence forms was limited.

Several analyses of interactional parameters also were conducted. Ten-minute segments from each of the three samples were analyzed to verify earlier impressions of C.D.'s assertiveness. The resulting analysis is presented in Table 2. C.D. produced a healthy proportion of the utterances in each sample, and the majority of these utterances were assertive acts. However, in the mother–child dyad, the majority of C.D.'s utterances were elicited directly by his mother's questions.

Topic content analyses were performed on the entire child–clinician sample, 10 minutes of the mother–child sample, and 10 minutes of the child–child sample. These analyses were conducted by defining broad content areas as topics (e.g., toys, playing house). The analyses indicated that C.D. maintained over

Table 2. C.D.'s production of assertive acts across three samples

Dyad	% of utterances produced by C.D.	% of C.D.'s utterances that were assertive	% of C.D.'s utterances directly elicited
Mother–child	44	46	54
Peer–child	55	78	9
Clinician–child	40	61	31

75% of the topics that he introduced in all samples. He maintained over 75% of the topics introduced by his mother or the clinician. However, he maintained only 50% of the topics introduced by his peer. In the child–child interaction, only 27% of the topics that were introduced by the dyad were maintained by both speakers (collaborative maintenance).

Although the broad topic analyses revealed that C.D. could introduce and maintain general topical areas in conversation, finer analyses substantiated two difficulties suggested by earlier screening. First, C.D. rarely initiated or contributed to topics that concerned objects, events, or people that were outside of the current physical context. In the mother–child interaction, C.D. often responded inappropriately to questions or changed the topic abruptly. In clinician–child interactions, C.D. could not explain an incident so that the clinician could understand the basic sequence of events. The following segment is representative as C.D. attempted to explain that his family made dipped dessert bars, called "dippies," the previous evening:

C.D.:	I know make dippies.
Clinician:	You know how to make cookies by dipping?
C.D.:	Um hmm.
Clinician:	Really?
C.D.:	Um hmm, not cookies.
Clinician:	Tell me about it.
C.D.:	Last night I make a dippy and my mom taste it. Tastes good.
Clinician:	Really?
C.D.:	Um hmm.
Clinician:	Last night you made a dippy?
C.D.:	Dippy!
Clinician:	Dippy?
C.D.:	Not dippy.
Clinician:	Not dippy?
C.D.:	Hmmm.
Clinician:	What was it?
C.D.:	Ah, just kidding.
Clinician:	Just kidding? Okay.

The second area of topic difficulty concerned the fact that C.D. frequently failed to observe relevance constraints in responding to questions. He often changed or shaded the topic or continued a previous topic in response to direct questions. In C.D.'s conversation with his mother, he responded appropriately to 77% of her simple product (wh-) questions, to 79% of her choice (yes/no) questions, and to 28% of her explanation questions. When C.D. responded inappropriately to a question, his mother tended to rephrase the question and ask it again. The result was a labored interaction in which C.D.'s mother continually probed and C.D. "danced around" the questions. The following example was characteristic:

Mother:	Tell me about golf. How do you play golf?
C.D.:	Like ya, ya win!
Mother:	How do you win?
C.D.	Me.
Mother:	What do you have to do to play golf?
C.D.:	Oh, I missed.
Mother:	Can you tell me how to play golf?
C.D.:	I can show you.
Mother:	No, tell me. Can you tell me?
C.D.:	Uh-huh. Oh.
Mother:	What do you do?
C.D.:	Oh. I'm doing it.
Mother:	You're doing it? A hole in one?
C.D.:	No.
Mother:	Almost.
C.D.:	I almost made it. Oh.
Mother:	What's that called?
C.D.:	Win.
Mother:	Win?
C.D.:	(4 syllables) shoot it far away (2 syllables).
Mother:	How do you tell sister to play golf?
C.D.:	(4 syllables)
Mother:	Does sister know how to play golf?
C.D.:	It's your turn. Let's make it higher, higher.

C.D.'s mother reported that she needed to ask C.D. questions in order to stimulate his language. Clearly, their conversations were hard work for both mother and child. This pattern extended to other adults. Our clinicians found it necessary to make a conscious effort to avoid the same type of questioning.

Intervention Goals

Although both structural and pragmatic aspects of C.D.'s interaction were candidates for intervention, the most pressing concern was the effect of C.D.'s language impairment on his interactions with his mother and family. We suspected this pattern would extend to C.D.'s interaction with his classroom teacher (see Blank & White, 1986). C.D.'s mother was highly supportive and committed to him. However, in her efforts to draw him out, she inadvertently presented him with probes that he could not handle. Thus, we chose to focus a portion of our intervention on easing the conversations between C.D. and his mother. A second focus of intervention was C.D.'s ability to talk about topic matter that was not tied to the current context. Specifically, we wanted to help him sequence and describe past events clearly and discuss events, objects, or facts outside his immediate physical context. It was felt that these skills would be particularly important in C.D.'s classroom environment. Two structural goals also were selected: facilitation of complex sentence constructions and acquisition of new lexical items.

Service Delivery

A three-pronged service delivery model was instituted, focusing on direct work with C.D., collaboration with his mother, and communication with personnel in C.D.'s school. It was our assumption that C.D.'s needs would be served chiefly through his public school setting. C.D. was seen twice weekly in our clinic where his mother observed or participated in intervention sessions and played an active role in determining intervention goals and methods. We felt that our extensive evaluation (especially language sampling) and clinical observations would be useful to C.D.'s school personnel. In turn, we felt that the majority of C.D.'s intervention should be coordinated and carried out in the school setting, the context for so much of C.D.'s social and academic experience.

Time proved that our assumptions were overly idealistic. At the request of C.D.'s family, we initiated exchange of information as well as inservices and conferences with school personnel. The results were disappointing. C.D.'s kindergarten curriculum was fast paced and superficial. Although his classroom teacher was concerned and cooperative, his speech-language pathologist was resistant to working with his teacher and hesitant to consider the classroom as part of her professional domain. C.D.'s parents became frustrated with what they perceived to be constant drilling on fragmented skills and lack of attention to language-based goals. Given this scenario, C.D.'s parents asked us to: 1) design and carry out goals and procedures within our clinic, 2) train C.D.'s mother to carry out procedures, 3) continue efforts to interface services with the school, and 4) support and counsel them as C.D.'s advocates.

Intervention Methods

In intervention, C.D. was presented with interesting scenarios and activities that encouraged him to produce target behaviors in conversation. In addition, we made concentrated efforts to integrate conversational behaviors into a variety of literacy tasks. Some of the methods, procedures, and activities that were used for each intervention goal are listed below.

Improving Responsiveness to Questions

Intervention focused on improving responding to explanation questions. To work on these questions, we targeted C.D.'s conversational partners' production for change. The type of questions that we asked C.D. in the clinical setting were limited to choice and product questions that carried real communicative import. Rhetorical and "teaching" questions were restricted as much as possible. We also worked with C.D.'s mother in adjusting the way that she questioned C.D. She was not asked to eliminate questions, but C.D.'s difficulty with certain question forms was discussed. Alternative ways to interact with C.D. were suggested, including following his topical lead in conversation, expanding his utterances, and modeling forms he produced incorrectly (Fey, 1986; Mecham & Jones, 1981). It was suggested to the classroom teacher that classroom questioning be designed to elicit information familiar to, and easily expressed by, C.D. but not clearly obvious to the teacher. For example, we encouraged questions such as "What do you have in your lunch box?" and discouraged questions such as "How did we cut out our snowflakes yesterday?"

Discussion of Topics Outside the Current Context

The general procedure used to help C.D. talk about past events involved: 1) observing or setting up events, 2) providing a reason to describe these events, and 3) providing enough support so that C.D. could describe the events. Specific activities included cooking or crafts in plan–do formats. For example, C.D. and his clinician planned to make pudding (an activity that was highly motivating for C.D.). They collaborated on a list of ingredients, went to the store and purchased the ingredients from the list, read the directions from the pudding box, and then carried out the directions. The clinician provided cues during these steps and was responsible for all writing and reading. After the pudding was made, C.D.. recapped the events verbally. As C.D.'s proficiency with these kinds of activities improved, story and event retell activities were introduced as well. Books were emphasized in these activities in order to link oral language with print. We felt the use of print in intervention was particularly important because C.D.'s mother reported that he did not enjoy books or being read to at the onset of intervention.

One procedure used to support C.D.'s description of past events was a personal journal. Within C.D.'s culture (The Church of Jesus Christ of Latter-Day Saints), every literate member is encouraged to keep a personal journal (diary) to record events and feelings on a daily basis. Preliterate children often contribute to personal journals by drawing or dictating. Therefore, from C.D.'s perspective, it was perfectly reasonable for his clinician to ask him to recount his intervention activities so that she could write them in his journal. C.D. reported the events, the clinician wrote down his utterances, and the clinician read the journal entry back to C.D. The clinician provided sufficient support so that C.D. could revise his journal entry to his satisfaction. Frequently, C.D. added to the journal entry by drawing pictures, writing his name, or writing some letters on the page.

Increasing the Production of Complex Sentence Forms

A focused stimulation approach (Fey, 1986) was used within a variety of activities to increase the production of complex sentence forms. Some activities were designed specifically to facilitate complex constructions, some incorporated the broader intervention goals as well. Specific complex sentence types (e.g., full object relative constructions) were not singled out. Rather, the clinician modeled a variety of complex forms, concentrating on forms that expressed means to an end or cause–effect (e.g., object complement clauses such as "I made the clock slide off the table," coordinating clauses using "so" or "because" such as "We close the door so the turtle can't get out.").

Increasing Available Lexical Items

The purpose of increasing available lexical items was to facilitate word recognition and production skills and to support C.D.'s understanding of specific classroom routines and academic units. We suggested that the acquisition of new lexical items that were tied to academic units be a focus of C.D.'s school program. In our clinic, intervention with lexical items was conducted on a troubleshooting basis. In other words, when C.D.'s mother expressed concern about specific lexical items, we targeted those items in subsequent sessions.

Intervention Results

It should be recognized that C.D.'s course of intervention does not document efficacy using a carefully controlled time-series design. We offer C.D.'s case only as a clinical example. Intervention goals and methods were adjusted during the program to meet C.D.'s needs, and progress was assessed using a mixture of quantifiable and subjective measures.

Improved Responsiveness to Questions

Progress was monitored by assessing the questioning behavior of C.D.'s mother as well as C.D.'s responses to her questions. C.D.'s mother was adept at altering her interactional style, and within a few months she had decreased the number of explanation questions dramatically. Table 3 summarizes the proportion of C.D.'s appropriate responses and the number of questions C.D.'s mother asked. The initial sample was collected in July, and the final sample was collected the following May. C.D.'s level of appropriate responses to product and to choice questions remained quite stable, and his level of appropriate responses to explanation questions increased fairly steadily.

It seemed clear that the question-nonresponse patterns in C.D. and his mother's interactions had been interrupted. We felt confident that the conversational context was now more conducive to C.D.'s learning about communication. C.D.'s mother shared our conclusions. Seven months after C.D. began intervention, his mother began to report that it was easier for her to talk with her son, and

Table 3. C.D.'s proportion of appropriate response to his mother's questions

| Type of question | Proportion of appropriate responses (in %)[a] | | | | |
	Sample 1 (July 1991)	Sample 2 (Sept. 1991)	Sample 3 (Nov. 1991)	Sample 4 (Feb. 1992)	Sample 5 (May 1992)
Product	77% (13)	33% (3)	33% (6)	100% (5)	75% (4)
Choice	79% (33)	78% (18)	86% (21)	74% (39)	67% (9)
Explan.	28% (25)	39% (18)	56% (9)	78% (9)	67% (5)

[a]Numbers in parentheses indicate raw frequency total of questions asked.

she perceived that he was making significant gains in his ability to express his ideas. C.D.'s mother had no difficulty maintaining her new interactional style. She became an adept observer of C.D.'s behavior in conversation, and she frequently brought insightful comments and questions to the clinic. She also tutored other family members on their interactional styles.

Discussion of Topics Outside the Current Context

C.D.'s performance on discussing topics outside the current context was regularly probed in a variety of clinic activities as C.D. recounted events. C.D.'s production was transcribed and the entries kept in log form. In the initial stages of intervention, C.D. rarely recounted an event in an intelligible manner. As intervention progressed, he became more adept at recounting events and eventually was able to clearly sequence intervention activities for entry into his journal. The following example is C.D.'s description of a trip to the grocery store to buy pudding supplies. On this trip, a ladybug lit on C.D.'s arm, and he brought the bug back to the clinic in a cup. Afterward, C.D. dictated a series of events, the clinician transcribed from C.D.'s dictation, and then, at C.D.'s instigation, the two "read" the entry. Finally, C.D. took the journal in his own hands to "write" some information. It is interesting to note C.D.'s interest in the accurate transcription of his ideas. (Speaker overlaps are noted by < >.)

Clinician:	Now you tell me what we did at the store and I'll write it down.
C.D.:	Okay.
Clinician:	Okay.
C.D.:	Pudding. We get pudding. (pause)
Clinician:	(2 syllables) [Clinician is writing.]
C.D.:	And we get milk. And we saw a ladybug (pause). And we ask a girl to get a glass. And first we need a lid. And we carry it to BYU. What are you writing? [Clinician is writing.]
Clinician:	[Clinician is reading journal entry.] First we get a lid and <get a lid>
C.D.:	<get a lid.>
Clinician:	We <we>
C.D.:	<We>
Clinician:	Carry it <carry it>
C.D.:	<Carry it>
Clinician:	to B<YU>
C.D.:	<YU>
Clinician:	What else?
C.D.:	That's all.
Clinician:	That's all.
C.D.:	Yeah.
Clinician:	That's pretty good.
C.D.:	What's this said? [pointing to sentence in journal]

Clinician: That says, "We got pudding. And we got milk."
C.D.: And this one? [pointing to sentence]
Clinician: Um, "and we saw a ladybug."
C.D.: A baby one.
Clinician: Okay. [inserts "baby" on page]
C.D.: I, I know how to write a ladybug.
Clinician: Baby. Would you like to draw a picture of a ladybug?
C.D.: No, I know, I gonna write her name. [takes journal]
Clinician: Oh, okay.
C.D.: I gonna write a ladybug's name. [writes letters in journal]

Another measure of discussing topics outside the current context was obtained from C.D.'s interactions with his mother. During language sampling, interactions that involved topics outside the current context were identified. Interactions were identified according to the speaker who initiated the outside topic (C.D. or his mother) and according to whether the exchange was felicitous. Felicitous exchanges ranged from 3 to 18 utterances in length and represented segments where C.D. and his mother collaborated successfully on outside topics. Felicitous exchanges contained a variety of contributions including exchanges of information, acknowledgment of one another's contributions, questions and responses, and collaborative topic development and shifts. Nonfelicitous exchanges ranged from 3 to 39 utterances and contained instances in which topic initiations were ignored or continuing topics were disrupted. These sequences sometimes contained nonfelicitous question–answer sequences as well (this measure overlaps somewhat with the question–response results reported above because most of the samples were used for both analyses). Data on the number of utterances comprising felicitous and nonfelicitous exchanges are presented in Table 4.

It was recognized that the immediate physical context would be important to a discussion of outside topics. The setting of each sample used in the above analysis was held constant (clinic room). However, the materials available varied. In most of the first four samples, C.D. and his mother used a number of toys. In the September 1991 sample, C.D. had just finished making cookies. He had

Table 4. Utterances within felicitous and nonfelicitous exchanges involving outside topics

Type of exchange	Number of utterances					
	July 91	Sept.	Nov.	Feb. 92	May	Dec.
C.D.—F[a]	0	0	5	0	11	66
M.—F[b]	6	32	0	8	20	60
C.D.—NF[c]	0	5	0	0	0	4
M.—NF[d]	103	151	0	11	0	2

[a]Felicitous exchanges initiated by C.D.
[b]Felicitous exchanges initiated by C.D.'s mother.
[c]Nonfelicitous exchanges initiated by C.D.
[d]Nonfelicitous exchanges initiated by C.D.'s mother.

the materials still present and was asked to tell his mother how the cookies were made. In the final, December 1992 sample, C.D. and his mother had art supplies, and they made a Christmas card. Although the contexts varied somewhat, the number of felicitous exchanges involving outside topics increased in C.D.'s conversations with his mother over the 18 months sampled. Conversely, the number of nonfelicitous exchanges decreased. The final sample shows a fairly large number of utterances devoted to outside topics. These utterances occurred almost equally in sequences initiated by C.D. and in those initiated by his mother. In other words, both C.D. and his mother learned to initiate and collaborate on outside topics. This result is particularly noteworthy in light of the fact that C.D. and his mother were engaged in an activity closely tied to the materials in front of them.

Increasing the Production of Complex Sentence Forms

C.D.'s production of complex sentences was assessed in four of the samples used previously. The total number of C.D.'s complex utterances, the percent of total utterances that were complex, and the percent of total utterances that were well-formed complex utterances are presented in Table 5. These utterances were largely instances of complementation or coordination. Few relative clauses were produced in any of the samples. Only a modest increase in the percentage of complex utterances and in the percentage of well-formed complex utterances was noted between the initial and final samples.

Increasing Available Lexical Items

As previously mentioned, we worked on increasing available lexical items when C.D.'s mother and teachers suggested difficulties with specific items. We also probed and targeted some items important to his school setting. Examples of items that C.D. did not know in probes but learned to recognize and name included classroom items (chalk, chalkboard, eraser, stapler, tape, pencil, pen), cooking items (bowl, paper towel, sink, measuring cup), and activity items (throw, jump).

One particularly troublesome lexical item for C.D.'s mother was his use of the word "liar." She reported that he used the word "liar" in a socially penalizing way. For example, C.D. asked for milk and his mother told him that there was

Table 5.   C.D.'s production of complex sentence forms

Type of utterance	Number of utterances[a]			
	Sample 1 (July 1991)	Sample 2 (Nov. 1991)	Sample 3 (May 1992)	Sample 4 (Dec. 1992)
Complex	5 (3%)	30 (13%)	18 (10%)	51 (17%)
Grammatically well-formed complex	4 (2%)	19 (8%)	9 (5%)	33 (11%)
Total utterances	186	242	185	300

[a]Numbers in parentheses are the percentages of total of that type of utterance.

some in the refrigerator. When C.D. looked in the refrigerator, there was no milk. C.D. then responded, "Liar." It was subsequently ascertained that C.D. used this term with a number of individuals both at home and at school. After considering the contexts in which C.D. used the word "liar," it was clear that C.D. meant something similar to "you made a mistake." C.D.'s mother and clinician agreed to handle occurrences of "liar" in the following way: When C.D. called his mother or clinician a liar, she would respond, "I feel bad when you call me a liar. If I say something that's not right, you could say, 'You made a mistake.'" If the context permitted, C.D.'s mother or the clinician would then direct C.D. to repeat the liar exchange using an alternative form such as "You made a mistake," or "That's not right." Within a 3-week period, C.D. ceased using "liar" inappropriately.

Formal Testing

Formal testing was administered to C.D. on a yearly basis in our clinic. These results are presented in Table 6. This testing was not conducted as a measure of progress in intervention, but rather to compare C.D.'s skills with those of children his age as he developed. The test scores in Table 6 were obtained 11–13 months following the initial formal measures reported in Table 1. Although we do not use these scores to "measure" growth, several of the same tests were repeated. C.D.'s scores on these formal measures are encouraging.

Table 6.   Formal testing measures and results for C.D.

Test	Age at administration	Standard score	Test mean	SD
PPVT–R	6;4	74	100	15
CELF–R	5;11	71 total	100	15
		80 receptive	100	15
		64 expressive	100	15
Linguistic concepts	5;11	7	10	3
Sentence structure	5;11	7	10	3
Oral directions	5;11	7	10	3
Word structure	5;11	3	10	3
Formulated sentences	5;11	7	10	3
Recalling sentences	5;11	3	10	3
TOLD-P[a]				
Picture vocabulary	6;0	6	10	3
Oral vocabulary	6;0	7	10	3
Grammatic vocabulary	6;0	9	10	3
Sentence imitation	6;0	3	10	3
Grammatic completion	6;0	7	10	3
Word discrimination	6;0	15	10	3
Word articulation	6;0	7	10	3

[a]Test of Language Development-2–Primary (Newcomer & Hammill, 1988)

C.D.: A Retrospective Look at the First 18 Months of Intervention

C.D.'s range of strengths and difficulties was representative of the strengths and difficulties of many children with SLI whom we have seen. From a traditional perspective, it might be argued that the core of C.D.'s difficulty lay in his obvious structural language problems, and any interactional problems could be considered as secondary. It would follow, then, that addressing the structural problems would alleviate any conversational limitations.

We viewed C.D.'s difficulty from a different perspective. We considered C.D.'s conversational and structural problems as intertwined. We focused on the impact of C.D.'s communicative skills on his social and academic functioning, and we did not feel that improvement in interactional skills hinged solely on improvement in language structure. We were most interested in facilitating behaviors that would directly help his interactions with his family, friends, and teachers. In this way, we hoped to intervene in a manner that would be most likely to enhance C.D.'s quality of life.

We felt that C.D.'s language impairment had its most devastating impact on his interaction with his mother. The relationship between child and parent is compromised if their conversational exchanges are constant work for each participant. Procedures were designed to facilitate the interaction between C.D. and his mother by interrupting their question-nonresponse pattern. Over several months of intervention, C.D.'s mother asked far fewer questions and C.D.'s responsiveness increased. Samples of their conversations revealed that C.D.'s assertiveness remained intact, the proportion of utterances produced by each partner remained about the same, but C.D. and his mother were more responsive to each other. It seems unlikely that such an interactional shift (which has since proved stable) would evolve spontaneously. The change in behavior was quantified with counts (see Table 3), but the impact of the change on C.D.'s quality of life was assessed by interviewing his mother, whose perceptions were considered as a legitimate source of information. She felt that her interactions with C.D. were much easier and more pleasant, she indicated that she and C.D. enjoyed activities (such as book sharing) that had previously been stressful, and she explained how she tutored other family members on the interactional techniques she felt were most effective.

Our second interactional goal focused on discussing topics outside the current physical context. We judged that his difficulty in this area seriously hindered C.D.'s ability to share information, explain his feelings, and justify his behaviors at home and school. In addition, describing past events was a central component in many of C.D.'s academic experiences. C.D.'s progress on this goal was measured by logging his instances of retelling events in the clinic, especially in his personal journal, and by quantifying utterances in exchanges concerning outside topics in conversations between C.D. and his mother. A dramatic increase in successful discussion on outside topics by C.D. and his mother was noted.

The impact of C.D.'s growing facility with discussing outside topics on his quality of life was assessed by interviewing C.D.'s parents and classroom teacher. His mother was impressed that C.D. could recount and explain past and outside events more clearly. His teacher was pleased at his improved performance in activities such as show-and-tell.

Although these interactional goals took priority, we also were concerned about C.D.'s structural language problems. We targeted the production of complex sentence forms and specific lexical items for intervention. With regard to lexical items, we wanted to see C.D. provided with a concentrated program to familiarize him with lexical items that would support his academic units. The school setting seemed the ideal place for this program to be implemented, and school personnel agreed. Unfortunately, the necessary coordination of services did not occur. In our clinic, we worked with a fairly small set of lexical items within larger lexical categories. C.D. acquired these targeted forms as demonstrated in probes. The effect of working on some of these items (i.e., learning when not to say liar) was readily apparent. However, intervention for C.D.'s lexical problems fell far short of our expectations. We saw little evidence of systematic attempts in the school setting to probe for and address problematic lexical items that might be important to academic units.

C.D.'s production of complex sentence forms was also a concern when we looked at the first 18 months of intervention. His modest growth in the percentage of well-formed complex structures is not readily attributable to intervention and might have occurred in the absence of intervention. However, C.D.'s use of structural complexity should be considered in light of the overall complexity of his language production. Over the course of intervention, C.D. engaged in much more difficult discussion (i.e., of topics outside the current physical context) than he had done previously. It is conceivable that C.D.. might manifest some overload syntactically as the complexity of the topical matter increased (see Kamhi, 1988). Therefore, we were pleased to see C.D.'s language forms hold steady and inch forward. In any event, a dramatic increase in structural complexity was evidently not necessary to effect the interactional changes noted. However, C.D.'s language structure requires continued monitoring. More concentrated procedures should be initiated (e.g., Camarata & Nelson, 1992; Fey, Cleave, Long, & Hughes, 1993) if it becomes apparent that structure is a chief factor inhibiting C.D.'s social or academic functioning (see also Gillam, McFadden, & van Kleeck, chap. 6, this volume).

In conclusion, in designing C.D.'s intervention program, we focused on the negative impact of his impairment on his quality of life and the possible efficacy of intervention to alleviate that impact. We chose to prioritize interactional goals and concentrate our resources on improving C.D.'s conversational interaction, first within his home and then within his school. As intervention progressed, C.D.'s school personnel became more interested in coordinating his program (thanks to the advocacy and diplomacy of C.D.'s parents). In the future, we feel the key to managing C.D.'s intervention will be to coordinate services to continually monitor his functioning and to determine which behaviors will most positively affect his quality of life. Those behaviors must then become priorities for intervention.

CONCLUSION: DIRECTIONS FOR FUTURE RESEARCH

Work in the study of conversational language impairment and intervention has just begun. Future research is needed to: 1) further clarify the nature of conversational language impairment, 2) document the efficacy of intervention procedures to establish specific conversational behaviors, and 3) examine the impact of those behaviors on a child's overall quality of life.

Our understanding of the conversational abilities of children with SLI has been furthered by studies using both group and case-study designs. However, the information gleaned from these studies has been constrained by methodological limitations. In addition, much of the available research has used different methods of analysis to study children of different ability at different ages interacting in different contexts. As a result, direct comparison of individual studies is difficult. A coordinated investigation examining conversational performance across contexts by subjects at different ages would help to clarify current understanding.

It also might be considered that most of the research (including our own) examining the conversational performance of children with SLI has been performed from a modular perspective. Underlying this perspective is the idea that aspects of form, content, and use may be studied independently of each other and distinct from social skills. In practice, it is impossible to separate these components and inadvisable to ignore social functioning. Research examining these difficulties in a more integrated manner would provide a more holistic picture of language impairment.

Our knowledge of the efficacy of intervention with conversational language impairment is also limited. Few researchers have examined the efficacy of intervention procedures in establishing specific conversational behaviors in children with SLI. The social impact of behavior established in intervention has received even less attention (see also Fey, Catts, & Larrivee, chap. 1, this volume; Windsor, chap. 8, this volume). This is a serious limitation to planning intervention programs. Perhaps some direction for further investigations may be taken from researchers who study conversational behaviors and social skills as intertwined entities.

Research also is needed to probe the influence of conversational language impairment (and language impairment in general) on quality of life, addressing not only the question of whether problems in conversation impede language and academic growth, but also whether these problems result in strained relationships with peers and other individuals in the child's environment (e.g., parents, teachers). Although some recent research has been reported on the ability of children with SLI to perform basic social tasks (e.g., Craig & Washington, 1993; Rice, Sell, & Hadley, 1991), we are only currently beginning to understand how structural and pragmatic impairments affect a child's life.

It is difficult to assess the impact of language impairment on quality of life in a quantifiable manner. There are few objective instruments that measure the type of increases in social skills or the satisfaction that might result from enhanced conversational behaviors. Some of the studies described above probe the impact of new skills by asking community members to rate subjects' general conversational skills pre- and postintervention. Many studies mention reports of parents and teachers regarding the impact of generalized behaviors. However, parent and teacher reports usually are presented rather apologetically, not as solid evidence. In general, it seems that the closer the informant is to the child, the less that informant is to be trusted to evaluate the impact of the child's behaviors. Although we are committed to quantifiable methods of assessing the presence of specific behaviors within social contexts, we also agree with Duchan (1991) that aspects of ethnographic approaches can be borrowed to allow us "to regard information provided by an informant as legitimate and to include it as part of the record" (p. 92). When we are concerned with the impact of behaviors on a child's life, the perceptions of those with whom the child must demonstrate the behaviors, as well as the perceptions of the child (when metalinguistic and "metasocial" abilities permit), form a viable body of evidence.

A FINAL NOTE

In summary, efficacy is not just a matter of asking, "Does this intervention program improve language?" but also, "Does this intervention improve quality of life?" Research examining issues of efficacy in intervention must address this larger question. Working with conversational interactions in real contexts has forced us to widen our perspective to consider the broad implications of language impairment and language intervention. Conversational interaction constitutes a starting point from which to view the impact of language functioning on the lives of individuals. Research investigating how to identify critical problems in conversational interaction and methods designed to alleviate those problems are only beginning. We hope that further work will document the effectiveness of various approaches to identify and intervene with those aspects of conversation that are most influential in improving quality of life.

REFERENCES

Adams, C., & Bishop, D.V.M. (1989). Conversational characteristics of children with semantic-pragmatic disorders: I. Exchange structure, turn taking, repairs and cohesion. *British Journal of Disorders of Communication, 24*, 211–239.

Asher, S., & Renshaw, P. (1981). Children without friends: Social knowledge and social skills training. In S. Asher & J. Gottman (Eds.), *The development of children's friendships* (pp. 273–296). New York: Cambridge University Press.

Bedrosian, J.L., & Willis, T.L. (1987). Effects of treatment on the topic performance of a school age child. *Language, Speech, and Hearing Services in School, 18*, 158–167.

Bishop, D.V.M., & Adams, C. (1989). Conversational characteristics of children with semantic-pragmatic disorders: II. What features lead to a judgment of inappropriacy? *British Journal of Disorders of Communication, 24*, 241–263.

Black, B., & Hazen, N.L. (1990). Social status and patterns of communication in acquainted and unacquainted preschool children. *Developmental Psychology, 26*, 379–387.

Blank, M., Gessner, M., & Esposito, A. (1979). Language without communication: A case study. *Journal of Child Language, 6*, 329–352.

Blank, M., Rose, S.A., & Berlin, L.J. (1978). *The language of learning: The preschool years*. New York: Grune & Stratton.

Blank, M., & White, S.J. (1986). Questions: A powerful form of classroom exchange. *Topics in Language Disorders, 6*(2), 1–12.

Bradlyn, A.S., Himadi, W.G., Crimmins, D.B., Christoff, K.A., Graves, K.G., & Kelly, J.A. (1983). Conversational skills training for retarded adolescents. *Behavior Therapy, 14*, 314–325.

Brinton, B., & Fujiki, M. (1982). A comparision of request-response sequences in the discourse of normal and language-disordered children. *Journal of Speech and Hearing Disorders, 47*, 57–62.

Brinton, B., & Fujiki, M. (1994). Ways to teach conversation. In J. Duchan, L. Hewitt, & R. Sonnenmeier (Eds.), *Pragmatics: From theory to practice* (59–71). Englewood Cliffs, NJ: Prentice Hall.

Brinton, B., Fujiki, M., & Sonnenberg, E.A. (1988). Responses to requests for clarification by linguistically normal and language-impaired children in conversation. *Journal of Speech and Hearing Disorders, 53*, 383–391.

Brinton, B., Fujiki, M., Winkler, E., & Loeb, D. (1986). Responses to requests for clarification in linguistically normal and language-impaired children. *Journal of Speech and Hearing Disorders, 51*, 370–378.

Camarata, S.M., & Nelson, K.E. (1992). Treatment efficiency as a function of target selection in the remediation of child language disorders. *Clinical Linguistics and Phonetics, 6*, 167–178.

Chadsey-Rusch, J., Karlan, G.R., Riva, M.T., & Rusch, F.R. (1984). Competitive employment: Teaching conversational skills to adults who are mentally retarded. *Mental Retardation, 22*, 218–225.

Charlop, M.H., & Milstein, J.P. (1989). Teaching autistic children conversational speech using video modeling. *Journal of Applied Behavior Analysis, 22*, 275–285.

Conti-Ramsden, G., & Friel-Patti, S. (1983). Mothers' discourse adjustments to language-impaired and non-language-impaired children. *Journal of Speech and Hearing Disorders, 48*, 360–367.

Conti-Ramsden, G., & Gunn, M. (1986). The development of conversational disability: A case study. *British Journal of Disorders of Communication, 21*, 339–351.

Craig, H.K. (1991). Pragmatic characteristics of the child with specific language impairment: An interactionist perspective. In T.M. Gallagher (Ed.), *Pragmatics of language: Clinical practice issues* (pp. 163–198). San Diego: Singular Publishing Group.

Craig, H.K., & Evans, J. (1989). Turn exchange characteristics of SLI children's simultaneous and nonsimultaneous speech. *Journal of Speech and Hearing Disorders, 54*, 334–347.

Craig, H.K., & Evans, J.L. (1993). Pragmatics and SLI: Within-group variations in discourse behaviors. *Journal of Speech and Hearing Research, 36,* 777–789.

Craig, H.K., & Gallagher, T. (1986). Interactive play: The frequency of related verbal responses. *Journal of Speech and Hearing Research, 29,* 375–383.

Craig, H.K., & Washington, J.A. (1993). The access behaviors of children with specific language impairment. *Journal of Speech and Hearing Research, 36,* 322–336.

Dodge, K.A., Pettit, G.S., McClaskey, C.L., & Brown, M.N. (1986). Social competence in children. *Monographs of the Society for Research in Child Development, 51* (2, Serial No. 213).

Dollaghan, C., & Kaston, N. (1986). A comprehension monitoring program for language-impaired children. *Journal of Speech and Hearing Disorders, 51,* 264–271.

Duchan, J. (1984). Language assessment: The pragmatics revolution. In R. Naremore (Ed.), *Language science* (pp. 147–180). San Diego: College-Hill Press.

Duchan, J. (1991). Everyday events: Their role in language assessment and intervention. In T.M. Gallagher (Ed.), *Pragmatics of language: Clinical practice issues* (pp. 43–98). San Diego: Singular Publishing Group.

Dunn, L., & Dunn, L. (1981). *Peabody Picture Vocabulary Test–Revised.* Circle Pines, MN: American Guidance Service.

Fey, M.E. (1986). *Language intervention with young children.* Newton, MA: Allyn & Bacon.

Fey, M.E., Cleave, P.L., Long, S.H., & Hughes, D.L. (1993). Two approaches to the facilitation of grammar in children with language impairment. An experimental evaluation. *Journal of Speech and Hearing Research, 36,* 141–157.

Fey, M.E., & Leonard, L. (1983). Pragmatic skills of children with specific language impairment. In T. Gallagher & C. Prutting (Eds.), *Pragmatic assessment and intervention issues in language* (p. 65–82). San Diego: College-Hill Press.

Fey, M.E., & Leonard, L. (1984). Partner age as a variable in the conversational performance of specifically language-impaired and normal-language children. *Journal of Speech and Hearing Research, 27,* 413–423.

Fujiki, M., & Brinton, B. (1991). The verbal noncommunicator: A case study. *Language, Speech, and Hearing Services in Schools, 22,* 322–333.

Gallagher, T. (1977). Revision behaviors in the speech of normal children developing language. *Journal of Speech and Hearing Research, 20,* 303–318.

Gallagher, T., & Darnton, B. (1978). Conversational aspects of the speech of language-disordered children: Revision behaviors. *Journal of Speech and Hearing Research, 21,* 118–135.

Gardner, M. (1979). *Expressive One-Word Picture Vocabulary Test.* Novato, CA: Academic Therapy Publications.

Gottman, J.M. (1983). How children become friends. *Monographs of the Society for Research in Child Development, 48*(2, Serial No. 201).

Hadley, P.A., & Rice, M.L. (1991). Conversational responsiveness of speech- and language-impaired preschoolers. *Journal of Speech and Hearing Research, 34,* 1308–1317.

Haring, T.G., Roger, B., Lee, M., Breen, C., & Gaylord-Ross, R. (1986). Teaching social language to moderately handicapped students. *Journal of Applied Behavior Analysis, 19,* 159–171.

Hazen, N.L., & Black, B. (1989). Preschool peer communication skills: The role of social status and interaction context. *Child Development, 60,* 867–876.

Hunt, P., Alwell, M., & Goetz, L. (1991). Interacting with peers through conversation turntaking with a communication book adaptation. *Augmentative and Alternative Communication, 7,* 117–126.

Hunt, P., Alwell, M., Goetz, L., & Sailor, W. (1990). Generalized effects of conversation skill training. *Journal of The Association for Persons with Severe Handicaps, 15,* 250–260.

Johnston, J.R. (1985). The discourse symptoms of developmental disorders. In T.A. Van Dijk (Ed.), *Handbook of discourse analysis: Vol: 3. Discourse and dialogue* (pp. 79–93). Orlando, FL: Academic Press.

Kamhi, A.G. (1988). A reconceptualization of generalization and generalization problems. *Language, Speech, and Hearing Services in Schools, 19,* 304–313.

Kelly, J.A., Furman, W., Phillips J., Hathorn, S., & Wilson, T. (1979). Teaching conversational skills to retarded adolescents. *Child Behavior Therapy, 1,* 85–97.

Lahey, M. (1988). *Language disorders and language development.* New York: Macmillan.

Leonard, L.B. (1986). Conversational replies of children with specific language impairment. *Journal of Speech and Hearing Research, 29,* 114–119.

McTear, M.F. (1985a). Pragmatic disorders: A case study of conversational disability. *British Journal of Disorders of Communication, 20,* 129–142.

McTear, M.F. (1985b). Pragmatic disorders: A question of direction. *British Journal of Disorders of Communication, 20,* 119–127.

McTear, M., & Conti-Ramsden, G. (1992). *Pragmatic disability in children.* San Diego: Singular Publishing Group.

Mecham, M.J., & Jones, J.D. (1981). *Modeling language: A participation booklet for parents.* Salt Lake City, UT: Communication Research Associates.

Nelson, K.E. (1989). Strategies for first language teaching. In M.L. Rice & R.L Schiefelbusch (Eds.), *The teachability of language* (pp. 263–310). Baltimore: Paul H. Brookes Publishing Co.

Nelson, N.W. (1993). *Childhood language disorders in context: Infancy through adolescence.* New York: Macmillan.

Nelson, R., Gibson, F., Jr., & Cutting, D.S. (1973). Video taped modeling: The development of three appropriate social responses in a mildly retarded child. *Mental Retardation, 11,* 24–28.

Newcomer, P., & Hammill, D. (1988). *Test of Language Development-2–Primary (TOLD2–P).* Austin, TX: PRO-ED.

Nippold, M.A. (1988). *Later language development: Ages nine through nineteen.* Austin, TX: PRO-ED.

Plante, E., Swisher, L., Kiernan, B., & Restrepo, M.A. (1993). Language matches, Illuminating or confounding? *Journal of Speech and Hearing Research, 36,* 772–776.

Prutting, C.A., & Kirchner, D.M. (1987). A clinical appraisal of the pragmatic aspects of language. *Journal of Speech and Hearing Disorders, 52,* 105–119.

Rice, M.L., Sell, M.A., & Hadley, P.A. (1991). Social interactions of speech- and language-impaired children. *Journal of Speech and Hearing Research, 34,* 1299–1307.

Rosinski-McClendon, M.K., & Newhoff, M. (1987). Conversational responsiveness and assertiveness in language-impaired children. *Language, Speech, and Hearing Services in Schools, 18,* 53–62.

Roessler, R.T., & Lewis, F.D. (1984, January). Conversation skill training with mentally retarded and learning disabled sheltered workshop clients. *Rehabilitation Counseling Bulletin,* pp. 161–171.

Rowan, L.E., Leonard, L.B., Chapman, K., & Weiss, A.L. (1983). Performative and presuppositional skills in language-disordered and normal children. *Journal of Speech and Hearing Research, 26,* 97–106.

Rychtarik, R.G., & Bornstein, P.H. (1979). Training conversational skills in mentally retarded adults: A multiple baseline analysis. *Mental Retardation, 17,* 289–293.

Schloss, P.J., & Wood, C.E. (1990). Effect of self-monitoring on maintenance and generalization of conversational skills of persons with mental retardation. *Mental Retardation, 28,* 105–113.

Semel, E., Wiig, E., & Secord, W. (1987). *Clinical Evaluation of Language Fundamentals–Revised.* New York: The Psychology Corporation.

Silliman, E.R., & Cherry Wilkinson, L. (1991). *Communicating for learning: Classroom observation and collaboration.* Gaithersburg, MD: Aspen Publishers, Inc.

Snyder, L. (1978). Communicative and cognitive abilities and disabilities in the sensorimotor period. *Merrill-Palmer Quarterly, 24,* 161–180.

Speidel, G.E. (1987). Conversation and language learning in the classroom. In K.E. Nelson and A. van Kleeck (Eds.), *Children's language* (Vol. 6, pp. 99–135). Hillsdale, NJ: Lawrence Erlbaum Associates.

Tomblin, J.B. (1983). An examination of the concept of disorder in the study of language variation. *Proceedings from the Fourth Wisconsin Symposium on Research in Child Language Disorders* (pp. 81–109). Madison: Department of Communicative Disorders, University of Wisconsin.

Tomblin, J.B., & Liljegreen, S.J. (1985). The identification of socially significant communication needs in older language impaired children: A case example. In D.N. Ripich & F.M. Spinelli (Eds.), *School discourse problems* (pp. 219–230). San Diego: College-Hill Press.

Wechsler, D. (1989). *Wechsler Preschool and Primary Scale of Intelligence–Revised.* San Antonio, TX: Psychological Corporation.

Wildman, B.G., Wildman, H.E., & Kelly, J. (1986). Group conversational-skills training and social validation with mentally retarded adults. *Applied Research in Mental Retardation, 7,* 443–458.

8

Language Impairment
and Social Competence

Jennifer Windsor

THE ABILITY TO COMMUNICATE FOR social purposes is of paramount importance for school-age children. During the school years, competent social interaction is fundamental to the development of friendships, positive evaluations by others, and academic achievement. In a real sense, to be socially competent is to be successful. For those students with less communicative competence than their peers, such success may be more difficult to achieve. Because of this, many professionals involved in intervention with children with language impairments now are being called on to address these children's social skills also (Brinton & Fujiki, chap. 7, this volume; Fey, Catts, & Larrivee, chap. 1, this volume; Fujiki & Brinton, 1994; Gallagher, 1991; Goldstein & Gallagher, 1992). The purpose of this chapter is to discuss the relationship between social skills and language skills and to address the educational implications of social skills impairments. The scope and limitations of current intervention strategies for social skills impairments and future research needs are highlighted.

THE CORRELATION BETWEEN
SOCIAL SKILLS AND LANGUAGE SKILLS

Multiple definitions of social competence exist, many referring to a set of social skills such as role perception and appreciation, control of attention, problem solving, understanding social relationships, adjustment, self-help skills, and everyday coping skills (e.g., Anderson & Messick, 1974). The key features of these definitions of social competence are the effectiveness and appropriateness of interpersonal interactions (Guralnick, 1992). Language skills are an integral part of interpersonal interactions. Certainly, the distinction between pragmatic aspects of language and some social skills is nebulous. Not only does language occur in a social context and act as the major medium of social interaction, the appropriate use of language is in itself a social skill. Many researchers and clinicians view language development as an inherent part of social development rather than as a completely independent phenomenon (cf. Gallagher, 1991).

It may well be that language skills and social skills are different views of the same animal. The very least that may be said is that neither social nor linguistic competence is a unitary phenomenon, but each encompasses multifaceted, overlapping developmental skills and knowledge. Although the degree of overlap between language skills and social skills is debatable, there is no question that the presence of language impairments is correlated with social skills impairments. Evidence for this link comes from several sources, including research on behavior and emotional disorders, challenging behaviors and other behaviors eliciting negative responses, and from research on learning disabilities.

An established correlation exists between language skills and behavior and emotional disorders. The incidence of both behavior and emotional disorders is higher for children with speech and language impairments than for children with typical language skills (Baker & Cantwell, 1982a, 1982b, 1987; Baltaxe & Simmons, 1988; Beitchman, Nair, Clegg, Ferguson, & Patel, 1986; Stevenson & Richman, 1978). Baker and Cantwell (1982a) investigated the incidence of behavior and emotional disorders in 180 children ages 1–12 years enrolled in a community speech-language clinic. Children were identified as having speech and/or language impairments on the basis of standardized test scores. Baker and Cantwell found that 25% of the children with speech impairments and 65% of the children with speech and language impairments had a diagnosable behavior disorder. Most of these children were diagnosed with attention deficit disorder. In a population-based study, Beitchman et al. (1986) found that 5-year-olds scoring below the normal range on standardized language tests were more likely to be classified by teacher reports as showing some type of behavior disorder (especially attention deficit disorder) or emotional disorder (e.g., anxiety, depression) than typical peers. Thirty-four percent of children with language impairments, compared to 22% of their typical peers, were classified as having a behavior or emotional disorder.

Similarly, children diagnosed with behavior or emotional disorders often are found to have language impairments (Camarata, Hughes, & Ruhl, 1988; Gualtieri, Koriath, Van Bourgondien, & Saleeby, 1983; Mack & Warr-Leeper, 1992; Miniutti, 1991). Gualtieri et al. (1983) found that 11 of 22 children with behavior disorders scored at least one standard deviation lower than would be expected from their verbal IQ scores on at least one standardized language test. More recently, Mack and Warr-Leeper (1992) compared the performance of 20 adolescent boys with chronic behavior disorders on a battery of standardized language tests with the performance of the normative samples used in each test. Seventeen of the 20 adolescents were identified as having speech and/or language impairments on the test battery. Mack and Warr-Leeper concluded that this rate of occurrence was about 10 times higher than the prevalence of speech and language impairments in the general population.

Because of potentially confounding variables (e.g., socioeconomic class, willingness to seek help), the generalizability of this type of institution-based study to the population at large may be limited. Moreover, in a number of institution- and population-based studies, information on subjects' cognitive levels is absent or is apparently not partialled out from language performance (e.g., Beitchman et al., 1986). Despite these limitations, there remains substantial evidence of a robust positive correlation between behavior and emotional disorders and language skills.

A second source of evidence for the link between social and language skills is apparent in the challenging behaviors of some students with disabilities. The occurrence of marked deficits in social interaction, including disruptive behaviors such as hitting and biting, has been documented for many children with severe disabilities (Donoghue & Abbas, 1971). There is increasing evidence that these challenging behaviors serve communicative functions. When more socially appropriate forms of communication are learned, the challenging behaviors decrease (Carr & Durand, 1985; Hunt, Alwell, Goetz, & Sailor, 1990). A similar link exists between language impairment and negative behaviors. For example, in a study with a 4-year-old boy with specific language impairment (SLI), Gallagher and Craig (1984) found that the boy's repeated use of a particular phrase elicited negative peer reactions. Establishing functional equivalence between this phrase and an alternative, less socially penalizing phrase improved the boy's social acceptance.

A third source of evidence for the link between language and social skills stems from the established relationship between learning disabilities and social skills. This relationship is reflected in the position statements of professional organizations. In the definition of learning disabilities proposed by the Interagency Committee on Learning Disabilities (Silver, 1988) the concept of significant deficits in social skills is included as part of the definition. Although this is not the case in the definition of learning disabilities proposed by the National Joint Committee on Learning Disabilities (1991), the frequent co-occurrence of language and social deficits is recognized here also. In this definition (adopted by the American Speech-Language-Hearing Association), "problems in self-regulatory behaviors, social perception, and social interaction may exist with learning disabilities but do not by themselves constitute a learning disability" (p. 19).

Part of the reason for the difference between definitions of learning disabilities is that there are no uniformly accepted diagnostic criteria for learning disabilities. Also, it is difficult to determine the specific behaviors that fall in the domain of social skills and difficult to determine how both social competence and communicative competence are defined distinctly. Aside from this definitional issue, many investigators see spoken language as the common thread linking different learning disabilities, including impairments of spoken language, reading, and mathematics (Stark, Tallal, & McCauley, 1988). It is accepted that an early impairment in the acquisition of language form may be predictive of a learning disability at a later point in development (especially involving reading)

(Aram & Nation, 1980; Fey et al., chap. 1, this volume). Given this link between language and learning disabilities, it is not surprising that researchers and clinicians are now attending more carefully to the social skills of children with language impairments.

POSSIBLE CAUSE–EFFECT RELATIONSHIPS
BETWEEN SOCIAL SKILLS AND LANGUAGE IMPAIRMENTS

Generally, it is agreed that language impairments and social skills impairments are not only correlated but, in most instances, are causally linked. There is less agreement about the exact nature and direction of the causal relationship. There are five distinct views of this cause–effect relationship: 1) no causal relationship between language impairments and social impairments exists, 2) language impairments cause social impairments, 3) social impairments cause language impairments, 4) a third variable causes both language impairments and social impairments, and 5) language impairments and social impairments interact over time. (See Prizant et al. [1990] for a review. See Nieves [1991] for a comprehensive overview of the cause–effect relationships hypothesized to exist between behavior and emotional disorders and learning disabilities.)

No Causal Relationship

In some instances, it is possible that no causal relationship exists between a particular language impairment and a particular social impairment (Prizant et al,. 1990). In this view, although they co-occur, the specific manifestations of the impairments are unrelated. For example, because a student who rarely initiates social interactions has a lateral lisp also does not necessarily imply that the lisp causes the low initiation level or vice versa.

Language Impairments Cause Social Impairments

When a cause–effect relationship is thought to exist, one view is that language impairments cause social impairments directly. For example, language impairments such as word retrieval deficits, difficulty constructing indirect requests, or difficulty taking a listener's perspective may predispose children to be less tactful than their peers (Bliss, 1992; Pearl, Donahue, & Bryan, 1985). In this view, any deficit in overall communication skills may adversely affect social skills. A student with poor language content and/or form (e.g., with poor comprehension, limited syntax, or unintelligible speech) may avoid peers because of the likely occurrence of communication breakdowns or because the strategies used to repair breakdowns are ineffective. In some instances, limited grammatical skills may lead to a pragmatic impairment (Fey & Leonard, 1991). For example, difficulty with certain constructions may lead to a child being less able to make repairs or be cohesive during conversation. Pragmatic impairments may predispose a child to be identified as having a social impairment (Blank, Gessner, &

Esposito, 1979; Fujiki & Brinton, 1991). Fujiki and Brinton (1991) reported a case study of a 9-year-old with a language impairment who was outgoing and very verbal but who was not well-accepted by his peers. The impression of the boy as "socially inept" was traced to his overly assertive conversational style (e.g., his high proportion of utterances and requests and low proportion of responses to requests).

The view that language impairments precede social impairments does not imply that all children with language impairments will have social impairments also. However, this view suggests that more severe language impairments may be associated with more severe social impairments and/or that, for a given child, there is a minimum level of communicative competence that is necessary to avoid difficulties in social interaction. Fey (Fey, 1986; Fey & Leonard, 1983) proposed that children with language impairments who have similar profiles of language form may differ from each other in their conversational assertiveness and responsiveness. For example, some children may have high levels of assertiveness and responsiveness and may be effective communicators even though they demonstrate impairments in language form. Conversely, some children may have low levels of assertiveness and/or responsiveness, thus presenting social-communicative profiles that reveal serious disabilities and who require intervention.

Social Impairments Cause Language Impairments

The third cause–effect view of the language–social skills relationship is that social skills impairments predispose children to develop learning problems, including language impairments (Patterson, DeBaryshe, & Ramsey, 1989; Walker, Shinn, O'Neill, & Ramsey, 1987). This view has received less support than the previous view that language impairments precede social impairments. However, some students' language difficulties may be traced to social impairments. Patterson et al. (1989) hypothesized that antisocial behavior is likely to lead to both rejection by peers and chronic academic failure. Similarly, a lack of emotional identification with peers and teachers could create an environment in which the child does not want to learn (Connolly, 1971). In this realization of the cause–effect relationship, a students's noncompliant behavior or emotional disorder precludes optimal learning experiences. For example, a student who does not attend, stays seated only for short periods, or who does not remain on task is less likely to successfully learn both the explicit academic curriculum and the implicit social rules of a classroom.

A Third Variable Causes Both
Language Impairments and Social Impairments

The fourth view is derived chiefly from research on the link between behavior and emotional disorders and the academic performance of students with learning disabilities. In this view, a third variable is considered to underlie both social and academic (including linguistic) competence. Although factors such as social class and family history have been suggested also (Baltaxe & Simmons, 1988), two hypotheses of this third variable have emerged as primary.

First, it has been suggested that some students with learning disabilities have a fundamentally different social cognition, or way of representing the social world (Johnson & Myklebust, 1971; Myklebust, 1975; Semrud-Clikeman & Hynd, 1991). This includes a decreased ability to understand the environment; differences from typically developing peers in interpreting gestures, prosody, and facial expressions; difficulty in conceptualizing alternatives, pretending and anticipating, and recognizing cause–effect relationships. In support of this description, Axelrod (1982) found that eight- and ninth-graders with learning disabilities were rated by teachers as showing lower levels of nonverbal social perception than typically developing peers. These differences in social cognition are considered to motivate both social and language impairments. Although there is some support for this hypothesis (see Pearl, 1987, for a review), the factors underlying differences in social cognition are unclear. Because it is possible that differences in social cognition are a consequence of different social interaction experiences, this hypothesis is in some ways linked to the preceding two views of the causal relationship between language impairments and social impairments.

The implication of a biological or neurophysiological factor is the basis of the second major hypothesis for the variable underlying both linguistic and social competence (Geschwind & Galaburda, 1985; Spreen, 1989). In this view, hormonal factors cause defective cell migration in the embryo, resulting in minor abnormalities in cerebral tissue growth and blood flow, particularly in the left hemisphere. These abnormalities lead to behavior, emotional, and learning disabilities among a variety of other concomitant disorders. Currently, this view of the cause–effect relationship is limited in that the mechanisms linking biological factors and specific behavioral subtypes are unclear. Moreover, there are few specific guidelines for intervention provided by this view. However, some learning disabilities and some behavior and emotional disorders do appear to be biologically based (Ferguson & Rapoport, 1983; Geschwind & Galaburda, 1985). Thus, it is plausible that the same biological factor underlies both language impairments and social impairments.

Language Impairments and Social Impairments Interact

Currently, the predominant view of the cause–effect relationship is that, for many students with language and social impairments, the impairments interact and affect each other during development. This view stems from a transactional model of development in which children's development is seen as the outcome of continuous interactions between children and their families and other social contacts (Sameroff, 1987). In line with this type of transactional model, Rice and her colleagues (Hadley & Rice; 1991; Rice, 1993; Rice, Sell, & Hadley, 1991) have proposed a social consequences account of language.

In the social consequences account, it is suggested that children with limited language who lack conventional means for entering social interactions are likely to be ignored and excluded from interactions with peers. These children may develop strategies to compensate for being rebuffed socially (e.g., directing social overtures to adults rather than peers) and may not have the same opportunities to take advantage of socialization to support language learning. In support of the social consequences account, Fujiki and Brinton (1994) described the case of a 4-year-old boy with both expressive and receptive language impairments. The boy had difficulty initiating and responding to peer interactions and often rebuffed peers' attempts to interact with him. Fujiki and Brinton noted that the boy's language impairment appeared to restrict his ability to engage in conversation, and his social skills limited his opportunities to use language for communication.

To a large extent, success throughout the school years lies in the eyes of the beholder. Several studies support the notion that students with similar behavior and academic performance but who differ in speech, language, or hearing abilities tend to be evaluated differently by peers (Hall, 1991; Perrin, 1954; Silverman & Paulus, 1989; Vandell & George, 1991) and professionals (Lass et al., 1992; Silverman & Marik, 1993). The methods used in studies in this area generally have isolated speech and language characteristics from other attributes, such as physical attractiveness (e.g., showing videotaped segments of unfamiliar children with and without language impairments to typical peers or using questionnaire information about hypothetical scenarios). These studies have indicated consistently that students with language impairments tend to be perceived as, for example, less popular, less smart, less attractive and more insecure, more unpleasant, and more "weird" than students without language impairments (Rice, 1993). Hall (1991) found that even the presence of minor articulation errors (i.e., misarticulating /r/ or /s/ and /z/) was sufficient cause for fifth graders to be rated more negatively by peers on three 4-point scales addressing speaking skills, peer status, and prognosis as a teenager, respectively. On each scale, students with articulation errors tended to score about 1 point more negatively than typical peers.

As would be anticipated, negative personality traits are not assigned only to students whose sole difficulty is a language impairment. Students who are not identified as having language impairments but who have social skill impairments are evaluated negatively by others (Dodge, 1983; Horstman & Bornstein, 1985). Children with developmental delays (Hemphill & Siperstein, 1990; Rhyner, Lehr, & Pudlas, 1990) and physical disabilities (Centers & Centers, 1963) also are at risk for being perceived more negatively or interacted with in a less than optimal manner by other students and teachers. For example, Rhyner et al. (1990) found that two teachers of four young children with developmental delays were not very responsive to the children's initiations. Moreover, the teachers' contingent responses to initiations occurred twice as frequently in teacher- as opposed to child-directed activities (see Koppenhaver, Pierce, Steelman, & Yoder, chap. 9, this volume).

Although factors such as nonverbal communication, role-taking abilities, and academic performance also are implicated (Horne, 1985), spoken language skills, especially conversational competence, appear to play a primary role in peer acceptance. Studies by Black and Hazen (1990) and Hazen and Black (1989) indicated that familiar and unfamiliar typically achieving preschoolers classified peers as more liked when the peers were better able to initiate and respond in conversations, able to direct initiations to more than one listener at a time, and able to direct initiations to specific listeners when interacting with familiar peers. Hemphill and Siperstein (1990) found that fourth- and sixth-graders rated children with mild developmental delays less favorably when the children demonstrated poor discourse skills. Infrequent questioning and inappropriate pauses were key discourse features leading to unfavorable reactions. The typical students tended to characterize peers with poor discourse skills as being lonely, bored, and ashamed, that is, as individuals who would be on the periphery of social interactions.

Poor conversational skill is a primary characteristic of many children with language impairments (Craig & Evans, 1989; Craig & Washington, 1993; Hadley & Rice, 1991; Rice et al., 1991). Using the Social Interactive Coding System, an online coding system of initiations and responses (Rice, Sell, & Hadley, 1990), Rice et al. (1991) found that preschoolers with speech and language impairments and preschoolers learning English as a second language were more likely to use one-word or nonverbal initiations than children with language impairments, who, in turn, were more likely to use shorter initiations than typically developing children. Typically developing children directed a higher proportion of their initiations to peers (as opposed to adults) than did the other children, and all children's peer-directed initiations were directed most often to typically developing children. The similarity of results for the children with speech and language impairments and for the children learning English as a second language suggested to Rice and her colleagues that it is a general deficit in overall communicative competence rather than a language impairment per se that is linked to social skill impairments. Hadley and Rice (1991) found that children with language impairments only and children with both speech and language impairments used fewer initiations than typically developing peers. They suggested that one reason for this finding was a relative lack of responses by peers to initiations. Two factors were noted as possible causes of the low level of peer responses: the unintelligibility of the children with language impairments and their limited ability to gain peers' attention prior to initiations.

Craig and Evans (1989) found that four out of five 8- to 13-year-olds with language impairments did not interrupt an adult interactant during a conversation. Interrupting a speaker is characteristic of typically developing children and is one way of gaining a speaker turn. The one child with a language impairment who did interrupt was the only one with intact receptive language skills. Craig and Washington (1993) studied the ability of five 7- to 8-year-olds with language impairments and their typical peers to join established social interactions. All of the typically developing peers joined interactions successfully, nine doing so verbally. Two of the five children with language impairments joined interactions successfully and both did so nonverbally. These two children had higher receptive language skills than the other children with language impairments.

Coinciding with the view that language impairments and social impairments interact (and with the view that language impairments cause social impairments directly), there is a philosophy that a primary goal of intervention with students with language impairments is to achieve socially relevant goals; that is, to assist students in achieving social approval and avoiding social penalties (Tomblin & Liljegreen, 1985). A more specific implication is that opportunities to participate in situations in which successful social as well as linguistic communication skills can be learned should be increased (e.g., devising curricula that permit choices among activities and encourage interaction among peers) (Rice, 1993).

EDUCATIONAL IMPLICATIONS OF SOCIAL SKILL IMPAIRMENTS

Each type of cause–effect relationship examined here most likely underlies at least some language and social impairments, with the particular relationship(s) motivating a given student's acquisition of skills dependent on the student's individual history and development. For all individuals, language and social skills impairments must be addressed in educational contexts. Students with low social competence are likely to have a diminished self-concept, to be less motivated to achieve, and to show reduced academic achievement (Byrne, 1984; Weiner, 1984).

Self-concept, the perception of one's own abilities, feelings, and acceptability, is an important determinant of a student's motivation to persist in learning difficult tasks. If self-concept is poor, motivation tends to be poor also. If their motivation is poor, students with language impairments may develop negative attitudes toward schoolwork, and the probability of improving language and academic skills is lowered. Students with poor self-concept tend to attribute academic success to factors such as the ease of tasks or good luck, and they tend to attribute academic failure to low ability (Tollefson et al., 1982). Much of the relevant research in this area concerns students with learning disabilities.

From a meta-analysis of 41 studies on the self-concepts of students with learning disabilities, Chapman (1988) drew three conclusions. First, many of these students' academic self-concepts were poorer than their peers. However, findings about the general self-concepts of students with learning disabilities in relation to peers were equivocal. Indeed, although many of these students' general self-concepts were poorer than their higher-achieving peers, they still had an average self-concept. This finding is supported by more recent research (Priel & Leshem, 1990). Priel and Leshem found that the self-evaluations of cognitive competence by first and second graders with learning disabilities were poorer than the self-evaluations of their normally achieving peers. Teachers had low evaluations of peers' acceptance of students with learning disabilities. However, students with learning disabilities and typically developing students had similar perceptions of how well they would be accepted by peers.

Chapman's (1988) second conclusion was that for those students with poorer self-concepts, decrements in self-concept occurred by third grade. This result parallels the finding that for the majority of typical children it is not until age 7 or 8 that self-perceptions of ability coincide with actual abilities. Prior to this age, self-perceptions tend to be positively biased (Stipek & Tannatt, 1984). Although it might be expected that self-concept would become increasingly poor in later grades because of cumulative academic failure, Chapman found that self-concept among students with learning disabilities tended to remain stable until high school.

Chapman's (1988) third conclusion was that students with learning disabilities who were receiving intervention services tended to have higher self-concepts than those who were not. It has been suggested that children with disabilities may be expected to receive more negative evaluations from typically developing peers in mainstreamed settings than from other children with disabilities in special educations settings (Taylor, Asher, & Williams, 1987). However, Chapman found there was no difference in self-concept between students with learning disabilities who participated in regular classrooms and those in special education classrooms. This finding supports early research (Barksdale, 1961; Pandy, 1971) suggesting that the same variables accounting for social status in the regular education classroom (e.g., academic achievement, attractiveness) operate in special education classrooms also. By federal mandate (PL 102-119, the Individuals with Disabilities Education Act Amendments of 1991), many students with disabilities are integrated into regular education classrooms and have more opportunities for social interaction with typically developing peers. Some small benefits and no adverse effects on students' social behaviors have been found as a result of the policy of inclusion (Guralnick, 1990a).

INTERVENTIONS FOR CHILDREN WITH SOCIAL IMPAIRMENTS

A key motivation for the current research emphasis on social skills stems from the belief that competent social interaction skills may facilitate the integration of students with disabilities and their typically developing peers (Haring, 1993). An overview of the intervention studies aimed at increasing social skills is given in Table 1. This table is not intended to include a comprehensive list of the research in this area but rather is meant to highlight general characteristics of this research.

For the most part, the intervention research has been carried out with a small number of students, and few investigations have focused on students with

Table 1. Overview of intervention research

Authors	Subjects	Goals	Techniques	Results
Strain, Kerr, and Ragland (1979)	4 9- to 10-year-olds with autism and developmental delays, 1 peer without disabilities	Teach subjects to respond by peer initiations and prompts and praise	Intervention by peer	Increased responding by all subjects in both interventions, minimal generalization
Lancioni (1982)	9 8- to 13-year-olds with developmental delays, social withdrawal; 51 peers without disabilities	Teach basic social responses	Intervention by peers	All subjects learned social responses. Edible rather than social contingencies were important in initial intervention. Generalization to similar contexts occurred.
Bierman and Furman (1984)	56 fifth- and sixth-graders with low peer acceptance, 56 fifth- and sixth-graders with high peer acceptance	Test effects of conversation skill training and positive peer involvement on language skills	Conversation training, peer involvement	Conversation training improved language. Involvement of peers improved peer- and self-evaluations but not language.
Gaylord-Ross, Haring, Breen, and Pitts-Conway (1984)	3 7- to 20-year-olds with autism and developmental delays, 7 peers without disabilities	Teach subjects a set of social behaviors	Initiation training, peer training	Increased social interaction especially with familiar peers, some generalization to untrained contexts for 2 subjects
Odom, Hoyson, Jamieson, and Strain (1985)	3 4-year-olds with developmental delays, social withdrawal; 3 peers without disabilities	Teach subjects a set of social behaviors	Intervention by peers	Increased peer initiations and positive social interactions, initiations by peers dependent on teachers' prompts and did not generalize across settings
Peck (1985)	8 9- to 13-year-olds with autism, moderate to profound delays; 4 teachers/aides	Test effects of increased opportunities for student initiations on social-communicative behaviors	Teacher/aide training	Increased social-communicative behaviors by 6 students
Haring, Roger, Lee, Breen, and Gaylord-Ross (1986)	3 10- to 13-year-olds with moderate developmental delays	Teach subjects to initiate and expand topics	Conversation training	Increased initiation and expansion by all subjects

(continued)

223

Table 1. (continued)

Authors	Subjects	Goals	Techniques	Results
Goldstein and Ferrell (1987)	3 3- to 5-year-olds with behavior disorders, 2 of these with language delays; 6 peers without disabilities	Teach subjects to initiate and respond	Intervention by peers	Decreased initiation by 2 subjects and increased responding by 2 subjects, generalization to untrained contexts by 1 subject, some peers more effective than others in intervention
Haring, Neetz, and Lovinger (1987)	21 5- to 13-year-olds with severe disabilities, 3 teachers	Teach teachers to implement modified incidental procedures	Self-guided teacher training	Increased opportunities for student communication, high frequency of student responses
Hunt, Alwell, and Goetz (1988)	3 14 to 16-year-olds with severe disabilities, 6 peers without disabilities	Teach subjects to initiate and maintain conversations	Conversation training by peers	Conversational skills increased, inappropriate social interaction decreased
Haring and Lovinger (1989)	3 4- to 6-year-olds with cerebral palsy, autism, developmental delays; 5 peers without disabilities	Test effects of play initiation training for social interaction of subjects with disabilities	Initiation training, peer rewards and awareness training	Initiation training more effective than peer training
Hunt, Alwell, Goetz, and Sailor (1990)	3 17- to 18-year-olds with severe disabilities, 18 peers without disabilities	Teach subjects to initiate and maintain conversations and to decrease challenging behaviors	Conversation training by peers	Conversational skills increased with some generalization to other peers, challenging behaviors decreased
Basil (1992)	4 7-to 8-year-olds with cerebral palsy using communication boards	Test effects of parent intervention on frequency of conversational initiations and responses	Parent intervention program	Initiations and responses increased but were much lower than parent levels
Haring and Breen (1992)	2 13-year-olds with moderate delays, autism, 9 peers without disabilities	Increase frequency and quality of social interactions	Peer network intervention	Increased interaction with subjects with disabilities, improved peer ratings of friendship

language impairments in the absence of cognitive delays. The primary intervention goal has been to teach basic social skills, usually initiation of social behavior and contingent responding. Typically, intervention has been of short duration. For example, Bierman and Furman (1984) carried out intervention for 10 half-hour sessions over a 6-week period. Peck (1985) conducted intervention for 15–17 days, and Goldstein, Wickstrom, Hoyson, Jamieson, and Odom (1988) carried out intervention for 10–15 minutes each day for 8–10 days. In general, the findings indicate that basic social skills can be taught but that intervention gains may be small and skill generalization may be limited.

Several intervention approaches for social skills impairments have been proposed, including: 1) direct teaching of social communication skills, 2) enhancing motivation and self-concept, 3) whole language techniques, 4) cooperative group experiences, 5) teacher and parent training, and 6) peer-mediated intervention. Although little of the intervention research has focused on students with language impairments only, several of these interventions have been suggested as viable teaching strategies for these students (Goldstein & Gallagher, 1992).

Direct Teaching of Social Communication Skills

Traditionally, direct intervention for social skills focused on remediating students' presumed social skills deficits. Such deficits were considered to be due to underlying psychological processes (e.g., perceptual motor skills). However, to an increasing degree, competent social skills are seen as an outgrowth of social interactions and the social environment rather than an inherent feature of the individual (Haring, 1993). In line with this change in emphasis, the focus of intervention has shifted from teaching specific social skills to facilitating positive interactions.

Fey (1986) noted that the basic components of direct coaching of social skills include instructing students in skills such as asking questions, sharing, and cooperating; practicing these skills with a peer; and reviewing the peer interaction. Because coaching involves much verbal instruction, Fey suggested that this intervention may not be effective for children with poor comprehension or attention skills. Direct social skills intervention may involve all students in a classroom and may be administered collaboratively by teachers and other educators. This classroom-based intervention emphasizes fundamental social communication skills such as appropriate turn-taking, listening skills, and nonverbal communication (e.g., Dodge & Mallard, 1992).

Some intervention research in this area has been performed with typically developing children (Bierman & Furman, 1984), students with disabilities (Haring, Roger, Lee, Breen, & Gaylord-Ross, 1986), and students with language impairments (Goldstein et al., 1988). Typically, conversational skills have been taught, such as initiating and expanding topics and responding appropriately to others' initiations. One intervention that has received attention as a technique to facilitate social interaction is script training (Goldstein & Gallagher, 1992; Goldstein et al., 1988). Script training is a form of sociodramatic play in which students are taught to carry out social roles (e.g., going shopping, going to a restaurant, getting a haircut) and learn the expectations implicit in a given role. It has been hypothesized that script training enhances social skills by providing opportunities for interactants to practice social roles, to observe play and language skills of interactants, and to solve interpersonal conflicts (e.g., over role assignments) (Goldstein et al., 1988). Although script training may for some students be focused on nonverbal contributions, conversational skills are a central focus of many scripts. Goldstein et al. (1988) studied triads of preschoolers who were taught to follow "hamburger stand" and "barber shop" scripts. They concluded that script training increased the frequency and quality of interaction among children with disabilities and among children with and without disabilities. However, although the children were able to learn the social roles in the scripts, script training was not very successful unless the children were prompted to stay in their assigned roles. Learning a single script took between 3 and 14 sessions for the triads of children.

Enhancing Motivation and Self-Concept

Generally, enhancing motivation is seen as a corollary of other forms of social skills intervention rather than the basis for a specific intervention per se. The general concept behind increasing students' motivation is that enhanced motivation leads to enhanced self-concept and to an increased ability to take full advantage of the learning environment. Based on this idea, intervention for a student or a group of students is achieved by helping students to identify, prioritize, and self-monitor intervention goals and to choose among intervention techniques, content, materials, schedules, and locations (Bos & Van Reusen, 1991). Enhancing motivation has been used most often with older students with learning disabilities, not only because of the self-monitoring and cognitive demands of structuring intervention activities, but also because younger children are less likely to experience motivational problems. The performance of such older students seems to improve when the students are involved in major decisions about the content and procedures of the intervention (Van Reusen, Deshler, & Schumaker, 1989). Performance improves also when students learn to attribute academic success to factors that are under their control (e.g., increased effort) (Adelman & Taylor, 1983; Licht & Kistner, 1986).

Whole Language Techniques

Providing intervention activities that are intrinsically motivating is one of the principles underlying whole language intervention (Reutzel & Hollingsworth, 1988). Highly motivating activities are created by focusing on events that are relevant to students' personal experiences, interests, and needs. Rather than focusing on discrete language forms and content or on discrete social skills, whole

language activities focus on the dynamic relationships among language components in both spoken and written language (Goodman, 1986). Gillam and his
colleagues (Gillam, 1994; Gillam, McFadden, & van Kleeck, chap. 6, this volume) and Norris and Hoffman (1993) described several whole language techniques used with children with language impairments. Gillam reported on
authorship as a form of language intervention. In the authorship intervention he
described, a demonstration book was read and discussed by students, the topic
and form of their own book was planned, and the story was drafted and revised
through conferences with other students and with teachers and clinicians. Then,
the book was printed, illustrated, and shared with others. An anticipated part of
this process was that students would have many opportunities to improve their
language form and content, problem-solving abilities, negotiation skills, and
peer relationships in a real-world communication situation.

Norris and Hoffman (1993) provided several suggestions for intervention
activities with spoken language that are in line with the philosophy of whole language. They noted that using scaffolding techniques (i.e., cues, prompts, models) in a variety of activities that are centered on the same topic or theme may
help to facilitate the ability of students to deal with more complex and more
abstract concepts. For example, they related a possible intervention in which students first read a story about buying and selling animals and then participate in a
"store" activity in which they learn to count money, negotiate buyer–seller relationships, divide merchandise into semantic categories, and purchase animal
cookies (that they learn how to bake). Similar to the intervention reported by
Gillam (1994), it is anticipated that such an activity would provide students with
structured experiences in conversational patterns, sensitivity to listener needs,
abstract thinking, and mental planning, for example.

Activities such as those described by Gillam (1994) and Norris and
Hoffman (1993) to facilitate children's social communication skills are intuitively appealing. However, whether they truly are effective in facilitating students'
communicative-social skills remains an empirical question. There is little objective information documenting the effectiveness of these techniques. In addition,
it is unclear that whole language activities enhance the syntax of children with
language impairments or their morphology without particular emphasis being
placed on these skills (Chaney, 1990).

Cooperative Group Experiences

Another intervention that focuses on the dynamic relationships among language
components is a cooperative group experience in which the successful completion of an activity depends on the contribution of each group member. Gallagher
(1991) described a cooperative experience in which a group of children was
asked to draw a picture of a sunny day. Each child was given a different colored
crayon in order to contribute to the picture. Because the yellow crayon was given
to the child in the group with a language impairment, it was essential that he

contribute to drawing the picture of a sunny day. Although some research indicates that cooperative group experiences are effective in improving typically developing children's self-evaluations and evaluations by other typical peers (Bierman & Furman, 1984), research is needed to investigate the effectiveness of this approach on the language and social skills of students with language impairments.

Teacher and Parent Training

Teacher and parent training is considered by some to be an effective way to increase optimal opportunities for students' social interaction, at least in the short term (Basil, 1992; Haring, Neetz, & Lovinger, 1987; Peck, 1985). For example, Peck (1985) taught teachers of students with autism to increase their rate of providing choices to students, to increase their compliance and responsiveness to student initiations, and to imitate or expand student initiations. Peck found that teacher interactions could be substantially modified to allow for more frequent student initiations and control of social interactions. Brinton and Fujiki (chapter 7, this volume) taught the mother of a 5-year-old boy with a language impairment to decrease the number of questions she asked her son during conversation. Brinton and Fujiki reported that the mother was successful in adapting her interaction style and that conversations with her son became more conducive to her son's learning. Patterson et al. (1989) suggested that parent training be included in intervention because of their speculation that the etiology of antisocial behavior lies in parental discipline and management techniques.

Peer-Mediated Intervention

By definition, social competence involves interaction with others, chiefly one's peers. Peer-mediated intervention has been much praised as an effective alternative to direct intervention by teachers and other professionals (Strain & Odom, 1986). Much of the initial work in this area was conducted by Strain and his colleagues, typically with preschoolers with severe disabilities (Strain, 1977; Strain & Fox, 1981; Strain, Kerr, & Ragland, 1979, 1981). Since that time, investigations of peer-mediated intervention have led to a burgeoning literature in this area.

In peer-mediated intervention, peers without disabilities are taught to direct positive social overtures to students with disabilities. In contrast to other interventions involving peers (e.g., script training, cooperative group experiences), peers have a primary role as facilitators rather than as participants only in peer-mediated intervention. Typically, students without disabilities are taught to organize and engage in play episodes with peers with disabilities, to share materials, and respond positively to peers' behaviors (Haring, 1993). In addition to the actual training of peers, selecting specific peer initiations (e.g., physical assistance, sharing materials), arranging the physical environment to promote interaction (e.g., providing toys that may be used cooperatively such as kitchen sets and cars), and conducting daily intervention sessions are seen as crucial components of this type of intervention (Strain & Odom, 1986). Strain and Odom (1986) suggested that each session should begin with the interventionist introducing the activity to all children, with and without disabilities, and then reminding the children without disabilities of their roles in the activity. If the children without disabilities do not make appropriate initiations, they are prompted to do so by the interventionist. All children are praised for their participation in the activity.

Goldstein and Ferrell (1987) taught six typically developing children in an integrated preschool four strategies to facilitate interaction with three children with disabilities. Each child with a disability was grouped with two of the typically developing children during structured free-play activities. Peers were taught to establish eye contact with the child with a disability, to suggest joint play, to respond to that child's verbal initiations, and to describe their own play. Goldstein and Ferrell (1987) found that all of the typically developing peers learned the intervention strategies but that there were individual differences in their effectiveness as facilitators. The intervention led to increased responses by two children with disabilities and decreased initiations (primarily requests) by two children. Only one child transferred intervention effects beyond the intervention activities.

Citing particularly the work of Hunt and Goldstein (e.g., Goldstein & Ferrell, 1987; Hunt, Alwell, & Goetz, 1988; Hunt et al., 1990), Ostrosky, Kaiser, and Odom (1993) proposed several intervention principles to promote positive social interaction among students with and without disabilities. These principles include the view that peers without disabilities are best seen as facilitators rather than primary interventionists, that all students in a classroom should be taught improved social-communicative strategies, that individualized instruction for initiating and responding is important, and that programmatic skill maintenance and generalization should be included. Ostrosky et al. (1993) suggested that preliminary, one-to-one intervention for social skills may enhance peer-mediated, classroom-based intervention.

These general intervention principles reflect the known strengths and limitations of peer-mediated intervention. For example, although direct intervention for social skills may be more effective than peer-awareness training (Haring & Lovinger, 1989), providing instruction for students with disabilities and not their peers may have limited success (Goldstein & Ferrell, 1987; Strain, Odom, & McConnell, 1984). Furthermore, providing no direct intervention for students with disabilities is likely to be unsuccessful (Guralnick, 1981). Some peers may be more successful facilitators than others (Goldstein & Ferrell, 1987). Also, generalization is unlikely to occur as an automatic consequence of social interaction training (Lancioni, 1982; Odom, Hoyson, Jamieson, & Strain, 1985).

Overall, it is not clear that peer-mediated intervention has had substantial, generalizable, long-term, or developmentally meaningful effects (Guralnick,

1990b). In addition, many peer-mediated interventions may require a great deal of time, effort, and specific expertise to implement successfully. Haring (1993) noted that it has yet to be demonstrated that the students without disabilities involved in peer-mediated intervention value their interaction with the students with disabilities, change their perceptions or attitudes toward them, or increase the frequency or quality of their interaction without being prompted to do so. The primary outcomes of successful peer interactions, that is, friendships and the nurturance and enhanced self-concept accompanying friendships, have yet to be achieved through current peer-mediated interventions.

CONCLUSION: FUTURE RESEARCH NEEDS

Most of the research on social skills has considered a small set of behaviors, mainly frequency of social initiations and conversational responses. Less research has focused on increasing the quality and acceptability to peers of social overtures. Although social skills can be taught and do transfer across some settings, the crucial limitation of social skills intervention is that it has not been adequately documented that fundamental, enduring change in social skills or social relationships takes place (Strain et al., 1984). This is especially true where children with language impairments are concerned.

Haring (1992) and Strain et al. (1984) have argued that social competence is a dynamic, contextually based relationship between an individual's behavior and the environment. Thus, the reduction of social competence to a catalog of discrete, static skills of an individual is unlikely to yield comprehensive and enduring clinical solutions. The current research trend is to design assessment and intervention studies focusing on social relationships rather than on discrete social skills (Ostrosky et al., 1993). In line with this approach, Haring (1992) suggested that intervention for social skills may be best implemented with naturalistic strategies, such as incidental teaching (e.g., Warren, McQuarter, & Rogers-Warren, 1984), in which social and linguistic behaviors are linked to the environment in which they occur. In general, whole language techniques, cooperative group experiences, and peer-mediated interventions each attempt to address dynamic relationships. However, there is a clear need for additional research to test the hypothesis that intervening with dynamic relationships leads to the significant changes in language form, content, and use that proponents of these approaches anticipate.

One avenue of research that appears promising is the investigation of behaviors that are pivotal to social competence, that is, behaviors that promote widespread changes in development and facilitate friendships (Haring, 1993). For example, Haring suggested that age-appropriate "hanging out" in a clique is a pivotal social skill for adolescents. Behaviors such as identifying clique members and where the clique hangs out, hanging out and looking cool, and following the clique as it moves are behaviors that could be learned to promote peer friendships. However, the effects of teaching such skills on the social and linguistic competence of students have yet to be determined. Ultimately, understanding a given student's individual characteristics may be the most valuable information for guiding selection of a particular intervention. However, factors such as the duration and intensity of the intervention needed to effect change, the relative benefits of different intervention strategies, and the types of behavior most amenable to change require additional investigation.

There remains a need for formal models of social competence within which different social behaviors, whether viewed as static or dynamic, can be better defined and understood. Ideally, such models would help to stimulate additional methods for measuring social competence, as well as for measuring the effects of intervention on social competence and the causal relationship between language impairments and social impairments. Although some models for determining intervention effectiveness and suggesting lines of research have appeared (Gaylord-Ross & Haring, 1987; Haring & Breen, 1989), more research is needed to document the conditions under which increases in social competence can be attained.

Very little research has focused on students who have language impairments in the absence of other disabilities. It is likely that students with different types and severities of language impairments will show different probabilities of having concomitant social skill impairments (Fey, 1986; Fey & Leonard, 1983). Although it may be that any deficit in communicative competence places a student at risk for social skills deficits, the research suggests that students with poor conversational skills, especially difficulty in initiating conversations, and students with poor comprehension are at risk for decreased social competence (Craig & Evans, 1989; Craig & Washington, 1993). Additional research directed toward children with SLI is needed to clarify the social skills of this population.

Research is needed also to further investigate the relative advantages and disadvantages of classroom type on improving social competence. The current idea that students with disabilities may learn social skills from peer models without disabilities is in line with the value-based argument that inclusion builds a greater sense of community and increases opportunities for incidental learning. However, this idea requires greater empirical documentation. For example, Weiss and Nakamura (1992) studied the effects of the inclusion of three typically developing preschoolers in a classroom of seven peers with language impairments (including one child with Down syndrome and one with a hearing impairment). They found that the typical children differed from each other in the amount of time they interacted with the children with language impairments and in how responsive they were to these children's conversational requests. Thus, as Weiss and Nakamura noted, selection of peer models without disabilities based solely on their language skills does not guarantee that these peers will interact in a uniform and desirable manner with their peers with language impairments.

Finally, the link between social skills and language skills must be addressed in future intervention research. Although some researchers have incorporated both social and language skills in the same intervention (e.g., Goldstein et al.,

1988; Haring et al., 1986), much of the existing research concerning social skills overlooks the language skills that students need to succeed in the intervention. For example, it is possible that children in some studies identified as without disabilities but with low peer acceptance (e.g., Bierman & Furman, 1984) actually have a language impairment in some sense. If the goal is to improve social-communicative competence, the relationship between social skills and language skills must be recognized explicitly.

REFERENCES

Adelman, H.S., & Taylor, L. (1983). Enhancing motivation and overcoming learning and behavior problems. *Journal of Learning Disabilities, 16,* 384–392.

Anderson, S., & Messick, S. (1974). Social competency in young children. *Developmental Psychology, 10,* 289–292.

Aram, D.M., & Nation, J.E. (1980). Preschool language disorders and subsequent language and academic difficulties. *Journal of Child Development, 13,* 159–170.

Axelrod, L. (1982). Social perception in learning disabled adolescents. *Journal of Learning Disabilities, 15,* 610–613.

Baker, L., & Cantwell, D.P. (1982a). Developmental, social and behavioral characteristics of speech and language disordered children. In S. Chess & A. Thomas (Eds.), *Annual progress in child psychiatry and child development* (pp. 205–216). New York: Brunner Mazel.

Baker, L., & Cantwell, D.P. (1982b). Psychiatric disorder in children with different types of communication disorders. *Journal of Communication Disorders, 15,* 113–126.

Baker, L., & Cantwell, D.P. (1987). A prospective psychiatric follow-up of children with speech/language disorders. *Journal of the American Academy of Child and Adolescent Psychiatry, 26,* 546–553.

Baltaxe, C.A., & Simmons, J.Q. (1988). Communication deficits in preschool children with psychiatric disorders. *Seminars in Speech and Language, 9,* 81–91.

Barksdale, M.W. (1961). Social problems of mentally retarded children. *Mental Hygiene, 45,* 509–512.

Basil, C. (1992). Social interaction and learned helplessness in severely disabled children. *Augmentative and Alternative Communication, 8,* 188–199.

Beitchman, J.H., Nair, R., Clegg, M., Ferguson, B., & Patel, P.G. (1986). Prevalence of psychiatric disorders in children with speech and language disorders. *Journal of the American Academy of Child Psychiatry, 25,* 528–535.

Bierman, K.L., & Furman, W.F. (1984). The effects of social skills training and peer involvement on the social adjustment of preadolescents. *Child Development, 55,* 151–162.

Black, B., & Hazen, N.L. (1990). Social status and patterns of communication in acquainted and unacquainted preschool children. *Developmental Psychology, 26,* 379–387.

Blank, M., Gessner, M., & Esposito, A. (1979). Language without communication: A case study. *Journal of Child Language, 6,* 329–352.

Bliss, L.S. (1992). A comparison of tactful messages by children with and without language impairment. *Language, Speech, and Hearing Services in Schools, 23,* 343–347.

Bos, C.S., & Van Reusen, A.K. (1991). Academic interventions with learning-disabled students: A cognitive/metacognitive approach. In J.E. Obrzut & G.W. Hynd (Eds.), *Neuropsychological foundations of learning disabilities* (pp. 659–683). San Diego: Academic Press.

Byrne, B.M. (1984). The general/academic self-concept nomological network: A review of construct validation research. *Review of Educational Research, 54,* 427–456.

Camarata, S.M., Hughes, C.A., & Ruhl, K.L. (1988). Mild/moderate behaviorally disordered students: A population at risk for language discorders. *Language, Speech, and Hearing Services in Schools, 19,* 191–200.

Carr, E.G., & Durand, V.M. (1985). Reducing behavior problems through functional communication training. *Journal of Applied Behavior Analysis, 18,* 111–126.

Centers, L., & Centers, R. (1963). Peer group attitudes toward the amputee child. *Journal of Social Psychology, 61,* 127–132.

Chaney, C. (1990). Evaluating the whole language approach to language arts: The pros and cons. *Language, Speech, and Hearing Services in Schools, 21,* 244–249.

Chapman, J.W. (1988). Learning disabled children's self-concepts. *Review of Educational Research, 58,* 347–371.

Connolly, C. (1971). Social and emotional factors in learning disabilities. In H.R. Myklebust (Ed.), *Progress in learning disabilities* (Vol. 2, pp. 151–178). New York: Grune & Stratton.

Craig, H.K., & Evans, J. (1989). Turn exchange characteristics of SLI children's simultaneous and nonsimultaneous speech. *Journal of Speech and Hearing Disorders, 54,* 334–347.

Craig, H.K., & Washington, J.A. (1993). Access behaviors of children with specific language impairment. *Journal of Speech and Hearing Research, 36,* 322–337.

Dodge, K.A. (1983). Behavioral antecedents of peer social status. *Child Development, 54,* 1386–1399.

Dodge, E.P., & Mallard, A.R. (1992). Social skills training using a collaborative service delivery model. *Language, Speech, and Hearing Services in Schools, 23,* 130–135.

Donoghue, E.C., & Abbas, K.A. (1971). Unstable behavior in severely subnormal children. *Developmental Medicine and Child Neurology, 13,* 512–519.

Ferguson, H.B., & Rapoport, J.L. (1983). Nosological issues and biological validation. In M. Rutter (Ed.), *Developmental neuropsychiatry* (pp. 369–384). New York: Guilford Press.

Fey, M.E. (1986). *Language intervention with young children.* Newton, MA: Allyn & Bacon.

Fey, M.E., & Leonard, L.B. (1983). Pragmatic skills of children with specific language impairment. In T.M. Gallagher & C.A. Prutting (Eds.), *Pragmatic assessment and intervention issues in language* (pp. 65–82). San Diego: College-Hill Press

Fey, M.E., & Leonard, L.B. (1991). Facilitating grammatical development: The contribution of pragmatics. In T.M. Gallagher (Ed.), *Pragmatics of language: Clinical practice issues* (pp. 333–355). San Diego: Singular Publishing Group.

Fujiki, M., & Brinton, B. (1991). The verbal noncommunicator: A case study. *Language, Speech, and Hearing Services in Schools, 22,* 322–333.

Fujiki, M., & Brinton, B. (1994). Social competence and language impairment in children. In R.V. Watkins & M.L. Rice (Eds.) *Communication and language intervention series: Vol. 4. Specific language impairments in children* (pp. 123–143). Baltimore: Paul H. Brookes Publishing Co.

Gallagher, T.M. (1991). Language and social skills: Implications for clinical assessment and intervention with school-age children. In T.M. Gallagher (Ed.), *Pragmatics of language: Clinical practice issues* (pp. 11–41). San Diego: Singular Publishing Group.

Gallagher, T., & Craig, H. (1984). Pragmatic assessment: Analysis of a highly frequent repeated utterance. *Journal of Speech and Hearing Disorders, 49,* 368–377.

Gaylord-Ross, R., & Haring, T.G. (1987). Social interaction research for adolescents with severe handicaps. *Behavioral Disorders, 12,* 264–275.

Gaylord-Ross, R., Haring, T.G., Breen, C., & Pitts-Conway, V. (1984). The training and generalization of social interaction skills with autistic youths. *Journal of Applied Behavior Analysis, 17,* 229–247.

Geschwind, N., & Galaburda, A.M. (1985). Cerebral lateralization, biological mechanisms, associations, and pathology. *Archives of Neurology, 42,* 428–459, 521–552, 634–654.

Gillam, R.B. (1994). Whole language principles at work in language intervention. In D. Tibbits (Ed.), *Language intervention: Beyond the primary grades.* Austin, TX: PRO-ED.

Goldstein, H., & Ferrell, D.R. (1987). Augmenting communicative interaction between handicapped and nonhandicapped preschool children. *Journal of Speech and Hearing Disorders, 52,* 200–211.

Goldstein, H., & Gallagher, T.M. (1992). Strategies for promoting the social-communicative competence of young children with specific language impairment. In S.L. Odom, S.R. McConnell, & M.A. McEvoy (Eds.), *Social competence of young children with disabilities* (pp. 189–213). Baltimore: Paul H. Brookes Publishing Co.

Goldstein, H., Wickstrom, S., Hoyson, M., Jamieson, B., & Odom, S.L. (1988). Effects of sociodramatic script training on social and communicative interaction. *Education and Treatment of Children, 11,* 97–117.

Goodman, K.S. (1986). *What's whole in whole language?* Portsmouth, NH: Heinemann.

Gualtieri, C.T., Koriath, U., Van Bourgondien, M., & Saleeby, N. (1983). Language disorders in children referred for psychiatric services. *Journal of the American Academy of Child Psychiatry, 22,* 165–171.

Guralnick, M.J. (1981). Peer influences on the development of communicative competence. In P.S. Strain (Ed.), *The utilization of peers as behavior change agents* (pp. 51–68). New York: Plenum.

Guralnick, M.J. (1990a). Peer interactions and the development of handicapped children's social and communicative competence. In H.C. Foot, M.J. Morgan, & R.H. Shute (Eds.), *Children helping children* (pp. 275–305). New York: John Wiley & Sons.

Guralnick, M.J. (1990b). Social competence and early intervention. *Journal of Early Intervention, 14,* 3–14.

Guralnick, M.J. (1992). A hierarchical model for understanding children's peer-related social competence. In S.L. Odom, S.R. McConnell, & M.A. McEvoy (Eds.), *Social competence of young children with disabilities* (pp. 37–64). Baltimore: Paul H. Brookes Publishing Co.

Hadley, P.A., & Rice, M.L. (1991). Conversational responsiveness of speech- and language-impaired preschoolers. *Journal of Speech and Hearing Research, 34,* 1308–1317.

Hall, B.J. (1991). Attitudes of fourth and sixth graders toward peers with mild articulation disorders. *Language, Speech, and Hearing Services in Schools, 22,* 334–340.

Haring, T.G. (1991). Social relationships. In L.H. Meyer, C.A. Peck, & L. Brown (Eds.), *Critical issues in the lives of people with severe disabilities* (pp. 195–218). Baltimore: Paul H. Brookes Publishing Co.

Haring, T.G. (1992). The context of social competence: Relations, relationships, and generalizations. In S.L. Odom, S.R. McConnell, & M.A. McEvoy (Eds.), *Social competence of young children with disabilities* (pp. 307–320). Baltimore: Paul H. Brookes Publishing Co.

Haring, T.G. (1993). Research basis of instructional procedures to promote social interaction and integration. In R.D. Gable & S.F. Warren (Eds.), *Strategies for teaching students with mild to severe mental retardation* (pp. 129–164). Baltimore: Paul H. Brookes Publishing Co.

Haring, T.G., & Breen, C.G. (1989). Units of analysis of social interaction outcomes in supported education. *Journal of The Association for Persons with Severe Handicaps, 14,* 255–262.

Haring, T.G., & Breen, C.G. (1992). A peer-mediated social network intervention to enhance the social integration of persons with moderate and severe disabilities. *Journal of Applied Behavior Analysis, 25,* 319–333.

Haring, T.G., & Lovinger, L. (1989). Promoting social interaction through teaching generalized play initiation responses to preschool children with autism. *Journal of The Association for Persons with Severe Handicaps, 14,* 58–67.

Haring, T.G., Neetz, J.A., & Lovinger, L. (1987). Effects of four modified incidental teaching procedures to create opportunities for communication. *Journal of The Association for Persons with Severe Handicaps, 12,* 218–226.

Haring, T.G., Roger, B., Lee, M., Breen, C., & Gaylord-Ross, R. (1986). Teaching social language to moderately handicapped students. *Journal of Applied Behavior Analysis, 19,* 159–171.

Hazen, N.L., & Black, B. (1989). Preschool peer communication skills: The role of social status and interaction context. *Child Development, 60,* 867–876.

Hemphill, L., & Siperstein, G.N. (1990). Conversational competence and peer response to mildly retarded children. *Journal of Educational Psychology, 82,* 128–134.

Horne, M.D. (1985). *Attitudes toward handicapped students: Professional, peer, and parent reactions.* Hillsdale, NJ: Lawrence Erlbaum Associates.

Horstman, A.M., & Bornstein, P.H. (1985). Children's judgments of socially skilled versus socially deficient female peers. *Child and Family Behavior Therapy, 7,* 51–64.

Hunt, P., Alwell, M., & Goetz, L. (1988). Acquisition of conversation skills and the reduction of inappropriate social interaction behaviors. *Journal of The Association for Persons with Severe Handicaps, 13,* 20–27.

Hunt, P., Alwell, M., Goetz, L., & Sailor, W. (1990). Generalized effects of conversation skill training. *Journal of The Association for Persons with Severe Handicaps, 15,* 250–260.

Johnson, D.J., & Myklebust, H.R. (1971). *Learning disabilities.* New York: Grune & Stratton.

Lancioni, G.E. (1982). Normal children as tutors to teach social responses to withdrawn mentally retarded schoolmates: Training, maintenance and generalization. *Journal of Applied Behavior Analysis, 15,* 17–40.

Lass, N.J., Ruscello, D.M., Schmitt, J.F., Pannabacker, M.D., Orlando, M.B., Dean, K.A., Ruziaska, J.C., & Bradshaw, K.H. (1992). Teachers' perceptions of stutterers. *Language, Speech, and Hearing Services in Schools, 23,* 78–81.

Licht, B.G., & Kistner, J.A. (1986). Motivational problems of the learning-disabled child: Individual differences and their implications for treatment. In J.K. Torgeson & B.Y. Wong (Eds.), *Psychological and educational perspectives on learning disabilities* (pp. 225–255). Orlando, FL: Academic Press.

Mack, A.E., & Warr-Leeper, G.A. (1992). Language abilities in boys with chronic behavior disorders. *Language, Speech, and Hearing Services in Schools, 23,* 214–223.

Miniutti, A.M. (1991). Language deficiencies in inner-city children with learning and behavioral problems. *Language, Speech, and Hearing Services in Schools, 22,* 31–38.

Myklebust, H.R. (1975). Nonverbal learning difficulties: Assessment and intervention. In H.R. Myklebust (Ed.), *Progress in learning disabilities* (Vol. 3, pp. 85–121). New York: Grune & Stratton.

National Joint Committee on Learning Disabilities. (1991). Learning disabilities: Issues on definition. *Asha, 33,* (Suppl. 5), 18–20.

Nieves, N. (1991). Childhood psychopathology and learning disabilities: Neuropsychological relationships. In J.E. Obrzut & G.W. Hynd (Eds.), *Neuropsy-*

chological foundations of learning disabilities (pp. 113–145). San Diego: Academic Press.

Norris, J., & Hoffman, P. (1993). Whole language intervention for school-age children. San Diego: Singular Publishing Group.

Odom, S.L., Hoyson, M., Jamieson, B., & Strain, P.S. (1985). Increasing handicapped preschoolers' peer social interactions: Cross setting and component analysis. Journal of Applied Behavior Analysis, 18, 3–16.

Ostrosky, M.M., Kaiser, A.P., & Odom, S.L. (1993). Facilitating children's social-communicative interactions through the use of peer-mediated interventions. In A.P. Kaiser & D.B. Gray (Eds.) Communication and language intervention series: Vol. 2. Enhancing children's communication: Research foundations for intervention (pp. 159–185). Baltimore: Paul H. Brookes Publishing Co.

Pandy, C. (1971). Popularity, rebelliousness, and happiness among institutionalized retarded males. American Journal of Mental Deficiency, 26, 325–331.

Patterson, G.R., DeBaryshe, B.D., & Ramsey, E. (1989). A developmental perspective on antisocial behavior. American Psychologist, 44, 329–335.

Pearl, R. (1987). Social cognitive factors in learning-disabled children's social problems. In S. Ceci (Ed.), Handbook of cognitive, social, and neuropsychological aspects of learning disabilities (Vol. 2, pp. 273–294). Hillsdale, NJ: Lawrence Erlbaum Associates.

Pearl, R., Donahue, M., & Bryan, T. (1985). The development of tact: Children's strategies for delivering bad news. Journal of Applied Developmental Psychology, 6, 141–149.

Peck, C.A. (1985). Increasing opportunities for social control by children with autism and severe handicaps: Effects on student behavior and perceived classroom climate. Journal of The Association for Persons with Severe Handicaps, 10, 183–193.

Perrin, E.H. (1954). The social position of the speech defective child. Journal of Speech and Hearing Disorders, 19, 250–252.

Priel, B., & Leshem, T. (1990). Self-perceptions of first- and second-grade children with learning disabilities. Journal of Learning Disabilities, 23, 637–642.

Prizant, B.M., Audet, L.R., Burke, G.M., Hummel, L.J., Maher, S.R., & Theadore, G., (1990). Communication disorders and emotional/behavioral disorders in children and adolescents. Journal of Speech and Hearing Disorders, 55, 179–191.

Reutzel, D.R., & Hollingsworth, P.M. (1988). Whole language and the practitioner. Academic Therapy, 23, 405–416.

Rhyner, P.M., Lehr, D.H., & Pudlas, K.A. (1990). An analysis of teacher responsiveness to communicative initiations of preschool children with handicaps. Language, Speech, and Hearing Services in Schools, 21, 91–97.

Rice, M.L. (1993). "Don't talk to him; he's weird": A social consequences account of language and social interaction. In A.P. Kaiser & D.B. Gray (Eds.), Communication and language interventions series: Vol. 2. Enhancing children's communication: Research foundations for intervention (pp. 139–158). Baltimore: Paul H. Brookes Publishing Co.

Rice, M.L., Sell, M.A., & Hadley, P.A. (1990). The social interactive coding system (SICS): An on-line, clinically relevant descriptive tool. Language, Speech, and Hearing Services in Schools, 21, 2–14.

Rice, M.L., Sell, M.A., & Hadley, P.A. (1991). Social interactions of speech- and language-impaired children. Journal of Speech and Hearing Research, 34, 1299–1307.

Sameroff, A.J. (1987). The social context of development. In N. Eisenberg (Ed.), Contemporary topics in developmental psychology (pp. 273–291). New York: John Wiley & Sons.

Semrud-Clikeman, M., & Hynd, G.W. (1991). Specific nonverbal and social-skills deficits in children with learning disabilities. In J.E. Obrzut & G.W. Hynd (Eds.),

Neuropsychological foundations of learning disabilities (pp. 603–629). San Diego: Academic Press.

Silver, L. (1988). A review of the federal government's Interagency Committee on Learning Disabilities: Report to the U.S. Congress. *Learning Disabilities Focus, 3,* 73–81.

Silverman, F.H., & Marik, J.H. (1993). "Teachers' perceptions of stutterers": A replication. *Language, Speech, and Hearing Services in Schools, 24,* 108.

Silverman, F.H., & Paulus, P.G. (1989). Peer reactions to teenagers who substitute /w/ for /r/. *Language, Speech, and Hearing Services in Schools, 20,* 219–220.

Spreen, O. (1989). The relationship between learning disability, emotional disorders, and neuropsychology: Some results and observations. *Journal of Clinical and Experimental Neuropsychology, 11,* 117–140.

Stark, R.E., Tallal, P., & McCauley, R.J. (1988). *Language, speech, and reading disorders in children: Neuropsychological studies.* Boston: College-Hill Press.

Stevenson, J., & Richman, N. (1978). Behavior, language, and development in three-year-old children. *Journal of Autism and Childhood Schizophrenia, 8,* 299–313.

Stipek, D.J., & Tannatt, L.M. (1984). Children's judgments of their own and their peers' academic competence. *Journal of Educational Psychology, 76,* 75–84.

Strain, P.S. (1977). An experimental analysis for peer social initiations on the behavior of withdrawn preschool children: Some training and generalization effects. *Journal of Abnormal Child Psychology, 6,* 203–209.

Strain, P.S., & Fox, J.J. (1981). Peer social interactions and the modification of social withdrawal: A review and future perspective. *Journal of Pediatric Psychology, 6,* 417–443.

Strain, P.S., Kerr, M.M., & Ragland, E.U. (1979). Effects of peer-mediated social initiations and prompt reinforcement procedures on the social behavior of autistic children. *Journal of Autism and Developmental Disorders, 9,* 41–54.

Strain, P.S., Kerr, M.M., & Ragland, E.U. (1981). The use of peer social initiations in the treatment of social withdrawal. In P.S. Strain (Ed.), *The utilization of classroom peers as behavior change agents* (pp. 101–128). New York: Plenum Press.

Strain, P.S., & Odom, S.L. (1986). Peer social initiations: Effective intervention for social skills development of exceptional children. *Exceptional Children, 52,* 543–551.

Strain, P.S., Odom, S.C., & McConnell, S.R. (1984). Promoting social reciprocity of exceptional children: Identification, target behavior selection, and intervention. *Remedial and Special Education, 5,* 21–28.

Taylor, A.R., Asher, S.R., & Williams, G.A. (1987). The social adaptation of mainstreamed mildly retarded children. *Child Development, 58,* 1321–1334.

Tollefson, N., Tracy, D.B., Johnsen, E.P., Buenning, M., Farmer, A., & Barke, C.R. (1982). Attribution patterns of learning disabled adolescents. *Learning Disabilities Quarterly, 5,* 14–20.

Tomblin, J., & Liljegreen, S. (1985). The identification of socially significant communication needs in older language impaired children: A case example. In D. Ripich & F. Spinelli (Eds.), *School discourse problems* (pp. 219–230). San Diego: College Hill Press.

Vandell, D.L., & George, L.B. (1991). Social interaction in hearing and deaf preschoolers: Successes and failures in initiation. *Child Development, 52,* 627–635.

Van Reusen, A.K., Deshler, D.D., & Schumaker, J.B. (1989). Effects of a student participation strategy in facilitating the involvement of learning disabled adolescents in the IEP planning process. *Learning Disabilities: A Multidisciplinary Journal, 1,* 23–34.

Walker, H.M., Shinn, M.R., O'Neill, R.E., & Ramsey, E. (1987). Longitudinal assessment of the development of antisocial behaviors in boys: Rationale, methodology, measures, and first-year results. *Remedial and Special Education, 8,* 7–16.

Warren, S.F., McQuarter, R.J., & Rogers-Warren, A.K. (1984). The effects of mands and models on the speech of unresponsive language delayed preschool children. *Journal of Speech and Hearing Disorders, 49,* 43–52.

Weiner, B. (1984). Principles for a theory of student motivation and their application within an attributional framework. In R. Ames & C. Ames (Eds.), *Research on motivation in education: Vol. 1. Student motivation* (pp. 15–38). Orlando, FL: Academic Press.

Weiss, A.L., & Nakamura, M. (1992). Children with normal language skills in preschool classrooms for children with language impairments: Differences in modeling styles. *Language, Speech, and Hearing Services in Schools, 23,* 64–70.

PART III

Issues in Language Intervention with School-Age Children

9

Contexts of Early Literacy Intervention for Children with Developmental Disabilities

David A. Koppenhaver, Patsy L. Pierce,
Jane D. Steelman, and David E. Yoder

THE LITERACY-LEARNING DIFFICULTIES OF children with developmental disabilities have been observed widely and documented by researchers (e.g., Schonell, 1956), educators (e.g., Perry, 1960), parents (e.g., Killilea, 1983), and the individuals with developmental disabilities themselves (e.g., Rush, 1986). The prevalence of such difficulties is unusually high. In children with cerebral palsy, for example, 50% of those with average or above average intelligence experience severe literacy-learning difficulties (Barsch & Rudell, 1962; Center & Ward, 1984; Danilova,1983; Seidel, Chadwick, & Rutter, 1975). Historically, these difficulties have been attributed to the nature and degree of the individual's impairments (e.g., Bowley, 1967; Dorman, 1985; Hopkins, Bice, & Colton, 1954). However, research in the 1980s and 1990s suggests that literacy-learning difficulties may be attributable not only to the individual's impairment but also to the ways in which parents and professionals respond to those disabilities (e.g., Light & McNaughton, 1993) and the contexts within which learning occurs (e.g., Koppenhaver & Yoder, 1993).

In this chapter, we first present a model for organizing thinking about the literacy-learning difficulties of children with a range of developmental disabilities including cerebral palsy, mental retardation, and autism.We focus especially on individuals who require augmentative communication (AAC) systems because they require literacy not only for communication over time and distance but also for face-to-face interaction. Next, we review literacy research in children with developmental disabilities with reference to the model and discuss the educational and pyschosocial implications. We then highlight some of the inter-

Preparation of this manuscript was made possible in part by a grant from the U.S.. Department of Education (#H180G20016). However, the contents do not necessarily represent the policy of the Department of Education, and endorsement by the federal government should not be assumed.

vention research efforts in this area before concluding with recommendations for future study.

Throughout the chapter, we discuss *literacy* and young children with *developmental disabilities*. Definitions of each, particularly *literacy*, often vary from author to author. In this chapter, *literacy* refers to reading and writing, which are viewed as complex and related processes that are constructive, interactive, strategic, and social. Both processes are constructive in that readers and writers create meaning based on their understandings of the world and their commands of a range of written and oral language skills (Anderson & Pearson, 1984; Hayes & Flower, 1980). Both reading and writing are interactive in two senses. First, individuals use what they have learned about reading to improve their writing (e.g., reading comprehension can aid revision) and what they have learned about writing to improve their reading (e.g., spelling skill can aid word identification) (Shanahan & Lomax, 1986). Second, and perhaps more important in thinking about the literacy difficulties of children with developmental disabilities, reading and writing are learned in social interactions with others who are literate. These interpersonal experiences are ultimately internalized as the individual's personal reading and writing capability (Vygotsky, 1978). Both reading and writing are strategic in that readers and writers must monitor their comprehension or composition processes and select tactics or strategies appropriate to a variety of texts, purposes, and occasions (Paris, Wasik, & Turner, 1991). Finally, both reading and writing are social processes in that they are learned in social contexts (e.g., parent–child storybook reading and interaction) and "used to establish, structure, and maintain social relationships between and among people" (Bloom & Green, 1984, p. 395). In fact, literacy development has been conceptualized by some researchers as the acquisition of culture (Teale, 1987).

Developmental disabilities has been popularly used as a synonym for mental retardation. In this chapter we refer to the broader definition found in the Developmental Disabilities Assistance and Bill of Rights Act of 1990 (PL 101-496), which refers to a range of mental or physical disabilities. Although diverse in their capabilities, individuals with developmental disabilities share two characteristics of particular relevance to this chapter and text: they are at risk for lesser educational achievement in general (McLean, Smith, McCormick, Schakel, & McEvoy, 1991) and for greater literacy difficulties in particular (Koppenhaver, Coleman, Kalman, & Yoder, 1991). As stated above, our discussion covers a range of young children with developmental disabilities but centers particularly on those who use AAC systems because of the severity of their speech impairments.

A CONTEXTUAL MODEL OF WRITTEN COMMUNICATION IN CHILDREN WITH DEVELOPMENTAL DISABILITIES

In this section, we describe a model of literacy use (see Figure 1). The model illustrates in broad strokes the relationship between readers, writers, and the

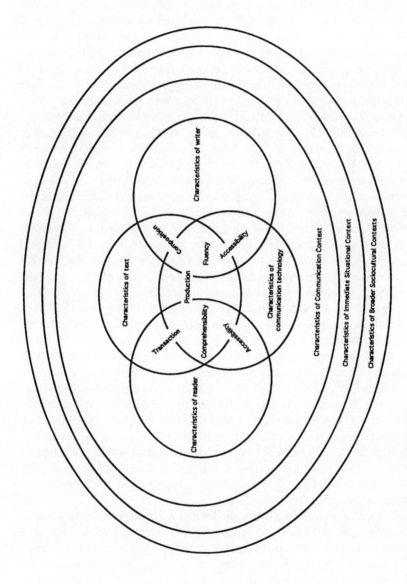

Figure 1.   Contextual model of written communication.

texts and tools that they use in reading and writing. It places readers, writers, their texts, and tools within the multiple contexts that may influence the success with which literacy is used to accomplish a variety of tasks. We know of no research specifically validating the model, but we have found that it serves a heuristic purpose, enabling us to think more broadly about the many different and interactive causes of literacy difficulties in children with developmental disabilities rather than to ascribe the difficulties solely to within-child factors such as cognition or physical capability (Koppenhaver & Pierce, 1992). The model serves additionally in this chapter to organize our discussion of literacy research.

The model in Figure 1 is based on the belief that written communication is made possible because of an implicit contract between readers and writers (Pappas, Kiefer, & Levstik, 1990). That is, writers have an implicit responsibility to consider their readers continually, just as readers have an implicit duty to construct from a text the meaning that they believe is consistent with the writer's intentions. The model illustrates that readers and writers carry on this communication with one another over time, distance, and disability by means of a text and a communications technology. That is, a writer can compose a text at a particular time and in a particular place, and an audience may read it much later in another location. Or, in the case of a child who relies on AAC, the individual may compose a text (i.e., sequence pictures, logographs, icons, or traditional orthography) for face-to-face interaction. Both *readers* and *writers* have characteristics that influence their development and use of literacy (e.g., cognitive, sensory, physical, and speech abilities; background knowledge and interests gained from experience; awareness of author or audience).

Likewise, texts and communication technology have characteristics that influence readers' and writers' development and use of literacy. *Texts* may be written on topics of great personal interest and knowledge (e.g., texts dictated by a child about a personal experience to a teacher) or on topics of little interest and complete unfamiliarity (e.g., a statistics text for many undergraduates). Texts may be logically organized and "reader-friendly," containing developmentally appropriate pictures and concepts, or be quite disorganized and difficult to read. *Communication technology* refers to the devices used to create a text. These may be as basic as an unadapted pencil or keyboard, as sophisticated as a computer with word-processing software, or as complex as a word processor with voice output that is accessed by an eyeblink switch and uses software with spelling and grammar assistance.

The reader encounters a text in the form of a *transaction* (i.e., both reader and text are changed by the experience). For example, the reader may gain knowledge or enjoyment from the text but at the same time transform the text by interpreting it with reference to personal and cultural knowledge and experiences. Some software programs allow the reader more literally to change the text by highlighting words or sentences by having text spoken aloud, or by animating static illustrations on command. Writers construct texts in the form of *composi-*

tion (i.e., the writer creates a text in order to communicate a message). Writers begin with the goal of communicating, plan how to accomplish that goal, consider the audience's needs and background understanding, create a text, edit and revise their message in response to anticipated audience reaction, and share the text with the intended audience.

The means by which a text is created physically, *production,* is formed by intersection of the communication technology and the text. The text may be produced in various forms included printed output on paper, a liquid crystal display on a dedicated voice-output communication aid, a visual display on a computer monitor, or as a series of word cards or letter tiles sequenced on a child's desk. The more reliable the writing device and the better the auditory, visual, or tactile quality of the subsequent text, the greater the *comprehensibility* of the message or successful communication between readers and writers. No matter how effective the writer, how skilled the reader, or how accessible the communication technology, if the text produced is not of sufficient quality (e.g., a smudged writing assignment, poor voice output in a talking book, or a worn braille page), written communication can break down (Koppenhaver & Pierce, 1992).

In individuals without disabilities, once handwriting or touch-typing have been mastered, the composition process is characterized by *fluency.* That is, the individual can focus almost complete attention on the meaning-making process. In the case of many individuals with disabilities, however, particularly those who require assistive technology in order to write, conscious attention must always be directed to the technology used to produce the text. For example, it is exceptionally difficult with current technology for children who access computer keyboards through scanning programs ever to become automatic or fluent enough to ignore the scanning process while composing. They must continually attend to the progress of the visual or auditory cue; engage in motor planning to activate the row, column, block, or key they desire; and simultaneously plan and sequence a message for a particular audience while retaining it in their memory.

Communication technology demonstrates varying degrees of *accessibility* for both readers and writers. For example, devices incorporating optical scanners, optical character recognition software, and speech synthesizers make independent reading possible for many individuals with visual impairments. High technology (e.g., eyebrow switches) and low technology adaptions (e.g., pencils, pens, markers with adapted holders) make writing tools accessible to individuals with physical disabilities. In every case, the easier and more rapid the access and the greater the operational competence of the user, the more fluent or comprehensible the reading and writing process, and the greater the attention that can be directed toward communicating meaning in print. The more difficult, unreliable, or slow the access, the greater the attention that must be directed to operating the device and the less attention that can be focused on communicating meaning.

Each of these central components is situated within *communication, situational,* and *sociocultural contexts.* The *communication context* refers to the speaking, listening, and other forms of communication that occur during and surrounding any given literacy event. It is these communications that enable children to make sense of literacy events, to incorporate content and process into their understanding of the uses of print, and to develop increasingly conventional forms of reading and writing. The *situational context* refers to the physical location in which literacy experiences or instruction occur and the nature and frequency of the available learning opportunities. For example, how conducive is the home or classroom to literacy learning? Is it print-rich? Are materials accessible? Are models of appropriate use available to the young child? Is the child given frequent opportunities to use existing materials for a range of functional purposes?

The *sociocultural context* encompasses all of the other components of the model and refers essentially to societal and cultural views toward people with disabilities (including those held by people with disabilities themselves), about their potential for contributing to the society or culture, and about their learning capabilities. That is, do parents, teachers, therapists, and the community value people with disabilities, and *literacy* in relation to people with disabilities? Do they expect individuals with disabilities to learn? Do they perceive them as competent individuals with a range of strengths and weaknesses? In short, just as context has proven critical in research efforts to understand the more general nature of developmental disabilities (e.g., Sameroff, 1982), context also seems essential in understanding the development and use of literacy in children with developmental disabilities.

In summary, the model serves a dual heuristic function in this chapter. It serves as an organizer for discussion of research to follow, but, more important, it is meant to encourage readers to think broadly about potential sources of literary learning difficulty rather than searching only within the child who is experiencing the difficulties.

WHAT DO WE KNOW ABOUT LITERACY AND CHILDREN WITH DEVELOPMENTAL DISABILITIES?

In this section, we selectively review the literature on literacy and children with developmental disabilities with respect to the contextual model described above. On the whole, the research is fraught with substantial methodological errors and does not paint a rosy picture of literacy learning success (see Koppenhaver & Yoder, 1992, for a fuller discussion), but it does suggest important directions for future research and development efforts that we describe later. The research also holds important lessons for practitioners planning to incorporate literacy into their early intervention or elementary-grade classrooms.

Readers and Writers

As we said in the introduction, studies show that children with developmental disabilities consistently exhibit significant difficulties in learning to read and write under a variety of experimental conditions. These conditions include: 1) when intelligence is controlled for (Barsch & Rudell, 1962; Seidel et al., 1975); 2) when individuals with disabilities are compared to same-age peers without disabilities (Cartwright, 1968), peers without disabilities of similar intelligence (Sedlak & Cartwright, 1972), and same-age peers without disabilities of similar intelligence in comparable instructional settings (Smith, 1990; Wolfe, 1950); 3) when their abilities are compared to reading or writing norms of individuals without disabilities (Berninger & Gans, 1986; Kelford Smith, Thurston, Light, Parnes, & O'Keefe, 1989; Schonell, 1956); and 4) when performance is examined in various countries (Center & Ward, 1984; Danilova, 1983; Kristensen, 1972, cited in Lademann, 1978). There is little evidence to determine conclusively the sources of these literacy-learning difficulties, although studies have demonstrated significant relationships between literacy and intelligence (Dorman, 1987), degree of physical impairment (Schonell, 1956), and degree of speech impairment (Barsch & Rudell, 1962). We know also that language impairments (e.g., Yoder & Calculator, 1981), sensory impairments, health impairments, and seizure activity (Mirenda & Mathy-Laikko, 1989) are prevalent in children with developmental disabilities. We can speculate that these and other factors intrinsic to the individual are related to observed literacy-learning difficulties. However, each of these potential relationships has yet to be tested empirically in this population.

Many individuals with severe and multiple impairments have successfully learned to read and write (e.g., Brown, 1954; Butler, 1979; Rush, 1986). How these individuals "beat the odds" remains an area for future study, with important implications for all young children with developmental disabilities. In their responses to an open-ended question in a retrospective survey, adults with severe speech and physical impairments attributed their literacy-learning success not only to their own talents and abilities but also to the support of their parents (i.e., an aspect of the sociocultural context) (Koppenhaver, Evans, & Yoder, 1991). In two case studies, Smith (1992) attributed the performance of individuals with severe cerebral palsy who scored within the average range of reading performance to their relative strength in language, good hand function allowing independent access to print materials, and supportive homes (again, an aspect of the sociocultural context). At present, we can conclude only that impairments impede literacy learning in many instances but are not necessarily insurmountable when severe or multiple.

One popular explanation of the literacy-learning difficulties in individuals with cerebral palsy is that they are often unable to speak or to speak clearly. While it is true that spoken language problems are strongly linked to reading problems, the strength of the correlation varies depending on what aspects of spoken language are examined (Kamhi & Catts, 1986). Recent research suggests that children with phonological disorders only are at less risk for learning-literacy difficulties than children with a broader range of phonological, semantic, and syntactic language disorders (Bishop & Adams, 1990). Furthermore, while early measures of language awareness are effective in identifying later literacy difficulties, the same measures do not apply equally well to all children (Menyuk et al., 1991). It is true that a strong predictor of conventional literacy achievement is phonemic awareness, or the ability to distinguish individual sounds in words (see Adams, 1990, for a review). Research involving literate adults with cerebral palsy who have varying degrees of dysarthia and anarthria consistently demonstrates their ability to distinguish individual sounds within words (e.g., Bishop, Brown, & Robson, 1990; Foley, 1993). What *is* unclear, because the research is done with adults, is whether their phonemic awareness led their literacy achievement or vice versa.

Texts and Communication Technology

We discuss communication technology and texts together because they are integrally related in the literacy activities of many children with developmental disabilities. This is particularly true for children with severe disabilities and for all children who require AAC systems or other assistive technology. There is little research to date, however, to indicate which characteristics of texts make them interesting to, or readily learned by, young children with developmental disabilities, or which technology implementations might enhance literacy learning in young children with developmental disabilities. Studies of the use of speech synthesis and digitization have received much of the research attention. The results of these studies suggest that speech feedback with computer use has several positive effects. For example, it increases: 1) spelling accuracy during composition activity in young adults with severe speech and physical impairments (Koke & Neilson, 1987), 2) quantity of writing and motivation in children with communication disorders (Norton & Heiman, 1988; Rosegrant, 1984), and 3) frequency of self-correction by young school-age children without disabilities (Borgh & Dickson, 1992). Furthermore, speech feedback has been shown to enhance reading efficiency in typically developing first-graders when paired with self-selection of the types of feedback desired (Reitsma, 1988) and to improve word recognition in context for school-age children with learning disabilities (Olson & Wise, 1987). Studies of the use of audiotapes accompanying text reading report similar findings, suggesting that it enhances reading comprehension (de Hoop, 1965) and word recognition in context (Koppenhaver & Yoder, 1988) of school-age children with cerebral palsy. Each of these strategies stems from research suggesting that pairing speech representations with print enables children to develop or build upon their phonological awareness more effectively and become successful readers (e.g., Wagner & Torgesen, 1987).

Software and CD-ROM versions of interactive storybooks are widely available that enable the reader to animate illustrations, hear portions of text spoken aloud, or incorporate multimedia. These tools have been created on the premise that they will make texts more accessible, interesting, and comprehensible to children with or without disabilities. While research has demonstrated that computers in general are highly motivating to a wide range of children with disabilities (e.g., MacArthur, 1988; Manion, 1986; Meyers, 1984), the specific influence of many aspects of computer-based reading and writing are based more on clinical and classroom observation than on empirical data. Given the cost of software relative to paperbacks, adapted pencils, or paper, the effects of computer intervention require careful investigation (see Schery and O'Connor, chap. 10, this volume).

One crucial component of communications technology to be explored empirically is the effect of the various graphic representation systems employed in AAC systems on literacy learning. Such picture-based or icon-based graphic representation systems are employed for a variety of reasons including circumventing an individual's inability to spell conventionally, saving keystrokes for individuals who may easily fatigue, enhancing the rate of communication, or providing access to expressive communication. It is critical that researchers explore the knowledge that is required to use such systems successfully as well as the knowledge that may be gained through the use of such systems because either or both may have an impact upon literacy learning (McNaughton, 1993). Based on their review of the research literature, Bishop, Rankin, and Mirenda (1994) concluded that graphic representation systems could play a role in the development of word recognition skills. Bishop et al. (1994) proposed that the real value of graphic representation systems may be in providing general access to language for children who use AAC.The more comprehensible a symbol system is to the child and to the communication partners, the greater the likelihood the child will become a competent language user across audiences and contexts. Substantial empirical efforts must be undertaken to explore these and other issues.

Automaticity and Accuracy

Both reading comprehension and written composition depend upon accurate and automatic application of subskills (e.g., spelling or word recognition). We noted earlier in describing the components of the contextual model that automaticity can be particularly difficult to achieve. Factors that influence achieving automaticity include the nature of the individual's disabilities (e.g., a child with cerebral palsy may be unable to keep his or her eyes trained on a page of text), the nature of the technology employed (e.g., an automatic page turner), or an interaction of the two (e.g., an individual who voluntarily can control only his or her head and must type via a scanning program).

Researchers and developers have made substantial progress in addressing the need for automaticity. For example, McNaughton and Drynan (1990) increased the composition rate of an 11-year-old boy with cerebral palsy from three words per minute to eight words per minute and produced a keystroke savings of 25% by using a programmable keyboard with letters, verb endings, and high-frequency written vocabulary grouped by grammatical function. A wide variety of technologies and techniques are available that can increase the speed and accuracy of text generation. Typical rate enhancement techniques include word prediction, icon pediction, and abbreviation expansion, and these produce keystroke savings ranging between 31% and 48% in a controlled comparison (Higginbotham, 1992). Word prediction systems operate on a variety of algorithms (e.g., grammatical appropriateness, recency of use, frequency of use) to provide word lists in an on-screen window at the press of a key. A writer can then compose a word in as few as two keystrokes regardless of its length. Icon prediction techniques highlight possible choices following the selection of any given icon or icon sequence. Abbreviation expansion allows the writer to select stored messages with relatively few keystrokes (e.g., typing RT might yield "Read this, please, and suggest how I can improve it.").

A variety of unanswered questions revolves around the use of rate enhancement technology and techniques in young children with developmental disabilities. Of particular importance is the question of what are the demands of the technology and the understandings and skills a child must have or develop for its successful use. McNaughton and Drynan (1990) incorporated into their word prediction system only words that the child knew how to spell. Pierce and Kublin (1993a, 1993b) incorporated vocabulary generated through classroom brainstorming activities. Both strategies make sense intuitively, but neither is systematic enough for maximum efficiency. For example, rate enhancement should be achievable if children can accurately spell the initial letter of a word and then accurately identify the word when it is juxtaposed against five other words in a prediction list. Perhaps the use of a prediction system could enhance accuracy over time if lists progressed gradually from words that shared only initial letter similarity (e.g., take and trip) to words that shared more letters (e.g., take, talk, tape, taste, tackle, tickle). How do we systematically determine which words to most effectively add to rate enhancement files for writing purposes? For example, it may not be necessary to add "goblin" to the system if the child uses it only in a few writings in October. These and other questions become increasingly important to children who fatigue easily, are reluctant writers, or who have severe physical disabilities or cognitive impairments.

Communication Context

Children's communication abilities, the interactive styles of their communication partners, and the overall supportiveness of the communication environment make up the multifaceted communicative context surrounding print experiences in which literacy learning may flourish or perish. A supportive communication environment offers ample opportunities for children to communicate, ways for them to communicate, motivating and functional activities for them to communicate about, and consistent reinforcing responses to their communication attempts (Tronick, 1981). Children with developmental disabilities often have communication impairments that may restrict the quality and quantity of their early literacy experiences. They may be unable to ask that stories be read to them (Coleman, 1991) or exhibit limited, idiosyncratic, or inconsistent responses that may in turn reduce the interest of their communication partners in talking or reading with them (Bricker & Lewis, 1982; Rogow, 1982).

Children's abilities also may affect their level of engagement and interaction during literacy experiences. In typically developing children, the total number of words spoken and the total number of questions asked and answered by a child during storybook reading highly correlate with developing reading skills (Flood, 1977). Children with developmental disabilities, however, are often passive or unable to interact during literacy activities because of their own difficulties in accessing communication devices or because of the difficulties that others encounter in interpreting their nonverbal signals or in understanding their speech (Coleman, 1991; Fitzgerald, Roberts, Pierce, & Schuele, in press; Light & Kelford Smith, 1993). Often they are restricted to pointing, gesturing, or answering yes/no questions.

The reader's communication style also may influence a child's future literacy learning (Martinez & Teale, 1993). For example, children who regularly have story events explained to them with reference to their own personal experiences typically develop conventional literacy at expected ages and levels (Flood, 1977; Wells, 1985). Applebee's (1978) work suggests that a child should participate actively in storybook reading activities and that adults must carefully select developmentally appropriate books or paraphrase text to meet a child's linguistic needs. Empirical studies of typically developing children have shown that storybook sharing enhances vocabulary development (Sulzby & Teale, 1991; Templin, 1957), general language development (Heath, 1982; Whitehurst et al., 1988), and future success in reading with comprehension (Wells, 1985).

Recent studies of children with developmental disabilities indicate that their communicative contexts are less than optimally supportive of literacy learning. For example, Fitzgerald et al. (in press) observed and audiotaped all activities of three children with Down syndrome for 6–10 hours across 2 days in the children's homes. Mothers' interactions with their children were found to be more likely to constrain than to encourage elaborated responses by the children. Typical parent comments to their child with Down syndrome included directives (e.g., "Do this,") test questions (e.g., "Is this a spoon?") or attention devices (e.g., "Look at that.").

Coleman (1991) analyzed videotaped interactions of preschool-age children with severe speech and physical impairments in classrooms with their teachers and at home with their parents during storybook reading. Using the Engagement and OBSERVE Coding System (Parsons, McWilliam, & Buysse, 1990), she found that the children were engaged during most literacy activities but that they did not interact at levels comparable to their cognitive abilities. Coleman attributed this to the absence of AAC systems and the types of questions that parents and teachers asked (primarily picture identification).

Wasson and Keeler (1984) conducted the only comparative observational study in school settings involving an AAC user that we can find. Subjects were a 6-year-old child with severe speech and physical impairments in a self-contained special education classroom and her typically developing twin, who was of equal intelligence and was placed in a mainstreamed first-grade class. The child with disabilities was found to experience, on average, only two opportunities to make comments or ask questions for every ten that her sibling had.

Harris (1982) conducted the first published interaction study of AAC users in classrooms. Three children, ages 6–7 years, with severe speech and physical impairments and their teachers were observed and videotaped during three types of classroom activities including one-to-one language experience, story generation, and small-group reading comprehension lessons. Teachers contributed more information per turn than the children in all contexts and primarily initiated. The children never contributed more than one word per turn, primarily responded, and seldom interacted with peers or persons other than the teacher.

Employing ethnographic methods, Mike (1991) observed student interactions during literacy events in a self-contained classroom for children with cerebral palsy and a range of multiple disabilities. In all, more than 120 hours of observations were conducted across a 4-month period in the fall semester. Mike reported that students interacted with one another less than once per hour on average over the course of the study. Koppenhaver's (1991) descriptive analysis of more than 70 hours of literacy instruction provided by exemplary teachers to children with severe speech and physical impairments likewise found little student–student interaction as well as a strong curricular emphasis on listening and reading to the near exclusion of writing and communicating.

Finally, Koppenhaver, Abraham, and Yoder (1994) conducted a microanalysis of the nature of teacher–student interactions and the ways that teachers sequence instruction during text composition activities for children with severe speech and physical impairments. Analysis of social participation structures (Au & Mason, 1982) in three teacher–student dyads suggested that composition lessons consisted largely of the Teacher Initiation-Student Reply-Teacher Evaluation sequence previously identified in regular education classrooms (e.g., Mehan, 1979). In conducting composition lessons, teachers consistently maintained control of topic, thematic unity, syntax, and cohesion by asking a series of wh- questions and then converting the student responses into a text. They further controlled the text creation process by acting as scribes for the students, although two of the three target students were capable of independently composing text. Academic task structure (i.e., the sequence of instruction) analysis (Erickson, 1982) of these composition lessons suggested that the students were provided little information and few strategies for independently communicating written messages. Activities were more effectively designed to complete texts in a limited time than to provide students with control over their own learning.

Children with a range of disabilities spend limited amounts of time in school reading, writing, or discussing texts of a paragraph or longer (Haynes &

Jenkins, 1986; Koppenhaver, 1991; Leinhardt, Zigmond, & Cooley, 1981). This is unfortunate given growing evidence of the positive influence of text reading and discussion on oral and augmented language learning in children with disabilities (e.g., Butler, 1979; Rogow, 1982; Steelman et al., 1992–1993). Commercially available texts such as *Storytime* (King-DeBaun, 1989) and the *O.W.L. curriculum* (oral and written language) (Pierce & Steelman, 1994) reduce the burden of teacher planning and preparation with the aim of achieving higher levels of interaction in text-centered activities for children with developmental disabilities.

In summary, existing research suggests that parents and teachers often do not use the children's communication devices, tend to dominate the content and sequence of interactions during literacy activities, ask many questions that require short responses, focus on end products (i.e., giving the right answer), and often provide verbatim text renderings. Additional research is required to determine if such observations are true in the general population of children with developmental disabilities in order to ascertain the causes of such conditions and to develop and test solutions.

Situational Context

In examining the home and school contexts in which literacy learning takes place, it seems that parents and teachers can have a substantial and lasting impact on individual children's literacy learning regardless of the severity of their disabilities (e.g., Fourcin, 1975). In home environments, researchers have found young children with severe speech, physical, and health impairments demonstrating surprising gains in their understanding of the form, content, and use of literacy materials and tools. Butler (1979), for example, reported the case of Cushla, who was immersed in a print-rich environment from birth. Cushla's parents read with her often and provided her with encouragement to explore independently a wealth of print materials and tools. While developmental tests revealed the child had severe delays in most areas, her language abilities were on par with typically developing peers, and her responses to written language were considered advanced for her age. In a retrospective survey, literate adults with severe speech and physical impairments recalled growing up in homes similar to Cushla's where they were surrounded by print materials, were read with regularly, and frequently observed others in their homes reading and writing for a variety of purposes (Koppenhaver, Evans, & Yoder, 1991).

A recent survey conducted by Light and Kelford Smith (1993) demonstrated the critical importance of the availability of materials *and* opportunities and encouragement to use them. While parents of typically developing preschoolers and of preschoolers with disabilities reported similar print-rich environments, the experiences of the two groups of children were quite different. The children with severe speech and physical impairments had far fewer opportunities to use the print materials or to engage in writing and drawing activities. Koppenhaver, Evans, and Yoder (1991) likewise found that highly literate adults with severe disabilities recalled that as children they rarely had engaged in writing or drawing experiences either at home or in school, and the researchers speculated that many individuals with disabilities who do not successfully become literate may have found such an imbalance in their learning experiences difficult to overcome.

Marvin and Mirenda (1993, 1994) conducted parallel surveys of parents and teachers of children in Head Start (HS) preschool programs and early childhood special education (ECSE) classrooms (which included both children with disabilities and typically developing peer models). Parents of children with disabilities in ECSE classrooms reported providing fewer types of early literacy experiences to their children than parents of typically developing peers in the same classrooms or parents of children in HS programs. Fewer children with disabilities in ECSE classrooms were taken by their parents to the library, had rhymes or poetry read to them, were asked to retell or predict story events during storybook reading, or had access to writing and drawing implements.

Two observational studies have been conducted in classrooms of children with developmental disabilities. First, Mike (1991), in addition to studying classroom interaction, observed classroom literacy events in order to determine factors that either impeded or aided literacy acquisition by children with multiple disabilities. Factors identified as aiding literacy acquisition by the children included regular story reading, student choice of literacy-related activities, and the presence of a wide array of print materials. Impediments to literacy learning included the small amount of time provided for literacy instruction (less than 15 minutes per day on average), instructional emphasis on acquisition of literacy subskills (e.g., identifying suffixes), and instruction organized around one-to-one seatwork done with the teacher.

Second, Koppenhaver (1991) observed and videotaped three teachers of children with severe speech and physical impairments for a full week of instruction in the fall, winter, and spring of one year. Teacher interviews, student work samples, and student records provided additional data. While teachers allocated substantial amounts of time for literacy instruction (an average of 75–105 minutes daily), the vast majority of that instruction was focused on words and sentences in isolation (i.e., worksheets and spelling lists) rather than on contextual and functional reading or writing. Teachers tended to work one-to-one with students in completing workbook activities. Similar findings of skills instruction isolated from contextual reading or writing are reported in the classroom experiences of children with mild mental retardation, behavior disorders, and learning disabilities (Haynes & Jenkins, 1986; Leinhardt et al., 1981; Ysseldyke, Thurlow, Christensen, & Weiss, 1987).

Sociocultural Context

Our perceptions, expectations, and values influence our behavior in ways that may in turn influence the behavior of others (Good & Brophy, 1984). Parent and teacher expectations strongly influence student outcomes in reading and writing achievements (Cooper, 1979; Durkin, 1984; Seigner, 1983). With typically developing children, parental and teacher expectations directly influence the priority given to literacy activities as well as to the quality and quantity of literacy interactions (Light & McNaughton, 1993). Parental and teacher expectations also may be communicated to children and influence the child's motivation level of self-confidence, which can in turn influence achievement (Cohen, McDonnell, & Osborn, 1989; Light & McNaughton, 1993).

Researchers are just beginning to investigate how parental and teacher expectations affect literacy outcomes in children with developmental disabilities. As noted in the previous section on situational context, Koppenhaver, Evans, and Yoder (1991) surveyed highly literate adults who use AAC systems. These adults exhibited high degrees of self-confidence and noted that their families had been highly supportive of their early literacy learning. Survey respondents wrote responses such as "My parents knew I could learn to read," and "They never babied me." Light and Kelford Smith's (1993) survey revealed that parents of speaking children consistently rated literacy achievement as a high priority, whereas parents of children who used AAC devices were more concerned with face-to-face communication proficiency and development of self-help skills. These priorities were evidenced in the literary experiences of the two groups. Children without disabilities tended to have more frequent access to writing and drawing materials, independent use of print materials, and parental storybook reading.

Parent and teacher priorities and expectations may not be tied so much to the severity of the disability as to the presence of the disability. Marvin and Mirenda (1993) conducted a comparative survey in a midwestern school district of the parents of the children in Head Start (HS) preschool programs ($N=112$), early childhood special education (ECSE) programs ($N=151$), and parents of children without disabilities enrolled as peer models (PM) in ECSE programs ($N=28$). While learning to read and write were identified as high priorities by 50% or more of the parents of children in HS or PM programs, they were identified as high priorities by less than 33% of the parents in ECSE programs. In a parallel survey of the children's teachers, Marvin and Mirenda (1994) report even more disturbing findings. Only one of 20 respondents listed reading as a high priority and none identified writing as a high priority for these children.

Light, Koppenhaver, Lee, and Riffle (1994) conducted a survey of parents ($N=66$) and teachers ($N=41$) to explore their expectations for children, ages 3–21 years, who use AAC devices. The study found that 24% of both parents and teachers had no expectations that their children and students would evidence improvement in their current literacy skills by age 25. Furthermore, there was a mismatch not only in parent and teacher expectations (congruent in only 33% of the parents and teachers) but also in parent and teacher priorities (congruent in 47% of the parents and teachers). Teachers' expectations generally appeared to be higher, with 64% of the teachers (versus 48% of the parents) predicting the achievement of functional literacy skills by age 25 for the students. In identifying highest priorities for the students, 63% of the teachers chose learning to read and 44% selected learning to write. Significantly fewer parents identified learning to read (41%) or learning to write (less than 25%) as high priorities. Given the current emphasis and support for family-focused intervention in the preschool years (e.g., Dunst, Trivette, & Deal, 1988), and a public policy of parental involvement in all of their children's education, public schools may need to explore systematic ways of identifying and addressing potential differences in parents' and teachers' expectations. Researchers need to explore the sources of these differences.

Coleman (1991) interviewed parents and teachers of preschool children with developmental disabilities regarding their perceptions of the children's current cognitive and communication abilities and their expectations for future literacy learning. She also observed and videotaped literacy experiences daily for several weeks in the children's homes and preschools. Parents and teachers completed a literacy event frequency checklist and kept a diary of literacy-related activities for an additional week after the observation period. When the children were perceived as having mental retardation, they were not expected to become literate, and the children had very few opportunities to participate in the literacy-related activities. One child, who was viewed as being "bright" and capable of becoming conventionally literate by both parents and teachers, was read to daily and regularly had environmental print pointed out to them. Perceptions and expectations appear to influence the amount of early literacy opportunities that are afforded to young children with disabilities, but none of the studies to date has explored a causal connection.

In addition to our perceptions and expectations for children, the value we place on literacy also may influence the quality and quantity of literacy-related experiences offered to children (Coleman, 1991). If parents or teachers do not value literacy, they are less likely to model varied and appropriate uses of literacy. If literacy activities (e.g., reading newspapers, using recipes, playing school) are not available for children to observe and participate in, they may have difficulty learning the functions and personal meanings of literacy that are the foundation for the development of conventional literacy. Children with developmental disabilities are often at a further disadvantage because their impairments may hinder incidental learning. Situations such as developing and using a shopping list often must be contrived so that the child with physical, cognitive, or sensory impairments can observe and participate in everyday print use.

Research suggests, then, that low expectations for literary achievements may translate into a child's lowered self-esteem regarding reading and writing, limited opportunities to interact with print-related materials, lack of participation in literacy-related activities, and a devaluing of literacy in general for children with disabilities. Low expectations may become a self-fulfilling prophecy and further the observed trend for children with developmental disabilities to experience significant and lasting literacy-learning difficulties. While further empirical testing is necessary, it may prove to be the case that for some children it is not so much the nature of their disabilities as our own expectations and responses in relation to those disabilities that lead to lowered literacy performance.

Educational and Psychosocial Implications

The contextual model used as an organizer for the research review above highlights the importance of considering a range of factors as we attempt to improve the purposeful use of literacy by children with developmental disabilities. The model grew out of our own experiences in creating the Center for Literacy and Disability Studies and from our conversations with parents, teachers, and administrators who were battling a popular view that literacy is irrelevant to children with developmental disabilities. For that reason, we believe it is necessary to conclude this literature review by briefly recapitulating some of the reasons we believe that literacy is vitally important to children with developmental disabilities.

In a society that is increasingly technology- and communication-driven, there is little debate that literacy skills are important to individuals without disabilities and can affect all life domains including education, vocation, and recreation (Applebee, Langer, & Mullis, 1987; Hallihan, Kauffman, & Lloyd, 1985). It is only quite recently, however, that the central necessity of literacy for persons with developmental disabilities has begun receiving more widespread support (e.g., Blackstone & Cassatt-James, 1988; Greer, 1991; Koppenhaver, Coleman, & Yoder, 1991; National Institute on Disability and Rehabilitation Research, 1992).

The abilities to read and write offer a number of important benefits to persons with disabilities. For example, for persons with severe speech and physical impairments, spelling skills can provide contextual clues to listeners that may clarify dysarthric speech (Beukelman & Yorkston, 1977). Likewise, spelling skills can provide unlimited access to vocabulary for persons with more severe speech impairments who use AAC devices. Being literate can provide access to powerful assistive technologies that can enable persons with developmental disabilities to listen, speak, read, and write better. Persons with severe cognitive impairments may be better able to communicate by pointing to logographs of foods and other items that are often recognizable in context to typically developing children 2 years old and younger (Masonheimer, Drum, & Ehri, 1984).

Ultimately, literacy gives substance to the implementation of national policies and legislation such as the Regular Education Initiative (Davis, 1989) or the Americans with Disabilities Act of 1990 (PL 101-336), because of its potential to increase peer acceptance in mainstream classrooms (Donahue & Prescott, 1988), to support independent and academic learning (Chall, 1983), and to develop employability and expand vocational options (Pierce & Kublin, 1993a;

Richardson, Koller, & Katz, 1988). Legislators and policymakers recognize the central importance of literacy, which is evidenced in the plethora of national literacy centers (e.g., Carolina Literacy Center for Literacy and Disability Studies, Center for the Study of Writing, National Center on Adult Literacy, National Center for Family Literacy, National Reading Research Center, among others) and the presence of universal literacy among adults in the United States as one of eight national education goals in Goals 2000: Educate America Act of 1994 (PL 103-227). Finally, and perhaps most often overlooked, literacy skills improve public and self-perceptions of individual competence. Killilea (1983) concludes the biography of her daughter, Karen, born with severe speech and physical impairments, with a quote from Karen: "I can walk. I can talk. I can read. I can write....I can do anything!" (p. 286).

LITERACY INTERVENTION STUDIES

Literacy intervention studies involving children with developmental disabilities are few in number and nearly uniform in their attention to improving literacy subskills (e.g., word identification, spelling, handwriting) while ignoring the impact of that improvement on the individual's ability to comprehend or compose texts.

Children with Mental Retardation

Studies of students with mental retardation have tended to explore the effectiveness of various methods of teaching sight words (e.g., Calhoun, 1985; Dorry & Zeaman, 1975; Gast, Ault, Wolery, Doyle, & Berlanger, 1988; Koury & Browder, 1986). Singh and Singh (1988), for example, compared the effectiveness of overcorrection and phonic analysis in improving oral reading errors of three children, ages 9–12 years, with moderate mental retardation. In the overcorrection condition, each oral reading error resulted in the teacher providing the correct word, followed by the child pointing to the word, saying it correctly five times, and then rereading the sentence. In the phonic analysis condition, the teacher directed the child to attend to various phonetic elements of the error word and sound it out. Both interventions proved effective, but phonic analysis was more effective over time, probably because it provides the reader with an independent strategy that can by employed in all reading situations. Overcorrection requires the presence of another person to highlight errors and produce the correct model.

Educators seeking to implement such word identification strategies in their own classrooms should bear several cautions in mind. First, care should be taken in selecting texts of appropriate difficulty. The texts employed in the Singh and Singh study (1988) were too difficult for the children. A substantial body of research suggests that children must be able to read successfully at least 95 of every 100 words encountered in a text if they are to read with comprehension (e.g., Betts, 1946; Cooper, 1952; Davis & Ekwall, 1976). Second, teachers should question their motives in improving students' word-reading skills. Prior to this study, these children received an average of 10 minutes of reading instruction three times per week. If so little emphasis is placed on literacy instruction in their own programs, educators should question whether reducing oral reading errors should be a high priority.

Calhoun (1985) compared handwriting and typing in a copying task as a means of improving sight-word recognition. Seven students with moderate mental retardation, ages 12–14 years, who read at the first grade level, were taught a set of five words in daily 30-minute instructional sessions followed by 10 minutes of practice in copying them. Typing proved consistently superior to handwriting in speed and accuracy, but word recognition scores did not differ by transcription method. Educators could implement such a strategy in their own classrooms with greater success by adapting some of its features. First, words should be selected that students need in their daily reading and writing tasks. Second, students should be taught an independent study strategy for studying and remembering the words (e.g., Koppenhaver & Yoder, 1989). Third, words should be introduced at a pace that students can manage easily (i.e., five words per day clearly exceeded these students' capabilities because they could retain only an average of 13–14 words after 20 days of intervention).

Dorry and Zeaman (1975) compared the effectiveness of four sight-word teaching approaches: consistently pairing the words with black-and-white line drawings, systematically fading the picture presentation, alternately presenting words alone or words-and-pictures, and alternately presenting words or pictures alone. Subjects were 35 children with moderate mental retardation who reportedly were nonreaders. Fading proved the most efficient technique. Again, educators might question their motives in implementing this strategy if they, too, are working with individuals who are unable to read conventional print. Instructional activities might be better aimed first at encouraging the exploration of print forms and uses so that students understand the utility of what they are attempting to learn.

Koury and Browder (1986) trained sight words to peer tutors, ages 9–11 years, with moderate mental retardation, using a time delay procedure (introducing increments of time between stimulus and prompt). Tutors then applied the procedure in teaching younger peers, ages 6–9 years, with moderate mental retardation. All of these students and tutors had been placed in the preprimer level of a basal reading series, could identify a few sight words, and could recognize most of the alphabet. Younger peers learned five sight words in one to three sessions of 10–20 minutes each. However, educators seeking to implement this procedure should consider a meaningful measure of success (e.g., ability to read the words in context or use them to accomplish a classroom task, not the ability to identify the words when presented on flash cards).

Gast et al. (1988) compared the effectiveness and efficiency of constant time delay and a system of least prompts in teaching four students, ages 8–13 years, with moderate mental retardation to read food words found in grocery stores. The words were presented on flash cards. Both procedures were effective, but the constant time delay was more efficient. Educators employing strategies such as these might consider more functional presentation and use of the words to be learned if their students' literacy skills are as rudimentary as those of the subjects of this study (described as knowing how to identify and spell a few high frequency, short words).

Raver and Dwyer (1986) provided a useful model in regard to a more functional presentation. The subjects in their study were five children with cognitive and language delays, ages 3–5 years, in a program for children with various disabilities. Teachers presented sight words, but did so in the context of functional use. For example, in teaching the word "puzzle," the teacher presented the word on a card, said the word, went to the toy cabinet and got out a puzzle, and then played with the puzzle while repeating the word. Trial-and-error learning was permitted as the children learned the words, and then sentence-building activities were added using similar methods. The children learned to read and use 25 words in their daily activities over a period of 49 days. The word cards were used throughout the day whenever appropriate. The students were able to generalize their learning to use the words and sentences in new settings and situations.

Taken as a whole, these studies suggest that there are many different ways of teaching sight words to children with mental retardation, most of them focusing on efficient memorization of lists of words. Raver and Dwyer (1986) suggest that drill and practice may not be the only intervention strategy available to educators and that researchers may need to broaden the range of their literacy explorations within this population. Much work remains to be done in examining effective means of not only teaching functional use of sight words but also of improving text composition and comprehension skills. In investigating these issues, researchers must consider how quickly students learn the words (or skills) and how appropriately students use the words in the new settings and situations within and beyond the classroom walls.

Children with Cerebral Palsy

Intervention studies of children with cerebral palsy are also focused on literacy subskills, divided broadly into methods of increasing children's rate of response and methods of increasing their accuracy of response. Studies of methods to increase rate of response have increased response efficiency in literacy drill-and-practice activities by relying on multiple choice and eye-pointing (Wasson & Keeler, 1984), increasing typing speed with rate enhancement techniques (McNaughton & Drynan, 1990), and providing longer wait time following teacher questions (Harris, 1982). Studies of methods to increase accuracy of response have employed auditory feedback of various sorts including synthetic speech, audiotapes, and voice to increase spelling accuracy in natural writing contexts, word identification in context, reading rate and time on task, and reading comprehension (Block, 1978; de Hoop, 1965; Koke & Neilson, 1987; Koppenhaver & Yoder, 1988, 1989).

Promising Directions

One very interesting study investigated the use of a literacy event, nursery rhyme reading, to develop intentional and communication behavior in young children with blindness and multiple disabilities, ages 15 months to 7 years (Rogow, 1982). Mothers were videotaped in their homes as they read nursery rhymes with their children. Data included videotapes of parent–child interactions during the nursery rhyme activities, weekly anecdotal records, audiotapes of play sessions in school, and a weekly checklist of behaviors. While the study is not experimental, observational data suggest that all of the children demonstrated growth in a variety of social responses using the modalities most accessible to each of them (e.g., vocalizations, gestures, postures).

Perhaps the most comprehensive intervention study to date involving literacy and children with developmental disabilities was conducted by Katims (1991). In a year-long experimental investigation, Katims examined the effect of a literacy enriched classroom on young children, ages 4–6 years, with mild to moderate retardation, behavior disorders, and learning disabilities. A statistically significant improvement was found in the experimental group's understanding of concepts of print (e.g., that print goes left to right or that words are a group of letters with white space on either side). He also documented a clear progression in the complexity and sustained attention of the children in their independent use of storybooks as well as in the complexity, variety, and structure of their independent writing.

DeCoste's (1993) study represents the first experimental comparison of the effects of modifying the instructional environment on the literacy learning of children with developmental disabilities. She employed a single-subject design in order to assess whether a whole language-oriented program or a skills-oriented program was more effective in improving the writing and spelling skills of three children, ages 9–11 years, with severe speech and physical impairments. The principal dependent measure was spelling accuracy measured at weekly intervals. At four intervals during the school year, writing data also were collected and analyzed for developmental spelling level, spelling accuracy in context, fluency (i.e., number of words written), and sentence complexity. Over the course of the school year, the children demonstrated gains under both instructional conditions, with a slightly higher increase under the skills condition for all three children, although all three reported a preference for the whole language approach.

This study is important for two reasons. First, it demonstrates that providing systematic instruction (of at least two types) to children with severe disabilities does improve their literacy skills (at least spelling and writing). Second, it highlights some of the difficulties intervention research with this population presents: that single-subject designs may be more conducive to studying specific literacy subskills (e.g., spelling accuracy) than to studying the overall effects (e.g., whether whole language-oriented or skills-oriented instruction is more effective), and that there are no currently available literacy assessments that have been validated for use with children with developmental disabilities. For example, the repeated spelling measures used by DeCoste (1993) address only a very narrow outcome of two broader instructional programs, and the four interval measures of three individuals yield little in the way of conclusive evidence of programmatic effects. Future intervention designs must take into account individual differences. At the same time, a wider array of valid literacy measures that can be administered repeatedly must be developed. For example, some single-subject designs have relied on administration of a set of passages controlled for length and reading difficulty in order to measure gains in reading comprehension (Mudre & McCormick, 1989; Palincsar & Brown, 1984). In this way, the researchers are able to attribute student gains to intervention effects and not to differences in text difficulty or student familiarity with a text or topic.

Toward More Comprehensive Intervention

Four pilot efforts have been undertaken to outline the characteristics of more comprehensive approaches to literacy intervention in preschool/kindergarten (Katims & Pierce, 1993; Pierce & Steelman, 1993) and elementary school (Cousin, Weekley, & Gerard, 1993; Erickson & Koppenhaver, 1994). Katims and Pierce (1993) concluded from their own (Katims, 1991; Steelman et al., 1992–1993) and existing research (e.g., Palloway, 1987) that children with disabilities must be prepared in at least four areas in order to succeed in public school. These include basic academic readiness, prosocial and age-appropriate social skills, appropriate responsiveness to a variety of instructional styles, and appropriate responsiveness to new and different environmental structures. Katims and Pierce (1993) proposed that a balanced emergent literacy curriculum that includes print-related activities accomplishing real purposes and predictable, repeated story readings can provide the classroom context necessary to develop each of these essential understandings and skills.

Pierce and Steelman (1994) have been developing a curriculum in Project O.W.L. that addresses the need for a structured approach to fostering emergent language and literacy development in the birth-to-5 population. Five principal goals guide their effort. First, developmentally appropriate activities, instructional strategies, and learning support are offered to young children with developmental disabilities, which foster all four modes of communication (i.e., listening, speaking, reading, and writing). Second, early learning is optimized by generalizing concepts across contexts rather than by focusing on specific skills training (e.g., use of communication targets is encouraged in a variety of related activities rather than in specific, nonrelated drill-and-practice sessions). Third, an abundance of purposeful, print-related experience is provided to help children understand the functions of print and to spur their natural curiosity to learn about written language (Hohmann, 1993). Fourth, a thematic approach is used to integrate classroom experiences and to provide the consistency, relatedness, and familiarity that support learning (Norris, 1989). Finally, collaboration between preschool teachers, therapists, and family members is stressed to incorporate emergent literacy activities into existing curricula and daily routines.

A variety of assessments were developed or adapted to monitor student progress during initial pilot testing of Project O.W.L. in a self-contained classroom for children ages 2–8 years with severe cognitive, speech, or physical impairments. The Concepts About Print Test (Clay, 1979) was used to explore changes in the children's understanding of various print features. An adaptation of Sulzby's (1989) categories of independent reading and independent writing and Katims' (1991) categories of independent book use were used to document growth in the children's independent literacy behaviors. Nonconventional child responsiveness (e.g., vocalizations or eye-pointing) during literacy events was recorded using a brief checklist (Pierce, 1992). Finally, a literacy artifact and events checklist (Coleman, 1991) was used to monitor changes in materials and activities in the classroom during the course of the school year. Validity and reliability of each of these assessments remain to be empirically demonstrated. However, triangulation of researcher observational notes, informal teacher observations, and the outcomes of the assessments mentioned above suggest that the children increased their understanding of the concepts and functions of print (Steelman et al., 1992–1993). Additionally, the pilot classroom became increasingly more print-rich and literacy-centered as teachers added software, books, and other reading materials; adapted writing and drawing materials for the children's independent use; and increasingly incorporated their instructional goals into interactions around print.

Cousin and Weekley (1993) investigated historical precedents to current instructional beliefs related to students with moderate and severe disabilities. Their curriculum development efforts are founded upon three central ideas: 1) the need for planned and varied demonstrations of print use so that children with disabilities can come to understand the range of functions print can serve in their lives, 2) the need to support development through greater involvement with proficient learners, and 3) a belief that literacy is learned holistically rather than the study of specific skills in isolation. The resultant curriculum attempts to immerse students in print-rich environments, provide students with frequent opportunities to hear text read aloud and to talk about what is to be learned, use peers and teachers to model varied and functional print use, encourage personal construction of print understanding, organize the curriculum into themes, and implement it in both mainstream and special education classrooms.

Erickson and Koppenhaver (1994) focused their curriculum development efforts on implementation issues within a self-contained classroom, encouraging educators and researchers to develop their own curricula to address the needs of all children. Key components of their effort included: 1) strong administrative support that facilitated acquisition of needed equipment and instructional freedom to respond to each student's individual needs; 2) availability of a wide array of hardware and software that provided independent access to reading, writing, and communication otherwise unavailable to the students with severe speech and physical impairments; and 3) a transdisciplinary planning and implementation process in which a special educator, a speech-language pathologist, two teacher's assistants, and a teacher's aide integrated instructional and therapeutic goals. Over the course of a school year, students with severe disabilities in the classroom learned letter names, letter-sound correspondences, and sight words. Students also learned to comprehend text that was read aloud to them and became able to compose simple texts using the computer. Five of the eight children in the self-contained program were sufficiently successful to be fully included in the regular education curriculum during the following school year.

NEED FOR RESEARCH

There is a tremendous need for research into effective methods for developing emergent and conventional literacy in children with all types of developmental disabilities. The works cited in this chapter only begin to explore explanations of why children with developmental disabilities have significant literacy-learning difficulties and how to prevent or overcome these problems. As research proceeds, we urge wider consideration of the individual and interactive effects on literacy learning and use of the various components of the contextual model and the multiple contexts in which literacy use occurs. It is also critical that researchers begin to develop more valid and reliable measures of literacy performance in individuals with developmental disabilities. The vast majority of current instruments and techniques used with children without disabilities penalize children with severe speech or physical impairments because of the demands for speech or motor performance, often under time restrictions.

We specifically urge increased research efforts in four areas. First, observational and descriptive studies are needed to determine the dimensions and characteristics of literacy learning in children with developmental disabilities. Such studies should begin to delineate particularly the roles of assistive technologies in facilitating learning from and about print. These technologies are now widely used and strongly advocated, but educational applications and implications are little understood. Efforts to date have focused on the development of a wider variety of better tools and on increasingly organized efforts to provide access to these tools by individuals with disabilities (e.g., RESNA, 1992). It is incumbent upon researchers and educators to explore how such tools can best be used to enhance literacy learning, participation in literacy events, or communication in and around literacy events by children with developmental disabilities. Special efforts should also be made to understand and explain literacy learning from the child's perspective. An adult explanation of literacy learning in typically developing children led to the readiness perspective, still prevalent in many special education programs, that has historically excluded many children with developmental disabilities from school-based literacy instruction and experience. It is only when researchers attempted to understand literacy from the young child's perspective that we came to value the information provided by the nonconventional readings and writings of young children and to recognize that literacy is relevant to all individuals, regardless of severity of disability (Koppenhaver, Coleman, Kalman, & Yoder, 1991).

Second, research-based intervention models are needed to develop successful and efficient programs for children with developmental disabilities. We need to understand better what works for whom, under what conditions, and for how long. But we also need to learn more specifically what is central to the literacy-learning process. We have found that it is not possible to expect the same quantity of experience or classwork from children with developmental disabilities that children without disabilities demonstrate. We must, consequently, continually refine our programs and strategies and materials to optimize learning.

Third, longitudinal and follow-up studies of children with developmental disabilities who receive early literacy intervention are greatly needed, as are investigations into the long-term effects of literacy learning on vocational, educational, and life choices and performance across the life span. Essentially this is an efficacy issue. We must understand the effects of early literacy intervention, if we are to provide the best possible programs for young children. Likewise, we must speculate less and understand more the consequences of literacy learning in the lives of individuals with developmental disabilities.

Fourth and finally, the effects of literacy learning on oral language development and cognitive development must be better understood. Emergent literacy theory argues that written and oral language development are concurrent and interrelated (e.g., Teale & Sulzby, 1989), and research with typically developing young children is beginning to provide supporting evidence (e.g., Allen et al., 1989; Sulzby & Teale, 1987). Likewise, theorists in cognitive psychology have proposed that written language developmental qualitatively changes the way an individual thinks (e.g., Vygotsky, 1978). The vast majority of early intervention programs for children with developmental disabilities include language and cognitive goals but include little in the way of substantial literacy experience. In so doing, such programs may omit a significant vehicle for obtaining the very language and cognitive goals they seek to achieve.

CONCLUSION

Language and literacy are simultaneously learned and mutually beneficial processes. Early studies of children with developmental disabilities suggest that print-related activities not only seem to help a child's ability to understand and use written language, but also to develop content, form, and use of their oral or augmented communications (e.g., Katims, 1991). Whether or not children with developmental disabilities attain high literacy levels, their understanding and use of more complex language structures, syntax, and vocabulary can be enhanced by participating in story reading and writing activities. These children can learn concepts and functions of print that will allow them to use print more independently to order foods, shop, use public transportation, or find favorite programs in a television guide. It is critical that early intervention programs increasingly include print-related activities in early childhood curricula (Bredekamp, 1992).

As we think long term about the consequences of literacy learning, it has been argued that literate children with developmental disabilities will be more successful in the educational and vocational mainstream. It is clear that while the abilities to read and to write are essential across educational and vocational settings, they are not sufficient for inclusion as evidenced by the experiences of the 22 literate adults with severe speech and physical impairments in the Koppenhaver, Evans, and Yoder (1991) study reported earlier in this chapter. Only one of those individuals was employed full time, and three others were employed part time. Successful full inclusion requires a constellation of skills in persons with disabilities as in persons without disabilities, as well as recognition by employers and educators of the array of relative strengths and weaknesses evidenced by all persons, including those with disabilities. Laws such as the Individuals with Disabilities Education Act of 1990 (IDEA) (PL 101-476) and the Americans with Disabilities Act of 1990 (ADA) (PL 101-336) ensure equal access and opportunity. These laws also provide the supports needed for inclusion to succeed and to encourage programs to increasingly address literacy, employment, and independence as they prepare children with disabilities for life beyond the program.

We are excited by the surge of interest in literacy as it pertains to individuals with developmental disabilities. Goals 2000 (PL 103-227) addresses all children and adults, including people with disabilities. The U.S. Department of Education now issues requests for proposals that directly link literacy and individuals with disabilities, a practice unheard of before 1992. The National Center to Improve Practice has convened an interdisciplinary working group of researchers and practitioners to establish a knowledge base linking literacy, disabilities, technology, and classroom instructional practices. The Center for Literacy Studies at the University of North Carolina at Chapel Hill has expanded research and education efforts to begin to address not only individuals with severe speech and physical impairments but other developmental disabilities as well.

All of this activity is recent, having been initiated largely since 1990. New ideas and efforts inevitably encounter difficulties and opposition. Therefore, it remains incumbent upon practitioners, families, researchers, and policymakers to further the breadth and depth of these efforts. Practitioners must share successes and be receptive to innovation. Families must be unwavering advocates for their children. Researchers must assist in explaining learning processes and in developing and evaluating effective intervention strategies and materials. Policymakers must continue to develop inclusive mandates. The potential rewards of success in these areas are too great and the likely consequences of failure too severe to do otherwise.

REFERENCES

Adams, M.J. (1990). *Beginning to read: Thinking and learning about print.* Cambridge, MA: MIT Press.

Allen, J.B., Clark, W., Cook, M., Crane, P., Fallon, I., Hoffman, L., Jennings, K.S., & Sours, M.A. (1989). Reading and writing development in whole language kindergartens. In J. Mason (Ed.), *Reading and writing connections* (pp. 121–146). Newton MA: Allyn & Bacon.

Anderson, R.C., & Pearson, P.D. (1984). A schema-theoretic view of basic processes in reading. In P.D. Pearson (Ed.), *Handbook of reading research* (pp. 255–291). New York: Longman.

Applebee, A.N., (1978). *The child's concept of story.* Chicago: University of Chicago Press.

Applebee, A.N., Langer, J.A., & Mullis, I. (1987). *Learning to be literate in America: Reading, writing, and reasoning.* Princeton, NJ: National Assessment of Educational Progress and Educational Testing Service.

Au, K.H., & Mason, J.M. (1982). *A microethnographic approach to the study of classroom reading education: Rationale and procedures.* Champaign: Center for the Study of Reading, University of Illinois. (ERIC Document Reproduction Service No. ED 215 314)

Barsch, R.H., & Rudell, B. (1962). A study of reading development among 77 children with cerebral palsy. *Cerebral Palsy Review, 23*(2), 3–12.

Berninger, V.W., & Gans, B.M. (1986). Language profiles in nonspeaking individuals of normal intelligence with severe cerebral palsy. *Augmentative and Alternative Communication, 2,* 45–50.

Betts, E.A. (1946). *Foundations of reading instruction.* New York: American Book.

Beukelman, D.R., & Yorkston, K. (1977). A communication system for the severely dysarthric speaker with an intact language system. *Journal of Speech and Hearing Disorders, 42,* 265–270.

Bishop, D., & Adams, C. (1990). A prospective study of the relationship between specific language impairment, phonological disorders and reading retardation. *Journal of Child Psychology and Psychiatry, 31,* 1,027–1,050.

Bishop, D.V.M., Brown, B.B., & Robson, J. (1990). The relationship between phoneme discrimination, speech production, and language comprehension in cerebral-palsied individuals. *Journal of Speech and Hearing Research, 33,* 210–219.

Bishop, K., Rankin, J.L., & Mirenda, P. (1994). Impact of graphic symbol use on reading acquisition. *Augmentative and Alternative Communication, 10,* 113–125.

Blackstone, S.W., & Cassatt-James, E.L. (1988). Augmentative communication. In N.J. Lass, L.V. McReynolds, J.L. Northern, & D.E. Yoder (eds.), *Handbook of speech-language pathology and audiology* (pp. 986–1013). Toronto: B.C. Decker.

Block, J.D. (1978). Teaching reading and writing skills to a teenaged spastic cerebral palsied person: A long-term case study. *Perceptual and Motors Skills, 46,* 31–41.

Bloom, D., & Green, J. (1984). Directions in the sociolinguistic study of reading. In P.D. Pearson (Ed.), *Handbook of reading research* (pp. 395–421). New York: Longman.

Borgh, K., & Dickson, W.P. (1992). The effects on children's writing of adding speech synthesis to a word processor. *Journal of Research on Computing in Education, 24,* 533–544.

Bowley, A.H. (1967). A follow-up study of 64 children with cerebral palsy. *Developmental Medicine and Child Neurology, 9,* 172–182.

Bredekamp, S. (Ed.). (1992). *Developmentally appropriate practice in early childhood programs serving children birth through age 8.* Washington, DC: National Association for the Education of Young Children.

Bricker, R.P., & Lewis, M. (1982). Co-occurrence and intervention. *Topics in Early Childhood Special Education, 2*(2), 1–16.

Brown, C. (1954). *My left foot.* London: Secker and Warburg.

Butler, D. (1979). *Cushla and her books.* Boston: The Horn Book.

Calhoun, M.L. (1985). Typing contrasted with handwriting in language arts instruction for moderately mentally retarded students. *Education and Training of the Mentally Retarded, 20,* 48–52.

Cartwright, G.P. (1968). Written language abilities of educable mentally retarded and normal children. *American Journal of Mental Deficiency, 72,* 499–505.

Center, Y., & Ward, J. (1984). Integration of mildly handicapped cerebral palsied children into regular schools. *Exceptional Child, 31,* 104–113.

Chall, J.S. (1983). Literacy: Trends and explanations. *Educational Researcher, 12,* 3–8.

Clay, M. (1979). *The early detection of reading difficulties.* Portsmouth, NH: Heinemann.

Cohen, S.G., McDonnell, G., & Osborn, B. (1989). Self-perception of "at-risk" and high achieving readers: Beyond reading recovery achievement data. In S. McCormick & J. Zutell (Eds.), *Cognitive and social perspectives for literacy research and instruction* (38th yearbook of the National Reading Conference) (pp. 117–122). Chicago. National Reading Conference.

Coleman, P.P. (1991). *Literacy lost: A qualitative analysis of the early literacy experiences of young children with severe speech and physical impairments.* Unpublished doctoral dissertation, University of North Carolina at Chapel Hill.

Cooper, H.M. (1979). Pygmalion grows up: A model for teacher expectation communication and performance influence. *Review of Educational Research, 49,* 389–410.

Cooper, J.L. (1952). *The effect of adjustment of basal reading materials on reading achievement.* Unpublished doctoral dissertation, Boston University.

Cousin, P.T., Weekley, T., & Gerard, J. (1993). The functional uses of language and literacy by students with severe language and learning problems. *Language Arts, 70,* 548–556.

Danilova, L.A. (1983). *Methods of improving the cognitive and verbal development of children with cerebral palsy* (R.H. Silverman, Trans., Monograph No. 23). New York: World Rehabilitative Fund.

Davis, E.E., & Ekwall, E.E. (1976). Mode of perception and frustration in reading. *Journal of Learning Disabilities, 9,* 448–454.

Davis, W. (1989). The regular education initiative debate: Its promises and problems. *Exceptional Children, 55,* 440–446.

DeCoste, D.C. (1993). *Effects of intervention on the writing and spelling skills of elementary school students with severe speech and physical impairments.* Unpublished doctoral dissertation, George Washington University, Washington, DC.

de Hoop, W. (1965). Listening comprehension of cerebral palsied and other crippled children as a function of two speaking rates. *Exceptional Children, 31,* 233–244.

Donahue, M., & Prescott, B. (1988). Reading-disabled children's conversational participation in dispute episodes with peers. *First Language, 8,* 247–258.

Dorman, C. (1985). Classification of reading disability in a case of congenital brain damage. *Neuropsychologia, 23*, 393–402.

Dorman, C. (1987). Verbal, perceptual and intellectual factors associated with reading achievement in adolescents using neuropsychological tests. *International Journal of Clinical Neuropsychology, 6*, 142–144.

Dorry, G.W., & Zeaman, D. (1975). Teaching a simple reading vocabulary to retarded children: Effectiveness of fading and nonfading procedures. *American Journal of Mental Deficiency, 79*, 711–716.

Dunst, C., Trivette, C., & Deal, A. (1988). *Enabling and empowering families: Principles and guidelines for practice.* Cambridge, MA: Brookline.

Durkin, D. (1984). Poor black children who are successful readers: An investigation. *Urban Education, 19*, 53–76.

Erickson, F. (1982). Classroom discourse as improvisation: Relationships between academic task structure and social participation structure in lessons. In L.C. Wilkinson (Ed.), *Communicating in the classroom* (pp. 153–181). New York: Academic Press.

Erickson, K.A., & Koppenhaver, D.A. (1994). *Developing a literacy program for children with severe disabilities.* Manuscript submitted for publication.

Fitzgerald, J., Roberts, J., Pierce, P., & Schuele, M. (in press). Literacy in the homes of preschool children with Down syndrome. *Reading & Writing Quarterly.*

Foley, B.E. (1993). The development of literacy in individuals with severe congenital speech and motor impairments. *Topics in Language Disorders, 13*(2), 16–32.

Flood, J.E. (1977). Parental styles in reading episodes with young children. *The Reading Teacher, 30*, 846–867.

Fourcin, A.J. (1975). Language development in the absence of expressive speech. In E.H. Lenneberg & E. Lenneberg (Eds.), *Foundations of language development: A multidisciplinary approach* (Vol. 2, pp. 263–268). New York: Academic Press.

Gast, D.L., Ault, M.J., Wolery, M., Doyle, P.M., & Berlanger, S. (1988). Comparison of constant time delay and the system of least prompts in teaching sight word reading to students with moderate retardation. *Education and Training in Mental Retardation, 23*, 117–128.

Good, T.L., & Brophy, J.E. (1984). *Looking in classrooms* (3rd ed.). New York: Harper & Row.

Greer, J.V. (1991). The tyranny of words. *Exceptional Children, 57*, 486–487.

Hallihan, D.P., Kauffman, J.M., & Lloyd, J.W. (1985). *Introduction to learning disabilities.* Englewood Cliffs, NJ: Prentice Hall.

Harris, D. (1982). Communicative interaction processes involving nonvocal physically handicapped children. *Topics in Language Disorders, 2*(2), 21–37.

Hayes, J.R., & Flower, L.S. (1980). Writing as problem solving. *Visible Language, 14*, 388–399.

Haynes, M.C., & Jenkins, J.R. (1986). Reading instruction in special education resource rooms. *American Educational Research Journal, 23*, 161–190.

Heath, S.B. (1982). What no bedtime story means. *Language and Society, 2*, 49–76.

Higginbotham, D.J. (1992). Evaluation of keystroke savings across five assistive communication technologies. *Augmentative and Alternative Communication, 8*, 258–272.

Hohmann, M. (1993, Winter). Supporting young writers. *High Scope Resource*, 19–20.

Hopkins, T.W., Bice, H.V., & Colton, K.C. (1954). *Evaluation and education of the cerebral palsied child.* Arlington, VA: Council for Exceptional Children.

Kamhi, A., & Catts, H. (1986). Toward an understanding of developmental language and reading disorders. *Journal of Speech and Hearing Disorders, 53*, 337–347.

Katims, D.S. (1991). Emergent literacy in early childhood special education: Curriculum and instruction. *Topics in Early Childhood Special Education, 11*(1), 69–84.

Katims, D.S., & Pierce, P.L. (1993). *Literacy-rich environments and the transition of young children with special needs.* Manuscript submitted for publication.

Kelford Smith, A., Thurston, S., Light, J., Parnes, P., & O'Keefe, B. (1989). The form and use of written communication produced by physically disabled individuals using microcomputers. *Augmentative and Alternative Communication, 5,* 115–124.

Killilea, M. (1983). *Karen.* New York: Dell.

King-DeBaun, P. (1989). *Storytime: Stories, symbols and emergent literacy activities for young, special needs children.* Acworth, GA: Pati King-DeBaun.

Koke, S., & Neilson, J. (1987). *The effect of auditory feedback on the spelling of non-speaking physically disabled individuals.* Unpublished master's thesis, University of Toronto.

Koppenhaver, D.A. (1991). *A descriptive analysis of classroom literacy instruction provided to children with severe speech and physical impairments.* Unpublished doctoral dissertation, University of North Carolina at Chapel Hill.

Koppenhaver, D.A., Abraham, L.M., & Yoder, D.E. (1994). *Social and academic organization of composition lessons for AAC users.* Manuscript in preparation.

Koppenhaver, D.A., Coleman, P.P., Kalman, S., & Yoder, D.E. (1991). The implication of emergent literacy research for children with developmental disabilities. *American Journal of Speech-Language Pathology, 1*(1), 38–44.

Koppenhaver, D.A., Evans, D.A., & Yoder, D.E. (1991). Childhood reading and writing experiences of literate adults with severe speech and motor impairments. *Augmentative and Alternative Communication, 7,* 20–33.

Koppenhaver, D.A., & Pierce, P.P. (1992). Literacy and AAC: Communicating every which way we can. In *Proceedings of the 13th Annual Southeast Augmentative Communication Conference* (pp. 71–93). Birmingham, AL: United Cerebral Palsy of Greater Birmingham.

Koppenhaver, D.A., & Yoder, D.E. (1988, October). Independent reading practice. *Aug-Communique: North Carolina Augmentative Communication Association Newsletter, 6*(3), 9–11.

Koppenhaver, D.A., & Yoder, D.E. (1989). Study of a spelling strategy for physically disabled augmentative communication users. *Communication Outlook, 10*(3), 10–12.

Koppenhaver, D.A., & Yoder, D.E. (1992). Literacy issues in persons with severe disabilities. In R. Gaylord-Ross (Ed.), *Issues and research in special education* (Vol. 2, pp. 156–201). New York: Teachers College Press.

Koppenhaver, D.A., & Yoder, D.E. (1993). Classroom literacy instruction for children with severe speech and language impairments (SSPI): What is and what might be. *Topics in Language Disorders, 13*(2), 1–15.

Koury, M., & Browder, D.M. (1986). The use of delay to teach sight words by peer tutors classified as moderately mentally retarded. *Education and Training of the Mentally Retarded, 21,* 252–258.

Lademann, A. (1978). Postneonatally acquired cerebral palsy: A study of the aetiology, clinical findings and prognosis in 170 cases. *Acta Neurological Scandinavica, 57* (Suppl. 65). 1–146.

Leinhardt, G., Zigmond, N., & Cooley, W.W. (1981). Reading instruction and its effects. *American Educational Research Journal, 18,* 343–361.

Light, J., & Kelford Smith, A. (1993). Home literacy experiences of preschoolers who use AAC systems and of their nondisabled peers. *Augmentative and Alternative Communications, 9,* 10–25.

Light, J., Koppenhaver, D., Lee, E., & Riffle, L. (1994). *The home and school literacy experiences of students who use AAC systems.* Manuscript in preparation.

Light, J., & McNaughton, D. (1993). Literacy and augmentative communications and alternative communications (AAC): The expectations and priorities of parents and teachers. *Topics in Language Disorders, 13*(2), 33–46.

MacArthur, C.A. (1988). The impact of computers on the writing process. *Exceptional Children, 54,* 536–542.

Manion, M.H. (1986). Computers and behavior-disordered students: A rationale and review of the literature. *Educational Technology, 26*(7), 20–24.

Martinez, M.G., & Teale, W.H. (1993). Teacher storybook reading style: A comparison of six teachers. *Research in the Teaching of English, 27*, 175–199.

Marvin, C., & Mirenda, P. (1993). Home literary experiences of preschoolers enrolled in Head Start and special education programs. *Journal of Early Intervention, 17,* 351–367.

Marvin, C., & Mirenda, P. (1994). Literacy practice in Head Start and early childhood special education classrooms. *Early Education and Development, 5,* 289–300.

Masonheimer, P.E., Drum, P.A., & Ehri, L.C. (1984). Does environmental print indentification lead children into word reading? *Journal of Reading Behavior, 16,* 257–271.

McLean, M., Smith, B. J., McCormick, K., Schakel, J., & McEvoy, M. (1991). *Developmental delay: Establishing parameters for a preschool category of exceptionality.* Reston, VA: Division for Early Children, Council for Exceptional Children.

McNaughton, D., & Drynan, D. (1990, August). *Assessment and intervention issues for written communication: A case study.* Paper presented at the International Society for Augmentative and Alternative Communication biennial meeting, Stockholm.

McNaughton, S. (1993). Graphic representational systems and literacy learning. *Topics in Language Disorders, 13*(2), 58–75.

Mehan, H. (1979). *Learning lessons: Social organization in the classroom.* Cambridge, MA: Harvard University Press.

Menyuk, P., Chesnick, M., Liebergott, J.W., Korngold, B., D'Agostino, R., & Belanger, A. (1991). Predicting reading problems in at-risk children. *Journal of Speech and Hearing Research, 34,* 893–903.

Meyers, L.F. (1984). Unique contributions of microcomputers to language intervention with handicapped children. *Seminars in Speech and Language, 5*(1), 23–34.

Mike, D.G. (1991). *Literacy and the multiply disabled: An ethnography of classroom interaction.* Unpublished doctoral dissertation, State University of New York at Albany.

Mirenda, P., & Mathy-Laikko, P. (1989). Augmentative and alternative communication applications for persons with severe congenital communication disorders. *Augmentative and Alternative Communication, 5,* 3–13.

Mudre, L.H., & McCormick, S. (1989). Effects of meaning-focused cues on underachieving readers' context use, self-corrections, and literal comprehension. *Reading Research Quarterly, 24,* 89–113.

National Institute on Disability and Rehabilitation Research. (1992). *Consensus statement: Augmentative and alternative communication* (Vol. 1, No. 2). Washington, DC: Author.

Norris, J. (1989). Providing language remediation in the classroom: An integrated language-to-reading intervention method. *Language, Speech, and Hearing Services in Schools, 20,* 205–218.

Norton, P., & Heiman, B. (1988). Computer literacy and communication disordered students: A research study. *Educational Technology, 28,* 36–41.

Olson, R.K., & Wise, B. (1987). Computer speech in reading instruction. In D. Reinking (Ed.), *Reading and computers: Issues for theory and practice* (pp. 156–177). New York: Teachers College Press.

Palincsar, A.S., & Brown, A.L. (1984). Reciprocal teaching of comprehension-fostering and comprehension-monitoring activities. *Cognition and Instruction, 1,* 117–175.

Palloway, E.A. (1987). Transition services for early age individuals with mild mental retardation. In R.N. Ianacone & R.A. Stodden (Eds.), *Transition issues and directions* (pp. 11–24). Reston, VA: Division of Mental Retardation, Council for Exceptional Children.

Pappas, C.C., Kiefer, B.Z., & Levstik, L.S. (1990). *An integrated language perspective in the elementary school.* New York: Longman.

Paris, S.G., Wasik, B.A., & Turner, J.C. (1991). The development of strategic readers. In R. Barr, M.L. Kamil, P.B. Mosenthal, & P.D. Pearson (Eds.), *Handbook of reading research* (Vol. 2, pp. 609–640). New York: Longman.

Parsons, A., McWilliam, R., & Buysse, V. (1990). *A manual for the Engagement and OBSERVE Coding System.* Chapel Hill: Frank Porter Graham Child Development Center, University of North Carolina.

Perry, N. (1960). *Training and the mentally retarded child.* New York: Columbia University Press.

Pierce, P.L. (1992). *Child responsiveness during literacy events.* (Available from the Center for Literacy and Disability Studies, University of North Carolina at Chapel Hill.)

Pierce, P., & Kublin, K. (1993a). Employment and independence through literacy training and computer access. *Team Rehab Report, 4*(5), 16–17.

Pierce, P., & Kublin, K. (1993b). Learning independence: The case of Terry Lee. *Team Rehab Report, 4*(5), 16–17.

Pierce, P.L., & Steelman, J.D. (1993). *The O.W.L. (oral and written language) curriculum for young children with disabilities.* Chapel Hill: Center for Literacy and Disability Studies, University of North Carolina.

Raver, S.A., & Dwyer, R.C. (1986). Teaching handicapped preschoolers to sight read using language training procedures. *Reading Teacher, 40,* 314–321.

Reitsma, P. (1988). Reading practice for beginners: Effects of guided reading, reading-while-listening, and independent reading with computer-based speech feedback. *Reading Research Quarterly, 23,* 219–235.

RESNA. (1992, April). *Technology and the individualized education program.* Washington, DC: Author.

Richardson, S.A., Koller, H., & Katz, M. (1988). Job histories in open employment of a population of young adults with mental retardation. *American Journal on Mental Retardation, 92,* 483–491.

Rogow, S.M. (1982). Rhythms and rhymes: Developing communication in very young blind and multihandicapped children. *Child: Care, Health and Development, 5*(2), 59–62.

Rosegrant, T.J. (1984). Fostering progress in literacy development: Technology and social interaction. *Seminars in Speech and Language, 5*(1), 47–58.

Rush, W.L. (1986) *Journey out of silence.* Lincoln, NE: Media Productions and Marketing.

Sameroff, A.J. (1982). The environmental context of developmental disabilities. In D.D. Bricker (Ed.), *Intervention with at-risk and handicapped infants: From research to application* (pp. 141–152). Baltimore: University Park Press.

Schonell, F.E. (1956). *Educating spastic children: The education and guidance of the cerebral palsied.* London: Oliver and Boyd.

Sedlak, R.A., & Cartwright, G.P. (1972). Written language abilities of EMR and nonretarded children with the same mental ages. *American Journal of Mental Deficiency, 77,* 95–99.

Seidel. U.P., Chadwick, O.F.D., & Rutter, M. (1975). Psychological disorders in crippled children. A comparative study of children with and without brain damage. *Developmental Medicine and Child Neurology, 17,* 563–573.

Seigner, R. (1983). Parents' educational expectations and childrens' academic achievements: A literature review. *Merrill-Palmer Quarterly, 29,* 1–23.

Shanahan, T., & Lomax, R. G. (1986). An analysis and comparison of theoretical models of the reading-writing relationship. *Journal of Educational Psychology, 78,* 116–123.

Singh, N.N., & Singh, J. (1988). Increasing oral reading proficiency through overcorrection and phonic analysis. *American Journal on Mental Retardation, 93,* 312–319.

Smith, M.M. (1990, August). *Reading achievement in non-speaking children: A comparative study.* Paper presented at the International Society for Augmentative and Alternative Communication biennial meeting, Stockholm.

Smith, M.M. (1992). Reading abilities of nonspeaking students: Two case studies. *Augmentative and Alternative Communication, 8,* 57–66.

Steelman, J.D. Pierce, P.L., Alger, M.J., Shannon, J., Koppenhaver, D.A., & Yoder, D.E. (1992–1993, Winter). Developing an emergent literacy curriculum for children with developmental disabilities. *The Clinical Connection, 6*(4), 10–15.

Sulzby, E. (1989). Forms of writing and rereading from writing. In J. Mason (Ed.), *Reading and writing connections* (pp. 51–63). Newton, MA: Allyn & Bacon.

Sulzby, E., & Teale, W. (1991). Emergent literacy. In R. Barr, M.L. Kamil, P.B. Mosenthal, & D. Pearson (Eds.), *Handbook of reading research* (Vol. 2, pp. 727–758). New York: Longman.

Sulzby, E., & Teale, W. (1987). *Young children's storybook reading: Longitudinal study of parent-child interaction and children's independent functioning.* Ann Arbor: University of Michigan.

Teale, W. (1987). Emergent literacy: Reading and writing development in early childhood. In J.E. Readence, R.S. Baldwin, J.P. Konopak, & H. Newton (Eds.), *Research in literacy: Merging perspectives* (36th yearbook of the National Reading Conference, pp. 45–74). Rochester, NY: The National Reading Conference.

Teale, W., & Sulzby, E. (1989). Emergent literacy: New perspectives. In D.S. Strickland & L.M. Morrow (Eds.), *Emergent literacy: Young children learn to read and write* (pp. 1–15). Newark, DE: International Reading Association.

Templin, M. (1957). *Certain language skills in children.* Minneapolis: University of Minnesota Press.

Tronick, E. (1981). Infant communicative intent: The infant's reference to social interaction. In R.E. Stark (Ed.), *Language behavior in infancy and early childhood* (pp. 5–39). New York: Elsevier/North Holland.

Vygotsky, L. (1978). *Mind in society: The development of higher psychological process.* Cambridge, MA: Harvard University Press.

Wagner, R.K., & Torgesen, J.K. (1987). The nature of phonological processing and its causal role in the acquisition of reading skills. *Psychological Bulletin, 101,* 192–212.

Wasson, P., & Keeler, J. (1984). [Changing response ratios of normal and handicapped children]. Unpublished raw data.

Wells, G. (1985). Preschool literacy-related activities and success in school. In D.R. Olson, N. Torrance, & A. Hildyard (Eds.), *Literacy, language, and learning: The nature and consequences of reading and writing.* New York: Cambridge University Press.

Whitehurst, G.J., Falco, F.L., Lonigan, C.J., Fischel, J.E., BeBaryshe, B.D., Valdez-Menchaca, M.C., & Caulfield, M. (1988). Accelerating language development through picture book reading. *Developmental Psychology, 24,* 552–559.

Wolfe, W.G. (1950) A comprehensive evaluation of 50 cases of cerebral palsy. *Journal of Speech and Hearing Disorders, 15,* 234–251.

Yoder, D.E., & Calculator, S. (1981). Some perspectives on intervention strategies for persons with developmental disorders. *Journal of Autism and Developmental Disorders, 11,* 107–123.

Yssedyke, J.E., Thurlow, M. L., Christensen, S. L., & Weiss, J. (1987). Time allocation to instruction of mentally retarded, learning disabled, emotionally disturbed and non-handicapped elementary students. *Journal of Special Education, 21*(3), 43–55.

10

Computers as a Context
for Language Intervention

Teris K. Schery and Lisa C. O'Connor

SINCE THE 1980S, MUCH ATTENTION has been given to developing technologies for use in the education of young children, including children with special learning needs. Although the effectiveness of much of this effort has not been examined systematically, there is a growing literature (aided by meta-analytic methodologies) suggesting that carefully designed and implemented computer-based instruction provides a detectable learning advantage in comparison with more traditional approaches, at least for academic subjects and for children with normal learning potential or those who have mild to moderate learning disabilities. This generalization is encouraging for educators and interventionists who work with young children and computers; however, it is by no means a blanket endorsement of computer-based approaches. The various learning needs of children with language impairments (LI) are complex and multidimensional, and the facilitative role computers can play in their educational and clinical progress varies with the intervention context and application. In order to provide a clearer understanding of the nature of these relationships, this chapter reviews and integrates wide-ranging efficacy research that uses computer applications with young children. Research from both regular and special education provides background for consideration of computer-based training approaches for children with language impairments. Studies have been grouped into three general areas: social skills development, cognitive and academic achievement, and specific communication skills training. Each of these is important to the development of a young child with a communication disability, and each area may involve speech-language pathologists, along with special educators, in training and intervention programs. What research has to offer regarding the setting variables for most effective service delivery (including group size and use of paraprofessionals) is considered in the second section, and this is followed by a discussion of future research needs. The chapter concludes with a review of considerations in selecting software for use with children with language impairments.

THE TECHNOLOGICAL CONTEXT

The use of computer-based technology in education can take many forms, primarily influenced by the type of software chosen. Thus, before examining research literature, it seems appropriate to review the most common types of programs used for educational purposes. Available software can be grouped roughly into three categories: 1) computer-assisted instruction (CAI), 2) problem-solving or discovery programs, and 3) application or tool programs. Each of these is considered briefly in the following sections.

Computer-Assisted Instruction (CAI)

The term "computer-assisted instruction" commonly is used to refer to learning activities facilitated by a microcomputer and appropriate software. These tools are used for direct intervention with students to help them improve their ability to handle information, solve problems, communicate with people, and acquire an understanding of the world around them. At its best, CAI is an enticing, highly structured, self-pacing learning tool. At its worst, it is an expensive student worksheet. The effectiveness and the appropriateness of use with particular students depends, in part, on the type of CAI program used. The three main types of CAI programs are drill and practice, tutorial, and simulation (Cannings & Brown, 1986; Sarachan-Deily, 1990; Schmidt, Weinstein, Niemiec, & Walberg, 1985–1986).

Drill and Practice

The primary purpose of drill-and-practice software is to reinforce previously learned information. The use of such software permits extensive repetition and practice of newly learned behaviors. Almost all conventional educational procedures rely on drill and practice to some extent, as this routine gives the student immediate feedback, helping to minimize the amount of negative practice. In the field of communication disorders, drill-and-practice software is available to modify articulation as well as certain language behaviors (Larson & Steiner, 1988). Initially, the presence of the clinician may be necessary to be sure the student understands the rules and procedures, but later the student may become capable of using the program independently.

Tutorial

Tutorial programs facilitate the learning of new information through a step-by-step presentation. Usually, basic information and instructions are displayed on the computer monitor, and opportunities for "branching" are offered. This means that what happens next on the screen depends on the user's input. Appropriate responses to stimuli are reinforced. Branching programs are preferable to linear tutorial programs in which events occur incidentally each time the program is run, regardless of user response. Tutorial programs often use vivid graphic and auditory feedback to stimulate and motivate students (Cannings & Brown, 1986; Russell, Corwin, Mokros, & Kapisovsky, 1989).

Simulations

People learn about their environment through experiences, but for individuals with language impairments such learning is often hindered by difficulties in appropriately matching the environment with the learning sequence. Computer simulations can help to provide an artificial environment in which students can manipulate events, solving some kind of problem in that environment. Usually, they must make choices and live with the consequences of their decisions. For example, one such program involves running a lemonade stand (Minnesota Educational Computing Consortium, 1980). Students make business decisions and observe the outcomes of those decisions before attempting the less controlled real-life situation. Simulations thus offer a controllable world, and the computer becomes a tool for building insight, intuition, and pragmatic awareness. Such skills are often difficult to teach in the limited environment of the classroom or clinic. Although simulation programs are considered a type of CAI in many instances (Cannings & Brown; Sarachan-Deily, 1990; Schmidt et al., 1985–1986), these types of programs also come under the category of "problem solving" discussed in the next section. Simulation programs represent the most innovative type of CAI, but they are also the most expensive and least available.

In discussing programs that offer simulations, it is important to mention "hypermedia." Hypermedia is a way to create and access information electronically (Clymer, 1991; Dede, 1987; Hasselbring, Goin, & Wissick, 1989). It is a method of coordinating the presentation of different forms of information. Hypermedia software allows the user to bring text, picture, speech, graphics, slides, video, and other media together interactively. Multimedia presentations can help to create more enjoyable and meaningful learning experiences for students with language impairments (Hofmeister & Thorkildsen, 1993). One common hypermedia program is HyperCard (Apple Computer, Inc., 1989), designed for use with the Apple McIntosh computer. *Hyper* refers to the program's ability to create and link multiple sources of information; *Card* refers to information displayed on the screen in the form of a card. Cards are organized into stacks, just like a stack of index cards. The power of HyperCard is in its ability to link any piece of information on a card to any other piece of information on any other card in any other stack. While hundreds of stacks have been developed for HyperCard since its inception, relatively few hypermedia stacks currently are available for speech-language pathology and audiology.

Problem-Solving, Perception, and Discovery Programs

Problem-solving, perception, and discovery software give students a variety of experiences with unfamiliar problems as well as opportunities to develop the skills necessary to solve them. Drill-and-practice and tutorial programs structure each step of a student's work and provide few opportunities for independent deliberation or decision making. Such programs lead students through successive steps so that success at the task may seem to have little to do with their own effort. Both drill-and-practice and tutorial programs are recognition based (i.e., the user is provided with choices and needs only to recognize information to find the answer) and they provide largely passive learning experiences for the user. Alternatively, problem-solving, perception, and discovery programs require active participation from the learner. These programs allow for individual differences in learning rates and styles, and they are challenging to students of many different ability levels. Simulation programs, mentioned as a type of CAI above, fall into this category, as does any software that uses multiple routes for presenting information and/or encourages students to use different ways of thinking to solve problems. Such software is particularly beneficial for students with language impairments because it gives them an opportunity to learn the advantages and disadvantages of different strategies. For example, students can learn that no single approach is right for all situations. In the case of cooperative learning situations, they can learn to value the complementary strengths of others and be helped to take another's perspective. There are many software programs that provide problem-solving opportunities for young children. It is important, however, to scrutinize the program for its appropriateness to individual learners. For example, the language used in such programs may be abstract and, therefore, less appropriate for some children with language impairments.

Application or Tool Programs

Application or tool programs are forms of software designed to be used in real-world applications. Word processing programs are an example of this type of software. Application or tool programs not only help students master skills that might prove valuable in future career choices, but such mastery also promotes the development of other skills such as organizing, planning, analyzing, and communicating. As Robinson (1991) pointed out, the writing samples of students with language impairments often are described as being garbled with broken sequences, incomplete or omitted words, disjointed thoughts, and illegibility. It is no wonder, then, that we find many students with special needs, including learners with language impairments, reluctant to express themselves in written form. They may be worried about all the mistakes they make in spelling, grammar, and punctuation. Features offered by word processing programs can minimize some of these hurdles to writing. For example, words appear on the screen at the touch of a key and paragraphs can be marked and deleted, or copied and moved to other places within the document, allowing the student the psychological freedom to experiment with the text. Papert (1980) suggested that such a playful attitude toward words and sentences can enhance the writing process by allowing students the opportunity to play with the text until their inner sense of what is good is satisfied. A recent book compiled by a public school clinician provides ideas for hundreds of speech and language activities based on word processing, database, spreadsheet, and graphics software (Schrader, 1990). Cochran and Bull (1991) discussed rationale and also shared some excellent ideas for integrating word processing into language intervention. Resources such as these, combined with a thorough knowledge of empirical research, can help to provide clinicians and teachers with a theoretical framework as well as many practical ideas for using microcomputers to improve the language skills of their students. An examination of the research base for use of computer intervention for children with special language learning needs is provided in the following section.

EVALUATING THE EFFICACY OF COMPUTER TECHNOLOGIES FOR CHILDREN WITH LANGUAGE IMPAIRMENTS

The research evidence for the effectiveness of computer technologies for young learners with language impairments should be considered before such approaches are adopted. A broad search of the literature examining this issue with typically developing, special education, and specific language impaired populations underscores the paucity of such data (Baldry, 1991; Cheek & Kelly, 1993; Clements & Nastasi, 1992; Fujiura & Johnson, 1986; Goodwin, Goodwin, & Garel, 1986; Jolicoeur & Berger, 1986; Lieber & Semmel, 1985; Shlecter, 1988). The authors cited above point out that relatively few efficacy studies have been carried out and that many studies that claim to provide information on efficacy have methodological flaws (Jolicoeur & Berger, 1986) or are insensitive to the real outcomes children achieve (Lieber & Semmel, 1985). Concerns include the lack of experimental or quasi-experimental design (Cheek & Kelly, 1993; Goodwin et al., 1986), the reliance on standardized achievement tests only as outcome measures when a wide range of nonacademic abilities is at issue (Lieber & Semmel, 1985), and the absence of attempts to combine qualitative measures within rigorous experimental and quasi-experimental frameworks (Fujiura & Johnson, 1986).

In the review that follows, we include only studies that are data-based, although we have not attempted to critique the methodological rigor of individual studies. Continued scrutiny and monitoring of the most useful and effective applications of technologies for students with special needs are important. Enthusiasm and demand for high technology learning has developed very rapidly. Common sense suggests that we embrace and refine what is facilitative in these new technologies without succumbing wholesale to claims made by developers. Only by continuing to evaluate and examine the varied facets of computer use as a context for communication intervention can we hope to maximize the effectiveness and efficiency of this tool in clinical and educational settings.

Meta-analyses

At least three related meta-analyses of CAI have been reported. Niemiec and Walberg (1987) evaluated 16 summary reviews comprising over 200 studies of

CAI effectiveness in the areas of reading, spelling, and math with typically developing children. They concluded that the typical effect of this technology was to raise outcome measures by 0.42 standard deviation units, a moderate improvement. Schmidt et al. (1985–1986) performed a meta-analysis of 22 summary studies of academic outcomes using CAI with exceptional children and also found a moderate positive effect. It is interesting to note that they concluded that the effect was most apparent for exceptional children at lower levels of learning and for those with language disorders. Finally, McDermid (1989) meta-analyzed 15 quantitative studies of CAI application with students with learning disabilities and students with mental retardation. The results suggested that CAI was moderately effective with these populations and that authors were more likely to discuss CAI applications with the students with learning disabilities than with the students with mental retardation.

Despite the above-mentioned paucity of well-designed studies addressing the effectiveness of computer technology with student populations, preliminary synthesis of research in the academic areas indicates a moderate positive effect of instruction by computers over more traditional methods. The next section provides a detailed examination of the three most pertinent areas in which such technology has been utilized; social skills development, cognitive and academic achievement, and communication skills training.

Social Skills Development

The importance of good interactive social skills for developing communication abilities has been emphasized in much of the recent psycholinguistic literature (Bates, Bretherton, Beeghley-Smith, & McNew, 1982; Berko-Gleason, 1992; Holzman, 1984). Young children's communication development is anchored in appropriate and supportive social exchanges, first with their primary caregivers and later with peers and teachers. Computer-based training has presented evidence of two ways in which social interactions of young children can be influenced by direct social skills training and by the more indirect influence provided during cooperative computer activities with peers.

Direct Training

There have been some attempts to use computer technology to train social skills directly in individuals with social learning difficulties (Hedley, 1987), including children with mental retardation and behavior disorders (Elting & Eisenbarth, 1986) and elementary school–age children with mild learning disabilities (Thorkildsen, 1985; Thorkildsen, Fodor-Davis, & Morgan, 1989). Thorkildsen and his colleagues developed a videodisc program that presented examples of appropriate and inappropriate social behaviors along with models to imitate in subsequent role-playing activities. Subjects were 30 elementary school students with mild disabilities enrolled in six resource rooms. Half of the students were assigned randomly to the computer intervention while the other half continued the regular resource room program. After 4 months, the students in the experimental group scored significantly higher on measures of classroom peer acceptance and observed classroom social skills than did the control group. A trend was noted toward carryover into natural settings, although these differences were not statistically significant (Thorkildsen et al., 1989).

Social Interaction During Cooperative Tasks

Researchers in both regular and special education have considered the indirect role computer-based learning can have in fostering social skills development through cooperative learning. Early predictions that computer education with young children would lead to isolation, diminished social interaction, and deficiencies in language (Barnes & Hill, 1983) have proven to have no empirical basis. In fact, recent reviews suggest that computer exercises in early childhood educational settings seem to foster social interaction (Clements & Nastasi, 1992; Watson, Chadwick, & Brinkley, 1986). Young children prefer the social use of computers and, given a choice, rarely work alone (Shade, Nida, Lipinski, & Watson, 1986). Existing patterns of social participation apparently are enhanced rather than disrupted when computers are introduced into the early childhood classrooms of typical learners (Swigger & Swigger, 1984). Compared to other preschool activities, computers support a much larger proportion of cooperative, turn-taking interactions (e.g., 63% of the time working with a peer at a computer compared with 7% when working with puzzles [Muller & Perlmutter, 1985]). Mulhstein and Croft (1986) found that the frequency of cooperative play was higher for computer use than any other preschool activity except a fishing game (96% and 98%, respectively) and resulted in the highest level of accompanying language use. Other studies have found that primary age children in regular educational settings engage in more collaborative social interaction on assigned tasks while working at a computer (Clements & Nastasi, 1985; Dickinson, 1986; Hawisher, 1989). If the computer seems to facilitate social interaction (including language output) among children in regular preschool and primary grades, can the same be said for children with learning and communication impairments?

Most research with atypical populations has examined the social consequences of being assigned to cooperative learning groups to carry out a computer task. Studies using elementary school–age students with learning disabilities have suggested that positive social interaction and peer support are increased when these students work in dyads and small groups to learn LOGO (a programming language for producing graphic displays [Papert, 1980]) (Chiang, 1992; Chiang, Thorpe, & Lubke, 1984). Social skills and self-esteem of older school-age students with learning difficulties increased measurably after 4 months of small group training in LOGO programming. The most positive results occurred when subjects were given a chance to share their computer skills with other students through a tutoring program (Larson & Roberts, 1986). Malouf, Wizer, Pilato, and Grogan (1990) found that older elementary school–age children with learning disabilities who were trained in small-group learning strategies displayed cooperative approaches to a proofreading task when compared with similar students trained in an individual learning computer approach. However, the mean posttest scores were not significantly higher for the experimental group, suggesting that the main effect of such training may be to facilitate social approaches to problem solving rather than to increase achievement per se. Arguing for increased achievement effects, Lieber and Semmel (1987) found that fourth- through sixth-grade boys with learning disabilities were able to solve more difficult math problems on paper and pencil tasks after a 4-week computer training period working with a partner (either with a learning impairment *or* without a learning impairment). After intensive observation over several weeks of two children with mild impairments who were exposed to a supplementary computer intervention, Goldman and Rueda (1988) observed that the children produced longer and more complex stories on the computer when working together than either did when working alone. Thus, it appears that the potential benefits of cooperative computer-based learning *may* include increases in both social skills and cognitive and academic achievement for children with disabilities who have carefully structured and monitored group learning experiences.

For children with disabilities, perhaps one of the most important outcomes of cooperative learning that can be facilitated through computer instruction is the modification of stereotypic or negative attitudes on the part of regular education peers. By carefully structuring the computer workgroups for children, combining those with and without mild learning disabilities, Mevarech, Stern, and Levita (1987) found that subjects came to perceive their own team members more favorably, regardless of impairment. Care must be taken in composing and supervising such workgroups, however, as studies have shown that low-achieving students in regular education are less likely to contribute to cooperative computer activities and are more likely to be subjects of peer ridicule under competitive conditions (Hativa, 1988).

To summarize, most of the evidence has suggested that the use of computers as an educational format has a generally positive social effect. Direct social skills training can be accomplished with elementary school–age children who demonstrate socially inappropriate behaviors. If indirect social benefit from group computer tasks is the goal, care must be taken in composing the group (e.g., avoid putting a child with a learning impairment with peers of notably more ability) and the nature of the task (e.g., avoid competitive formats). With care, such social groupings can lead to increased acceptance of children with learning disabilities by their peers without disabilities and to positive feelings of self-worth and achievement by all of the children involved in such collaborative learning.

The social benefits considered above may well facilitate the development of young children's speech and language skills by improving the interpersonal context in which the children communicate (see Windsor, chap. 8, this volume). It is worthwhile for clinicians and special educators to take such information into account when planning interventions utilizing computers. It is interesting that little attention has been given to examining the effects of the social and communicative impetus that computers seem to provide in typical preschool classrooms when designing programs for preschool children with language difficulties. Would the presence of a computer and developmentally appropriate software attract youngsters with speech and language impairments and provide the relatively intense, naturalistic opportunities for peer-based social and communicative interactions that have been documented in regular preschool settings? In one related study, Fazio and Rieth (1986) found that the use of commercial software in preschool situations with children with developmental disabilities increased the social interaction among peers. Little direct attention was paid, however, to the kinds of communication interchanges such encounters generated. It would be interesting to observe such interactions for their specific effects on social communication.

Cognitive and Academic Achievement

The majority of research examining computer instructional effects on the cognitive and academic achievements of young children has been carried out in the areas of math, reading, composition, and spelling. In a recent review of data-based research, Clements and Nastasi (1992) summarized the results of such studies with typically developing children and concluded:

> Appropriate use of computers is effective in facilitating young children's development of a variety of academic and cognitive abilities. Computer environments can strengthen expressive and receptive oral language, and prereading and reading skills....Technological tools such as word processors amplify children's writing abilities, encouraging them to write and revise more, experiment with and reflect on their writing, and develop a sense of audience....Some reports suggest that the greatest gains in the use of CAI [computer assisted instruction] across all ages and students and all subject areas have been in mathematics skills for primary grade children. (p. 233)

Clements and Nastasi point out that not all studies have shown positive effects, and they emphasize that the less well-researched higher-order thinking and problem-solving applications perhaps provide more exciting potential outcomes than the familiar drill-and-practice or tutorial uses represented in most of the literature on instructional computing. Considerable computer research effort also has been directed toward fostering cognitive and academic skills for children with learning difficulties. The following section reviews studies with special needs populations in the areas of math, reading, composition, and spelling. Finally, we consider some research on cognitive skills and problem solving that has been carried out with children with language impairments.

Mathematics CAI for Children with Disabilities

Mathematics CAI seems to be an especially effective means of computational instruction for nontypical learners of all types (Hotard & Cortez, 1983: Lavin & Sanders, 1983; Mevarech, 1985). Elliott and Hall (1990) implemented a computer-based program for early math skill development with preschool children who were judged "at risk" because of their poor language use, poor social skills, and emotional immaturity. A total of 140–240 minutes of computer intervention over a 6- to 8-week period yielded dramatic gains in mathematical skills and understanding for the experimental group compared to the control group, which had equivalent access to nonmathematical computer-based activities. Primary school–age children from disadvantaged environments who were low achieving not only showed greater mathematics achievement when using CAI (on an individualized basis), but also reported reduced math anxiety (Mevarech, 1985). Chiang (1986) trained fourth-grade children with learning disabilities for 12 days on multiplication skills on the computer. Skills generalized to paper-and-pencil worksheet performance. Hasselbring, Goin, and Bransford (1988) emphasized the effectiveness of such drill and practice mathematics learning for developing math automaticity with primary school–age children with learning disabilities.

Not all studies have shown marked advantages of CAI for math achievement with youngsters with learning disabilities. McDermott and Watkins (1983) assigned 205 first- through sixth-graders identified as having learning disabilities to either CAI instruction or a conventional instruction control group. After 1 school year, standardized achievement tests, covaried for initial group pretest differences, IQ, and time in remedial instruction, indicated that gains were essentially equivalent. Therefore, although the results are not uniform, the use of structured computer drill-and-practice programs in mathematics computation seems to be helpful with young elementary school–age children with learning difficulties when used in an individualized, noncompetitive manner. Perhaps one of the major factors is the increased time these children spend on task when compared with independent seatwork (MacArthur, Haynes, & Malouf, 1986).

Reading Skills CAI for Children with Disabilities

CAI has been used to improve several aspects of reading skills with young children who are at risk and elementary school–age children with identified learning disabilities. The most frequent and most straightforward application has been the use of drill-and-practice programs to increase decoding skills or sight word recognition. Torgesen and his colleagues have shown that accuracy and speed of word recognition can be improved with individualized computer instruction for young primary school–age pupils with learning disabilities (Jones, Torgesen, & Sexton, 1987; Torgeson, 1986a, 1986b; Torgeson, Waters, Cohen, & Torgeson, 1988). Thorkildsen and Friedman (1986) used an interactive video-disc system for beginning sight reading (BSR) for 5- to 9-year-old children with academic difficulties. Posttest scores doubled from those of the pretest. McGregor, Drossner, and Axelrod (1990) found that voice plus text enhanced word recognition in this population more than text alone.

There has been far less research examining the effectiveness of the use of computers in delivering a more holistic or problem-solving approach to reading development (as opposed to the skill-development approach discussed above). A few studies on typically developing children suggest that computer technology can be effective in facilitating this type of higher order reading approach. Moxley and Barry (1986) used single-subject methodology with four 4-year-olds who were seen individually for 20- to 30-minute sessions over a semester at a university nursery school. Programs focused on composing pictures with letter and word commands (e.g., moving the cursor to the desired location and typing a letter or short word to bring up the graphic) and adding verbal text to the resulting pictures. Results indicated that all children improved their literacy skills. Sharp et al. (1993) have been undertaking a longitudinal study using interactive videodisc technology with kindergarten and first-grade children from low socioeconomic backgrounds. Small groups of children working with a teacher create "language experience" stories that they compose, refine, and view together. Videodisc technology allows the viewer to individualize the video and to combine or review segments as frequently as desired. The group creation of this video story allows for a shared experience that is also produced in printed format for the children to read and share with peers and family. These children are being followed for 3 years to see what effects this training has on their acquisition of literacy by the time they reach third grade.

Finally, instruction in LOGO programming has been offered as an *indirect* method of improving reading skills through training comprehension monitoring and general problem solving (Clements & Nastasi, 1992). A longitudinal study by Clements (1987) showed moderate-to-strong positive effects on reading vocabulary, comprehension, and language mechanics by third grade for those children who were trained in LOGO in first grade. None of the studies examining computer-based whole language approaches to reading has considered children with language impairments.

The one group of youngsters with severe language disabilities on whom computer research in literacy training has been carried out is children who are deaf. Prinz, Nelson, and Stedt (1982) demonstrated significant improvement in word recognition and identification with 3- to 6-year-old deaf children after 6 weeks of reading instruction using a microcomputer (ALPHA Program). The children were exposed to a sight-word computer program that used printed words, graphic pictures, and graphic representations of the manual sign for each word in an interactive format where messages in the student's best communicative mode were exchanged with an adult. Subsequent research with higher levels of the ALPHA program, including a Storyteller routine, and supplemented by videodisc still and action sequences (Nelson, Prinz, & Dalke, 1989; Prinz & Nelson, 1985), showed that deaf children between the ages of 3 and 11 years made significant improvement in reading and writing for individual words and short sentences using the microcomputer. Children wrote sentences to describe meaningful animations they had just seen on the video monitor by pressing word keys on their keyboards. Recent work has focused on the replication of early results with 12 5- to 10-year-old children with severe motor disabilities (Prinz, 1991), with 10 primary school–age children with hearing impairments, and with three children diagnosed with autism, mental retardation, and severe language disabilities, respectively (Prinz, Nelson, Loncke, Geysels, & Willems, 1993). Although the reported outcomes of these studies focused on reading abilities, the authors assert that the multimodality input and the interactive nature of the programs (requiring a teacher to work alongside the child) facilitate *all* forms of communication, including oral language discourse. No direct evidence is provided for this latter claim in the current study, however.

One program, Writing to Read, developed by IBM (Martin, 1986), links reading and composition directly. Children work with computers, typewriters, tape recorders, and a simplified phonetic alphabet to write simple stories, in addition to doing preparatory drill-and-practice exercises. Evaluations have shown generally positive results with 5- to 7-year-old children both in regular education programs and in programs for learners at risk (Murphy & Appel, 1984; Shaver & Wise, 1990). Caution must be used in the interpretation of results, however. Gains may be due to the increased amount of structured time spent on reading and writing with these young children. Critics have suggested that the program avoids real communication in favor of drilling a narrow set of skills out of context and that the program deemphasizes the use of oral language and may not be effective with children with language impairments (Clements & Nastasi, 1992).

In summary, computer-based approaches to reading facilitation for children with language impairments have focused predominantly on drill-and-practice word recognition programs (decoding) for learners with mild disabilities. Computers also have been used, although infrequently, as an aid in holistic or whole language approaches to reading development with young, typically developing children. To date, the use of such technological applications with children with language impairments has not been examined systematically. However, a multimodality, multimedia reading program for young children who are deaf has shown promising success, and preliminary evidence of usefulness with young children with cognitive, social, and language impairments has recently been reported (Prinz et al., 1993).

Composition CAI for Children with Disabilities

The editing and revision capabilities of word processors can simplify writing production. Perhaps the main benefit of using word processors with very young writers is the provision of support in the form of a physical tool that allows children, from the beginning, to focus on and experiment with letters and words without being distracted by the motoric requirements of handwriting (MacArthur, 1988; Rosegrant, 1986). Studies with primary grade students with learning disabilities have shown that keyboarding skills can be learned within a reasonable time frame (approximately 9 hours of instruction over 27 days in a study by Tenney & Osguthorpe, 1990), and that these students develop more positive attitudes about writing, write more, and are more independent in writing tasks (MacArthur & Schneiderman, 1986; Riel, 1985). Grandgenett, Lloyd, and Hill (1991) compared the quality of written output of 7- and 8-year-old students with learning disabilities under two conditions. A program of wordprocessor instruction was compared with a carefully structured, equally intense, traditional paper-and-pencil program. After 4 weeks of 16, 45-minute sessions, there was consistent and significant improvement for both groups. Although the results achieved by the two groups were not significantly different, the generally higher scores of the word processing group suggested that some difference might be found in a study that considered more subjects or was of longer duration. MacArthur and Graham (1987) found that dictated stories of fifth- and sixth-grade students with learning disabilities were longer, of higher quality, and contained fewer errors than either handwritten or word-processed stories. This finding suggests that the students' oral language skills were ahead of their written language abilities, regardless of the output format (see also Gillam, McFadden, & van Kleeck, chap. 6, this volume). The word-processed stories were significantly longer, however, than the handwritten versions. Hine and Goldman (1990) found that a collaborative writing assignment for dyads of students with learning disabilities (ages 8–13 years) facilitated editing and monitoring behaviors, useful skills for developing compositions. Ward (1989) reported that the use of computer-based written dialogues about on-screen graphics improved use of trained vocabulary in oral language interactions and the improved vocabulary use showed some evidence of carryover into structured verbal communication in a group of 10- to 13-year-old children with language impairments.

A related line of inquiry has compared the effectiveness of voice-aided word processing programs with standard word processing programs. Lehrer, Levin, DeHart, and Comeaux (1987) randomly assigned preschool and kindergarten children to three conditions of writing instruction: paper and pencil, word processor, and word processor with voice-aided feedback. Results suggested that the voice-aided word processing was superior in promoting acquisition of sound-symbol associations and metacognitive awareness of the writing process. The use of "talking computers" has a surprisingly long history. Over 3 decades ago, in the 1960s, Moore's Talking Typewriter (Israel, 1968) was shown to increase significantly alphabet recognition and verbal abilities of inner city, at-risk preschool children. Follow-up studies have documented continued reading achievement gains for these children (Steg, Lazar, & Boyce, 1993; Steg, Vaidya, & Hamdan, 1982).

Although there appear to be no studies comparing the efficacy of word processing with and without voice output for children with language impairments, the inclusion of multiple input modalities for this population is thought to be beneficial (Cochran & Bull, 1991; Meyers, 1990). Overall, it seems that providing elementary school–age children who have mild to moderate learning disabilities with access to a wordprocessing program may help to support a context for increasing written output, both in the amount and quality of the text. Any advantage to voice-accompanied word processing as compared to a standard program needs to be empirically verified, although there is certainly a theoretical rationale for its use.

Spelling CAI for Children with Disabilities

Research on the effectiveness of CAI for spelling achievement with children with learning disabilities is inconsistent. Some studies have found significant achievement differences favoring CAI (Hasselbring, 1982; MacArthur, Haynes, Malouf, & Harris, 1990), especially for children with attentional difficulties (Fitzgerald, Fick, & Milich, 1986). However, other research has suggested that letter search time on the keyboard may interfere with cognitive processes and have negative effects on spelling performance (English, Gerber, & Semmel, 1985; Varnhagan & Gerber, 1984). Certainly, more systematic inquiry is needed before the effectiveness of this aspect of CAI can be assessed with pupils with language impairments.

In reviewing the varied studies on CAI learning, it appears that academic achievement has been fostered, at least for young elementary school–age children with mild disabilities. The learning factors of individualization, active responding, immediate feedback, reinforcement and self-pacing seem to match well with the learning style needs of many children with mild to moderate disabilities (Clark, 1986; Vockell & Mihail, 1993). Although the results are not completely uniform, a majority of studies suggest that the individualized, tutorial, and self-pacing nature of much of CAI in reading and math can be helpful for a wide variety of young children with learning difficulties, including language-learning disabilities. Evidence of effectiveness for spelling CAI is equivocal. Introduction of word processing by age 6 (or perhaps younger) may serve to encourage composition by deemphasizing the motoric requirements of handwriting and allowing revisions to be made with little effort. Computer training as a method of developing more generic cognitive skills, including problem solving, with young children with disabilities is briefly reviewed in the following section.

Cognitive and Problem-Solving
Computer-Based Training for Children with Disabilities

Microcomputer research on LOGO programming has produced most of the literature on problem solving with young typically developing learners as well as those with mild disabilities. Studies examining the effect that LOGO Turtle Graphics instruction has on young children's problem-solving skills have been divided almost equally between those finding negative results and those finding positive results (see Watson et al., 1986, for a review). However, a meta-analysis in 1988 (Roblyer, Castine, & King) showed a substantial and homogeneous positive effect on LOGO's influence on problem-solving performance. One specific positive effect has been to increase higher order (metacognitive) processes, so that preschool and elementary school–age children are better able to monitor their own comprehension; that is, to realize when they don't understand (Clements, 1990). A few studies have examined comprehension with students with learning disabilities. Lehrer, Harckham, Archer, and Pruzek (1986) found positive benefits of training in LOGO for problem-solving abilities and the acquisition of linguistic pragmatics with preschoolers (4–6 years old) with special needs. Mathinos (1990) found that fourth- to sixth-grade children with learning disabilities were able to refine and extend their use of problem-solving skills within and across computer and noncomputer contexts after training in LOGO.

Simulation programs and discovery learning offer similar opportunities for problem-solving and higher order cognitive learning. No studies have examined directly the effects of such programs with young children who have learning difficulties. The language demands and abstraction requirements may make such programs especially challenging for many pupils with significant language learning disabilities.

Next, studies of microcomputer technologies that have been used to influence directly the language and speech development of children with special learning needs are reviewed. Although an increasingly large body of published information discusses the potential applications of computer technology to the clinical practice of speech-language pathology, there is still relatively little data-based information that can be examined. Studies that train language skills are considered separately from efforts to improve articulation (although these two aspects of communication are closely related).

Communication Skills

Language Development

Limited attention has been given to specific outcomes of computer training on language comprehension and production in research with young, typically developing children. McCormick (1987) compared the social and language effects of microcomputer activity with playing with toys in a regular preschool environment and found that the computer activity was slightly more effective in stimulating vocalization. In another study, 3- to 7-year-old children using computer graphics and robots in structured and spontaneous play showed enhanced oral language use (Forman, 1986).

Recently, several authors have reviewed the limited empirical research on computer-based language interventions (Bull, Cochran, & Snell, 1988; Iacono & Miller, 1989; Steiner & Larson, 1991). Although all are generally positive regarding the potential for computer-based applications, each author cautions that insufficient information is available regarding many aspects of computer usage and stresses the importance of using computer training only with a communication partner (teacher or clinician), rather than as a stand-alone procedure.

Much of the software that has been used with children with language impairments is based on the learning theory principles of immediate feedback and reinforcement of specific academic skills. However, some attempts have been made to incorporate current knowledge of cognitive and language development with computer technology. Two such programs that have been subjected to empirical scrutiny include the Programs for Early Acquisition of Language (PEAL) (Meyers, 1985) and the ALPHA Program (Nelson et al., 1989; Prinz, Pemberton, & Nelson, 1985). Meyers (1984, 1987) designed the PEAL to develop initial communication skills by scaffolding the vocabulary of young children's natural play routines with computer-generated graphics, printed text, and speech output. She felt this would allow children in the initial stages of language acquisition to communicate by using an expanded keyboard with graphic symbols as support while their own language skills developed. The programs included five levels in two play contexts, progressing from initial vocabulary to combinations of this vocabulary into 3- to 5-word phrases.

Studies utilizing the PEAL software have focused on very young children and children with severe disabilities at the initial stages of language acquisition. O'Connor and Schery (1986) compared PEAL computer-based language intervention with traditional individual language intervention by a speech-language pathologist, using as subjects eight 2- to 3-year-old children with diagnoses of Down syndrome and developmental delay. All subjects were trained over 8–10 weeks in each condition and served as their own controls. Outcome measures included a criterion-referenced test of the actual vocabulary trained, as well as composite scores of formal language tests and social skills as rated by teachers and parents. Subjects made significant progress in *both* conditions with no significant differences between them. In other words, these young children were able to make notable language gains when using the PEAL software in an interactive format with a graduate student in speech-language pathology comparable to those made in traditional individual language intervention. However, no distinct advantage was demonstrated for the computer condition.

These results were essentially replicated in a study by Houghton, Warr-Leeper, Archer, and Henry (1992) using 14 children with Down syndrome (with a mean age of 6 years, 9 months). The researchers used language samples and a social outcome rating questionnaire as the dependent measures and found significant increases over time in each condition.

Schery and O'Connor (1992) evaluated the effectiveness of adding computer-based language training (PEAL) to the ongoing special class curriculum for 52 children (ages 3–12 years) who had severe disabilities (including autism, developmental delay, and cerebral palsy). Again, each subject served as his or her own control by a comparison of each child's progress during equivalent time periods (10–12 weeks) in the regular classroom program and when receiving additional computer training. The children made significantly more progress when they were receiving the additional computer training, suggesting the efficacy of utilizing such a supplementary intervention with this group of youngsters. Effects were most apparent on the trained PEAL vocabulary. Effects were attenuated on general language measures given by researchers and the classroom teachers, and they were weakest (yet still detectable) on social interactive skills as measured by parents and teachers. These results suggest that there was some generalizing effect on the specific vocabulary training provided in the computer condition to the general communication skills of these children.

The ALPHA program initially was designed to develop basic sight word literacy with young children who are deaf. It has since been expanded to incorporate storytelling dialogue, including oral language, with a variety of children with disabilities (Prinz et al., 1993). Children using these programs interact with the microcomputer and/or videodisc through a special keyboard that displays pictures and/or words as well as graphic symbols of American Sign Language. Initial vocabulary is combined into subject + verb + (object) (S + V + [O]) patterns. An integral part of the program involves an interactive dialogue between adult (teacher or clinician) and child, exchanged in the child's best communicative mode (speech, sign language, or text). Literacy gains have been reported for several samples of young children who are deaf (Prinz, 1991; Prinz et al., 1993). Prinz et al. (1993) cited evidence of gains in general language skills (measured by sentence imitation, receptive and productive vocabulary, and grammatical comprehension) for 10 children who were deaf as well as for 12 5- to 10-year-olds with significant motoric impairments and three 6-year-olds with language and/or emotional disabilities. The authors reported that gains in conversational discourse were especially salient, although no supporting data were provided.

The results of the research on both PEAL and the ALPHA programs are promising. This suggests that computer technology, when combined with software designed to support interactive, developmentally appropriate communication exchanges, can facilitate language development in a variety of children with special learning needs as they move from early symbolic skills to acquisition of initial vocabulary and early syntactic patterns expressed in verbal, written, or signed form. However, there is clearly a need for software that builds on this initial base and extends the syntactic and discourse potential while remaining interactive and allowing individualization of vocabulary.

Attempts have been made to utilize the animation capabilities of computer technology to teach verbs to young children. Harn (1986) taught S + V sentences to 12 young (24- to 41-month-old) children operating at Brown's (1973) Stage I. Harn compared learning when subjects were given as stimuli enactments of the actual event, computer animations, or static pictures. Children learned best given the enactment condition, the results of the computer animation condition were a close approximation, and the static picture condition was a distant third. Ott-Rose and Cochran (1992) compared use of still pictures and computer-controlled videodiscs to teach action verbs to five preschoolers with language impairments in two separate single subject–design studies. Results suggested that both the traditional pictures and videodisc stimuli were effective in teaching and eliciting present progressive verbs and that four out of five of the children performed as well or better when responding to the videodisc segments. The child who responded better to the picture stimuli nevertheless expressed a preference for the videodisc presentation, suggesting that children appreciate a variety of materials in a clinical situation.

Several other studies of computer efficacy in developing language skills in children with disabilities have been published. Two 6-year-old girls who were deaf were given 12 weeks of computer training to improve language, attention, and attitude toward learning (Bailey & Weippert, 1992). Both reportedly increased language competence as expressed through manual signs and developed more positive attitudes toward school, although no controls were employed. Lehrer and deBernard (1987) compared the effectiveness of LOGO training, commercial preschool software (such as color naming), and no computer intervention (teacher-directed activities in the learning center) on the perceptual language development of 120 preschool children with language impairments in the New York metropolitan area (ages 2;7–4;9 years). Results suggested that training in LOGO programming facilitated the development of perceptual language skills compared with either of the other two conditions. The authors felt that the LOGO context offered more opportunities for scaffolded instruction in which concepts are elaborated upon or extended by an instructor. They pointed out, however, that more research was necessary to distinguish the most important components of the child-teacher-software match.

Research on new and innovative methods for using the SpeechViewer system in clinical environments (Allen, 1991; Mahaffrey, 1991) has recently been conducted. (SpeechViewer is a combination hardware and software product that uses color graphics and synchronized playback of speech to provide visual feedback on fundamental frequency, loudness, voicing aspects, timing, and vowel accuracy.) Most of the applications of this system are relevant to aspects of speech production, but one study has looked at its potential in stimulating lexical inventories of 2- and 3-year-olds with expressive language delay (Dollaghan, 1991). Although the lack of formal conditions of experimental control precluded reporting group results, Dollaghan noted that there was a great deal of individual difference in the response of these young children to the system, with some children responding quite positively while others responded negatively.

A primary application of computer technology with children with severe disabilities is the development of cause-and-effect relationships, in which the computer is used as the mechanism for a child to activate an event in the environment (see Iacono & Miller, 1989, for a review). Perhaps the most widespread and well-examined application of computer technology to populations with severe disabilities (including children with severe physical limitations and normal cognitive potential) is augmentative and alternative communication (AAC). Koppenhaver, Pierce, Steelman, and Yoder (chap. 9, this volume) examine this literature in some depth. Speech output systems have been especially useful in designing intervention programs for individuals with severe intellectual disabilities. For example, Romski, Sevcik, and Pate (1988) described the successful implementation of a system using portable, battery-operated speech output computer devices in homes and classrooms in order to facilitate the communication skills of 13 youngsters with mental retardation.

In summary, computer technology for language intervention has been used with various populations, including toddlers at risk and young children with hearing impairments, developmental disabilities (especially Down syndrome), specific language impairments (SLI), and multiple disabilities. Most of the studies report positive effects of the computer intervention (at least for many of the children), but there is little direct evidence about which aspects of the procedure are most useful in promoting specific parameters of language development. Virtually all of the computer-based intervention studies with young children with language impairments have been carried out in an interactive environment with a responsive adult monitoring and encouraging the child's efforts. When compared with traditional individual language therapy, the computer-based approach showed similar results. In this respect, the use of computer-based language programs appears to offer an additional tool that clinicians and teachers can employ in helping and motivating young children in the task of learning language skills during interactive communication exchanges. The continuing development of videodisc technology will allow a wider range of motivating and realistic images to be used as a resource for linguistic mapping. Improvements in voice output capabilities will provide more natural and responsive verbal interchanges. However, despite the envisioned refinement and improvement in the technology (Cochran & Bull, 1993; Fitch, 1993), it seems clear that, for the foreseeable future at least, the use of computers as a context for language intervention with young school-age children depends upon the sensitivity and judgment of skilled communication partners.

Speech Production and Articulation

Research on applications of microcomputer technology for intervention to facilitate speech production in school-age children has been very limited. Theoretically, speech recognition devices, which recently have become available, would be ideal for providing feedback on aspects of phoneme production to a child with a speech disorder. A device that could monitor speech attempts and assess the accuracy of production would be of enormous assistance to clinicians working on the time-consuming task of correcting sound production errors in children's speech. Unfortunately, the capability of current speech recognition devices is not very useful for clinical purposes (Shriberg, Kwiatkowski, & Snyder, 1990). Fitch (1989) assessed the accuracy of one recent program for speech recognition, the Computer-Aided Speech Production and Training program (CASPT) (Cooper & Neilson, 1986). He found that the program was able to identify correctly only 20.2%–64.4% of groups of phoneme targets when they were produced by 12 normal speakers (six of them children). This suggests extremely limited application for articulation intervention.

Shriberg, Kwiatkowski, and Snyder (1986, 1989, 1990) have compared the efficacy of microcomputer-assisted intervention with "tabletop" (traditional) management of childhood articulation disorders. In the initial study, the responses of children with speech delays (3–8 years of age) to articulation testing were compared using a microcomputer and a pencil-and-paper booklet. Results indicated that there was no difference in the accuracy of articulation assessment in either condition. However, the computer-assisted testing was associated with better attention and task persistence. The second series of studies looked at microcomputer assisted and tabletop procedures during the stabilization phase of speech sound development and, once again, found no significant difference in effectiveness between the two training approaches. There was support for the higher motivational or engagement value of the microcomputer for many (although not all) of the children, as well as an expressed preference for the computer condition by the majority of the clinicians. The final series of studies examined the usefulness of computer technology during the response evocation phase of articulation training, or when the child is just learning to produce a phoneme correctly. Once again, the modes of presentation (computer-assisted or tabletop) were found to be equally effective, efficient, and engaging. The authors noted that the microprocessor software was especially useful in engaging children in drill-and-practice sessions when the target sound was stimulable. However, the multiple cuing of the interacting clinician was necessary in early phases of evocation. This research purposefully utilized the technology that is most routinely available to speech-language pathologists in school settings, and the authors felt that some negative aspects noted in the computer-assisted intervention condition (time delays for graphic displays, poor intelligibility of synthesized speech) were attributable to technical limitations of this hardware.

Ruscello, Cartwright, Haines, and Shuster (1993) utilized the IBM SpeechViewer to allow parents of a group of 12 preschoolers with speech delays in a rural area to augment the limited training time available from professional speech-language pathologists. These parent volunteers were able to use the hardware and software systems to help train their children's articulation by using minimal pair contrasts to eliminate developmentally inappropriate phonological processes. Other pilot studies using the SpeechViewer suggest that the system may be useful in helping children with cleft palate detect hypernasality in their speech (Horii, Osredkar, Moore, & Huddleston, 1991) and in shaping fluency for dysfluent children (McGuire, Hageman, & Highnam, 1991). Somewhat less success has been reported for productive vowel training studies with young children with hearing impairment (Guilford & Hnath-Chisolm, 1991; Pratt, Heintzelman, & Ensrud, 1991).

In summary, it seems that application of computer technology to direct training of speech production has, until quite recently, been limited to presentation of stimulus materials and reinforcement activities through use of innovative graphic effects. The need for a clinician to be centrally involved in assessing and shaping speech production attempts is stressed, at least until more discriminating speech recognition software becomes available. Computerized approaches to articulation training appear to result in outcomes very similar to those achieved in traditional intervention. There may be some motivational enhancements from the use of computer technology in this training and the nature of individual learner's response to specific aspects of such training needs to be examined further.

SETTING VARIABLES FOR EFFECTIVE SERVICE DELIVERY

In this section, the role of the teacher or clinician in classroom and clinical settings in which computer technology is used is examined. In addition, the possibility of using nonprofessionals to provide computer intervention with children with language learning disorders is considered.

Teacher and Clinician Roles in Computer Intervention

Robinson (1991) has pointed out that as computers became available in education, teachers were led to believe that they would serve as free-standing, auto-instructional aids to the classroom that would decrease their instructional burdens. Although an occasional program has proven to be successful without teacher monitoring (Friedman & Hofmeister, 1984), in fact, actual teacher engagement and instructional decision-making may be tripled when comparing a lecture-discussion format of teaching with computer-assisted-instruction (Robinson 1991).

The role that a teacher or clinician takes in facilitating group use of computer technology appears to vary depending on the age of the students involved, at least for children who function predominantly in a mainstream setting. Preschool children can work at the computer cooperatively with minimal supervision, generating their own rules of turn-taking and sharing (Shade et al., 1986). Peer collaboration apparently is facilitated by the inaccessibility of a teacher at this stage (Genishi, 1988); however, aggressive behavior of 3- to 5-year olds as they jockeyed for access to the computer declined when teachers were present (Lipinski, Nida, Shade, & Watson, 1986). Clements and Nastasi (1992) suggest that "an optimal level of teacher intervention might be one that inhibits inappropriate behaviors while not interfering with peer conferencing and peer instruction" (p. 199).

Fazio and Rieth (1986) studied the characteristics of microcomputer use of children with disabilities in a special education preschool. They found that the children with the lowest functional levels needed teacher assistance throughout, although children with mild to moderate disabilities developed some independence and cooperative learning strategies. Thus, it appears that even for preschoolers with mild to moderate disabilities in a group setting, social interaction, turn-taking, and exploration/discovery are maximized by allowing them to interact on the computer with minimal direct interaction from the supervising adult. Youngsters with more severe disabilities seem to require much more direct support from the teacher or clinician in this setting.

Young school-age children apparently need teacher guidance in structuring use of microcomputers for curricular activities, even those involving social outcomes. Haynes and Malouf (1986) argued that providing the children with clear metacognitive strategies for use of the computer is essential for success. They included the following among the primary responsibilities of the teacher: making students aware of the task goals, helping students select appropriate learning strategies (including whether to collaborate or work independently), and developing students' self-monitoring skills. Lipinski et al. (1986) pointed out that teachers need to structure the basic rules clearly for computer learning in groups and then remain available to monitor these rules, especially in initial stages. They have found that the need for teacher guidance is likely to decrease as children develop effective collaboration and problem-solving skills. However, Robinson (1991) pointed out that for pupils with learning disabilities, the teacher's ability to be an interface between the student and the computer is the most critical element in the successful application of instructional technology.

The use of computers in clinical settings almost universally has been based on one-to-one interaction with a knowledgeable adult who can use the computer as a context for communicative dialogue (O'Connor & Schery, 1986; Prinz, 1991), or who can lead the child through a tutorial program while providing additional monitoring, support, and examples (Ott-Rose & Cochran, 1992; Shriberg et al.,1989). Virtually no research has investigated the usefulness of group computer use (pairs of ability-matched children) for stimulating socialization and problem-solving skills. Such applications of group computer intervention appear warranted in clinical settings as well as in classroom environments, based on the positive outcomes reported earlier (Clements & Nastasi, 1992; Larson & Roberts, 1986). Although most computer-based clinical work with children who have significant communication disabilities will continue to be individualized and interactive with an adult (Bull et al., 1988; Iacono & Miller, 1989; Steiner & Larson, 1991), speech-language pathologists should consider incorporating some social and problem-solving goals into aspects of their practice. In addition, the inclusion of more interactive computer interventions within the classroom or resource room may be helpful by providing opportunities for building peer communication for children who have language-learning difficulties. As collaborative services among regular education, special education, and speech-language pathology expand, opportunities to incorporate a continuum of communication and socialization activities based on computer technology may likewise expand to bridge classroom and clinical settings.

Using Nonprofessionals to Deliver Microcomputer Intervention

The need for individual, one-to-one interaction in order to utilize microcomputers for intervention with children with language impairments places additional time demands on clinicians and special educators already overburdened by large caseloads and class enrollments. All of the efficacy studies cited in the earlier section on facilitating communication skills utilized professional speech-language pathologists or trained graduate students. It is supposed that these individuals have the necessary sensitivity to pupils' communication styles as well as knowledge of the course of communication development to provide the maximum support for and encouragement of speech and language growth. If software can be identified that is appropriate for a child's developmental needs and is sufficiently specific in its directions, communication partners with less formal training should be able to interact effectively with pupils with language impairments. Various authors have suggested this strategy for delivering more cost-effective communication training (Schery & O'Connor, 1992; Schetz, 1989), but little systematic inquiry of the relative efficacy of this approach has been made. Fitch (1984) compared screening results for language and speech problems within Head Start classes when assessments were conducted by paraprofessionals using a computerized screening instrument with assessments conducted by graduate students in speech-language pathology using a paper-and-pencil version. They found that satisfactory results were obtained for the language screening in the paraprofessional/computer version, but that the speech screening judgments were unclear. Schetz (1989) used nonprofessional volunteers to administer commercial software for "concept enrichment" (quantity, time, nouns, verbs) for 22 kindergarteners who were at risk for language difficulties. Follow-up questionnaires to teachers indicated that 80% thought that the program was beneficial. Teachers felt that 41% of the children had improved, although no data-based verification of this improvement was provided. Recently, Schery and Spaw (1993) compared directly the results of computer-based language intervention with five 2-year-olds who were at risk when the training was administered by a trained speech-language pathologist with the training administered by a paraprofessional (a mother of a toddler with a disability) given 1 hour of training. All subjects made progress in general language skills measured with classroom observational ratings and formal testing, as well as in the recognition of vocabulary items specifically from the computer training program. Four of the five subjects made measurably greater progress in acquisition of the trained vocabulary when working with the paraprofessional compared to the same amount of training (three 20-minute sessions per week over 8–10 weeks) with the speech-language pathologist. There was possibly an issue of "cultural match" in the study. The four toddlers who made the most progress were Hispanic, as were the two paraprofessionals. In contrast, the fifth toddler and the speech-language pathologist were not Hispanic (although the speech-language pathologist spoke Spanish).

It is possible that subtle contextual differences in interaction styles and the ability to support English language acquisition with a second language (Spanish) in a natural fashion contributed to the acquisition of English vocabulary for these very young children (see Kayser, chap. 11, this volume). Nevertheless, the immediate result of this formal comparison indicated that, at least for circumscribed specific language acquisition goals (vocabulary), intervention administered by trained paraprofessionals can be as effective as similarly intense training delivered by a professional.

The type of nonprofessional who can be effective at administering computer-assisted intervention and the degree of training and supervision that are necessary are questions that remain to be explored. If, however, it is important that children with language impairments receive individualized, interactive training for the majority of their intervention program, it seems worthwhile to explore further the use of nonprofessionals (including older, able peer tutors) in helping to provide such training. The need for cost effectiveness in the provision of clinical services is increasingly emphasized (Harden, 1991; Powell, 1991). If computer intervention programs administered by nonprofessionals could be integrated into clinical and educational environments, the professional (special education teacher or speech-language pathologist) might well be able to spend individual time with a child more efficiently. The professional serving in such a consultative, decision-making capacity could select the appropriate software to meet each child's communication training needs and then concentrate on monitoring change and on shaping new speech and language behaviors while the nonprofessional carried out the tasks of stabilizing and generalizing the more routine or straightforward aspects of the training.

It seems, then, that the current research on the setting variables that make for the most effective use of computers to teach youngsters with language-learning impairments gives only limited direction for teachers and clinicians. If social communication is an important goal of the intervention, group learning (usually pairs of children of similar ability) seems to facilitate turn-taking, problem solving, and natural dialogue. Limited structure and limited teacher direction are facilitory for preschoolers in this situation. If the children have severe impairments, however, teacher support will be needed continuously. In comparison, school-age children seem to work best in a group situation where the rules are explicit, and they are encouraged to monitor their own performances as well as to access the supervising adult as frequently as needed. Under these conditions, even students with moderate disabilities can make progress in collaborative learning, problem-solving, and independence, and the need for the professional to be part of the interaction may gradually fade.

Individual interactive exchanges with a professional who can support and expand upon communication behaviors are clearly the mainstay of clinical service delivery that uses computers for intervention with children with language impairments. In such interventions, the computer supplies material that provides a motivating and dynamic alternative to more traditional therapy activities, although the necessity for simultaneous "live" support and modeling of language is stressed by all authors. The level of training needed in order to provide this interactive support, however, is an area for future consideration. As more explicit and developmentally appropriate software programs become available, the use of nonprofessionals to augment the professional in the more routine aspects of language and speech intervention becomes a definite consideration. Given the cost-effectiveness issues that face specialized service providers, this development should be explored empirically to determine the most effective ways in which nonprofessionals can be trained and utilized to complement the efforts of professional practitioners.

SUMMARY REFLECTIONS

The literature reviewed in this chapter has focused on three general areas in which existing research on computer-based learning is most pertinent to the training needs of children with language impairments: social skills development, cognitive and academic learning, and specific training approaches for developing speech and language skills. The following key points reiterate some of the main conclusions supported by the literature. First, group tasks assigned on the computer can facilitate interaction and communication between children, especially where joint problem-solving or turn-taking are necessary. For preschoolers, little structure or adult direction is needed for children to engage in cooperative interaction. If the children have severe disabilities, consistent teacher support is necessary. School-age children interact better if clear task guidelines are communicated before beginning the task, and teacher or clinician support is available when needed. Children of similar ability levels working in a noncompetitive format stimulate the most positive cooperative interactions. Direct social skills training can be carried out for children who have mild to moderate learning difficulties that include socially inappropriate behaviors.

Second, computer-based academic skill learning —especially math, reading, and composition—have proven beneficial for children with mild to moderate disabilities, including language disorders. The learning principles embodied in good academic drill-and-practice software (learner-paced instruction, immediate reinforcement, nonjudgmental presentation, and the ability to provide multimodality information) are well-suited to the learning needs of these children. The speech-language pathologist, working in collaboration with the classroom teacher, may be able to arrange for computer tutorial practice in academic skill areas where the child needs extra support. The objectives of much of reading and composition instruction are highly appropriate for implementation by a communications specialist, and knowledge of the software in this area can help match student needs to an efficient and proven approach to intervention. LOGO programming appears to be useful for learners with mild disabilities in facilitating general problem-solving strategies as well as social interaction. Access to word processing is generally helpful to students with mild to moderate disabilities.

Third, computer-based instruction to develop specific language or speech abilities is as effective as traditional individual therapy. Comparative efficacy studies looking at the development of speech sound production and at vocabulary and social language acquisition when using computer intervention compared to traditional therapy have shown similar outcomes. The variety provided by multimedia programs can increase motivation for some young children with language disorders, although there appears to be considerable variation in this. Voice-processing capabilities of computers are not yet sufficient to provide feedback to young learners on their phoneme production. This aspect of intervention continues to depend on the availability of a knowledgeable listener, trained in speech sound discrimination.

Fourth, the use of nonprofessionals to provide circumscribed computer training for children with language disabilities may prove useful in increasing the amount of individualized intervention these children receive as well as increasing the cost effectiveness of computer-assisted intervention approaches. Much clinical speech and language intervention, even when presented via a computer, remains predominantly anchored in one-to-one social interchanges between the child and the clinician. Use of nonprofessionals to follow up needed communication skills practice with a structured computer program could be a cost-effective way of providing extended individualized practice. Information is needed on the amount and type of training necessary for the most effective utilization of such nonprofessionals.

NEED FOR FUTURE RESEARCH

Without a doubt, the availability and use of computer technology in the fields of education and special education will continue to increase dramatically as it has since the mid-1980s (Schwartz, 1989; Yin & Moore, 1987). As technological improvements continue to refine and increase the impact that computer-based learning can have on young language learners, there is a need for research on several other aspects of this intervention process. We already have pointed out some research needs in earlier sections of this chapter. Systematic examination of the use of computers for dyads or small groups of children with language impairments to increase socialization and problem-solving abilities is warranted. If this format can help children with language impairments increase successful peer interactions, it provides an excellent opportunity to extend such learning into the classroom or clinic environment. The development and evaluation of software that can be individually tailored to a student's language level, vocabulary, and developmental abilities are critical for the widest application and efficacy and very little has been done in this area. As we accumulate data on the general efficacy of computer-based approaches in learning for children with special educational requirements, we need to turn our inquiries to what aspects of the learning environment are most effective for individual children. Some studies have reported wide variability in children's interest in and success with technology (Dollaghan, 1991). What are the characteristics of the particular child-teacher-software match that are most useful in promoting specific parameters of language development? It is time that we begin to try to discriminate among some of these interactions. The cost effectiveness of computer-based intervention is another avenue for future exploration. As service delivery efficiency is questioned, we need to consider when and in what form paraprofessionals can begin to augment speech and language acquisition training for children with language impairment. What skills and training are necessary to prepare a nonprofessional to function effectively in this role? For example, would it be possible to use cross-age peer tutors from among children with typically developing language abilities? In addition, the longitudinal effect of computer technology should be examined. Are children with language impairments incorporating what they learn in the context of a computer environment into their language interactions in naturalistic settings? Are the targeted skills in social interaction, vocabulary and syntax acquisition, initial literacy, and later academic applications generalized over time to maintain a positive learning trajectory? We have only begun to consider questions such as these, yet they are critical to our overall understanding of the importance of technology in support of learning. Additionally, the possible novelty effects of computer presentations have not been examined. Will the reported motivational advantage of interactive media (Shriberg et al., 1989, 1990) for presentation of speech and language material be maintained over extended periods of intervention training or will children become saturated with this presentation mode and become less responsive over time?

Although this review of current research utilizing computer-based intervention methodologies has shown generally positive outcomes, there is still a need to evaluate and refine the technology as it develops. There are many questions that must be answered before we will know how best to utilize this tool of technology effectively in the service of helping young children with language impairments. The need for clinicians and teachers to be familiar with computer-based intervention approaches, including the ability to select and utilize appropriate software, will only increase as applications of computer technology expand. In the final section of this chapter, some guidelines for evaluating, selecting, and modifying software for use with young school-age children with communication disorders are reviewed. The appropriate use of computer-based intervention approaches for these children depends, in the final analysis, on well-informed and thoughtful clinicians and educators who utilize guidelines verified through research efforts, yet always hold the needs of each individual child foremost.

CONSIDERATIONS FOR SELECTING SOFTWARE
FOR CHILDREN WITH LANGUAGE IMPAIRMENTS

Steiner and Larson (1991) made the point that "As microcomputers infiltrate the profession, new technology must be integrated optimally with established procedures" (p. 18). They further reminded us that learning principles that guide the intervention process should not change when the computer is employed as a clinical tool. In other words, it is best to plan the intervention, and only then determine if computer use might enhance the remedial plan, not vice versa. The computer and software are simply tools, and their use must be accompanied by a clear understanding of how such tools can be effectively integrated into the comprehensive intervention process (Schwartz, 1990).

Because effective computer-based intervention is contingent upon the selection of appropriate software (Haugland, 1992; Lee, 1987; Majsterek & Wilson, 1989), choosing the right software for students with communication disabilities demands as much care and attention as planning their noncomputer-based intervention programs. For example, the content of the software in relationship to the developmental level of the students needs to be considered (Clements & Nastasi, 1992). Just as important, however, are the features the program offers. Distinct features of a program may create challenges and curiosity, enhance motivation, and foster independence, as well as provide successful learning experiences. Particular features also may emphasize competition or extended repetition, thereby contributing to negative attitudes on the part of the learner (Hativa, Swisa, & Lesgold, 1989). Choosing appropriate software, then, can present many challenges. A problem that continues to limit the use of computers as an intervention tool with individuals who demonstrate language impairments is the unavailability of well-designed, developmentally appropriate software (Mokros & Russell, 1986; Neuman, 1991; Robinson, 1991).

There are several software programs that have been designed specifically for use with individuals who demonstrate language impairments. Usually, the documentation for such "designer" software offers the professional thorough information regarding the theoretical rationale, as well as the procedures to be employed during program use. However, most of this software was developed to solve particular problems. Such programs tend to be relatively narrow in scope. Generic software, developed for the mass market, is usually less expensive and often can be adapted to meeting individual student needs. Often commercial software offers flexibility and can be used with students to meet multiple speech and language goals, regardless of the author's original intentions. For example, the Explore-A-Story series (Learning Ways, 1987) can help in meeting various clinical goals. This series, which is primarily designed to develop students' reading and writing skills, also can be used to help students learn to follow directions, to acquire new vocabulary, to reinforce the learning of spatial concepts, to expand language forms and structures (e.g., students describe what is happening by using key descriptive words and grammatical forms), and to promote discourse skills (e.g., students tell a story about the events displayed). Using "Rosie the Counting Rabbit," (Learning Ways, 1987), the lesson outlined in Table 1 provides an example of possible activities that could be included in a child's intervention program. These include "pre-computer" lessons, the actual computer-based intervention, and then "post-computer lessons," or follow-up activities.

During the computer lesson, children can be grouped or paired as they collaborate in the development of the story. This offers a learning environment where positive social skills are facilitated and reinforced. These joint learning activities may help children develop the social skills necessary for cooperative learning (e.g., turn-taking, listening, learning to consider another's perspective).

Table 1. Sample language lessons that include computer activities

Materials and software
"Rosie the Counting Rabbit" (D.C. Heath & Co., 1987)
Storybook from the software program (program comes with five books)
Color printer
Various objects and action pictures

Goals
Production of appropriate answers to *wh-* questions
Expansion of sentence structure using prepositional phrases
Production of discourse to tell a story about the picture created

Pre-computer lessons
1. Use pictures and/or objects and ask the child to tell *who* is doing the action or identify where the action is taking place.
2. Use objects or pictures and ask the child to talk about *where* the objects are located (e.g., on, under, behind).
3. Use sequenced picture cards that tell a story and ask the child to appropriately sequence the cards and tell a brief story.
4. Read and discuss the storybook that comes with the software program.

Computer lesson
1. The child chooses an object or story character to talk about (this is done following step 4 above). While using the program, he or she manipulates the figure/object in the graphic picture and is encouraged to talk about what is happening. The child can be requested to answer who and where questions.
2. The child can be asked to identify the location of various objects or people.
3. The child can be asked to combine action and location into one sentence. Sentence can be written under the picture.
4. Print the story and ask the child to tell the story using the pictures as a guide.

Post-computer lesson
1. The child can share the storybook and story with classmates and/or family.
2. The child's book can be included in the classroom library.
3. The child can select an age-appropriate book from the library, preferably without many words, and tell a story about what is happening. *Good Dog, Carl* (Day, 1985) is an excellent example of this type of book.
4. The child can be asked to describe events that are happening in the classroom.

Selecting software that can be maximally useful in working with children with language impairments is important. The following section briefly describes some of the initial steps that clinicians and teachers should take to ensure that they are selecting tools that are functional, adaptable, and effective in providing computer-based intervention support for children with language impairments.

1. Examine communication goals and objectives. It is advisable to examine closely the specific learning needs of individual students with speech and/or language impairments before selecting software.
2. Preview software and explore its use with a knowledge of the learning sequences planned for the students. Previewing software should be part of the selection process whenever possible. Many companies offer a trial period in which to preview their software products. Another excellent opportunity to preview software is presented at conferences where software demonstrations are often available in the exhibit area. Reviews in journals and computer publications that focus on students with special needs are available. The Appendix contains a step-by-step procedure to assist in the evaluation and selection of software for use in communication intervention programs.
3. Learn more about how computers can be used as an intervention tool. Although in this chapter studies have been reviewed that can guide applications of computer use with special learners, current research cannot provide all the answers. Interventionists need to know more about how to make sound judgments regarding software and to place this information in a coherent context of knowledge regarding good teaching and learning principles. Look for publications that can help to increase an understanding of the appropriate use of computers and that can help to provide knowledge sufficient for making sound judgments. One such publication is *Beyond Drill and Practice: Expanding the Computer Mainstream* (Russel et al., 1989).

A Final Word

It is hoped that by reviewing the broad scope of research in computer intervention since the 1980s, and by providing a framework for evaluating and selecting software, we have helped to facilitate the making of informed choices concerning the application of this technology. There is much that has been shown to be helpful and effective, and most of it is applicable for children with language impairments. New technologies are adding rapidly to the realism, variety, and motivational properties of computer-based approaches. Yet, computers remain, and always will remain, a tool—a tool to be used within the total *context of language intervention* in the preschool and elementary school years. We must not forget that this context must have as its primary underpinning professional expertise and support for the individual learning needs of the children we serve.

REFERENCES

Allen, B. (1991). People helping people through research. *IBM Speech Viewer Times,* *1*(1), 8–10.

Apple Computer, Inc. (1989). *HyperCard user's guide.* Cupertino, CA: Author.

Bailey, J., & Weippert, H. (1992). Using computers to improve the language competence and attending behaviour of deaf aboriginal children. *Journal of Computer-Assisted Learning, 8*(2), 118–127.

Baldry, S. (1991). Microcomputer applications for people with learning difficulties. In A. Ager & L. Bendall (Eds.), *Microcomputers and clinical psychology* (pp. 139–154). New York: John Wiley & Sons.

Barnes, B., & Hill, S. (1983). Should young children work with microcomputers— LOGO before Lego? *The Computing Teacher, 10*(9), 11–14.

Bates, E., Bretherton, I., Beeghley-Smith, M., & McNew, S. (1982). Social basis of language development: A reassessment. In H. Reese & L. Lipsitt (Eds.), *Advances in child development and behavior, 16* (vol. 16, pp. 8–68). New York: Academic Press.

Berko-Gleason, J. (1992). *The development of language.* Columbus, OH: Merrill/ Macmillan.

Brown, R. (1973). *A first language: The early stages.* Cambridge, MA: Harvard University Press.

Bull, G., Cochran, P., & Snell, M. (1988). Beyond CAI: Computers, language, and persons with mental retardation. *Topics in Language Disorders, 8*(4), 55–76.

Cannings, T., & Brown, S. (1986). *The information age classroom: Using the computer as a tool.* Irvine, CA: Franklin Beedle & Associates.

Cheek, E., & Kelly, R. (1993). Evaluation models for technology applications. In J. Lindsey (Ed.), *Computers and exceptional individuals* (2nd ed., pp. 311–331). Austin, TX: PRO-ED.

Chiang, B. (1986). Initial learning and transfer effects of microcomputer drills on LD students' multiplication skills. *Learning Disabilities Quarterly, 9*(2), 118–123.

Chiang, B. (1992). Microcomputer applications for teaching students with exceptional needs in the regular classroom. In L. Cohen (Ed.), *Children with exceptional needs in regular classrooms* (pp. 163–181). Washington, DC: National Education Association.

Chiang, B., Thorpe, H., & Lubke, M. (1984). Learning disabled students tackle the LOGO language. *Journal of Learning Disabilities, 17*(5), 303–304.

Clark, M. (1986). Educational technology and children with moderate learning difficulties. *Exceptional Child, 33*(1), 28–34.

Clements, D. (1987). Computers and literacy. In J. Vacca, R. Vacca, & M. Gove (Eds.), *Reading and learning to read* (pp. 338–372). Boston: Little, Brown.

Clements, D. (1990). Metacomponential development in a LOGO programming environment. *Journal of Educational Psychology, 82,* 141–149.

Clements, D., & Nastasi, B. (1985). Effects of computer environments on social-emotional development: LOGO and computer-assisted instruction. *Computers in the Schools, 2*(2–3), 11–31.

Clements, D., & Nastasi, B. (1992). Computers and early childhood education. In M. Gettinger, S. Elliott, & T. Kratochwill (Eds.), *Preschool and early childhood treatment disorders* (pp. 187–246). Hillsdale NJ: Lawrence Erlbaum Associates.

Closing the Gap. (Available from P.O. Box 68, Henderson, MN 56044)

Clymer, E. (1991). Using hypermedia to develop and deliver assessment or intervention services. *Topics in Language Disorders, 11*(2), 50–64.

Cochran, P., & Bull, G. (1991). Integrating word processing into language intervention. *Topics in Language Disorders, 11*(2), 31–48.

Cochran, P., & Bull, G. (1993). Computers and individuals with speech and language disorders. In J. Lindsey (Ed.), *Computers and exceptional individuals* (2nd ed., pp. 143–157). Austin, TX: PRO-ED.

Cooper, R., & Neilson, H. (1986). *Computer-aided speech production and training program [Computer Program].* Los Angeles: Voice Learning Systems.

Day, A. (1985). *Good dog, Carl.* Hong Kong: Green Tiger Press.

Dede, C. (1987). Empowering environments, hypermedia and microworlds. *The Computing Teacher, 15*(3), 29–34.

Dickinson, D. (1986). Cooperation, collaboration and a computer: Integrating a computer into a first-second grade writing program. *Research in the Teaching of English, 20*(4), 357–378.

Dollaghan, C. (1991). Clinical problem: Expressive language impairments. In R. Mahaffey (Ed.), *Methods for using SpeechViewer: Final project summary report* (p. 9). Boca Raton, FL: IBM Special Needs Systems.

Elliott, A., & Hall, N. (1990). *An evaluation of computer based activities in an early intervention program: A report to the early special education program.* New South Wales, Australia: Wollogong University. (ERIC Document Reproduction Service No. ED 323 028)

Elting, S., & Eisenbarth, J. (1986). *Interactive video for special education.* Reston, VA: The Center for Education Technology, Council for Exceptional Children. (ERIC Document Reproduction Service)

English, J., Gerber, M., & Semmel, M. (1985). Microcomputer-administered spelling tests: Effects on learning handicapped and normally achieving students. *Journal of Reading, Writing, and Learning Disabilities International, 1*(2), 165–176.

Fazio, R., & Rieth, H. (1986). Characteristics of preschool handicapped children's microcomputer use during free-choice periods. *Journal of the Division for Early Childhood, 10,* 247–254.

Fitch, J. (1984). Computer-managed screening for communication disorders. *Language, Speech, and Hearing Services in Schools, 15*(2), 66–69.

Fitch, J. (1989). Computer recognition of correct sound productions in articulation treatment. *Journal for Computer Users in Speech and Hearing, 5*(1), 80–83.

Fitch, J. (1993, September). Computer technology: History and overview. *Asha, 36–37.*

Fitzgerald, G., Fick, L., & Milich, R. (1986). Computer-assisted instruction for students with attentional difficulties. *Journal of Learning Disabilities, 19,* 376–379.

Forman, G. (1986). Observations of young children solving problems with computers and robots. *Journal of Research in Childhood Education, 1*(2), 60–74.

Friedman, S., & Hofmeister, A. (1984). Matching technology to content and learners: A case study. *Exceptional Children, 51*(2), 130–134.

Fujiura, G., & Johnson, L. (1986). Methods of microcomputer research in early childhood special education. *Journal of the Division for Early Childhood, 10,* 264–269.

Genishi, C. (1988). Kindergartners and computers: A case study of six children. *The Elementary School Journal, 89,* 184–201.

Goldman, S., & Rueda, R. (1988). Developing writing skills in bilingual exceptional children. *Exceptional Children, 54,* 543–557.

Goodwin, L., Goodwin, L., & Garel, M. (1986). Use of microcomputers with preschoolers: A review of the literature. *Early Childhood Research Quarterly, 1,* 269–286.

Grandgenett, N., Lloyd, C., & Hill, J. (1991). The effect of computer use on the process writing of learning disabled students. *Journal of Computing in Childhood Education, 2*(2), 63–71.

Guilford, A., & Hnath-Chisolm, T. (1991). Clinical population: Apraxic children and hearing impaired. In R. Mahaffrey (Ed.), *Methods for using SpeechViewer: Final project summary report* (pp. 3–4). Boca Raton, FL: IBM Special Needs Systems.

Harden, S. (1991 June). Confronting the health care crisis. *State Legislatures, 33–34.*

Harn, W. (1986). Facilitating acquisition of S-V utterances in children: Actions, animations and pictures. *Journal for Computer Users in Speech and Hearing (CUSH), 2*(2), 95–101.

Hasselbring, T. (1982). Remediating spelling problems of learning handicapped students through the use of microcomputers. *Educational Technology, 1,* 31–32.

Hasselbring, T., Goin, L., & Bransford, J. (1988). Developing math automaticity in learning handicapped children: The role of computerized drill and practice. *Focus on Exceptional Children, 20,* 1–7.

Hasselbring, T., Goin, L., & Wissick, C. (1989). Making knowledge meaningful: Applications of hypermedia. *Journal of Special Education Technology, 10*(2), 61–72.

Hativa, N. (1988). Computer-based drill and practice in arithmetic: Widening the gap between high- and low-achieving students. *American Educational Research Journal, 25,* 366–397.

Hativa, N., Swisa, S., & Lesgold, A. (1989, April). *Competition in individualized CAI.* Paper presented at the American Educational Research Association annual meeting, San Francisco.

Haugland, S. W. (1992). The effect of computer software on preschool children's developmental gains. *Journal of Computing in Childhood Education, 3,* 15–30.

Hawisher, G. (1989). Research and recommendations for computers and composition. In G. Hawisher & C. Selfe (Eds.), *Critical perspectives on computers and composition instruction* (pp. 44–69). New York: Teachers College Press.

Haynes, J., & Malouf, D. (1986). Computer-assisted instruction needs help. *Academic Therapy, 22*(2), 157–164.

Hedley, C. (1987). What's new in software? Computer programs for social skills. *Journal of Reading, Writing and Learning Disabilities International, 3*(2), 187–191.

Hine, M., & Goldman, S. (1990). Error monitoring by learning handicapped students engaged in collaborative microcomputer-based writing. *Journal of Special Education, 23*(4), 407–422.

Hofmeister, A., & Thorkildsen, R. (1993). Interactive videodisc and exceptional individuals. In J. Lindsay (Ed.), *Computers and exceptional individuals* (pp. 87–107). Austin, TX: PRO-ED.

Holzman, M. (1984). Evidence for a reciprocal model of language development. *Journal of Psycholinguistic Research, 13,* 119–146.

Horii, Y., Osredkar, M., Moore, S., & Huddleston, R. (1991). Clinical population: Cleft-palate/hypernasality. *IBM SpeechViewer Times, 1*(1), 8.

Hotard, S., & Cortez, M. (1983). *Computer-assisted instruction as an enhancer of remediation.* Lafayette LA: Lafayette Parish.

Houghton, C., Warr-Leeper, G., Archer, A., & Henry, S. (1992, November). *Computer-assisted language training for children with Down syndrome.* Paper presented at the American Speech-Language-Hearing Association annual convention, San Antonio, TX.

Iacono, T., & Miller, J. (1989). Can microcomputers be used to teach communication skills to students with mental retardation? *Education and Training of the Mentally Retarded, 24*(1), 32–44.

Israel, B. (1968). *Responsive environment program: Brooklyn, N.Y.: Report of the first full year of operation with the talking typewriter.* Brooklyn NY: Office of Economic Opportunity.

Jolicoeur, K., & Berger, D. (1986). Do we really know what makes educational software effective? A call for empirical research on effectiveness. *Educational Technology, 21,* 7–11.

Jones, K., Torgesen, J., & Sexton, M. (1987). Using computer guided practice to increase decoding fluency in learning disabled children: A study using the Hint and Hunt I program. *Journal of Learning Disabilities, 20*(2), 122–128.

Larson, B., & Roberts, B. (1986). The computer as a catalyst for mutual support and empowerment among learning disabled students. *Journal of Learning Disabilities, 19*(1), 52–55.

Larson, V., & Steiner, S. (1985). Microcomputer use in assessment and intervention with speech and language disorders. In N. Lass, L. McReynolds, J. Northern, & D. Yoder (Eds.), *Handbook of speech pathology and audiology* (pp. 395–418). Philadelphia: B.C. Decker.

Lavin, R., & Sanders, J. (1983). *Longitudinal evaluation of the C/A/I computer assisted instruction.* Chelmsford MA: Merrimack Education Center.

Learning Ways, Inc. (1987). *Explore-a-story: Rosie the counting rabbit* [Computer program]. Lexington, MA: Author.

Lee, W. (1987). Microcomputer courseware production and evaluation guidelines for students with learning disabilities. *Journal of Learning Disabilities, 20*(7), 436–438.

Lehrer, R., & deBernard, A. (1987). Language of learning and language of computing. *Journal of Educational Psychology, 79,* 41–48.

Lehrer, R., Harckham, L., Archer, P., & Pruzek, R. (1986). Microcomputer-based instruction in special education. *Journal of Educational Computing Research, 2,* 337–355.

Lehrer, R., Levin, B., DeHart, P., & Comeaux, M. (1987). Voice-feedback as a scaffold for writing: A comparative study. *Journal of Educational Computing Research, 3*(3), 335–352.

Lieber, J., & Semmel, M. (1985). Effectiveness of computer application to instruction with mildly handicapped learners: A review. *Remedial and Special Education, 6,* 5–14.

Lieber, J., & Semmel, M. (1987). The relationship between group size and performance on a microcomputer problem-solving task for learning handicapped and nonhandicapped students. *Journal of Educational Computing Research, 3*(2), 171–187.

Lipinski, J., Nida, R., Shade, D., & Watson, J. (1986). The effects of microcomputers on young children: An examination of free-play choices, sex differences, and social interactions. *Journal of Educational Computing Research, 2,* 147–168.

MacArthur, C. (1988). The impact of computers on the writing process. *Exceptional Children, 54*(6), 536–542.

MacArthur, C., & Graham, S. (1987). Learning disabled students' composing under three methods of text production: Handwriting, word processing and dictation. *Journal of Special Education, 21*(3), 22–42.

MacArthur, C., Haynes, J., & Malouf, D. (1986). Learning disabled students' engaged time and classroom interaction: The impact of computer assisted instruction. *Journal of Educational Computing Research, 2*(2), 189–198.

MacArthur, C., Haynes, J., Malouf, D., & Harris, K. (1990). Computer assisted instruction with learning disabled students: Achievement, engagement, and other factors that influence achievement. *Journal of Educational Computing Research, 6*(3), 311–328.

MacArthur, C., & Schneiderman, B. (1986). Learning disabled students' difficulties in learning to use a word processor: Implications for instruction and software evaluation. *Journal of Learning Disabilities, 19,* 248–253.

Mahaffrey, R. (1991). *Methods for using SpeechViewer: Final project summary report.* Boca Raton FL: IBM Special Needs Systems.

Majsterek, D., & Wilson, R. (1989). Computer-assisted instruction for students with learning disabilities: Considerations for practitioners. *Learning Disabilities Focus, 5*(1), 18–27.

Malouf, D., Wizer, D., Pilato, V., & Grogan, M. (1990). Computer-assisted instruction with small groups of mildly handicapped students. *Journal of Special Education, 24*(1), 51–68.

Martin, J.G. (1986). *Writing-to-read program* [Computer program]. Dayton, NJ: Entry Systems Division, PC Software Department, International Business Machines, Inc.

Mathinos, D. (1990). LOGO programming and the refinement of problem-solving skills in disabled and nondisabled children. *Journal of Educational Computing Research, 6*(4), 429–446.

McCormick, L. (1987). Comparison of the effects of a microcomputer activity and toy play on social and communicative behaviors of young children. *Journal of the Division of Early Childhood, 11,* 195–205.

McDermid, R. (1989). *A quantitative analysis of the literature on computer-assisted instruction with the learning disabled and educable mentally retarded.* Unpublished doctoral dissertation, University of Kansas, Lawrence.

McDermott, P., & Watkins, M. (1983). Computerized vs. conventional remedial instruction for learning-disabled pupils. *Journal of Special Education, 17*(1), 81–88.

McGregor, G., Drossner, D., & Axelrod, S. (1990). Increasing instructional efficiency: A comparison of voice plus text vs. text alone on the error rate of students with mild disabilities during CAI. *Journal of Special Education Technology, 10*(4), 192–197.

McGuire, R., Hageman, C., & Highnam, C. (1991). Clinical population: Fluency disorders. *IBM SpeechViewer Times, 1*(1), 8–9.

Mevarech, Z. (1985). Computer-assisted instructional methods: A factorial study within mathematics disadvantaged classrooms. *Journal of Experimental Education, 54,* 22–27.

Mevarech, Z., Stern, D., & Levita, I. (1987). To cooperate or not to cooperate in CAI: That is the question. *Journal of Educational Research, 80*(3), 164–167.

Meyers, L. (1984). Unique contributions of microcomputers to language intervention with handicapped children. *Seminars in Speech and Language, 5,* 23–33.

Meyers, L. (1985). *Programs for Early Acquisition of Language* (PEAL) [Computer program]. Calabasas, CA: PEAL Software.

Meyers, L. (1987). Bypassing the prerequisites: The computer as a language scaffold. *Closing the Gap, 5,* 1–20.

Meyers, L. (1990). Technology: A powerful tool for children learning language. *News In Print, 3*(2), 5. Washington, DC: Office of Special Education and Rehabilitative Services (OSERS), U.S. Department of Education.

Minnesota Educational Computing Consortium. (1980). *Sell lemonade* [Computer program]. St. Paul, MN: Author.

Mokros, J., & Russell, M. (1986). Learner centered software: A survey of microcomputer use with special needs students. *Journal of Learning Disabilities, 19*(3), 185–190.

Moxley, R., & Barry, P. (1986). *Developing micocomputer programs for early literacy.* (ERIC Document Reproduction Service No. ED 279 397).

Muhlstein, E., & Croft, D. (1986). *Using the microcomputer to enhance language experiences and the development of cooperative play among preschool children.* Cupertino, CA: DeAnza College Press.

Muller, A., & Perlmutter, M. (1985). Preschool children's problem-solving interactions at computers and jigsaw puzzles. *Journal of Applied Developmental Psychology, 6,* 173–186.

Murphy, R., & Appel, L. (1984). *Evaluation of writing to read.* Princeton, NJ: Educational Testing Service.

Nelson, K., Prinz, P., & Dalke, D. (1989). Transitions from sign language to text via an interactive microcomputer system. In B. Woll (Ed.), *Papers from the Seminar on*

Language Development and Sign Language (Monograph 1, International Sign Linguistics Association). Bristol, UK: Centre for Deaf Studies, University of Bristol.

Neuman, D. (1991). Learning disabled students' interactions with commercial courseware: A naturalistic study. *Education-Technology-Research-and-Development, 39*(1), 31–49.

Niemiec, R., & Walberg, H. (1987). Comparative effects of computer-assisted instruction: A synthesis of reviews. *Journal of Educational Computing Research, 3*(1), 19–38.

O'Connor, L., & Schery, T. (1986). A comparison of microcomputer-aided and traditional language therapy for developing communication skills in non-oral toddlers. *Journal of Speech and Hearing Disorders, 51*, 356–361.

Ott-Rose, M., & Cochran, P. (1992). Teaching action verbs with computer-controlled videodisc vs. traditional picture stimuli. *Journal for Computer Users in Speech and Hearing, 8,* (1–2), 244–301.

Papert, S. (1980). *Mindstorms: Children, computers and powerful ideas.* New York: Basic Books.

Powell, R. (1991, September-October). Update: Everyone agrees on need for health care reform, but no consensus on how to pay for solutions. *California Speech-Language-Hearing Association Bulletin, 2,* 15.

Pratt, S., Heintzelman, A., & Ensrud, S. (1991). Clinical population: Young hearing impaired children. In R. Mahaffrey, *Methods for using Speech Viewer: Final project summary report* (pp. 17–18). Boca Raton, FL: IBM Special Needs Systems.

Prinz, P. (1991). Literacy and language development within microcomputer-videodisc-assisted interactive contexts. *Journal of Childhood Communication Disorders, 14*(1), 67–80.

Prinz, P., & Nelson, K. (1985). Alligator eats cookie: Acquisition of writing and reading skills by deaf children using the microcomputer. *Applied Psycholinguistics, 6,* 283–306.

Prinz, P., Nelson, K., Loncke, F., Geysels, G., & Willems, C. (1993). A multimodality and multimedia approach to language, discourse, and literacy development. In F. Coninx & B. Elsendoorn (Eds.), *Interactive learning technology for the deaf.* New York: Springer-Verlag.

Prinz, P., Nelson, K., & Stedt, J. (1982). Early reading in young deaf children using microcomputer technology. *American Annals of the Deaf, 127,* 529–535.

Prinz, P., Pemberton, E., & Nelson, K. (1985). The ALPHA interactive microcomputer system for teaching reading, writing and communication skills to hearing impaired children. *American Annals of the Deaf, 130,* 444–461.

Riel, M. (1985). The computer chronicles newswire: A functional learning environment for acquiring literacy skills. *Journal of Educational Computing Research, 1,* 317–337.

Robinson, S. (1991). Computer-based instruction in special education. In T. Schlecter (Ed.), *Problems and promises of computer-based training* (pp. 39–60). Norwood, NJ: Ablex.

Roblyer, M., Castine, W., & King, F. (1988). *Assessing the impact of computer-based instruction: A review of recent research.* New York: Haworth Press.

Romski, M.A., Sevcik, R.A., & Pate, J.L. (1988). The establishment of symbolic communication in persons with severe mental retardation. *Journal of Speech and Hearing Disorders, 59,* 94–107.

Rosegrant, T. (1986). Using the microcomputer as a scaffold for assisting beginning readers and writers. In J. Hoot (Ed.), *Computers in early childhood education: Issues and practices* (pp. 128–143). New York: Teachers College Press.

Ruscello, D., Cartwright, L., Haines, K., & Shuster, L. (1993). The use of different service delivery models for children with phonological disorders. *Journal of Communication Disorders, 26*(3), 193–205.

Russell, S., Corwin, R., Mokros, J., & Kapisovsky, P. (1989). *Beyond drill and practice: Expanding the computer mainstream.* Reston, VA: The Council for Exceptional Children.

Sarachan-Deily, A. (1990). Can microcomputers help the school speech-language pathologist? *Journal for Computer Users in Speech and Hearing, 6*(1), 57–62.

Schery, T., & O'Connor, L. (1992). The effectiveness of school-based computer language intervention with severely handicapped children. *Language, Speech, and Hearing Services in Schools, 23*(1), 43–47.

Schery, T., & Spaw, L. (1993). The effectiveness of paraprofessionals in computer intervention with handicapped toddlers. *Infant Toddler Intervention, 3,* 51–61.

Schetz, K. (1989). Computer-aided language/concept enrichment in kindergarten: Consultation program model. *Language, Speech, and Hearing Services in Schools, 20,* 2–10.

Schmidt, M., Weinstein, T., Niemic, R., & Walberg, H. (1985–1986). Computer-assisted instruction with exceptional children. *Journal of Special Education, 19,* 493–502.

Schrader, M. (1990). *Computer applications for language learning.* Tucson, AZ: Communication Skill Builders.

Schwartz, A. (1989). A look at the needs for the application of microcomputers in the 1990s. *Journal for Computer Users in Speech and Hearing, 5,* 114–124.

Schwartz, A. (1990). *The role of the speech therapist in technology acquisition and use.* Tech use guide: Using computer technology. Reston, VA: Council for Exceptional Children. (ERIC Document Reproduction Service No. ED 339 154)

Shade, D., Nida, R., Lipinski, J., & Watson, J. (1986). Microcomputers and preschoolers: Working together in a classroom setting. *Computers in Schools, 3,* 53–61.

Sharp, D., Goldman, S., Bransford, J., Hasselbring, T., Vye, N., and the Cognition and Technology Group at Vanderbilt. (1993, April). *Developing strategic approaches to narrative structures with integrated-media environments for young, at-risk children.* Paper presented at the American Educational Research Association annual meeting, Atlanta, GA.

Shaver, J., & Wise, B. (1990, December). *The impact of technology on early reading.* Paper presented at the American Reading Forum annual meeting, Sarasota, FL. (ERIC Document Reproduction Service No. ED 327 832)

Shlechter, T. (1988). An examination of the research evidence for computer-based instruction. In R. Hartson & D. Hix (Eds.), *Advances in human–computer interactions* (pp. 316–367). Norwood, NJ: Ablex.

Shriberg, L., Kwiatkowski, J., & Snyder, T. (1986). Articulation testing by microcomputer. *Journal of Speech and Hearing Disorders, 51,* 309–321.

Shriberg, L., Kwiatkowski, J., & Snyder, T. (1989). Tabletop versus microcomputer-assisted speech management: Stabilization phase. *Journal of Speech and Hearing Disorders, 54,* 233–248.

Shriberg, L., Kwiatkowski, J., & Snyder, T. (1990). Tabletop versus microcomputer-assisted speech management: Response evocation phase. *Journal of Speech and Hearing Disorders, 55,* 635–655.

Steg, D., Lazar, I., & Boyce, C. (1993). *Computer assisted education: A communication approach.* Philadelphia: Center for School Study Councils, University of Pennsylvania.

Steg, D., Vaidya, S., & Hamdan, P. (1982). Long term gains from early intervention through technology: An eleven-year report. *Journal of Educational Technology Systems, 11,* 203–214.

Steiner, S., & Larson, V. (1991). Integrating microcomputers into a language intervention with children. *Topics in Language Disorders, 11*(2), 18–30.

Swigger, K., & Swigger, B. (1984). Social patterns and computer use among preschool children. *Association for Educational Data Systems Journal, 17,* 35–41.

Tenney, R., & Osguthorpe, R. (1990). Elementary age special education students using self-directed or tutor-assisted computer-aided instruction to develop keyboarding skills. *Journal of Educational Computing Research, 6*(2), 215–229.

Thorkildsen, R. (1985). Using an interactive videodisc program to teach social skills to handicapped children. *American Annals of the Deaf, 130*(5), 383–385.

Thorkildsen, R., Fodor-Davis, J., & Morgan, D. (1989). Evaluation of a videodisc-based social skills training program. *Journal of Special Education Technology, 10*(2), 91–98.

Thorkildsen, R., & Friedman, S. (1986). Interactive videodisc: Instructional design of a beginning reading program. *Learning Disability Quarterly, 9*(2), 111–117.

Torgesen, J. (1986a). Computers and cognition in reading: A focus on decoding fluency [Special issue]. *Exceptional Children, 53*(2), 157–162.

Torgesen, J. (1986b). Using computers to help learning disabled children practice reading: A research-based perspective. *Learning Disabilities Focus, 1*(2), 72–81.

Torgesen, J.K., Waters, M., Cohen, A., & Torgesen, J. (1988). Improving sight-word recognition skills in LD children: An evaluation of three computer program variations. *Learning Disability Quarterly, 11*(2), 125–132.

Varnhagen, S., & Gerber, M. (1984). Use of microcomputers for spelling assessment: Reasons to be cautious. *Learning Disability Quarterly, 7*(3), 266–270.

Vockell, E., & Mihail, T. (1993, Spring). Principles behind computerized instruction for students with exceptionalities. *Teaching Exceptional Children,* 38–43.

Ward, R. (1989). Some uses of natural language interfaces in computer assisted language learning. *Instructional Science, 18*(1), 45–61.

Watson, J., Chadwick, S., & Brinkley, V. (1986). Special education technologies for young children: Present and future learning scenarios with related research literature. *Journal of the Division for Early Childhood, 10,* 197–208.

Yin, R., & Moore, G. (1987). The use of advanced technologies in special education: Prospects from robotics, artificial intelligence, and computer simulation. *Journal of Learning Disabilities, 20*(1), 60–63.

Appendix

Software Evaluation Guidelines

Evaluation

TECHNICAL REQUIREMENTS

1. Is the type of computer, memory requirements, and/or
   system requirements compatible with your system?   Yes   No

2. Is any additional hardware necessary (e.g., extra
   disk drive)?   Yes   No

3. Can adaptive devices be used (e.g., Unicorn Key-
   board™, Muppet Learning Keys™, Power Pad™)?   Yes   No

4. Is any technical support available from the company?   Yes   No

DOCUMENTATION

1. Are the manuals and/or program directions written in
   clear, easy to follow language?   Yes   No

2. Are the age ranges and/or developmental levels stated?   Yes   No

3. Are the instructions and options displayed on-screen
   (menu options, keyboard command options)?   Yes   No

4. Are replacement copies available for damaged or
   outdated programs?   Yes   No

5. Is the program copy protected?   Yes   No

6. Is the cost of the program appropriate for what it does
   (i.e., is the cost high and the application limited)?   Yes   No

PROGRAM FORMAT

1. Is the program design flexible? (Can you use the pro-
   gram for students functioning at different ability levels?)   Yes   No

2. Can the program be easily operated by the students?   Yes   No

3. Is the program user-friendly (e.g., what happens when
   you hit an incorrect key or make a mistake?)   Yes   No

Evaluation

4. Are the directions on the screen easy to follow? Yes No

5. Does it allow students to make choices? Yes No

6. Does it set limits on time, or number of turns one can take before coming up with a solution? Yes No

7. Does the program offer successive levels of difficulty? Yes No

8. Does this program provide feedback to students? (If so, be sure to examine the type of feedback provided. Audible responses associated with errors can embarrass a student). Yes No

9. Does the program lend itself to instructional strategies that are useful to students with special needs? Yes No

FEATURES AFFECTING MOTIVATION/INTEREST

1. Does the software present an appropriate level of challenge? Yes No

2. Do the motivational features distract from the task at hand? Yes No

3. Do the motivational features facilitate attention to relevant dimensions of the task? Yes No

4. Does the subject matter stimulate interest? Yes No

5. Does the software build on the existing interests of students? Yes No

6. Does the software create a desire to learn about new information? Yes No

CONTENT

1. Are off-computer activities compatible with this software? (Make a list) Yes No

2. Does the program offer something worthwhile for students? Yes No

3. Can activities be tailor-made for students? Yes No

4. Does the software support the instructional scenarios frequently used with students? Yes No

11

Intervention with Children from Linguistically and Culturally Diverse Backgrounds

Hortencia Kayser

LANGUAGE INTERVENTION WITH CHILDREN FROM linguistically and culturally diverse populations is a challenge to many speech-language pathologists. Logically, we may believe that language intervention that is known to be effective with mainstream English-speaking children also should be effective with children from other cultural groups. But if we assume what is good for one child is good for another, we will have difficulty rationalizing why children from linguistically and culturally diverse backgrounds do not appear to make progress in our language intervention programs (Kayser, 1985; Ortiz, Garcia, Wheeler, & Maldonado-Colon, 1986). The goal of any intervention program is to meet the specific language needs of the child. In order to fulfill this goal, the child's cultural and linguistic background must be considered and acknowledged beyond the surface features of culture, such as foods and holidays. This chapter reviews issues of multiculturalism and multilingualism that are likely to affect intervention programs. The child's cultural background and how this could affect interactions with the clinician are discussed. Through this discussion, it is shown that different cultures have different learning and teaching styles that affect the style of communication during a clinical event. The language of instruction during intervention also affects the rate of learning new concepts and may determine the extent of parent involvement in developing a child's language abilities. Case studies, primarily of Mexican-American children, are presented to illustrate these issues and to demonstrate how existing intervention programs can be modified successfully by carefully considering the child's cultural and linguistic background.

Funded in part by Research and Training Center Grant #1P60 DC-01409 from the National Institute on Deafness and Other Communication Disorders, National Center for Neurogenic Communication Disorders and Stroke.

THE CHILD'S CULTURE

What aspects of culture does a child bring into the clinical setting that may affect the teaching and learning outcomes of the clinical session? Unfortunately, we cannot always determine precisely how a child's cultural knowledge and background may affect an intervention program. Nevertheless, it is impossible to separate language intervention from the context of culture. For example, the culture of the clinician determines a number of cultural variables such as the language of instruction and sociocultural rules for who should speak what to whom. The child's and clinician's cultures define for each of them what must be known about the use of language in order that each can be an accepted participant and member of their own communities.

Culture encompasses all of the behaviors, values, and beliefs that serve as a foundation for individual behavior and regulation of interactions with other community members and nonmembers (Saville-Troike, 1986). Saville-Troike suggested that our knowledge, perceptions, and behaviors are influenced by our culture. Modes of thinking, feeling, perceiving, and behaving are characteristic not just of individuals but of whole groups and are learned by being a member of a given group. How individuals learn these behaviors depends upon the culture's understanding of learning and teaching as well as how these are transmitted to the young members.

Culture and language use also include the repertoire of nonverbal behaviors, such as intonation, eye contact, touch, social distance, posture, and facial and body gestures (Pennycook, 1985). Birdwhistell (1970) suggested that the interaction between culture and language is such that cultural groups possess a unique nonverbal behavioral repertoire inseparable from language. Speakers of the same language then may use nonverbal behaviors that may be considered appropriate, acceptable, and within norms of a particular community. As an example, Garcia Coll (1990) states that mother and infant interactions among Mexican-Americans are predominantly nonverbal. These mothers use tactile stimulation more often than vocalization with their 2- and 4-week-olds infants. In addition, mothers talk less to their 12-month-old infants than when the child is 8 months old. Steward and Steward, as reported in Garcia Coll (1990), found that Mexican-American mothers often presented nonverbal instructions to their children as an adjunct to, or instead of, spoken instructions. For example, gesture may be used with an imperative to communicate a directive, or eye gaze is used to direct the child to sit appropriately in a chair. Valdes (1986) reported that Mexican-born parents who live in the United States emphasize observation of competent models of an activity and independent learning rather than direct teaching and explanation of a new activity to their children. Adults provide guidance if requested, but the parent rarely offers much in the way of unsolicited verbal instructions. These observed behaviors of Mexican-born parents in regard to their children's interactions with them and with language-learning environments contrast markedly with those of mainstream American parents that emphasize direct teaching and explanation of a new skill or activity (Owens, 1988).

Thus, the content of intervention programs, as well as the method of instruction, might be affected by the child's cultural understanding of how learning and teaching should be accomplished. In the following case study, a clinician modified her procedures to increase the use of requests and labeling with an Hispanic child.

Case Example

A bilingual Anglo clinician attempted to increase labeling and requesting behaviors of a Spanish-speaking 4-year-old boy with a language impairment. The clinician used a craft project to elicit these behaviors and used a set of materials that was kept on her side of the work table. The child had to request these art materials from the clinician so that he could construct his art work. The clinician was concerned because she could not elicit the child's participation. The usual response for this child was to sit on his side of the table and look at the clinician and the materials. He did not verbally request to use the materials nor did he label the objects.

These initial sessions were observed by an Hispanic supervisor who recognized that the child was requesting these materials from the clinician through the use of alternating gaze. When a Hispanic child requests an object or asks permission from an adult stranger, eye gaze may be used to execute this illocutionary act. This nonverbal requesting is less likely to occur with familiar adults, such as the child's parents. In this case, the child appeared to recognize that it was inappropriate to make a verbal request to a stranger for an object that does not belong to him. In addition, for this Spanish-speaking child, verbal requesting and labeling was not used even with his mother. Because this child used gaze exclusively to request and to label or reference objects, the intervention plan was modified to focus on comprehension of the names of objects until the child recognized that spoken language was necessary for requesting these items. The child was allowed to use eye gaze to label objects. The clinician modeled labels of objects the child requested nonverbally until the child understood this different and verbal mode of labeling. Procedures were further modified so that the clinician was able to assess the child's comprehension while using interactive techniques such as parallel and self-talk. This allowed the child the opportunity to become accustomed to the clinician's expectation of "talk" during the session.

Verbal requesting behaviors also were modeled for the child by the clinician in parallel with the child's preferred nonverbal mode. The sequence of nonverbal requesting by this child was to look at the clinician, look at the object, and then look again at the clinician. The clinician had to observe the child's eye movements closely to determine if requesting was occurring. Once the clinician recognized that a request had taken place, she provided the verbal model for the child's request. This modification targeted an increase in the child's use of his preferred method of requesting and set the stage for targeting verbal requests at a later date.

This child had an illocutionary mode of requesting that was nonverbal and acceptable within his culture with adult strangers, but with familiar interactants such as his parents, verbal requests were obligatory. Recognition of this cultural difference led to the clinician's reevaluation of the child's competencies and modification of the specific intervention goals and procedures. Language intervention provided an alternative verbal form for what was appreciated as an already existing and acceptable form of requesting and labeling.

Selection of Materials

Advocates for individuals with language impairments from culturally and linguistically diverse backgrounds have emphasized the importance of cultural sensitivity in the use of materials during the intervention session (Harris, 1986; Kayser, 1985; Saville-Troike, 1986). Kayser (1993) stated that background research about a community and culture may be necessary in order to develop appropriate materials. This background preparation may include observations of the community and discussion with bilingual professionals and families to understand those aspects of the culture that may be familiar, meaningful, and appropriate for the children. Awareness of a child's culture can lead to major adaptations in the activities that serve as the context within which intervention procedures are employed. For example, Kayser (1985) described the participation of Hispanic children in a session with an Anglo clinician. This clinician had experienced some difficulty in getting the children to participate in the standard activities she normally used with children from mainstream American culture. She had learned about a local Mexican-American tradition where dried egg shells filled with confetti were cracked over a person's head during a festival. She decided to use these "cascarones" in an art activity for language development. The clinician was surprised and delighted to see the recognition, active response, and participation of the children in the session. In turn, the increase in participation by the students gave the clinician many more opportunities to employ the procedures she had selected to facilitate the children's language development.

Acknowledging a child's culture through the materials that are used for language intervention is likely to bring about a more positive response from children. Acknowledgment of the child's culture not only facilitates the objectives of the session, but it also may help to develop the children's sense of worth and pride in who they are. It also provides an opportunity for clinicians to incorporate the world knowledge that a child brings to the session.

THE CLINICIAN–CHILD INTERACTION

Taylor (1986) stated that all clinical interactions are cultural events. Therefore, the clinician should view the intervention situation as a social-communicative event that has cultural rules and guidelines for appropriate interactions between the clinician and the client. There may be miscommunications because of the assumptions and norms that the child brings to the clinical session. Recognizing that children from culturally and linguistically diverse backgrounds have different communication styles is the first step toward improving intervention programs with children from diverse backgrounds.

Adult and child interactions have been studied by a number of researchers interested in parent–child and clinician–child dyads. Heath (1986) reported in her ethnographic studies that, in Mexican-American families, children are not considered equal conversational partners. In mixed adult and child groups, adults rarely ask children to express their interpretation of events or their emotional evaluations. Additionally, if the parents know the occurrences in an event, there is a feeling that they do not need to ask a child, who also knows, to recount the event. Children will recount an event when the adult is not familiar with the details of the event. Blount (1982) compared parental speech to young children in English- and Spanish-speaking families. He reported that the Spanish-speaking parents used repetition, exaggerated intonation, and instructional and attentional devices more often than the English-speaking parents.

Scudder and Holmskog (1989) studied the repair strategies of Spanish-speaking children, ages 6–11 years, in interactions with Anglo and Hispanic adults. The results indicated that the children used more additions (adding information to the original response) and revisions (changing the form of the utterance but not the semantic content) with the Anglo listener, while repetitions (repeating all or part of the original utterance) were used more often during the children's interactions with the Hispanic listener. This might be interpreted to mean that these children viewed the nonnative listener as needing more clarification than the native Spanish listener. Scudder and Holmskog suggested that these Hispanic children changed their style of clarification based on the ethnicity of the listener.

In describing the behaviors of Anglo clinicians, Prutting, Bagshaw, and Goldstein (1978) reported that clinicians used descriptions, statements of explanation, and statements of intentions when they spoke to their English-speaking clients. These investigators found that the use of questions by these clinicians was limited predominantly to those in which both speaker and listener already knew the answer. Each of these types of statements and questions may be viewed as "different" or unusual during interactions by culturally and linguistically different groups between clients and clinicians (Heath, 1986).

Kayser (1989) described the interactions of 3 Anglo and 3 Hispanic clinicians as each screened Hispanic children for speech and language impairments. The verbal and nonverbal behaviors of the Anglo and Hispanic clinicians were strikingly different. The English-speaking clinicians kept a social distance of 48–60 inches from the children, while the Hispanic clinicians kept within a range of 18–48 inches. The Anglo clinicians did not touch the children, but the Hispanic clinicians used touch to control the children's behavior or to get their attention on an immediate task. The Hispanic clinicians used a number of facial gestures to communicate affirmation, confusion, agreement, and disagreement with the child while the Anglo clinicians primarily smiled and used no other facial expressions. The use of eye gaze by the Hispanic clinicians to control the children's behavior was of particular interest.

The verbal communication between the clinicians and children also was different for the two groups. The Anglo clinicians used verbal reinforcements, questions, permission statements, statements of need, hints, explanations concerning a task, and if–then statements, such as "if you show me the car, then we can play with the toys" to coax the child to complete a task. The Hispanic clinicians were much more directive, using primarily performatives, such as "di" (say), "ensename" (show me), and "haz esto" (do this). When the clinicians clarified their utterances, the Hispanic clinicians repeated the utterances while the Anglo clinicians rephrased the utterance. This style of clarification, repetition of the utterance, is similar to Scudder and Holmskog's (1989) results for Hispanic children's clarifications with Anglo and Hispanic adults.

Verbal behaviors also were found in the Hispanic clinicians' interactions that were not found in the Anglo clinicians' interactions. The Hispanic clinicians complimented the children's beauty, appearance, clothes, names, and names of family members. This was observed during the initial, middle, and final sections of the testing sessions. Additionally, the Hispanic clinicians were observed using attentional devices such as "mira" (look), "escuche" (listen), and "hey" to keep the children on task. The Hispanic clinicians' behaviors support observations by Blount (1982), Heath (1986), and Scudder and Holmskog (1989), suggesting differences in adult–child interactions between Anglo and Hispanic adults.

These studies and observations of children and clinician interactions also support Taylor's (1986) statements that the intervention session is a social clinical event that reflects each individual's knowledge of how the interaction should proceed. Mismatched assumptions can result in miscommunication that may affect the clinician's judgments about the child's learning potential, progress in intervention, and communicative competency.

LANGUAGE INTERVENTION WITH BILINGUAL CHILDREN

There has been considerable debate concerning the language of instruction for minority-language children in the United States. Should children be taught only in English? Or should the native language be used to teach academic subjects? The issues that surround language of instruction and bilingual education have been discussed in terms of legal, political, social, economic, and cultural ramifications since the 1960s.The debate now is focusing on those children with language impairments who come from a non–English-speaking background. This debate has caused some confusion in the general public about the relative effectiveness of English-only instruction versus native language instruction. This confusion may have its source in the relative effectiveness of the two different bilingual education systems that are found in the United States and Canada. Therefore, a description of these two systems is warranted.

Canadian Bilingual Education Programs

Many Canadian programs are "additive" immersion bilingual education programs. Majority-language children who speak English voluntarily enter kindergarten classrooms that are taught in French, the minority language. As the children progress through the grade levels, they are increasingly exposed to English, their home language, until they are receiving half of their education in English and half in French. The goal of these programs is to maintain the home language while helping children to acquire a valued second language. There are four important sociocultural features of such additive immersion programs: 1) they are intended for children from the majority group language (i.e., English); 2) teachers and administrators value and support the children's home language and culture; 3) the child and parents value their home language and culture; and 4) acquisition of the second language by the participants and parents is regarded as a positive skill (McLaughlin, 1985). The success of additive immersion bilingual education programs is believed to be due in large part to these features. Programs that share such features are found in target schools in major cities in the U. S. and throughout Canada and are considered to be enrichment programs for majority language children (Hakuta, 1986).

U. S. Bilingual Education Programs

In contrast, the U. S. has several predominant curriculum designs for bilingual education. These include: 1) the maintenance model, which is designed to develop bilingualism and biliteracy; 2) the transitional model, which is designed to use the non-English language to facilitate the learning of English through curriculum content; 3) the English as a second language (ESL) model, which is usually a component of the first two models; and 4) the high-intensity model, which is found in middle- and high schools where students are expected to learn English rapidly (Fradd, 1987). Transitional bilingual education is the model mandated by the Bilingual Education Act of 1976 (PL 95-561) and the *Lau v. Nichols* (1974) decision. Minority-language students are instructed in their home language until they are able to receive instruction exclusively in English (Hakuta, 1986). These children receive instruction beginning in kindergarten in the home language, and, as they progress through the grades, they are increasingly exposed to the majority language (English). When these children are determined to have adequate proficiency in English, they are transferred to English-only instruction. The home language is not maintained.

The Canadian programs have received positive evaluations through research that supports the effectiveness of additive immersion (Lambert & Tucker, 1972; Swain & Barik, 1978). In contrast, the effectiveness of transitional bilingual education in the U. S. has not been documented adequately (Hakuta, 1986; McLaughlin, 1985). Thus, there is the opinion that immersion should be used with minority-language children, at least partially because it has been documented to be effective in Canada. However, Hakuta (1986) stated that neither transitional bilingual education nor immersion will be effective with minority-language children in the U. S. As long as education is a subtractive, rather than an additive experience, one of assimilation at all costs and without respect for the child's home language and culture, minority-language children will not succeed in either of these models. This would seem to be the case especially for children who have difficulty acquiring their first language.

ABILITIES OF CHILDREN WITH LANGUAGE IMPAIRMENTS TO LEARN A SECOND LANGUAGE

Despite such legal mandates as the Education for All Handicapped Children Act of 1975 (PL 94-142), misconceptions remain about the ability of children with language impairments to learn more than one language and about the utility of the first language in helping minority-language children acquire English as a second language. Juarez (1983) stated that many speech-language pathologists believe that minority-language children who are experiencing difficulty in mastering language skills should receive intervention only in English. The argument has been that these children need to learn English to be able to communicate in the predominant language used in the school and throughout the country (Barclay, 1983). Ortiz (1984) added that among education and special education personnel, there is a belief that children are confused when both English and the home language are used for instruction. Couched in this belief is the assumption that bilingualism is difficult and not accessible for the individual with a language-learning impairment. Therefore, it is believed that these children are better served by English-only education and language intervention.

It is important to note, however, that such an immersion model lacks the feature deemed to be responsible for the success of the additive immersion programs in Canada and elsewhere. Furthermore, there is research that suggests that the assumptions on which the model is based are flawed. Bruck (1982) reported that a group of native English-speaking children with language impairments who attended 2 years of French immersion programs achieved cognitive, first-language, and academic test scores comparable to a control group of English-speaking children with language impairments who received English-only language instruction. Thus, these children had no deleterious effects from 2 years of instruction in a second language. Furthermore, the immersion programs were successful in helping these children to acquire some skills in French. Bruck argued that the positive psychosocial conditions that characterized the immersion program were responsible for its success. The children in this study were from middle-class homes, their home language and culture was valued by all parties, and the home language was maintained in the home.

In two follow-up studies, Bruck (1985a, 1985b) studied children who transferred out of French immersion programs. She found that transfer was not correlated with teachers' ratings of academic improvement or the children's actual academic performance. However, children's negative attitudes and classroom behavior were important factors associated with transfer. Although much of Bruck's data in these studies is descriptive rather than experimental, her results suggest that careful scrutiny of the factors predicting success in language learning is warranted.

Unlike the student population in the French immersion programs, however, the minority-language student in the U. S. typically does not have the same sociocultural, economic, political, or language status upon entering bilingual education or English-only classrooms as the children in French immersion programs. Therefore, native language instruction has been the focus for minority language students in the United States. The stated purpose of native language instruction has been to provide comprehensible input (Krashen, 1981) so that the child understands the nature and demands of the learning task. If the child is instructed in the unfamiliar language, the child's level of learning of the curriculum would be expected to be compromised by the child's lack of comprehension of the second language.

Research in speech-language pathology in the U. S. supports the hypothesis that the native language may be instrumental in helping minority-language children with language impairments develop skills in both the native and the majority language (Kiernan & Swisher, 1990; Perozzi, 1985; Perozzi & Chavez-Sanchez, 1992). Experimental single-subject designs by Kiernan and Swisher (1990) and Perozzi (1985) support the use of the first language before instructing in the second language, and suggest that a bilingual curriculum is better than teaching only in English.

Perozzi (1985) examined the learning of receptive vocabulary in the native language for six subjects who ranged in age from 4;0 to 5;5 years. The six subjects were three English speakers (one with a mild language delay and two with typically developing language) and three Spanish speakers (one with a mild language delay, one with a language impairment, and one with typically developing language). Using a within-subject design, there were two experimental conditions presented to these children. In Condition A, receptive vocabulary was first taught in the child's native language. Then, instruction was provided in the second language. Once the child was able to identify correctly all the items in a set, the same set was taught in the child's second language. Condition B involved the initial presentation of new vocabulary in the child's second language. When these vocabulary items were learned, they were presented in the first language. The results indicated that learning a set of words initially in the first language resulted in fewer trials to criterion in learning those same words in the second language than when words were learned initially in the second language. This finding held true for both the English-speaking and Spanish-speaking children. Based on these findings, Perozzi concluded that if there are bilingual goals for students, it is better to teach in the child's native language, as this facilitates learning the second language.

Kiernan and Swisher (1990) investigated the initial learning of novel words by minority-language children acquiring English as a second language in two experiments. The verbal stimuli consisted of two-syllable nonsense words designed to be phonemically and phonetically representative of English, Spanish, and Navajo words. The effectiveness of a daily bilingual training condition was compared with a daily English-only training condition. The Spanish-speaking subjects for the first experiment were three boys and one girl, ages 4;11 to 5;3. The Navajo-speaking subjects for the second experiment were two boys and one girl, ages 5;6 to 6;3. In both experiments, the bilingual and monolingual training conditions were presented during each session, with the order of the presentation switched on a daily basis. Each experiment supported the hypothesis that second-language (L2) word learning was superior in the bilingual condition of training when compared to the monolingual English condition. It took fewer trials for the children to learn an L2 word under the bilingual training program than in the English-only condition.

In a larger study, Perozzi and Chavez-Sanchez (1992) compared the rate of receptive acquisition of English prepositions and pronouns for two groups of bilingual first-grade children identified as having language delays. The subjects were 38 first graders with a mean age of 6;8. One half of the children (Group A) received instruction in Spanish prior to instruction in English, and the other half (Group B) received instruction in English only. All of the children were tested initially to identify prepositions that they erroneously identified in both languages. Therefore, the number of instructional stimuli varied from subject to subject. Results indicated that Group A (Spanish) learned the Spanish items and then the English equivalents twice as rapidly as those subjects who were instructed in English only.

The results of these three studies, each of which involved a small number of subjects, are limited to examination of receptive and expressive vocabulary and the comprehension of prepositions. Nevertheless, they show promise for a practice that has been accepted in the field of bilingual education. Despite this promise and legal mandates, the use of the native language in language intervention with children from language minorities is still not practiced widely within speech-language pathology. The paucity of bilingual clinicians may be the primary factor in not promoting language intervention programs in the home language. If this is the case, coordination of services among school professionals and cooperation with the family become critical avenues for intervening in a child's bilingual language development.

Case Example

Ernesto entered school at age 5 as a monolingual Spanish speaker, but with 2 years of school, he had lost his Spanish proficiency and was using primarily

English with friends, siblings, and in the classroom. At age 7, however, his Spanish comprehension was still better than his English comprehension. Ernesto's academic progress was slow, and, after diagnostic testing, he was determined to have a learning disability with a language impairment. The school professionals recommended language intervention in English by the speech-language pathologist and resource assistance from the special education and ESL teachers. There were no bilingual classrooms available in Ernesto's school district. Ernesto's parents were monolingual Spanish speakers, and they were concerned that he was not able to communicate effectively with the family.

Although Ernesto's receptive language skills were better in Spanish, this was not seen as a strength or as a potential mode to develop the child's cognitive and language learning skills. Bilingual children have different levels of competency in form, content, and use for the two languages, and these competencies change rapidly during the course of a school year (Grosjean, 1982; McLaughlin, 1985). For example, a child may be predominantly Spanish-speaking at the beginning of a school year but lose expressive abilities in the language within the year and prefer to speak English. The domains and environments in which children learn language determine their knowledge of each language. The child may be knowledgeable about home activities, tools, and religious events in the home language but prefer to use English to speak about academic and school events (Baetens Beardsmore, 1986). As children become more balanced in their bilingualism, or if they begin to shift dominance to the majority language, the guiding principle for bilingual children with language impairments may be to use the language that best assists the child's acquisition and retention of new information.

There are two major issues exemplified by Ernesto's situation. The first involves the loss of the home language, Spanish, and the second is the English-only programming offered by the school. What modifications could be implemented in this program to meet the needs of the family? In addition, what modifications could be implemented in the school program so that Ernesto would maximize his opportunities for language learning and academic success? For this child, the clinician's role should expand to include that of parent-program facilitator and coordinator of other services to meet the child's language intervention objectives. Through the use of an interpreter, the parents or caregivers can be included in the intervention program. They should receive information concerning the clinician's goals for intervention and the weekly objectives. These objectives can be explained and strategies for carryover in the home can be provided. Parents also can provide the speech-language pathologist with information concerning the home-language strengths and weaknesses of the child. This important information should be used to develop objectives in a cooperative effort with the special education teacher and other support personnel. This model for intervention provides the child with the opportunity to continue developing communication skills with the family. Such a model also provides the clinician with information about the child's first-language abilities so that English skills can be developed in parallel to what is already known in the home language. Additionally, new information introduced in English in the school environment can be discussed and taught in the home language with the parents cooperation and participation. For Ernesto, both English and Spanish must be used to develop his communication skills and language-learning abilities. Using only one language, English, could limit his language development to the weaker receptive language and neglect his strength in Spanish comprehension. This language strength, Spanish comprehension, could be used to develop academic language through the curriculum and, possibly, to increase the efficiency of Ernesto's acquisition of English.

FAMILY INVOLVEMENT IN INTERVENTION

Enhancing existing parent intervention programs may be an appropriate way to facilitate family involvement in language intervention programs. However, clinicians should be aware that the majority of parent training programs are based on research with mainstream English-speaking families. Research involving parents of children from multicultural populations with language impairments is nonexistent. Therefore, clinicians should modify existing parent intervention programs to meet the needs of families from culturally diverse groups.

Gutierrez and Saneroff (1990) and Gutierrez, Saneroff, and Krarer (1988) studied the belief systems and conceptualizations of child development of Mexican, Mexican-American, and Anglo mothers. They determined that the more the mother accepts the mainstream values related to child-rearing and culture, the more complex were her explanations of child development. Therefore, the educational level and acculturation of families must be considered when implementing parent training programs. A parent who is acculturated and has a high school education may accept readily the teaching role of many intervention programs. In contrast, the unacculturated and less educated parent may find this role uncomfortable and unfamiliar and may be less likely to participate actively in the program.

Developing rapport with a parent from a background that is culturally and linguistically different from the clinician's is the first step in increasing the chances of parent involvement. Juarez (1993) made three suggestions for establishing rapport. 1) Make the parent feel important. Parents may feel uneasy about visiting the clinician and school; therefore, conversations should be free of technical jargon that may confuse or alienate them. 2) Invite parents to visit periodically so that they are not called only when there is a problem. 3) Focus on the issue during conferences and do not "attack" the child, because the parent may interpret this to be an affront to the whole family. Each of these suggestions is appropriate for all families regardless of their cultural backgrounds, but for families from diverse linguistic and cultural backgrounds, these suggestions become more difficult to operationalize. Developing rapport takes time and effort and is not established immediately.

Communication with families is the foundation of an effective family intervention program. Every culture has values and mores concerning the "do's" and "don'ts" of communication between the family and professional. These cross-cultural differences in communication and interactional expectations need to be explored by speech-language pathologists as they work with culturally and linguistically diverse groups. Montecel et al. (1993) discussed several suggestions that may enhance communication with Hispanic parents. These researchers suggested that telephone contact and home visits are important in encouraging family participation in intervention. Among Hispanic families, the extended family may include religious leaders and neighbors. Montecel et al. suggested that these individuals should be included in attempts to communicate with the family. These individuals can deliver messages, interpret information from the school, or encourage the family to participate actively in the intervention program.

Parents feel more comfortable if they know that the agency or school they contact has someone who speaks their language. Ensuring that parents can call the school or agency will enhance communication. Written messages should be sent in English and the home language because, although some families may not have native language literacy, older children or friends may be able to read notes written in English and interpret these to the parents. Montecel et al. (1993) stated that meetings should not be announced; rather, families should be invited to participate. Formality is necessary and viewed as appropriate etiquette among parents from many Hispanic groups (i.e., Cuban, Mexican, Puerto Rican). Finally, parents may be sensitive concerning the language they use. They are aware that there is a standard language, and class distinctions are drawn in many societies by the type or dialect of the language a person speaks. Therefore, parents are aware if an interpreter or speaker depreciates them for speaking a nonstandard form of a language.

Parents may have perceptions of their own roles in the intervention program that differ from those of mainstream English-speaking parents. Therefore, communicating with parents requires efforts in searching for mechanisms to convey information successfully. Parents need sufficient information and instruction to participate in decision making. This may involve multiple presentations of goals and objectives through informational workshops. Because the clinic or school may appear distant or foreign to many of these parents, it is important that they be able to ask questions in a nonthreatening atmosphere, and they may need to be invited to participate in order to feel free to visit the school or clinic. They may need to be encouraged to become aides in the classroom or intervention session. Parents should receive many opportunities for learning techniques to help their children practice new skills (New Mexico State Department of Education, 1978). An aggressive education program is needed that introduces the rationale for parent training, early intervention, language facilitation, and other concepts that may be unfamiliar to the families (Neiderhauser, 1989).

The child's culture, clinician–child interactions, language of instruction, and family involvement are key issues that must be addressed each time that a child from a culturally and/or linguistically distinct population enters the clinic for language intervention. In contrast to Ernesto's example, which emphasized coordination of services among professionals within the school, the following is an illustration of a clinician's exploration of a family's culture in order to assist the family to facilitate the language development of their preschooler.

Case Example

Lee was a 3-year-old Chinese-American female whose parents were well-educated, bilingual immigrants. The home language was a dialect of Chinese, and there was a community of Chinese immigrants who served as an extended family. The parents recognized that their daughter was not developing the home language in a manner comparable to that of other children in their community. Therefore, the parents brought Lee to a neighborhood school for screening. The school speech-language pathologist recommended that Lee enter the English-only preschool classroom for children with language impairments and also suggested that the parents speak only English to her child. The parents were concerned that Lee would not learn Chinese and that their own English would not be adequate for her English-language development.

The family was seen at a university clinic in order to obtain a second opinion. The parents were advised that the learning of two languages simultaneously by their child with a language delay was possible. The parents agreed to enroll the child in two weekly 1-hour sessions that emphasized parent training. Additionally, Lee was enrolled in the preschool classroom for children with language impairments, where her mother volunteered daily.

The parent program developed for this family included videotaping common interactions in the clinic that the mother identified as daily routine activities in the home. These events were videotaped in the first 15 minutes or so of the session. The clinician and the mother then reviewed the videotape to identify what Lee was understanding and what she was expressing in the home language. The mother's interaction patterns, such as imitation, repetition of utterances, and expansions, were identified. Those facilitative interactions that appeared to be frequent occurrences were encouraged and practiced in the home environment during other activities. Specific vocabulary and semantic relations that the mother believed were important for the child to know were identified during conferences and included in these videotaped sessions. The mother also was encouraged to teach activities that were introduced in the preschool classroom, although this was not monitored. Therefore, Lee was being exposed to the classroom curriculum in the home language as well as in English. The primary focus of this intervention was to discover those form, content, and use categories that were of cultural and linguistic significance to this particular family and use these in intervention. Additionally, feedback and suggestions on the mother–child interactions were provided through videotaped sessions.

After 6 months of intervention, Lee had expanded her receptive and expressive skills in the home language, and she also had developed a rudimentary ability in English. One year after intervention was terminated, the mother reported that Lee was functioning at near-comparable levels to other children of her age and background, and she was expressing herself in English in her private preschool classroom. The parents' involvement in intervention made this a success story. What must be emphasized is that the objectives, materials, and procedures were developed from interviews with the parents. The family's culture, experiences, expectations, and desires were significant variables included in the language intervention plan.

CONCLUSION

This chapter has reviewed four critical aspects of intervention with children from culturally and linguistically diverse backgrounds: 1) culture, 2) clinician–child interactions, 3) language of intervention, and 4) parent involvement. For each of these aspects, there is limited research to support the clinical experiences that many master clinicians advocate. Empirical research is needed to support and/or to refute clinical intuitions, but the individual differences of children always leave the clinician with the final decision of whether to modify the intervention to meet the needs of the child.

Most of what is known about cultures and language groups other than our own comes from other professional fields such as bilingual education, second language acquisition, anthropology, sociology, and linguistics. We know very little about what modifications in the intervention program are necessary for children from other cultures and language groups. It is not known if these modifications will be effective and beneficial to these children. Therefore, intervention efficacy research is needed in all areas of language intervention, from early intervention and parent programs to issues that involve school-age children both in and out of the classroom. Language intervention with individuals from culturally and linguistically different backgrounds is a formidable assignment that involves many issues that may compromise the effectiveness of the intervention plan. The state of the art depends upon the creative research of clinicians and researchers, as well as on their willingness to understand cultural and linguistic perspectives that differ from their own.

REFERENCES

Baetens Beardsmore, H. (1986). *Bilingualism: Basic principles.* San Diego: College Hill Press.

Barclay, L.K. (1983). Using Spanish as the language of instruction with Mexican-American Head Start children: A reevaluation using meta-analysis. *Perceptual and Motor Skills, 56,* 359–366.

Birdwhistell, R. (1970). *Kinesics and context.* Philadelphia: University of Pennsylvania Press.

Blount, B. (1982). Culture and the language of socialization: Parental speech. In D.A. Wagner & H.W. Stevensen (Eds.), *Cultural perspectives on child development* (pp. 54–76). New York: W. H. Freeman.

Bruck, M. (1982). Language impaired children's performance in an additive bilingual education program. *Applied Psycholinguistics, 3,* 45–60.

Bruck, M. (1985a). Consequences of transfer out of early French immersion programs. *Applied Psycholinguistics, 6,* 101–120.

Bruck, M. (1985b). Predictors of transfer out of early French immersion programs. *Applied Psycholinguistics, 6,* 39–61.

Fradd, S.H. (1987). The changing focus of bilingual education. In S.H. Fradd & W.J. Tikunoff (Eds.), *Bilingual education and bilingual special education: A guide for administrators* (pp. 1–44). Boston: College-Hill Press.

Garcia Coll, C.T. (1990). Developmental outcome of minority infants: A process-oriented look into our beginnings. *Child Development, 61,* 270–289.

Grosjean, F. (1982). *Life with two languages: An introduction to bilingualism.* Cambridge, MA: Harvard University Press.

Gutierrez, J., & Saneroff, A. (1990). Determinants of complexity in Mexican-American and Anglo-American mothers' conceptions of child development. *Child Development,* 384–394.

Gutierrez, J., Saneroff, A., & Krarer, B.M. (1988). Acculturation and SES effects on Mexican-American parents' concepts of development. *Child Development,* 250–255.

Hakuta, K. (1986). *Mirror of language: The debate on bilingualism.* New York: Basic Books.

Harris, G. (1986). Barriers to the delivery of speech, language, and hearing services to Native Americans. In O. Taylor (Ed.), *Nature of communication disorders in culturally and linguistically diverse populations* (pp. 219–236). San Diego: College-Hill Press.

Heath, S.B. (1986). Social cultural contexts of language development. In *Social and cultural factors in schooling language minority students* (pp. 143–186). Los Angeles: Bilingual Education Office, California State Department of Education.

Juarez, M. (1983). Assessment and treatment of minority language-handicapped children: The role of the monolingual speech-language pathologist. *Topics in Language Disorders, 3,* 57–65.

Juarez, M. (1993, October). *Issues in family intervention.* Paper presented at "Bilingualism: What Every Clinician Needs to Know," American Speech-Language-Hearing Association, Washington, DC.

Kayser, H. (1985). *A study of speech language pathologists and their Mexican-American language disordered caseloads.* Unpublished doctoral dissertation, New Mexico State University, Las Cruces.

Kayser, H. (1989, November). *Communicative strategies of Anglo and Hispanic clinicians with Hispanic preschoolers.* Paper presented at the American Speech-Language-Hearing Association annual onvention, St. Louis, MO.

Kayser, H. (1993). Hispanic cultures. In D. Battle (Ed.), *Communication disorders in multicultural populations* (pp. 114–157). Boston: Andover Medical Publishers.

Kiernan, B., & Swisher, L. (1990). The initial learning of novel English words: Two single-subject experiments with minority-language children. *Journal of Speech and Hearing Research, 33,* 707–716.

Krashen, S. (1981). *Second language acquisition and second language learning.* Oxford: Pergamon.

Lambert, W.E., & Tucker, G.R. (1972). *Bilingual education of children: The St. Lambert experiment.* Rowley MA: Newbury House.

Lau v. Nichols. (1974). 414 U. S. 563, 39L Ed 2d 1, 94 S Ct. 786.

McLaughlin, B. (1985). *Second-language acquisition in childhood: Vol. 2. School-age children.* Hillsdale NJ: Lawrence Erlbaum Associates.

Montecel, M.R., Gallagher, A., Montemayor, A., Villareal, A., Adame-Reyna, N., & Supik, J.P. (1993). *Hispanic families as valued partners: An educator's guide.* San Antonio, TX: Intercultural Development Research Associates.

Neiderhauser, V.P. (1989). Health care of immigrant children: Incorporating culture into practice. *Pediatric Nursing, 15,* 569–574.

New Mexico State Department of Education. (1978). *State of New Mexico Title 1 Advisory Committee: A postion paper on parental involvement.* Santa Fe: Author.

Ortiz, A.A. (1984, Spring). Choosing the language of instruction for exceptional bilingual children. *Teaching Exceptional Children,* 208–212.

Ortiz, A.A., Garcia, S.B., Wheeler, D.S., & Maldonado-Colon, E. (1986). *Characteristics of limited English-proficient Hispanic students served in programs for the speech and language handicapped: Implications policy, practice, and research.* Austin: Handicapped Minority Research Institute on Language Proficiency, University of Texas.

Owens, R.E. (1988). *Language development: An introduction.* Columbus OH: Charles E. Merrill.

Pennycook, A. (1985). Actions speak louder than words: Paralanguage, communication and education. *TESOL Quarterly, 19,* 259–82.

Perozzi, J.A. (1985). A pilot study of language facilitation for bilingual, language handicapped children: Theoretical and intervention implications. *Journal of Speech and Hearing Disorders, 50,* 403–406.

Perozzi, J.A., & Chavez-Sanchez, M.L. (1992, October). The effect of instruction in L1 on receptive acquisition of L2 for bilingual children with language delay. *Language, Speech, and Hearing Services in Schools, 23,* 348–352.

Prutting, C., Bagshaw, N., & Goldstein, H. (1978). Clinician–child discourse: Some preliminary questions. *Journal of Speech and Hearing Disorders, 43,* 123–139.

Saville-Troike, M. (1986). Anthropological considerations in the study of communication. In O. Taylor (Ed.), *Nature of communication disorders in culturally and linguistically diverse populations* (pp. 47–72). San Diego: College-Hill Press.

Scudder, R., & Holmskog, S. (1989). *Spanish-speaking children's repairs during conversation with an Anglo adult.* Unpublished manuscript.

Swain, M., & Barik, H. (1978). Bilingual education in Canada: French and English. In B. Spolsky & R.L. Cooper (Eds.), *Case studies in bilingual education.* Rowley MA: Newbury House.

Taylor, O. (Ed.). (1986). *Nature of communication disorders in culturally and linguistically diverse populations.* San Diego: College-Hill Press.

Valdes, G. (1986, March). *Brothers and sisters: A closer look at the development of "cooperative" social orientation in Mexican-American children.* Paper presented at the California Association of School Psychologists Annual Convention, Oakland.

12

Classroom-Based and Consultative Service Delivery Models for Language Intervention

Frank M. Cirrin and Sharon G. Penner

Every day, Speech-Language Pathologists working in schools are faced with many decisions about how best to facilitate the language and learning skills of students with language impairment. One of the most important decisions, and one of the most difficult, is choosing the manner or model through which language intervention services are delivered. A service delivery model is more than an instructional method or a particular set of materials. A service delivery model can be conceptualized as an organized configuration of resources aimed at achieving a particular educational goal (Bennett, 1988). The resources, or variables, that are combined to create a service delivery model include facilities, personnel, materials, and the specific instructional or intervention procedure(s) to be used, as well as the schedule for provision of services. There are two other critical variables that make up a service delivery model, and these are the primary focus of the present chapter. These variables are the *setting(s)* in which intervention services will be delivered and the *direct and indirect role(s)* that service providers assume as they deliver language intervention to students with language impairments.

Traditionally, speech-language pathologists have used pullout rooms most frequently as contexts for providing language intervention services in schools. By "pullout rooms" we mean settings outside the regular or special education classroom where students receive most instruction. This practice has been prevalent for several reasons. First, services to students with language impairments have evolved out of a "speech clinic" model, where therapeutic interventions were provided in special rooms, either to individual children or to children in small groups (Miller, 1989). Second, the pullout setting provides certain advantages over the classroom with regard to the control that the speech-language pathologist can exert over communication contexts (Nelson, 1993). For example, auditory and visual distractions can be controlled in pullout rooms, and activities can be easily organized so that children have more opportunities to take turns and produce specific linguistic targets. Third, language and language problems often have been conceptualized in relatively simple fashion as being discrete linguistic units such as vocabulary or length or type of sentences (Damico, 1988; Miller, 1989), with relatively little attention paid to the relationship between language and learning in school contexts. This simplistic view of language, in combination with the history of clinic-based services in schools and the ability to control context, have contributed to the prevalence of pullout settings for the delivery of language intervention (see Miller, 1989, for a discussion of the background for language services in schools).

Recently, however, speech-language pathologists in schools throughout the country have been engaged in determined efforts to develop and implement alternative models for delivering language intervention services to students with language impairments *in their classrooms* (e.g., Achilles, Yates, & Freese, 1991; Borsch & Oaks, 1992; Ferguson, 1991, 1992a: Magnotta, 1991; Montgomery, 1992: Moore-Brown, 1991; Nelson, 1989; Roller, Rodriquez, Warner, & Lindahl, 1992: Silliman & Wilkinson, 1991). The impetus for developing alternative service models for language intervention has come from four sources: 1) growing evidence and concern regarding the efficacy of providing language intervention in pullout settings (Damico, 1988; Simon, 1987b), including concerns about students' lack of generalization of new skills to daily communication situations (Fey, 1986, 1988; Johnston, 1988), the reduced naturalness of pullout settings (Nelson, 1990), and negative effects of removing children with disabilities from the classroom (Andersen & Nelson, 1988); 2) holistic views of language and literacy that emphasize the role that language plays in learning and classroom success (Bashir, 1989; Wallach & Miller, 1988); 3) the emphasis and impact of collaboration in business and industry (Hoskins, 1990; Wiig, Secord, & Wiig, 1990); and 4) recent policy changes that have taken place in special education at the national, state, and local levels. With respect to this last factor, educators, researchers, and policymakers have called for an increase in the extent to which children with mild disabilities are served in general education settings (e.g., Biklen & Zollers, 1986; Reynolds, Wang, & Walberg, 1987; Will, 1986).

Alternative service delivery systems for students with language impairments include a variety of models that collectively have come to be labeled "classroom-based" and/or "collaborative" programs. Although different models each have their unique characteristics, all have the goal of moving the *setting* of language intervention from a separate therapy room into the student's ongoing educational experiences (Miller, 1989). In addition to an alternative, more naturalistic setting, these models also seek to expand the traditional, direct service *provider role* of the speech-language pathologist or language specialist. Miller (1989) has described a number of provider roles and formats that allow speech-language pathologists in schools to provide language intervention to students in general and special education classroom settings. For example, these roles include providing direct language intervention to individuals or to small groups of students in their classrooms (e.g., Norris, 1989), team teaching with general and special education classroom teachers on lessons that integrate language intervention targets into the regular curriculum (e. g., Brandel, 1992; Buttrill, Niizawa, Biemer, Takahashi, & Hearn, 1989; Christensen & Luckett, 1990; Despain & Simon, 1987; Dodge & Mallard, 1992; Ferguson, 1992b; Nelson, 1981; Norris & Hoffman, 1990, 1993, Simon, 1987b), and consulting with classroom teachers to provide indirect language intervention services to students (e.g., Creaghead, 1990; Damico, 1987; Damico & Nye, 1990: Dyer, Williams, & Luce, 1991; Gruenewald & Pollak, 1990; Marvin, 1987; Silliman, Wilkinson, Belkin & Hoffman, 1991; Simon, 1987b). Other variations of classroom-based and consultative models for delivering language intervention services in schools have been described also (e.g., American Speech-Language-Hearing Association [ASHA], 1991, 1993; Frassinelli, Superior, & Meyers, 1983; Marvin, 1987, 1990; Simon, 1987b; Simon & Myrold-Gunyuz, 1990).

The purpose of this chapter is to address selected critical questions about the use of alternative models to deliver language intervention in classroom settings to students with language impairments. We begin by briefly describing two main types of classroom-based service delivery models: classroom-based direct services and indirect consultation. We then review selected published research on outcomes of these two types of service delivery models as it pertains to children with language impairments and to children with learning and other disabilities. Finally, we discuss implications of this research for the choice of service delivery models from a continuum of service options that includes the use of pullout and classroom settings and direct and indirect provider roles.

TYPES OF CLASSROOM-BASED MODELS

Classroom-Based Direct Services

In classroom-based direct service delivery models, the emphasis is on the speech-language pathologist providing some regularly scheduled *direct* intervention services to students within the classroom. Intervention is provided in the natural classroom environment in order to integrate communication goals with the curriculum and to allow for collaboration with teachers. Direct service components of classroom-based models may include team teaching to the entire class by the speech-language pathologist and the regular and/or special education teacher, as well as the speech-language pathologist working in the classroom with individual students and/or groups of students with similar goals or curriculum expectations (ASHA, 1993). In addition, many language intervention programs implemented in classroom settings are based on important aspects of the curriculum content and classroom learning activities, such as students' reading or science textbooks or classroom communication rules and expectations. Thus, the regular or special education curriculum is viewed as a relevant context for determining a student's communication intervention needs and goals, for designing intervention activities, and for selecting and modifying materials, as well as for monitoring student progress (Nelson, 1990).

A representative example of a language intervention program designed to be implemented directly in the classroom may help illustrate some of the key concepts underlying this service provider role. Norris (1989) described a method termed Communicative Reading Strategies (CRS), which uses written text as a basis for direct language intervention provided in the regular classroom setting. In this method, the target child's small reading group within the regular classroom is used as a naturally occurring context for intervention. The group provides a social context in which information read by one child is viewed as communication directed to the other group members, who in turn may comment, ask for clarification, reiterate the information, or in other ways acknowledge the information that was exchanged. During the small group session, the clinician uses a variety of procedures to help the students interpret and comprehend the text. The student with a language impairment communicates the information by reading the relevant text to the group. The clinician listens for word miscues, poor intonation, or other indications that the child is continuing to experience difficulty with the language. Feedback is provided to the child in the form of acknowledgments and requests for clarification or an extension of an idea. This feedback serves as a natural consequence to the child based on what he or she communicated to the group. With this intervention procedure, the clinician provides direct service in the classroom by modifying a typical, already existing learning activity—small-group reading instruction.

Indirect Consultation Services

The service provider role for speech-language pathologists that is currently receiving much attention is that of consultant. Models using consultation methodologies are *indirect* in that the clinician interacts primarily with a client's care providers (consultees) rather than directly with the client. Service is delivered by a consultant to a client indirectly through a consultee. When children are the clients, the consultees are usually teachers and/or parents. In school settings, the consultants are typically specialists such as speech-language pathologists or special education/resource teachers.

Consultant roles may be divided into two main types: collaborative and expert models (see Frassinelli et al., 1983, and Marvin, 1987, 1990, for discussions of consultative services in speech-language pathology, and Idol, 1989, for a review of types of consultation models used in schools). *Collaborative consultation* models are those in which the speech-language pathologist and regular and/or special education teachers (and parents) voluntarily work together to produce solutions that are different from those that individual team members would have produced independently (Idol, Paolucci-Whitcomb, & Nevin, 1986). A major principle of this model is that shared decision making regarding the needs of students results in better solutions than decisions made by one person.

Therefore, within this model, the speech-language pathologist, educators, and parents share in developing goals, implementing programs, evaluating results, and making program revisions (ASHA, 1991). Many collaborative consultation models described in the literature on language intervention also include some direct classroom-based services provided jointly by the clinician and the classroom teacher (e.g., Silliman & Wilkinson, 1991). Another principle is that collaborative consultation can help teachers deal effectively with a targeted student's problems and avoid similar student problems that may arise in the future (Marvin, 1990).

An example of collaborative consultation was described by Silliman et al. (1991). A third-grade teacher volunteered to work with a speech-language clinician to learn more about a particular student's language-learning difficulties and how instruction for this student could be more effective. Initially, weekly meetings were held in which the clinician's and teacher's observations about the student's language and learning styles were jointly reviewed, possible language targets were identified, and current and potential teaching strategies were mutually evaluated in the context of the curriculum. The student was included in small-group and whole-class language lessons taught by the speech-language pathologist that were designed to encourage the teacher to join in and observe. As the teacher developed observational skills relative to student language-learning difficulties, the teacher and the clinician jointly prepared lessons. Over a 2-year period, the teacher became more independent in implementing language-based teaching strategies and began to transfer these new skills to other curriculum areas. For example, she learned to modify her own teaching discourse throughout the school day as she observed students who appeared to have difficulty with aspects of language.

Expert consultation models are those in which the consultant provides unidirectional services, including recommendations to the individuals responsible for implementing them. The expert consultant may: 1) serve as a short-term specialist to carry out assessment and trial intervention, which then forms the basis of recommendations to other service providers; 2) serve as a diagnostician, performing assessments that lead to intervention recommendations; and 3) serve as an information provider to those who ultimately will deliver intervention services (Marvin, 1987).

An example of a speech-language pathologist serving as an expert consultant is provided by Fujiki and Brinton (1984), who described the content of a consultative program designed to complement a child's language intervention program. Through inservice presentations, small group decisions, and individual conferences with teachers, the speech-language pathologist provides information on the nature of language and its relationship to academic success, as well as on the target child's specific language strengths and weaknesses. This background information is followed by demonstration teaching and specific recommendations for talking with children (e.g., the use of modeling and expansion techniques) and integrating language into the classroom curricula, as well as by specific activities that might be utilized by the classroom teacher to facilitate language learning with the student (e.g., sentence completion tasks, retelling stories). Expert consultation may include training teachers to monitor progress of both students (clients) and their own (consultee) target behaviors.

Presumed Advantages of Classroom-Based Service Delivery Models

The examples of classroom-based direct and indirect consultative delivery models described above are representative of a large number of program descriptions and opinion-based articles on classroom language models. These opinion-based papers, and a handful of empirical studies, reveal a strong consensus among authors as to the presumed advantages of these models. There are five areas in which there is almost universal agreement as to why these alternative models should be effective for delivering language intervention. It is important to realize that, while the advantages of classroom-based models are often stated as facts, most of these assumptions have not been tested adequately. Thus, these assumptions are more accurately viewed as hypotheses about the potential advantages of providing language intervention in classroom contexts.

Relevance of Language Goals

Classroom-based services may allow the speech-language clinician to better address the language skills that the child needs for understanding and responding to instructional content and for participating in teacher–student and student–student interactions that support learning. The natural learning context of the classroom may provide rich opportunities for developing language form, content, and use in both spoken and written language formats. The implementation of language intervention in the classroom may provide the context that enables students to see the relationship between language skills and learning strategies and their actual use in daily learning situations (Nelson, 1990). The integration of language intervention with general learning processes in the classroom also may facilitate a student's academic performance, given the interrelationship between language deficits, academic failure, and the role language proficiency plays in the educational process (Bashir, 1989; Dudley-Marling, 1987; Fey, Catts, & Larrivee, chap. 1, this volume; Gillam, McFadden, & van Kleeck, chap. 6, this volume; Miller, 1989; Nelson, 1981, 1989; Scott, chap. 5, this volume; Wallach & Miller, 1988).

Generalization to Natural Contexts

Conducting language intervention in the classroom environment may result in better generalization of newly learned communication skills to that and other educational environments than might occur with children receiving pullout intervention (Despain & Simon, 1987; Frassinelli et al., 1983; Hughes, 1989; Marvin, 1987; Miller, 1989; Nelson, 1990; Wilcox, Kouri, & Caswell, 1991).

Pullout contexts may be so different from the child's natural environments that newly learned skills do not transfer to the classroom. Natural reinforcement and consequences that encourage generalization of new skills may be facilitated when language intervention is incorporated into the classroom.

Frequency of Intervention

Consultative and classroom-based models may allow increased opportunities for educational personnel other than speech-language clinicians to become effective intervention agents (Damico, 1987; Marvin, 1987). When intervention is provided by clinicians in the classroom, their actions can serve as models for intervention strategies that teachers can use for facilitating language within the classroom. Therefore, a student might benefit from language intervention procedures throughout the day rather than only during scheduled pullout treatment sessions (Wilcox et al., 1991). Classroom contexts also have potential to provide children with numerous models of targeted language behaviors from adults and typical language peers in daily social and learning situations (Damico, 1987; Fey et al., chap. 1, this volume; Marvin, 1987; Miller, 1989; Wilcox et al., 1991; Windsor, chap. 8, this volume).

Alleviating Negative Effects of Pullout Models

When students are served exclusively in pullout settings, they may miss segments of the curriculum and be held responsible for the work that is missed in their general education classrooms. Consultation and classroom-based language services do not regularly remove students from their classrooms to receive language intervention, thus potential negative effects may be avoided (Anderson & Nelson, 1988; Christensen & Luckett, 1990; Damico, 1988; Despain & Simon, 1987; Marvin, 1987; Nelson, 1990; Simon, 1987b).

Prevention of Communication Problems

Traditional pullout intervention models, by definition, focus only on students already identified as having communication disabilities. Classroom-based services, however, may have potential to help teachers identify student communication problems, plan and implement solutions, and adapt teacher language and the language of the curriculum to meet individual student needs. Thus, the use of these models may have positive effects on students who are at risk for language and learning problems, but who either are not eligible to receive special education services or who have not been formally identified as having language impairments (Frassinelli et al., 1983).

Prevalence of Classroom-Based Language Intervention Models in the Schools

Based on the large number of recent articles and papers advocating the use of classroom-based service delivery models for language intervention, it would be reasonable to assume that a large number of speech-language pathologists working in the schools are using these alternative models with students with language impairments. Data supporting this assumption, however, are not widely available. Table 1 presents data on use of service delivery models from a random sample of licensed speech-language pathologists working in schools in Minnesota (Cirrin & Peters, 1992). Classroom-based direct and/or indirect consultative models were reported as used for almost one fourth of the students served, while direct intervention in a traditional pullout model was used for almost two thirds of the students with speech-language individualized education programs (IEPs).

These data were reported across areas of disorder (e.g., articulation, language, voice, fluency) and should not be generalized beyond the specific state where they were collected. The data provide some limited support, however, for the suggestion that school speech-language clinicians are attempting to provide classroom-based services to a substantial percentage of their students, although the majority of students with communication problems continue to be served in pullout settings. There are a number of factors that might influence whether classroom-based, collaborative, or consultative service delivery models are more widely implemented in a particular school, school district, or state. Some factors that have been proposed include administrative support (Goodin & Mehollin, 1990; Montgomery, 1990), collaborative and consultative competencies and beliefs of special educators (Damico, 1987; Friend & Cook, 1990; Marvin 1987), and state and local policies on consultation and collaboration in special education (West & Brown, 1987). This is an important area for future study.

Table 1. Students with speech-language IEPs who are served by various service delivery models (Cirrin & Peters, 1992[a])

Service delivery model	Percentage of students receiving service[b]
Direct intervention by speech-language pathologist with individual students or small groups in a general or special education classroom	5
Collaboration between speech-language pathologist and teacher to provide direct intervention in a general or special education classroom (including team teaching)	24
Indirect consultation services by a speech-language pathologist to general and/or special education teachers	12
Direct intervention by speech-language pathologist with individual students or small groups in a pullout room	64
Other (e.g., home based, community based)	8

[a]300 surveys were mailed to a random sample of school-based speech-language pathologists licensed in Minnesota during the 1992–1993 school year, and 209 were returned and used in this analysis.

[b]Students served by more than one type of service delivery model are counted in each category. For this reason the percentages do not equal 100%.

Prevalence data are a measure of frequency of use and, as such, do not constitute direct evidence supporting the effectiveness of classroom-based models over pullout models. In the next two sections, we first review available evidence on the effectiveness of classroom-based direct language intervention and then on indirect consultative service delivery models for language intervention with school-age students.

CLASSROOM-BASED DIRECT LANGUAGE INTERVENTION

Evidence from Studies with Students with Language Problems

Is there any evidence that the targeted language abilities of students with language impairments improve when direct intervention services are implemented in classroom settings? Although models that include direct classroom-based language services are receiving a great deal of attention, we are not aware of any experimental or quasi-experimental studies that support their general effectiveness as service delivery models for school-age children with language impairments (see Fey & Cleave, 1990, for a discussion of levels of effectiveness in efficacy research).

The available literature on school-age children is limited to anecdotal reports of student outcomes when direct services were provided through a variety of classroom-based models (e.g., Achilles et al., 1991; Buttrill et al., 1989; Christensen & Luckett, 1990; Dodge & Mallard, 1992; Magnotta, 1991; Roller et al., 1992). For example, Despain and Simon (1987) placed junior high–school students who were at risk for language and learning problems in special sections of science, social studies, and English. Teachers in these sections incorporated communication and study skills into the course content. In addition, the speech-language pathologist provided direct instruction in classroom communication skills on a weekly basis to the whole class. After one year, pre- and post-assessments revealed "modest average gains" for participating students on standardized reading tests and on curriculum-based measures of reading, vocabulary, and selected "classroom communication skills" (as measured by the Classroom Communication Screening Procedure for Early Adolescents, Simon, 1987a). Similarly, Andersen and Nelson (1988) placed junior high–school students with language and learning disabilities into a "language classroom" offered in a daily, 1-hour class period taught by the speech-language pathologist. Programming focused on strategies that included studying and test-taking, textbook analysis, metalinguistic awareness, classroom prag-matics, and syntactic and morphological skills. After 3 years, all five students who were enrolled in the program achieved C grades in regular education English classes, and evidenced modest gains on standardized reading tests. These authors also reported that both the students' attitudes towards school and the general education teachers' attitudes toward these students had changed from negative to positive.

These reports of improvements in the classroom language and reading skills of school-age children with language impairments are encouraging and may lend some very preliminary support to the hypothesis that academic performance (e.g., reading achievement) of students with language impairments can be influenced positively by direct instruction on related language skills. However, the anecdotal nature of the data does not constitute strong empirical support for the efficacy of providing language services in classrooms. Also, without an experimental or quasi-experimental design, it is impossible to sort out which service delivery variables, if any, were related to the reported increases in student outcomes.

To our knowledge, the only direct comparison between pullout (individual) and classroom settings for direct language intervention is a recent study with preschool children by Wilcox et al. (1991). This study is unique in that the authors used a group experimental design to investigate the role of setting directly, while controlling other confounding variables including intervention procedures and intervention goals. Twenty children with language impairments, ages 20–47 months, were assigned randomly to classroom and individual pullout intervention programs. The intervention goal for each child was to establish productive use of at least 10 new words, which were selected for each individual for ease of learning. All children were seen twice weekly for a total of 24 individual or classroom intervention sessions.

Intervention in both settings was based on an interactive modeling procedure that focused on learning language skills within the context of typical, natural, interpersonal interactions. Through this procedure, all children were exposed to a high density of lexical models, in a conversational format embedded into ongoing activities. Approximate 15 models for each target word were provided during each individual or classroom session. Intervention in the classroom was provided jointly by an early childhood special educator and a speech-language pathologist. The classroom contained both typically developing peers and peers with moderate to severe disabilities.

The primary measure of children's progress in intervention was the number of target words that were used productively in spontaneous speech. Data sampled in the two respective treatment settings showed that children in the classroom condition demonstrated target word use that was equal to that of children in the individual intervention condition, indicating that children made progress toward their goals in both settings. There were no differences in the average number of clinician models that were required before a child demonstrated productive use of target words in intervention. A fair amount of individual variation was observed, including three children (one in the classroom condition and two in the individual pullout condition) who demonstrated no productive target word use when sampled in either the treatment context or in their homes. In general, when data sampled in the treatment contexts were considered, the classroom-based lexical training appeared to be as effective as that provided in individual treatment.

Of equal importance, the authors collected generalization data by gathering mother–child language samples in the children's homes immediately following the conclusion of intervention. When these generalization data were examined (although no statistical test was applied to this comparison), classroom learners appeared to demonstrate more productive use of target words in the home setting than did children in the individual intervention condition. Wilcox et al. (1991) suggested several reasons for the differences they observed between the classroom and individual intervention settings. One difference was that children in the classroom condition participated in a broader range of activities (including snack time, circle time, story time, and free play) than did children in the individual intervention condition, who had only a free-play activity in which learning could take place. The authors raised the possibility that using the interactive modeling procedure in these ongoing classroom activities provided more diverse contexts in which to observe and use target words. This, in turn, may have facilitated the production of target words in those home activities that shared a degree of similarity to the classroom activities (e.g., bedtime story). Moreover, the classroom condition had more conversational partners for children than the individual intervention condition. Wilcox et al. (1991) reported that in the classroom setting, peers with age-appropriate language abilities participated in the same activities as the children with language impairments and often produced the children's target words. The children in the classroom may have been exposed to productions and models of the target words by diverse conversational partners, including both adults and peers. Several other studies with preschool children provide some limited support for the effectiveness of direct language instruction in a classroom setting (Cole & Dale, 1986; Yoder, Kaiser, & Alpert, 1991).

Conclusions based on these findings should be restricted to preschool children in need of lexical training, and generalization of these findings beyond this population (and to other language intervention procedures or language goals) is premature at this point. Thus, it cannot be concluded on the basis of these studies that direct intervention in a classroom setting is more effective than individual intervention in a pullout setting for children with language impairments in general. Nevertheless, the findings of Wilcox et al. (1991) illustrate one of several possible interactions that can take place between service delivery variables. In this case, a specific direct language intervention procedure (interactive modeling) and a specific language target (production of new vocabulary) appeared to interact with aspects of *setting* to produce differential intervention effects when generalization data were considered. Two aspects of the classroom setting (number of activities and number of conversational partners) may have allowed the lexical gains resulting from intervention in the classroom to be generalized to another naturalistic context (home). It seems plausible, given these results, that direct language intervention implemented in a classroom setting might be effective at increasing *school-age students'* use of certain communication skills. For example, it would be useful to know whether certain aspects of a classroom setting might facilitate remediation of classroom pragmatic skills (Creaghead &

Tattershall, 1985) such as knowledge of classroom routines, written language formats, and giving and following oral directions in the classroom.

Preschool classroom contexts, like the one used by Wilcox et al. (1991), may be different from elementary or secondary school classrooms in several respects. The biggest difference may be that preschool settings allow sufficient time for children to practice talking in a facilitative context, whereas classroom settings for school-age children may not. We know that children spend much more of their time in regular classrooms listening than talking. It has been estimated that elementary school students spend over 50% of their day listening to teachers talk, and estimates for high school students range as high as 90% (Lindfors, 1987). Therefore, it cannot be assumed that the factors that might lead to optimal language growth (e.g., number of conversational partners) are automatically present in every classroom.

It also might be anticipated that new language behaviors acquired in classroom contexts are long term and that students will continue to develop language skills over time. Further language growth would seem to depend on whether the classroom conditions that facilitated acquisition continue to be present. However, we are not aware of any study that has examined outcomes of classroom service delivery models in sufficient detail to conclude that this assumption is true.

Given the potential advantages of providing language intervention in classroom contexts and the number of authors, educators, and clinicians advocating alternative models, it is likely that attempts to implement classroom-based service delivery models will continue for the foreseeable future. However, we really do not know if their use helps to facilitate the growth of functional communication skills among school-age students with language impairments. This is not because these models have been shown to be ineffective, but because crucial testing of their effects on language use in classroom contexts has not been done.

Evidence from Studies with Students with Reading and Behavior Problems

As we have noted previously, the current emphasis on alternative service delivery models for language intervention is part of the movement in special education to serve children with disabilities in the least restrictive environment. We are aware of very few studies, however, that have examined effects of intervention setting variables on academic and behavioral outcomes for students with disabilities, although there has been considerable research on the efficacy of resource room (pullout) models (see Wiederholt & Chamberlain, 1989, for a critical analysis of resource programs). Several authors have described "collaborative" programs for students with learning disabilities that include some direct reading instruction in the classroom by a special education teacher (Deno, Maruyama, Espin, & Cohen, 1990; Wang & Zollers, 1990; Zigmond & Baker, 1990). For example, Zigmond and Baker (1990) used a time-series design to report on the progress at the end of 1 year of planning (baseline) and 1 year of implementation of a collaborative, classroom-based service delivery model for reading of 13 students with learning disabilities. After receiving instruction for reading in a pull-out resource room setting during the baseline year, these students were returned full time to mainstream classes. Supplemental direct instruction for reading was provided by special education teachers in the general classroom setting. Baseline- and implementation-year comparisons of standard scores for reading on standardized achievement tests were not significantly different. Similarly, there was no difference on curriculum-based measurement data for reading, suggesting that students made minimal progress in both settings.

Several authors (Deno et al., 1990; Wang & Zollers, 1990; Zigmond & Baker, 1990) have asserted that resource (pullout) programs do not produce clear evidence that warrant removing a student from class for remedial reading instruction. Unfortunately, the research designs used in these studies do not allow meaningful comparisons of alternative and traditional service delivery models, and it cannot be concluded that either a pullout (resource room) or a classroom service delivery model is more appropriate. In the case of Zigmond and Baker (1990), it appears that an attempt was made to evaluate outcomes before the alternative program had sufficient time to stabilize. The authors reported that the mainstream environments into which these students were placed had not fully implemented many important elements of their collaborative model, such as adapting reading instruction to a broad range of learning styles and skill levels and making instructional changes on the basis of student progress data. In effect, the program had yet to be delivered. These observations suggest that modifications of critical educational practices by regular classroom teachers may be as important to improved outcomes for students with disabilities as the direct intervention program implemented in the classroom by special education staff. Few studies have examined the basic assumption that providing special education services in the regular classroom can create an environment that facilitates learning for a wide range of students.

Conclusions on the Use of Classroom-Based Direct Service Models

In summary, direct language intervention procedures implemented in classroom settings have not been put to any adequate test to determine their effectiveness in facilitating development of specific language abilities in school-age children. However, evidence from studies with preschool children suggests that classroom-based direct language services are as effective as individual intervention for some intervention goals (Cole & Dale, 1986; Wilcox et al., 1991; Yoder et al., 1991), and that intervention in classroom settings may facilitate generalization of new skills to other natural settings (Wilcox et al., 1991). The limited research on the effectiveness of resource room (pullout) and classroom-based direct services for students with learning disabilities does not reveal the advantage of one model over the other (e.g., Deno et al., 1990), although it appears that modifications of the regular education classroom may be necessary for alternative models to affect student outcomes. In our view, the results of these few studies are sufficiently encouraging to warrant further experimentation and more intensive testing of classroom-based direct language intervention for school-age children, especially in light of the potential advantages of these service delivery models and recent trends in special education.

INDIRECT CONSULTATIVE LANGUAGE INTERVENTION

Evidence from Studies with Students with Language Problems

There is very little empirical research that supports the efficacy of consultation as a service delivery model for school-age children with language impairments. There are many more articles and reports available regarding how it is done (or should be done), in part because so many variables appear to influence consultative service provision. Several studies of children with severe communication disabilities and autism provide some support for the effectiveness of teacher consultation as a service delivery model for language intervention (Dyer et al., 1991; Peck & Schuler, 1983). For example, Dyer et al (1991) used a time-series design to determine effectiveness of an expert consultative program in which the speech-language pathologist trained four special education teachers to use naturalistic communicative intervention strategies in the classroom with eight students with autism. The teacher training program consisted of several stages. The speech-language pathologist: 1) assessed each student's current level of communicative functioning, 2) developed communication goals and short-term objectives that became part of the student's individualized education program (IEP), 3) provided inservice training to teachers on naturalistic intervention procedures (e.g., incidental teaching; see Warren & Kaiser, 1986) and functional communication goals, 4) provided classroom training and modeling of intervention techniques, and 5) provided maintenance and feedback sessions every 2 weeks once teachers met training criteria.

Ten-minute videotaped probes were collected several times a week for 3 months during baseline and intervention phases (classroom and inservice training), and once a month for 3 months during the follow-up phase (maintenance feedback). Data were taken on the number of communication goals exhibited by each child in the classroom and on whether each goal was elicited by the teacher or spontaneously produced without a teacher prompt. All children showed increases in the frequency of elicited communication goals from baseline to intervention, and all children but one maintained increases at the end of the follow-up phase. This suggests that these children were responsive to naturalistic prompts by their teachers in the classroom setting. Five children showed increases in spontaneous communication goals over baseline during the intervention phase, and six showed increases over baseline by the end of the follow-up phase.

This suggests that, in some situations, these students with autism produced targeted communication behaviors appropriately without teacher prompts.

Just as important as the gains made by students, Dyer et al. (1991) presented an in-depth analysis for one student that revealed that teachers increased the frequency of their attempts to elicit target goals (through the use of various naturalistic techniques) almost 25 times over baseline during the intervention phase. Unfortunately, there was a marked reduction in target goals elicited by teachers during subsequent follow-up observations. One factor that may have resulted in the positive effects during intervention was the presence of videotape equipment in the classrooms (Dyer et al., 1991). Once the follow-up phase began and the videotape equipment was removed, the fidelity of the intervention appeared to decrease, and teachers stopped using some of their newly learned skills. Fidelity of intervention refers to the quality, intensity, and consistency with which an intervention is implemented and is an issue that must be considered when using a consultative service delivery model.

Conclusions based on studies with children with autism (e.g., Dyer et al., 1991) must be limited to this population at the present time. Yet these studies provide some evidence that an expert consultation training model can be effective in: 1) increasing the frequency with which special education teachers use naturalistic techniques to elicit target language goals in the classroom, and 2) increasing the frequency with which students with severe disabilities produce both elicited and spontaneous productions of the target goals. However, it is not clear if this type of consultation can produce long-term changes in both teacher and student behaviors. Also, no data were collected to assess generalization of student skills to other contexts such as mealtime. In addition, we still do not know what variables affect the success of consultative models for language intervention in schools. For example, Dyer et al. (1991) used a highly prescriptive expert approach to consultation and teacher training. Collaborative consultation is the model most often recommended for school settings (e.g., Damico, 1987; Friend & Cook, 1990; Idol et al., 1986; Marvin, 1987, 1990; Secord, 1990), yet we have little empirical evidence that this consultation style is effective as a service delivery model for language intervention.

Evidence from Studies with
Students with Reading and Behavior Problems

Consultative services for students with learning disabilities and behavioral disorders are receiving much attention in the special education literature (see recent reviews by Idol, 1989; Kratochwill, Sheridan, & VanSomeren, 1988; West & Idol, 1987). Although there is rapidly growing interest among special educators concerning school consultation, the empirical base for evaluating its impact on teachers and students is limited. Nevertheless, there appear to be initial indications that positive changes at the teacher (consultee) and student (client) levels can result from consultative special education services, and such findings may have implications for how consultative services can be best implemented for students with language impairments. In a comprehensive review of recent studies of consultative intervention effects on students with learning disabilities in schools, Idol (1989) concluded that the existing school consultation research provides at least modest support for the use of consultation for students with learning disabilities. Specifically, in certain cases, consultation appears to result in: 1) decreases in referrals to special education after a number of years of using consultative services, 2) positive teacher attitudes toward consultative services as long as the consultant's recommendations were realistic, 3) student achievement outcomes on standardized tests equal to resource room (pullout) programs, and 4) gains that generalized to other students in the same class as a result of positive changes in teacher effectiveness via consultation. As with all attempts to study efficacy of educational service delivery, general conclusions from these various analyses are limited by several factors. For example, school consultation is exemplified by at least 10 different models of consultation (see West & Idol, 1987), and the efficacy results vary across models. Also, there are a variety of methodological issues that contribute to the difficulty of extending these claims to all students with learning disabilities, including lack of experimental and quasi-experimental designs to evaluate efficacy, inadequate control and description of consultee and consultant characteristics, and lack of follow-up data.

Several studies have compared academic outcomes for special education students receiving consultative versus resource room (pullout) services (Buffmire, 1977; Miller & Sabatino, 1978; Wixson, 1980). These studies found no differences in achievement outcomes when a consulting teacher model was compared with a traditional resource room approach to services. These studies also showed that children with learning disabilities and behavior disorders who received consultative services were subsequently more likely to return to the mainstream without any special education assistance than were children receiving resource services. However, none of these studies randomly assigned students to intervention conditions; instead, students were assigned to resource room or consulting services based on the severity of their problems. Thus, it is probable that students in the consultation conditions had less severe learning and behavior difficulties, which may have contributed to differential outcomes.

A recent study by Schulte, Osborne, and McKinney (1990) improved on these research methods by using an experimental design to compare achievement of elementary-school children identified as having learning disabilities in reading or writing. Students were randomly assigned to one of four models of special education service delivery. One group of students received one period per day of instruction in the resource room; a second group received two periods per day of resource room instruction. A third group received consultative services combined with a limited amount of direct instruction ("consultation + direct") by the special education teacher in the general education classroom. The fourth group of students received consultative services only. Experienced consulting teachers were hired by the project and underwent additional training in consultation. Resource services were provided by district-hired learning disabilities teachers assigned to the participating schools.

In both consultation models, consulting teachers collaborated with classroom teachers to identify instructional and behavioral objectives, developed lesson plans, and met weekly to review plans, procedures and instructional priorities. In the consultation + direct service model, the consulting teacher provided direct instruction in the classroom 1/2 hour per day, 2 or 3 days per week, modifying the regular teacher's lesson plans for the remainder of the class. Modifications included analyzing the lesson and teaching it in smaller steps, monitoring student comprehension, reteaching, reducing the quantity of independent work, using more manipulatives and concrete examples, and teaching student self-monitoring. Resource programs consisted of 45- to 50-minute periods of small-group instruction, either 4 or 5 days per week. The average number of weeks of intervention for all four conditions was 26 weeks. All groups improved from pretest to posttest on norm-referenced measures of achievement in reading and writing. Students assigned to the consultation + direct model made greater overall academic gains than students in any of the other conditions. Students in the consultation-only model made achievement gains comparable to those of students in the resource room. These findings provide modest support for two models of consultative service delivery for these students with learning disabilities.

Although the results of this experimental study are encouraging for those who advocate consultative models, the question of why these consultative models were effective remains unanswered. For example, the caseloads of the teachers providing consulting services were small, between 12 and 14 students per teacher, relative to the caseloads of district resource room teachers, who had average caseloads of 27 students (Schulte et al., 1990). We wonder if consultative services would lead to similar student achievement gains in schools with higher caseloads and complex schedules and in students with language or learning disabilities spread throughout many different classrooms. Also, both models of consultative services were delivered by teachers hired by the researchers rather than employed by the district. It is unclear where similar results would be obtained for district-employed special education teachers with less training and experience in consultation and collaboration.

Clinicians and teachers need much more information on the critical variables that can affect the success of consultative service delivery models. West and Idol (1990) reported that a majority of schools and school districts fail at initial attempts to implement consultative services in special education because they have not systematically assessed essential staff communicative interactive skills and collaborative skills. These authors stated that in order for a school consultative model to be successful, consulting teachers must have competencies in three areas: 1) essential communication and problem-solving skills involved in the collaborative consultation process, 2) empirically validated instructional strategies and interventions in their content area (e.g., reading disabilities, language impairments), and 3) experience in the presentation and training of skills and strategies to school-based staff members. Idol et al. (1986) suggested that regular education teachers were more likely to implement consultants' suggestions for instructional strategies for their students with mild disabilities if the strategies were easy to implement, based on general education curriculum and materials, could be used for group instruction, and included skills that could be taught directly to students.

Evidence from Studies on Consultation for Pre-referral Intervention

One potentially important use of consultation is for pre-referral intervention. Pre-referral intervention is a teacher's modification of instruction prior to referral for special education in order to better accommodate a student who has not yet been assessed as having a disability (Fuchs, Fuchs, & Bahr, 1990). Pre-referral intervention is supported by special education staff who work indirectly with the targeted student through consultation with his or her teacher. Pre-referral intervention is presumed to have a preventive effect by: 1) eliminating inappropriate referrals, and 2) reducing future student problems by strengthening the teacher's capacity to intervene effectively with a greater diversity of children. Damico and Nye (1990) viewed pre-referral intervention as an integral part of a collaborative language program in the schools, with special application for students from culturally and linguistically diverse backgrounds. Secord and Wiig (1991) advocated "communication assistance teams" operating in schools, in which team members led by the speech-language pathologist collaborate on developing and implementing classroom-based pre-referral strategies for students at risk for language and learning disabilities.

We are not aware of any experimental or quasi-experimental studies examining the use of consultation for pre-referral intervention for students with language impairments. However, several empirical studies have examined the effectiveness of pre-referral intervention for students with behavior and learning difficulties. Fuchs, Fuchs, Bahr, Fernstrom, and Stecker (1990) studied the effects of a highly structured expert consultation model. In this model, consultants guided teachers through a succession of scripted interviews that focused on the identification and analysis of the target student's problem behaviors, the development and implementation of an intervention plan, and the evaluation of the effects of the intervention on the student's behavior. Forty-three students were identified by their teachers as "difficult to teach" for reasons such as "off task," "poor academic work," and "poor interpersonal skills with adults," and served as targets of pre-referral intervention. Pre-referral intervention consisted of 10–16 activities/contacts (including meetings, observations, teacher–student contracts and classroom visits) occurring over 6–8 weeks. The fidelity of the pre-referral classroom interventions was demonstrated through frequent on-site monitoring by the authors. The average percentage of targeted student problem behaviors showed a significant decrease between pre-intervention and post-intervention for the consultant model, but not for a control group. Average teacher ratings of the severity, manageability, and tolerability of students' target behaviors showed reliable pre-intervention and postintervention differences in a positive direction for the consultation group, but not for the control group.

The authors speculated that one reason for the effectiveness of the pre-referral interventions might have been the high fidelity of implementation with which they were conducted. Fidelity of implementation was probably enhanced by the on-site presence of both graduate students and the authors. The prescriptiveness of the interventions (e.g., written scripts to guide the process of consultation) also may have been another reason for the apparent success. This structured "expert" approach to consultation is more directive than current descriptions of "collaborative consultation." It is interesting to note that Fuchs, Fuchs, Bahr, Fernstrom, and Stecker (1990) reported that they began the first year of their pre-referral research program using a collaborative consultation model. Despite expectations for success, they concluded that in-class interventions designed collaboratively were less effective than interventions prescribed by the expert consultants and that teachers were reluctant to commit blocks of time for collaborative problem-solving. Instead, teachers requested helpful suggestions from the consulting special education teachers.

Fuchs, Fuchs, Bahr, Fernstrom, and Stecker (1990) replicated and extended these findings and found that of 50 students receiving pre-referral consultation services for problem behaviors, 5 (10%) were referred for special education at the end of the school year. Among 12 control pupils, 6 (50%) were referred to special education. These studies provide support for the effectiveness of consultation as a pre-referral strategy with students whose teachers identify them as difficult to teach.

Conclusions on the Use of Indirect Consultative Service Models

Little empirical information is available about the effectiveness of consultation models in facilitating the acquisition of language in school-age children with language impairments. However, evidence from studies with students with autism suggest that consultative models may produce positive changes in these children's use of certain language targets in their classrooms and that teachers can integrate basic language facilitation strategies into their classroom teaching (Dyer et al., 1991). Also, evidence from students with learning disabilities suggests that some students can make progress toward academic and behavioral goals via consultative services that is at least equal to progress made when students are removed from their classrooms for special education instruction (Idol, 1989; Schulte et al., 1990). However, it is not clear whether expert or collaborative consultation models are differentially effective. Nor do we have the information needed to understand how teacher, clinician, and student characteristics affect the overall effectiveness of school consultation.

IMPLICATIONS FOR
THE CHOICE OF SERVICE DELIVERY MODELS

Accountability Issues

Clinicians must be cautious in assuming that classroom-based direct and indirect consultative models will automatically lead to significant and lasting changes in language skills for students with language impairments, even though the limited information available on these service options gives reason to be cautiously optimistic. Connell (1982) argued that clinicians should be skeptical toward any intervention procedures that are not firmly upheld by empirical evidence and should systematically monitor procedures as if they were *not* effective. Testing clinical hypotheses about combinations of intervention variables allows the clinician to make changes in aspects of service delivery when the data indicate that student progress is insufficient. The reader is referred to Fey (1986), Fey and Cleave (1990), McReynolds and Kearns (1983), and Olswang and Bain (1991) for descriptions of methods for testing clinical hypotheses and demonstrating intervention efficacy, such as the use of multiple-baseline, single-subject designs. The following discussion of factors that influence a clinician's choice of service delivery variables should be interpreted in light of this premise: It is necessary for clinicians to monitor and demonstrate the effectiveness of their service delivery models.

Choosing Service Delivery Options

The optimal combination of service delivery variables, such as intervention settings and service provider roles, is likely to differ for individual children. In addition, public education laws (i.e., PL 94-142, the Education for All Handicapped Children Act of 1975) require that the choices for language intervention services be based on the specific needs of each student. Nelson (1993) has suggested that the choice of specific service delivery variables can be guided by asking the following question: "How can we use intervention settings, people and schedules to maximize the opportunities for a child to acquire the language abilities the child needs for participating in important life contexts?" (Nelson, 1993, p. 164). Therefore, rather than looking at classroom-based models as replacing services provided through traditional pullout models, it may be more beneficial to view alternative models as a means of *extending language intervention services to the classroom and to other significant adults* (i.e., teachers) in order to enhance students' communication skills and academic learning (Ferguson, 1991).

The choice of a service delivery model for a particular student involves consideration of the advantages and limitations of both pullout and classroom contexts for language intervention. For a particular student (with specific language needs and intervention targets), it may be beneficial to provide intervention in a pullout setting that allows control of critical variables (e.g., providing maximal opportunities for focused practice of target skills). For another student in a different classroom with different intervention targets, the clinician might decide that the student's classroom could be modified to best afford multiple opportunities for use of target skills. Thus, the choice might be to provide services indirectly through the classroom teacher without initial use of a pullout model. A clinician also might hypothesize that a model that combines pullout and indirect consultative services may be beneficial for a student. For example, a student might need the controlled environment of the pullout room and profit from pre-teaching and practice of critical communication skills, perhaps once or twice each week. At the same time, indirect services provided through the classroom teacher on a daily basis might allow the child to integrate newly learned skills into the classroom during relevant learning opportunities.

Language Intervention Service Delivery: An Example

If all of the conditions that might lead to language gains could be brought to bear in classrooms (e.g., diversity of language models and opportunities for practice and use of communication targets), then it would be reasonable to assume that language intervention in these circumstances would be optimally effective. It may be quite difficult to deliver "ideal" interventions under ordinary circumstances, however. In our experience, the extent to which an ideal intervention can actually be accomplished depends on interactions between three sets of service delivery variables: setting characteristics (e.g., the opportunities for students to practice and use skills in functional contexts), clinician and teacher characteristics (e.g., the collaborative and consultative skills of staff), and student characteristics (e.g., the language and behavior needs of a student at a particular point in time).

The following example illustrates how these factors influence the decisions of speech-language clinicians as they try to integrate language intervention services into the classroom. Some of the students with whom we work have multiple language needs in the areas of comprehension and use curriculum vocabulary, sentence structure in speaking and writing, and conversational and classroom discourse (including understanding academic instruction). It is not uncommon for these students to have additional needs in the area of academics (e.g., reading and writing) and behavior. One of these students in particular (with a diagnosis of attention deficit disorder) had difficulty in focusing her attention on schoolwork, although she could sustain her focus of learning during experiential learning activities (as opposed to teacher lectures). For this reason, the student was placed in a fifth-grade class that had a high frequency of hands-on activities. Such classrooms also tend to be noisy, with students talking and moving between learning centers. Our plan was to capitalize on the experiential learning experiences and on the numerous opportunities for conversational interactions with peers by using a service delivery model that included both direct classroom-based and consultative indirect service. Within 1 month, however, it became obvious that the noise and movement in this classroom prevented the student from focusing on language and learning activities. Our progress monitoring data showed that our direct intervention and indirect intervention through the classroom teacher were having minimal effects on the student's use of target goals.

At this point, the classroom teacher and the speech-language clinicians attempted to design collaboratively a series of interventions intended to reduce auditory and visual distractions in the classroom and to increase the amount of external structure available to the student during learning activities. Unfortunately, the planned classroom modifications could not be implemented easily by the classroom teacher. Although the teacher was interested in working collaboratively to provide the student with opportunities for focused practice of language targets within the classroom, she was not able to modify consistently the structure of her class and still meet the needs of her other students. At the end of 3 months, the student had virtually stopped participating in learning activities. Data taken in the classroom indicated that no measurable progress had been made toward language goals.

A decision was made to change the setting of language intervention to the pullout room. In this setting, the clinician could exert greater control over auditory and visual distractions and provide a routine structure in which learning could take place. Direct intervention in the pullout room enabled the student to make progress on targeted language goals, as measured by data collected in the pullout room. Although we attempted to make intervention in the pullout room ecologically valid (e.g., by using materials from the classroom and incorporating normal language peer models when possible), classroom data continued to show slow progress toward goals in that setting.

This year the student was placed in a classroom with a high degree of structure and with minimal auditory and visual distractions. The student support team's hypothesis is that this setting will allow the student to focus her attention during the language and learning activities provided directly by the speech-language clinician in small-group and whole-class lessons. This particular classroom does not appear to afford multiple opportunities to practice new language skills at other times, however. We are in the process of implementing consultative services that include planning with the teacher to modify the classroom to provide peer models and opportunities for the student to practice conversational skills. Most of our discussions so far have focused on how language intervention can be integrated efficiently into this classroom's *existing* structure and routines, with *realistic* amounts of time invested by the classroom teacher and speech-language clinician.

This examples illustrates the need to balance the advantages and limitations of both pullout and classroom-based service delivery models depending on student needs and logistic limitations. It also illustrates how the effectiveness of any service delivery model is a function of the interactions between setting variables, clinician and teacher variables, and student variables. Figure 1 is a representation of the three groups of variables that operate in any service delivery model.

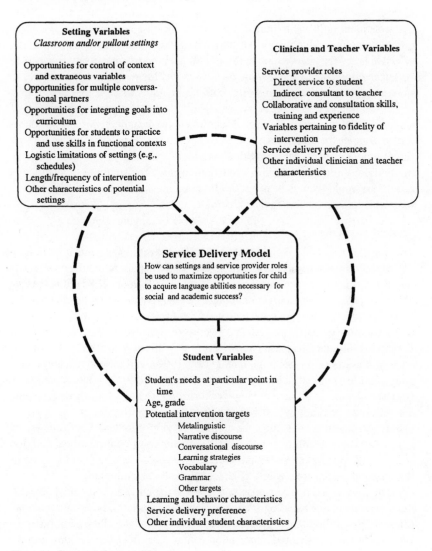

Setting Variables
Classroom and/or pullout settings

Opportunities for control of context
   and extraneous variables
Opportunities for multiple conversational partners
Opportunities for integrating goals into
   curriculum
Opportunities for students to practice
   and use skills in functional contexts
Logistic limitations of settings (e.g.,
   schedules)
Length/frequency of intervention
Other characteristics of potential
   settings

Clinician and Teacher Variables

Service provider roles
   Direct service to student
   Indirect consultant to teacher
Collaborative and consultation skills,
   training and experience
Variables pertaining to fidelity of
   intervention
Service delivery preferences
Other individual clinician and teacher
   characteristics

Service Delivery Model
How can settings and service provider roles
be used to maximize opportunities for child
to acquire language abilities necessary for
social and academic success?

Student Variables

Student's needs at particular point in
   time
Age, grade
Potential intervention targets
      Metalinguistic
      Narrative discourse
      Conversational discourse
      Learning strategies
      Vocabulary
      Grammar
      Other targets
Learning and behavior characteristics
Service delivery preference
Other individual student characteristics

Figure 1.   Service delivery variables.

SERVICE DELIVERY VARIABLES

Setting Variables

The language-learning environments of classrooms vary. In the example above, the effectiveness of classroom-based intervention for one student was very different in two classrooms with contrasting instructional environments. Although a quiet, structured classroom allowed one student to focus attention sufficiently to receive and respond to instruction, multiple opportunities for practice of target conversational skills were limited. We need to increase our understanding of the complex language-learning environments of classrooms if we are to provide effective language intervention in these settings. It may be necessary for speech-language clinicians to actively assess classrooms for potential opportunities to maximize student language skills. Ysseldyke and Christensen (1987) have argued for the need to describe systematically the instructional environments of students with learning disabilities. According to these authors, this allows educators to evaluate the effectiveness of instruction and to design appropriate instructional interventions for individual students. Similarly, a comprehensive methodology for assessing the language-learning environment in a student's classroom would seem to be necessary for planning and implementing direct and indirect language services in the classroom.

Student Variables

The population of school-age children with language impairments is extremely heterogeneous with respect to potential intervention goals, reflecting a variety of linguistic, pragmatic, and metalinguistic problems (Simon, 1985). It is reasonable to hypothesize that classroom language intervention might be effective for language targets that have immediate use in and relevance to ongoing classroom and curriculum demands, including conversational discourse skills (e.g., Brinton & Fujiki, 1989), metalinguistic awareness (e.g.,Wallach & Miller, 1988), knowledge of classroom scripts (e.g., Creaghead, 1990), and related academic language and learning strategies (e.g., Buttrill et al., 1989). In contrast, students who have deficits in the area of language form and structure and whose problems are reflected in reading and writing might need individual or small-group instruction in settings that allow the clinician to control context. For example, we have observed that children with targets in the areas of conversational and discourse skills participate and make progress in whole-class language lessons in this general target area. Some of these students take advantage of response opportunities to practice conversational skills in the classroom setting, both with the speech-language pathologist and the classroom teacher. These same students often do less well in small-group intervention outside the classroom, possibly because the more structured intervention context does not offer the same natural opportunities for modeling, practice, and feedback. We also observe the opposite pattern for students whose language deficits center on structural aspects of language. We find that, although these students may attempt to respond during whole-class language lessons, they tend to be unsuccessful. Also, the whole-class context limits the amount of individual assistance that can be given. Alternatively, these students can be focused and responsive and make acceptable progress toward objectives in small-group sessions held outside of the classroom. Much more research is needed to understand the interactions between student variables (e.g., language targets) and intervention setting.

Clinician and Teacher Variables

Clinician and teacher characteristics also may differentially affect the success of classroom-based intervention. In the above example of the student who was placed in two very different classrooms in successive years, the first teacher was interested in collaborating but lacked collaborative skills and experience in modifying a classroom environment to meet the needs of a student with a language impairment. The second teacher had collaborated with the speech-language pathologist for several years. She was likely to participate in a collaborative process that did not demand unrealistic amounts of time but that did include the regular and frequent exchange of information. At least as important as collaborative skills are the trust and commitment that can grow in professional relationships. Both collaborative skills and good professional relationships can affect the success of classroom-based intervention, and we need to understand more about these processes. Obviously, it will be necessary to apply this knowledge to our staff training efforts, both in university training and district staff development programs.

The successful studies discussed in this chapter consistently provided high levels of intervention fidelity, therefore the results reported for classroom-based service models must be considered within that framework. Consultative models are based partly on the assumption that indirect intervention can lead to positive changes in teacher attitudes and skills, which in turn can lead to consistency of indirect services provided through the teacher. We need information about the clinician and teacher characteristics that predict positive responses to consultation and subsequently to long-term commitment to intervention fidelity.

CONCLUSION

The importance of the classroom communicative environment to the school success of school-age children with language impairments has been highlighted by the current literature on classroom-based direct and indirect service options. However, despite this increased awareness, speech-language clinicians need more information on how they can use service delivery models to maximize a student's opportunities for acquiring needed language skills. To help students learn the language skills necessary for social and academic success, we need to know how to extend language intervention effectively into the classroom. In our view, no comprehensive language intervention plan can be considered complete without a plan that will enable the student to use newly learned target skills in the classroom and other natural environments. This view requires that we consider service delivery options from a continuum of services. The continuum of services appropriately includes direct and indirect services in the classroom and in pullout contexts designed to be as ecologically valid as possible. We must evaluate the effectiveness of *all* of the service delivery models that we use (classroom-based *and* pullout) by measuring student outcomes and progress toward intervention goals on a frequent and regular basis.

REFERENCES

Achilles, J., Yates, R., & Freese, J. (1991). Perspectives from the field: Collaborative consultation in the speech and language program of the Dallas Independent School District. *Language, Speech, and Hearing Services in Schools, 22,* 154–155.

American Speech-Language-Hearing Association. (1991). A model for collaborative service delivery for students with language-learning disorders in the public schools. *Asha, 33*(Suppl. 5), 44–50.

American Speech-Language-Hearing Association. (1993). Guidelines for caseload size and speech-language service delivery in the schools. *Asha, 35*(Suppl. 10), 33–39.

Anderson, G., & Nelson, N. (1988). Integrating language intervention and education in an alternate adolescent language classroom. *Seminars in Speech and Language, 9,* 341–352.

Bashir, A., (1989). Language intervention and the curriculum. *Seminars in Speech and Language, 10,* 181–189.

Bennett, R. (1988). Evaluating the effectiveness of alternate educational delivery systems. In J. Graden, J. Zins, & M Curtis (Eds.), *Alternative educational delivery systems: Enhancing instructional options for all students* (pp. 276–301). Washington, DC: National Association of School Psychologists.

Biklen, D., & Zollers, N. (1986). The focus of advocacy in the LD field. *Journal of Learning Disabilities, 19,* 579–586.

Borsch, J., & Oaks, R. (1992). Implementing collaborative consultation: Effective collaboration at Central Elementary School. *Language, Speech, and Hearing Services in Schools, 23,* 367–368.

Brandel, D. (1992). Implementing collaborative consultation: Collaboration—full steam ahead with no prior experience. *Language, Speech, and Hearing Services in Schools, 23,* 369–370.

Brinton, B., & Fujiki, M. (1989). *Conversational management with language-impaired children.* Rockville, MD: Aspen.

Buffmire, J. (1977). *Special education delivery alternatives.* Salt Lake City: Southwest Regional Resources Center.

Buttrill, J., Niizawa, J., Biemer, C., Takahashi, C., & Hearn, S., (1989). Serving the language-learning disabled adolescent: A strategies-based model. *Language, Speech, and Hearing Services in Schools, 20,* 185–204.

Christensen, S., & Luckett, C. (1990). Getting into the classroom and making it work! *Language, Speech, and Hearing Services in Schools, 21,* 110–113.

Cirrin, F., & Peters, A. (1992). MSHA School Services: 1992 public school caseload survey. *Minnesota Speech-Language-Hearing Association Newsletter, 13*(4), 3–4.

Cole, K., & Dale, P. (1986). Direct language instruction and interactive language instruction with language delayed preschool children: A comparison study. *Journal of Speech and Hearing Research, 29,* 206–217.

Connell, P. (1982). On training language rules. *Language, Speech, and Hearing Services in Schools, 13*, 231–248.

Creaghead, N. (1990). Mutual empowerment through collaboration: A new script for an old problem. *Best Practices in School Speech-Language Pathology, 1*, 109–115.

Creaghead, N., & Tattershall, S. (1985). Observation and assessment of classroom pragmatic skills. In C. Simon (Ed.), *Communication skills and classroom success: Assessment of language-learning disabled students* (105–134). San Diego: College-Hill Press.

Damico, J. (1987). Addressing language concerns in the schools: The SLP as consultant. *Journal of Childhood Communication Disorders, 11*(1), 17–40.

Damico, J. (1988). The lack of efficacy in language therapy: A case study. *Language, Speech, and Hearing Services in Schools, 19*, 51–66.

Damico, J., & Nye, C. (1990). Collaborative issues in multicultural populations. *Best Practices in School Speech-Language Pathology, 1*, 127–139.

Deno, S., Maruyama, G., Espin, C., & Cohen, C.(1990). Educating students with mild disabilities in general education classrooms: Minnesota alternatives. *Exceptional Children, 56*(2), 150–161.

Despain, A., & Simon, C. (1987). Alternative to failure: A junior high school language development-based curriculum. *Journal of Childhood Communication Disorders, 11*(1), 139–179.

Dodge, E., & Mallard, A. (1992). Social skills training using a collaborative service delivery model. *Language, Speech, and Hearing Services in Schools, 23*, 130–135.

Dudley-Marling, C. (1987). The role of SLPs in literacy learning. *Journal of Childhood Communication Disorders, 11*(1), 81–90.

Dyer, K., Williams, L., & Luce, S. (1991). Training teachers to use naturalistic communication strategies in classrooms for students with autism and other severe handicaps. *Language, Speech, and Hearing Services in Schools, 22*, 313–321.

Ferguson, M. (1991). Collaborative/consultative service delivery: An introduction. *Language, Speech, and Hearing Services in Schools, 23*, 361–362.

Ferguson, M. (1992a). Implementing collaborative consultation: An introduction. *Language, Speech, and Hearing Services in Schools, 23*, 361–362.

Ferguson, M. (1992b). Implementing collaborative consultation: The transition to collaborative teaching. *Language, Speech, and Hearing Services in Schools, 23*, 371–372.

Fey, M. (1986). *Language intervention for young children.* Newton, MA: Allyn & Bacon.

Fey, M. (1988). Generalization issues facing language interventionists: An introduction. *Language, Speech, and Hearing Services in Schools, 19*, 272–281.

Fey, M., & Cleave, P. (1990). Treatment efficacy: Early language intervention. *Seminars in Speech and Language, 11*, 165–179.

Frassinelli, L., Superior, K, & Meyers. J (1983). A consultation model for speech and language intervention. *Asha, 25*, 25–30.

Friend, M., & Cook, L. (1990). Assessing the climate for collaboration. *Best Practices in School Speech-Language Pathology, 1*, 67–73.

Fuchs, D., Fuchs, L., & Bahr, M. (1990). Mainstream assistance teams: A scientific basis for the art of consultation. *Exceptional Children, 56*(2), 128–138.

Fuchs, D., Fuchs, L., Bahr, M., Fernstrom, P., & Stecker, P. (1990). Prereferral intervention: A prescriptive approach. *Exceptional Children, 56*(6), 493–513.

Fujiki, M., & Brinton, B. (1984). Supplementing language therapy: Working with the classroom teacher. *Language, Speech, and Hearing Services in Schools, 15*, 98–109.

Goodin, G., & Mehollin, K. (1990). Developing a collaborative speech-language intervention program in the schools. *Best Practices in School Speech-Language Pathology, 1*, 89–99.

Gruenewald, L., & Pollak, S. (1990). *Language interaction in curriculum and instruction.* Austin, TX: PRO-ED.

Hoskins, B. (1990). Collaborative consultation: Designing the role of the the the speech-language pathologist in a new educational context. *Best Practices in School Speech-Language Pathology, 1,* 29–35.

Hughes, D. (1989). Generalization from language therapy to classroom academics. *Seminars in Speech and Language, 10,* 218–228.

Idol, L. (1989). The resource/consulting teacher: An integrated model of service delivery. *Remedial and Special Education, 10*(6), 38–48.

Idol, L., Paolucci-Whitcomb, P., & Nevin, A. (1986). *Collaborative consultation.* Austin, TX: PRO-ED.

Johnston, J. (1988). Generalization: The nature of change. *Language, Speech, and Hearing Services in Schools, 19,* 272–281.

Kratochwill, T., Sheridan, S., & Van Someren, K. (1988). Research in behavioral consultation: Current status and future directions. In J. West (Ed.), *School consultation: Interdisciplinary perspectives on theory, research, training, and practice* (pp. 345–372). Austin, TX: Association for Educational and Psychological Consultants.

Lindfors, J. (1987). *Children's language and learning* (2nd ed.). Englewood Cliffs, NJ: Prentice Hall.

Magnotta, O. (1991). Looking beyond tradition. *Language, Speech, and Hearing Services in Schools, 22,* 150–151.

Marvin, C. (1987). Consultation services: Changing roles for SLPs. *Journal of Childhood Communication Disorders, 11*(1), 1–15.

Marvin, C. (1990). Problems in school-based speech-language consultation and collaborative services: Defining the terms and improving the process. *Best Practices in School Speech-Language Pathology, 1,* 37–47.

McReynolds, L., & Kearns, K. (1983). *Single-subject experimental designs in communication disorders.* Baltimore: University Park Press.

Miller, L. (1989). Classroom-based language intervention. *Language, Speech, and Hearing Services in Schools, 20,* 153–169.

Miller, T., & Sabatino, D. (1978). An evaluation of the teacher consultant model as an approach to mainstreaming. *Exceptional Children, 45,* 86–91.

Montgomery, J. (1990). Building administrative support for collaboration. *Best Practices in School Speech-Language Pathology, 1,* 75–79.

Montgomery, J. (1992). Implementing collaborative consultation: Perspectives from the field—language, speech, and hearing services in schools. *Language, Speech, and Hearing Services in Schools, 23,* 363–364.

Moore-Brown, B. (1991). Moving in the direction of change: Thoughts for administrators and speech-language pathologists. *Language, Speech, and Hearing Services in Schools, 22,* 148–149.

Nelson, N. (1981). An eclectic model of language intervention for disorders of listening, speaking, reading, and writing. *Topics in Language Disorders, 1*(2), 1–23.

Nelson, N. (1989). Curriculum-based language assessment and intervention. *Language, Speech, and Hearing Services in Schools, 20,* 170–184.

Nelson, N. (1990). Only relevant practices can be best. *Best Practices in School Speech-Language Pathology, 1,* 15–27.

Nelson, N. (1993). *Childhood language disorders in context: Infancy through adolescence.* New York: Macmillan.

Norris, J. (1989). Providing language remediation in the classroom: An integrated language-to-reading intervention method. *Language, Speech, and Hearing Services in Schools, 20,* 205–218.

Norris, J., & Hoffman, P. (1990). Language intervention within naturalistic environments. *Language, Speech, and Hearing Services in Schools, 21,* 72–84.

Norris, J., & Hoffman, P. (1993). *Whole language intervention for school-age children.* San Diego: Singular Publishing Group.

Olswang, L., & Bain, B. (1991). When to recommend intervention. *Language, Speech, and Hearing Services in Schools, 22,* 255–263.

Peck, C., & Schuler, A. (1983). Classroom-based language intervention for students with autism. *Seminars in Speech and Language, 4,* 93–103.

Reynolds, M., Wang, M., & Walberg, H. (1987). The necessary restructuring of special and regular education. *Exceptional Children, 53,* 391–398.

Roller, E., Rodriquez, T., Warner, J., & Lindahl, P. (1992). Implementing collaborative consultation: Integration of self-contained children with severe speech-language needs into the regular education classroom. *Language, Speech, and Hearing Services in Schools, 23,* 365–366.

Schulte, A., Osborne, S., & McKinney, J. (1990). Academic outcomes for students with learning disabilities in consultation and resource programs. *Exceptional Children 56*(2), 162–171.

Secord, W. (Ed.). (1990). Best practices in school speech-language pathology. In *Collaborative programs in the schools: Concepts, models and procedures.* San Antonio, TX: The Psychological Corporation.

Secord, W., & Wiig, E. (1991). *Developing a collaborative language intervention program.* Buffalo, NY: Educom Associates.

Silliman, E., & Wilkinson, L. (1991). *Communicating for learning: Classroom observation and collaboration.* Gaithersberg, MD: Aspen Publications.

Silliman, E., Wilkinson, L., Belkin, A., & Hoffman, L. (1991). Facilitating collaboration through coparticipation. In E. Silliman & L. Wilkinson, *Communicating for learning: Classroom observation and collaboration.* Gaithersberg, MD: Aspen Publications.

Simon, C. (Ed.). (1985). *Communication skills and classroom success: Therapy methodologies for language-learning disabled students.* San Diego: College-Hill Press.

Simon, C. (1987a). *Classroom Communication Screening Procedure for Early Adolescence.* Tempe, AZ: Communi-Cog Publications.

Simon, C. (1987b). Out of the broom closet and into the classroom: The emerging SLP. *Journal of Childhood Communication Disorders, 11*(1), 41–66.

Simon, C., & Myrold-Gunyuz, P. (1990). *Into the classroom: The SLP in the the collaborative role.* Tuscon, AZ: Communication Skill Builders.

Wallach, G., & Miller, L. (1988). *Language intervention and academic success.* Boston: College-Hill Press.

Wang, M., & Zollers, N. (1990). Adaptive instruction: An alternative service delivery approach. *Remedial and Special Education, 11*(1), 7–21.

Warren, S., & Kaiser, A. (1986). Incidental language teaching: A critical review. *Journal of Speech and Hearing Disorders, 51,* 291–299.

West, J., & Brown, P. (1987). State departments of education policies on consultation in special education: The state of the the states. *Remedial and Special Education, 8*(3), 45–51.

West, J., & Idol, L. (1987). School consultation (part 1): An interdisciplinary perspective on theory, models, and research. *Journal of Learning Disabilities, 20*(7), 388–408.

West, J., & Idol, L. (1990). Collaborative consultation in the education of mildly handicapped and at-risk students. *Remedial and Special Education, 11*(1), 22–31.

Wiederholt, J., & Chamberlain, S. (1989). A critical analysis of resource programs. *Remedial and Special Education 10*(6), 15–37.

Wiig, K., Secord, W., & Wiig, E. (1990). Deming goes to school: Developing total quality services in speech-language pathology. *Best Practices in School Speech-Language Pathology, 1,* 1–14.

Wilcox, M., Kouri, T., & Caswell, S. (1991). Early language intervention: A comparison of classroom and individual treatment. *American Journal of Speech-Language Pathology, 1*(1), 49–62.

Will, M. (1986). *Educating students with learning problems: A shared responsibility.* Washington, DC: Office of Special Education and Rehabilitative Services (OSERS). U.S. Department of Education.

Wixson, S. (1980). Two resource room models for serving learning and behavior disordered pupils. *Behavior Disorders, 5,* 116–125.

Yoder, P., Kaiser, A., & Alpert, C. (1991). An exploratory study of the interaction between language teaching methods and child characteristics. *Journal of Speech and Hearing Research, 34,* 155–167.

Ysseldyke, J., & Christensen, S. (1987). Evaluating students' instructional environments. *Remedial and Special Education, 8*(3), 17–24.

Zigmond, N., & Baker, J. (1990). Mainstream experiences for learning disabled students (Project MELD): Preliminary report. *Exceptional Children, 56*(2), 176–185.

Author Index

Subject Index